The Right to a Fair Trial

EUROPEAN MONOGRAPHS

In the European Monographs series this book, *The Right to a Fair Trial: Article 6 of the European Convention on Human Rights*, is the eighty-seventh title. The titles published in this series are listed at the end of this volume.

The Right to a Fair Trial

Article 6 of the European Convention on Human Rights

Piero Leanza
Ondrej Pridal

Wolters Kluwer
Law & Business

Published by:
Kluwer Law International
PO Box 316
2400 AH Alphen aan den Rijn
The Netherlands
Website: www.kluwerlaw.com

Sold and distributed in North, Central and South America by:
Aspen Publishers, Inc.
7201 McKinney Circle
Frederick, MD 21704
United States of America
Email: customer.service@aspenpublishers.com

Sold and distributed in all other countries by:
Turpin Distribution Services Ltd
Stratton Business Park
Pegasus Drive, Biggleswade
Bedfordshire SG18 8TQ
United Kingdom
Email: kluwerlaw@turpin-distribution.com

Printed on acid-free paper.

ISBN 978-90-411-4855-1

Printed and Bound by CPI Group (UK) Ltd, Croydon, CR0 4YY.

To our wives Reňd’a and Natalia

About the Authors

Piero Leanza, *Doctor in Jurisprudence*, full time judge since 1997, after having served as civil judge in different District Courts in Italy, is currently serving as criminal judge in the District Court of Trieste, and has been recently appointed as member of the Provincial Tax Court of Gorizia. He worked as international judge at the *Special Chamber of the Supreme Court of Kosovo* from 2009 to 2013, within the European Union Rule of Law Mission in Kosovo.

Judge Leanza has published numerous monographs in civil law, employment law, and procedural law, with major Italian law publishers, and is the Author of a number of articles and contributions to law commentaries in his home country.

Ondrej Pridal, *Ph.D.*, is currently serving, since 2011, as international judge at the *Supreme Court of Kosovo*, within the European Union Rule of Law Mission in Kosovo. He previously worked as District Court judge in the Czech Republic, as well as in an Attorney's office. He achieved the Master of Laws and the Ph.D. at Masaryk University in Brno, and Doctor Juris at Charles University in Prague. His study interests focus particularly on the right to a fair trial, which was also the theme of his Ph.D. thesis, and in the interpretation of the law and swiftness and effectiveness in court's procedures.

Judge Pridal is Co-author of a Commentary to the Czech Civil Procedure Code and Author of numerous articles in law magazines.

Table of Contents

List of Abbreviations

ACHPR	African Charter on Human and People's Rights
ACHR	American Convention on Human Rights
CFREU	Charter of Fundamental Rights of the European Union
EC	European Community
ECJ	Court of Justice of the European Union
ECCC	Extraordinary Chambers in the Courts of Cambodia
ECHR	European Convention on Human Rights
ECtHR	European Court of Human Rights
EU	European Union
ICC	International Criminal Court
ICCPR	International Covenant on Civil and Political Rights
ICJ	International Court of Justice
ICTY	International Criminal Court for former Yugoslavia
ICTR	International Criminal Court for Rwanda
SCSC	Special Chamber of the Supreme Court of Kosovo
SCSL	Special Court for Sierra Leone
SOE	Socially Owned Enterprise
STL	Special Tribunal for Lebanon
TFEU	Treaty on the Functioning of the European Union
UDHR	Universal Declaration of Human Rights
UN	United Nations
UNMIK	United Nations Mission in Kosovo

Foreword

It is said that the seed from which the main principles of the European Convention on Human Rights (ECHR), as well as of all the modern international human rights treaties, have sprung is to be found in the *Magna Carta*, sealed by King John of England on 15 June 1215, which granted 'all free men' of the Kingdom a number of rights and liberties, including the archetype of the 'right to a fair trial'.

Since then many centuries have passed, and the right to any individual to a fair trial, in both civil and criminal proceedings, has been included in a vast number of international treaties, such as the International Covenant on Civil and Political Rights, the Universal Declaration of Human Rights, the Charter of Fundamental Rights of the European Union, the American Convention on Human Rights, the African Charter on Human and People's Rights, and the ECHR.

What makes the ECHR special, if compared with other international instruments, is undoubtedly the possibility granted to any individual to file a complaint to the European Court of Human Rights (ECtHR), which in the last fifty years has delivered more than 10,000 judgments, binding to the states concerned.

Today, it is not possible to overestimate the role and importance of Article 6 ECHR for the people of the 47 Member States of the Council of Europe. Not only for the high number of cases handled by the Court of Strasbourg during its functioning, but also for the 'preventive' impact of the provisions laid down in Article 6: each judge, court, and tribunal will have to take into consideration Article 6 and the ECtHR's case law when handling and deciding their cases.

It is a fact that the judicial systems of the States signatory to the Convention have a different approach with regard to the several aspects of the right to a fair trial (this phenomenon is due not only to the differences existing between common-law and civil-law systems, but also to the different legal traditions of the Member States of the Council of Europe). Nevertheless, the ECHR (and, in particular, Article 6) require from the judicial authorities to observe certain European standards. In this regard, it is interesting to note that there are States against which there are a few cases pending before the ECtHR and, on the contrary, States that are 'regular customers' in Strasbourg.

It was my pleasure to know in person the Authors of this book some years ago, when working together in the Special Chamber of the Supreme Court of Kosovo (on Kosovo Trust Agency Related Matters), within the EU Rule of Law Mission in Kosovo. We had the opportunity to discuss about fair trials and Article 6 almost on a daily basis. Kosovo is not a signatory State to the ECHR; however, according to the *Constitutional Framework for Provisional Self-Government in Kosovo*, promulgated by UNMIK on 15 May 2001 (UNMIK/REG/2001/9), the ECHR had direct legal effects also in Kosovo. More recently, the *Constitution of the Republic of Kosovo*, which entered into force on 15 June 2008, in its Article 22 provided that – among other instruments – the ECHR is '*directly applicable in the Republic of Kosovo and, in the case of conflict, have priority over provisions of laws and other acts of public institutions*'.

The Authors are two judges, with different background and experience, coming from two different countries, but who share the interest for the subject matter.

Their book focuses on a key right set forth in the ECHR, the 'right to a fair trial', and examines the guarantees provided by Article 6 both in civil and in criminal proceedings, with a hint to the possible application of the principles thereof also to international and 'hybrid' courts.

The book tackles the topic from a practical point of view, essentially, including in the text full paragraphs of important decisions of the ECtHR. It also provides two 'schemes' on possible steps that domestic courts should follow to keep the process within the boundaries of a 'fair trial' (the patterns are related to civil proceedings, and do not refer to any national procedure in particular, but are based on an abstract model).

As much as I had the pleasure to work with them, during our priceless experience abroad, it now gives me great pleasure to write the Foreword for this book.

Tapio Vanamo
Judge of the Court of Appeal of Helsinki

Acknowledgements

This book is the result of the friendship and fruitful cooperation of two judges from different countries and legal backgrounds, and professional experiences, who found themselves working together abroad, in a 'hybrid-court' set by the international community in a post-conflict country. Daily conversations on the subject of human rights and, in particular, on the right to due process, were the seeds which eventually germinated into this project. Our experiences in that hybrid-court, has had a significant influence on our decision to publish a book on the right to a fair trial, a subject more topical than ever in these times, more than half a century after the signing of the European Convention on Human Rights (ECHR) by the first States.

The style and format of this book might appear to the reader somewhat different from other publications on the same subject. We decided to proceed following a practical approach, by inserting in the body of the text passages of the case law of the European Court of Human Rights (ECtHR). The cases are cited in the way we believe to be most effective, yet simple, with the name of the parties and the full date, as well as the number of paragraphs. This, in our opinion, is of great utility to the reader, who will have at their disposal the relevant passages of the quoted decisions and judgments, without having to resort to long and tedious research. The reader may also decide to look for the full text of the decisions, searching online on the official website of the ECtHR (HUDOC).

We would like to thank, for their precious cooperation in this project, Agne Limante, Ph.D. in EU law (Vilnius University), and MA in EU law (King's College London), from Lithuania, who contributed to the book writing the part on the right of standing before the European Court of Justice (Chapter 3, § 3.09), and Timo Knäbe, lawyer from Germany, for his contribution in the revision of Chapters 5 and 6. A special thanks goes also to Jeffrey Green, MA, JD, from the United States, for his contributions in the revision of Chapters 3 and 4 (one sign that the interest in the topic of this work is not limited to the States signatory to the Convention).

Appreciation also goes to Tapio Vanamo, Judge of the Court of Appeal of Helsinki, for his helpful insights on the application of the principles set forth in the ECHR and its Protocols while he served as President of the Special Chamber of the Supreme Court of Kosovo, which provided inspiration in our daily work as judges.

Finally, we would like to thank our families, for their moral support, especially when, coming home from work, we had to 'steal' further hours from our 'family time', to finalize this project.

Piero Leanza
Ondrej Pridal

‘Justice must not only be done,
it must also be seen to be done’

CHAPTER 1

The Right to a Fair Trial

Piero Leanza & Ondrej Pridal

§1.01 JUSTICE AND THE RIGHT TO A FAIR TRIAL

When it comes to defining the 'right to a fair trial', the literature faces serious difficulties. Each Author has his own idea of what a fair trial should be and of its content, and, although jurists in general agree on the basic features of a fair trial, several aspects still remain controversial.[1]

In defining the term, one cannot fail to take into consideration philosophical concepts associated with the category of *justice* as well, if only for the adjective 'fair' placed before the word 'trial'. The concept of justice is intuitively understandable, but its definition poses no fewer problems than defining the concept of law itself.[2] Philosophers and jurists have been trying to agree on a common definition of justice for more than two thousand years, but the results are still unsatisfactory. Moreover, any attempt to define the concept of justice is complicated by the fact that the word has multiple meanings: quite often no distinction is made between justice in the legal sense, in the ethical sense, in the political sense, and in the sociological sense;[3] and different understandings of the concept of justice inevitably lead to different ideas of

1. The views expressed in this section are discussed, *amplius*, in O. Pridal, *Pravo na spravedlivy proces v. civilnim rizeni* (*The Right to a Fair Trial in Civil Procedure*), Ph.D. Thesis, Masaryk University in Brno, 2011.
2. On the definition of law, it is worth quoting the thought expressed by an eminent Author: 'I am gladly going to resist the temptation to embark on (another) definition of "law". What I mean is this: I conceive law mainly as a living set of norms which develops through its application, and more particularly through its application by the courts' (S. Trechsel & S.J. Summers, *Human Rights in Criminal Proceedings* (*Collected Courses in the Academy of European Law*) (Oxford: Oxford University Press, 2006), 4.
3. V. Knapp, *Teorie práva, 1. Vydání* (Prague: C. H. Beck, 1995), 86.

what it should entail: social order, the fair distribution of assets and values, righteous life, fair and just judicial activity, etc.[4]

The Christian concept of justice, for example, is based on charity and forgiveness. '*Do unto others as you would have them do unto you*'. Justice, in this sense, should be accompanied by compassion and mercy.[5]

As Plato had already remarked over 2,000 years ago, a just society exists only if citizens are born and live in a fair and just way.[6] Such a concept is not so dissimilar to the point stressed many centuries later by John Rawls, according to whom the stability of a society depends on whether its members feel that they are being treated justly or not.[7]

Applying the law in the exercise of judicial powers is, however, something quite different. In the administration of justice, although the sense of justice may often be intuitive, the possibility to use 'intuition' (as well as personal understanding bases on learnt expectations) in judicial decisions is questionable. A constructive model requires that judges act on the basis of legal principles rather than on faith and intuition. In fact, the potential hazards connected with intuitive decisions can easily be identified in terms of possible arbitrariness and abuse.

On the other hand, it is the duty of the judge not only to correctly apply the law, but also to find a 'just' solution to the case.[8] The logical corollary of this premise is that a fair court decision may objectively be defined as such when it has been reached through a fair trial. Indeed, a judge cannot draw a substantively fair decision if there has been a gross violation of the right to a fair trial.

---

4. Justice concerns also the allocation of certain values within social relations, be they positive or negative, related to material objects and benefits, to ethics or moral principles (M. Večeřa, *Spravedlnost v. právu* (Brno: Masarykova Univerzita, 1997), 16). Thus, if one wants to define the concept of justice, he has necessarily to deal also with the concept of 'equality'.
5. See, in this sense, J. Pieper, *The Four Cardinal Virtues* (Notre Dame, IN: University of Notre Dame Press: 1966), 112, wherein the Author states: 'For it is true, as Thomas says, that 'mercy without justice is the mother of dissolution'; but, also, that 'justice without mercy is cruelty'.
6. Plato, *Republic*, (369 B, 420 B). The work, written in 360 B.C., deals with the search after Justice, seen as the order of the State, the construction of which is its aim. Plato also described Justice as harmony, explaining that 'adherence to their own business on the part of the industrious, the military, and the guardian classes, each of these doing its own work in the state, is justice, and will render the state just' (Book 4, 434b-c, in Plato, *Republic*, as translated by John Llewelyn Davies & David James Vaughan, in *Wordsworth Classics of World Literature* (Ware: Wordsworth Editions Ltd., 1997), 131). For an analysis of the principle mentioned in the text, see T. Bubík, *Filosofický o spravedlnosti* (Pardubice: Univerzita Pardubice, 2007), 58.
7. J. Rawls, *A Theory of Justice* (Harvard University Press, 1971); J. Rawls, *Justice as Fairness: A Restatement* (Harvard University Press, 2001). The Author's idea of justice starts from the basic concept that all persons are free and equal. The Author also explains the notion of justice as fairness, stating – *inter alia* – that 'a basic liberty can be limited or denied solely for the sake of one or more other basic liberties' (J. Rawls, *Political Liberalism* (Columbia University Press, 1996), 294).
8. According to some Authors, justice is traditionally considered to be something that maintains or restores balance and proportion, and the main rule – at least within the judicial world – may be expressed by the sentence 'treat like cases alike; and treat different cases differently'. See, in this sense, H.L.A. Hart, *The Concept of Law*, 2nd edn (Oxford: Oxford University Press, 1994).

[A] Notion of Right to a Fair Trial

The right to a fair trial is, in a way, an intuitive concept: each party is aware that he is entitled to a fair trial, and is subjectively convinced of his knowledge of his rights, as well as of the fact that it is always possible to apply 'to Strasbourg'. However, when it comes to giving a common definition, valid throughout the Signatory States of the European Convention on Human Rights (ECHR), things start to get complicated,[9] and the interpretation becomes even more complex due to the differences between the common law and civil law systems, especially in the field of criminal law.[10]

The right to a fair trial is explicitly mentioned not only in Article 6 ECHR, but also in Article 10 of the Universal Declaration of Human Rights,[11] in Article 14 of the International Covenant on Civil and Political Rights,[12] in the Sixth Amendment to the

9. On the interpretation of the European Convention on Human Rights in general, see, among others, G. Letsas, *A Theory of Interpretation of the European Convention on Human Rights* (New York: Oxford University Press, 2007); G. Letsas, *The Truth in Autonomous Concepts: How to Interpret the ECHR*, 15(2) European Journal of International Law 279 (2004); F. Sudre, *L'interprétation de la Convention européenne des droits de l'homme* (Bruxelles: Brylant 1998).
10. See, among others, D.J. Harris, M. O'Boyle, E. Bates, C. Buckley, *Harris, O'Boyle & Warbrick: Law of the European Convention on Human Rights*, 2nd edn (New York: Oxford University Press, 2009), 203. The Authors stress the relevant differences in criminal proceedings between the 'adversarial' system of common law countries and the 'inquisitorial' system of civil law countries. These differences have an important impact both in the investigation phase and during the trial.
11. Article 10 of the Universal Declaration of Human Rights reads: 'Everyone is entitled in full equality to a fair and public hearing by an independent and impartial tribunal, in the determination of his rights and obligations and of any criminal charge against him.'
12. In particular, Article 14(1) of the Covenant provides:

> All persons shall be equal before the courts and tribunals. In the determination of any criminal charge against him, or of his rights and obligations in a suit at law, everyone shall be entitled to a fair and public hearing by a competent, independent and impartial tribunal established by law. The press and the public may be excluded from all or part of a trial for reasons of morals, public order or national security in a democratic society, or when the interest of the private lives of the parties so requires, or to the extent strictly necessary in the opinion of the court in special circumstances where publicity would prejudice the interests of justice; but any judgment rendered in a criminal case or in a suit at law shall be made public except where the interest of juvenile persons otherwise requires or the proceedings concern matrimonial disputes or the guardianship of children.

United States Constitution,[13] and in many other international conventions,[14] as well as in national legislations.[15]

The right to a fair trial generally comprises, according to the doctrine, the following basic fundamental rights: the right of access to court and, consequently, to be heard by a competent, independent and impartial tribunal; the right to 'equality of arms'; the right to a public hearing; the right to be heard within a reasonable time; the right to counsel; and the right to interpretation.[16] These rights are listed in almost all international conventions, however some provisions – such us Article 6 ECHR – provide more detailed hypotheses of specific rights.[17] Moreover, these rights have been the subject of a laborious activity of interpretation by the European Court of Human Rights (ECtHR), which has led to a copious case law, with consequent expansion of the number of specific rights deserving protection under the general category of the right to a fair trial. Indeed, as pointed out by the Court, 'the right to a fair trial holds so prominent a place in a democratic society that there can be no justification for interpreting Article 6 § 1 of the Convention restrictively'.[18]

---

13. The Sixth Amendment to the United States Constitution provides:

> In all criminal prosecutions, the accused shall enjoy the right to a speedy and public trial, by an impartial jury of the State and district wherein the crime shall have been committed, which district shall have been previously ascertained by law, and to be informed of the nature and cause of the accusation; to be confronted with the witnesses against him; to have compulsory process for obtaining witnesses in his favor, and to have the Assistance of Counsel for his defence.

The origins of the Sixth Amendment, as of almost all the provisions of the Bill of Rights, are to be found in the draft proposals by George Mason, which were used, with slight modifications, for the Virginia Declaration of Rights of 12 June 1776 (therefore, before the Declaration of Independence of the United States of America on 4 July 1776). See, on this point, R. Carter Pittman, *The Creation of the Sixth Amendment Right to a Fair Trial*, in *The Right to a Fair Trial*, ed. Enid W. Langbert, Esq. (series '*The Bill of Rights*') (Famington Hills: Greenhaven Press (Thomson Gale corp.), 2005), 29.

14. Such as in Articles 3, 7 and 26 of the African Charter on Human and Peoples' Rights and in Articles 3, 8, 9 and 10 of the American Convention on Human Rights. See, more in detail, Curtis F.J. Doebbler, *Introduction to International Human Rights Law* (Washington DC: CD Publishing, 2006), 108.
15. See, for example, Article 111 of the Italian Constitution (as amended by Constitutional Law No. 2/99), which, at paragraph 1, emphatically states: '*La giurisdizione si attua mediante il giusto processo regolato dalla legge*' ('The jurisdiction is implemented through a due process, as regulated by the law' – translation by the Author), and then lists a long series of guarantees in civil and criminal proceedings, basically modelled on Article 6 ECHR.
16. See, on the listing of these rights, Curtis F.J. Doebbler, *Introduction to International Human Rights Law*, cited above, 108, to which the Author adds the prohibition of an *ex post facto* law, explaining that the aim of the provision for such warranties is the proper administration of justice, either in administrative or judicial proceedings.
17. See, on this point, R. Clayton & H. Tomlinson, *Fair Trial Rights*, cited above, 120–121, where the Authors divide the rights provided for by Article 6 ECHR in two categories, 'express and implied rights'.
18. *Moreira de Azevedo v. Portugal*, Judgment of 23 October 1990, paragraph 66.

[B] Definitions in the Literature and in the Case Law

But what is the right to a 'fair trial' (in French, '*procès équitable*')? Have the literature and the jurisprudence defined a common concept, valid in the different national legal systems - belonging either to civil law or common law tradition - of the States signatory to the Convention?

The right to a fair trial, in accordance with the interpretation given by the Court of Strasbourg, is a basic principle of the Rule of Law in a democratic society and aims to secure the right to a proper administration of justice. The right in question includes, therefore, the right to an effective access to justice, to the equality of arms, to a fair composition of an independent court, to a public hearing, to a Judgment pronounced publicly within 'a reasonable time', etc.

Quite interesting, in this perspective, are the below-quoted paragraphs of a recent Judgment, wherein the Court summarizes the criteria to be used when interpreting and applying the provisions of the Convention, and lists several precedents on the subject matter:

> In order to determine the meaning of the terms and phrases used in the Convention, the Court is guided mainly by the rules of interpretation provided for in Articles 31 to 33 of the Vienna Convention on the Law of Treaties (see, for example, *Golder v. the United Kingdom*, 21 February 1975, § 29, Series A no. 18; *Johnston and others v. Ireland*, 18 December 1986, §§ 51 et seq., Series A no. 112; *Lithgow and others v. the United Kingdom*, 8 July 1986, §§ 114 and 117, Series A no. 102; and *Witold Litwa v. Poland*, no. 26629/95, §§ 57–59, ECHR 2000-III). In accordance with the Vienna Convention the Court is required to ascertain the ordinary meaning to be given to the words in their context and in the light of the object and purpose of the provision from which they are drawn (see *Golder*, cited above, § 29; *Johnston and others*, cited above, § 51; and Article 31 § 1 of the Vienna Convention). Recourse may also be had to supplementary means of interpretation, either to confirm a meaning determined in accordance with the above steps, or to establish the meaning where it would otherwise be ambiguous, obscure, or manifestly absurd or unreasonable (Article 32 of the Vienna Convention; see *Saadi v. the United Kingdom* [GC], no. 13229/03, § 62, ECHR 2008-....).
>
> Since the Convention is first and foremost a system for the protection of human rights, the Court must interpret and apply it in a manner which renders its rights practical and effective, not theoretical and illusory. The Convention must also be read as a whole, and interpreted in such a way as to promote internal consistency and harmony between its various provisions (see, among other authorities, *Stec and others v. the United Kingdom* (dec.) [GC], nos. 65731/01 and 65900/01, §§ 47–48, ECHR 2005-X).
>
> In addition, the Court has never considered the provisions of the Convention as the sole framework of reference for the interpretation of the rights and freedoms enshrined therein. On the contrary, it must also take into account any relevant rules and principles of international law applicable in relations between the Contracting Parties (see *Saadi*, cited above, § 62; *Al-Adsani*, cited above, § 55; and *Bosphorus Hava Yolları Turizm ve Ticaret Anonim Şirketi v. Ireland* [GC], no. 45036/98, § 150, ECHR 2005-VI; see also Article 31 § 3 (c) of the Vienna Convention).

> The Court further observes that it has always referred to the 'living' nature of the Convention, which must be interpreted in the light of present-day conditions, and that it has taken account of evolving norms of national and international law in its interpretation of Convention provisions (see *Soering v. the United Kingdom*, 7 July 1989, § 102, Series A no. 161; *Vo v. France* [GC], no. 53924/00, § 82, ECHR 2004-VIII; and *Mamatkulov and Askarov v. Turkey* [GC], nos. 46827/99 and 46951/99, § 121, ECHR 2005-I).
>
> (*Demir and Baykara v. Turkey*, Judgment 12 November 2008, paragraphs 65-68)

Such principles had already been stated quite clearly more than three decades earlier, when the Court ruled that there is no need to resort to 'supplementary means of interpretation' (as provided for by Article 32 of the Vienna Convention), in order to identify specific aspects (and meanings) of the right to a fair trial. In *Golder v. United Kingdom*[19] the Court stated that Article 6(1) envisages not only to right to a fair trial in an already pending lawsuit, but also the right of access to justice, since it would be inconceivable that the Convention should describe in detail the procedural guarantees accorded to the parties in a pending case and should not grant what comes first, i.e., the access to a court:

> Taking all the preceding considerations together, it follows that the right of access constitutes an element which is inherent in the right stated by Article 6 para. 1 (art. 6-1). This is not an extensive interpretation forcing new obligations on the Contracting States: it is based on the very terms of the first sentence of Article 6 para. 1 (art. 6-1) read in its context and having regard to the object and purpose of the Convention, a lawmaking treaty (see the Wemhoff Judgment of 27 June 1968, Series A no. 7, p. 23, para. 8), and to general principles of law.
>
> The Court thus reaches the conclusion, without needing to resort to 'supplementary means of interpretation' as envisaged at Article 32 of the Vienna Convention, that Article 6 para. 1 (art. 6-1) secures to everyone the right to have any claim relating to his civil rights and obligations brought before a court or tribunal. In this way the Article embodies the 'right to a court', of which the right of access, that is the right to institute proceedings before courts in civil matters, constitutes one aspect only. To this are added the guarantees laid down by Article 6 para. 1 (art. 6-1) as regards both the organisation and composition of the court, and the conduct of the proceedings. In sum, the whole makes up the right to a fair hearing. The Court has no need to ascertain in the present case whether and to what extent Article 6 para. 1 (art. 6-1) further requires a decision on the very substance of the dispute (English 'determination', French '*décidera*').
>
> (*Golder v. the United Kingdom*, Judgment of 21 February 1975, paragraph 36)

According to the prevailing interpretation, the right to a fair trial has two components: the right of access to court, and the right to a fair process, which is secured by a certain number of procedural safeguards.

19. *Golder v. the United Kingdom*, Judgment of 21 February 1975.

A support to the work of interpreting the meaning of the right to a fair trial can also be found, outside the European Convention on Human Rights, in article 14(1) of the International Covenant on Civil and Political Rights, with reference to which the Human Rights Committee has clarified that it 'must be interpreted as requiring a number of conditions, such as equality of arms and respect for the principle of adversary proceedings'.[20]

In conclusion, it might well be said that there is not a common, 'all-inclusive' and general definition of 'right to a fair trial', the meaning of which, on the contrary, has to be identified referring to specific aspects (*rectius*: rights) that form part of it, as listed in the same Article 6 and as resulting from the case law of the ECtHR.

The right to a fair trial covers indeed the entire proceedings, including the execution stage. It embodies all the basic principles of the Rule of Law in a democratic society. Consequently, it has to be recognized as a structured right, comprising several separate subjective fundamental rights, as mentioned above. Its content shall therefore include not only all the guarantees mentioned in Article 6, but also those principles which are not explicitly mentioned, but can, according to the circumstances, be identified by the Court in exercising its decision-making function.

§1.02 THE EUROPEAN CONVENTION ON HUMAN RIGHTS

The European Convention for the Protection of Human Rights and Fundamental Freedoms was signed in Rome on 4 November 1950 and entered into force on 3 September 1953, after being ratified by eight States.[21] It was drafted within the Council of Europe some years after the end of World War II (between 1949 and 1950), when Europe was engaged in a laborious work of reconstruction, both of its economy and material infrastructures and the lives of its people. It is in this period, when European countries were healing the still open wounds deriving from the war, that the notion (and the term itself) of 'human rights' became object of strong interest and study throughout the world.

Thus, short after that the United Nations (recently established for the main purpose of maintaining and promote international peace and security) had adopted the 'Universal Declaration on Human Rights' of 1948, in the 'old continent' the movement for an European integration was becoming stronger and stronger and, with it, also the will to create a common 'charter' for the protection of human rights and liberties. On 5 May 1949 the Council of Europe was formally created, with the signature in London

20. Communication No. 289/1988, *D. Wolf v. Panama*, in UN doc. *GAOR*, A/47/40, paragraph 6.6.
21. Denmark, the Federal Republic of Germany, Iceland, Ireland, Luxembourg, Norway, Sweden and the United Kingdom.

by ten founding States,[22] and the basis for a European Human Rights Convention was laid down.[23]

However, according to part of the literature, the seed of the principles set forth in the European Convention on Human Rights, as well as the concept itself of 'human rights protection', is to be found much earlier in time, probably already in 1215, when the Magna Charta (in the original, in Latin: *Magna Carta*) was sealed by King John (on 15 June 1215),[24] granting 'all free men' of his Kingdom a number of rights and liberties, including what is believed to be the archetype of the 'right to a fair trial'.[25]

In particular, Clause 39 of the Magna Charta states: '*Nullus liber homo capiatur, vel imprisonetur, aut desseisetur de libero tenemento, vel libertatibus, vel liberis consuetudinibus suis, sut utlagetur, aut exuletur, aut aliquo modo destruatur, nec super eum ibimus, nec super eum mittemus, nisi per legale judicium parium suorum, vel per legem terrae*' ('No free man shall be captured, and or imprisoned, or disseised of his freehold, and or of his liberties, or of his free customs, or be outlawed, or exiled, or in

22. The preamble of the Statute of the Council of Europe reads as follows:

> The Governments of the Kingdom of Belgium, the Kingdom of Denmark, the French Republic, the Irish Republic, the Italian Republic, the Grand Duchy of Luxembourg, the Kingdom of the Netherlands, the Kingdom of Norway, the Kingdom of Sweden and the United Kingdom of Great Britain and Northern Ireland,
>
> Convinced that the pursuit of peace based upon justice and international co-operation is vital for the preservation of human society and civilisation;
>
> Reaffirming their devotion to the spiritual and moral values which are the common heritage of their peoples and the true source of individual freedom, political liberty and the rule of law, principles which form the basis of all genuine democracy;
>
> Believing that, for the maintenance and further realisation of these ideals and in the interests of economic and social progress, there is a need of a closer unity between all like-minded countries of Europe;
>
> Considering that, to respond to this need and to the expressed aspirations of their peoples in this regard, it is necessary forthwith to create an organisation which will bring European States into closer association,
>
> Have in consequence decided to set up a Council of Europe consisting of a committee of representatives of governments and of a consultative assembly, and have for this purpose adopted the following Statute:....
>
> The Statute can be found, *inter alia*, at http://conventions.coe.int/Treaty/en/Treaties/html/001.htm (accessed on 1 November 2013).

23. Article 3 of the Statute of the Council of Europe reads:

> Every member of the Council of Europe must accept the principles of the rule of law and of the enjoyment by all persons within its jurisdiction of human rights and fundamental freedoms, and collaborate sincerely and effectively in the realisation of the aim of the Council as specified in Chapter I.

24. Actually, King John was forced by the feudal barons – who wanted to limit the King's powers and to protect their privileges - to accept the *Magna Carta*, and indeed soon after he withdrew from it. However, its principles remained alive and, with several amendments, were included in following editions of the Charter.
25. See, *ex multis*, A. Pallister, *Magna Carta: the Heritage of Liberty* (Oxford: Oxford University Press, 1971); A.D. Boyer (edited by), Essays by Thomas Garden Barnes, *Shaping the Common Law: from Glanvill to Hale, 1188–1688* (Stanford University Press, 2008), 27; G. Slapper & D. Kelly, *Sourcebook on the English Legal System* (London: Cavendish Publishing Limited, 2001), 487.

any way destroyed, nor will we proceed against him by force or proceed against him by arms, but by the lawful Judgment of his peers, and or by the law of the land').[26]

The principle according to which man is born 'free' and has a number of rights and liberties developed across the centuries, also with the help of the work of writers and philosophers (among which we cannot avoid to mention Grotius, Hobbes, Locke, Smith, Montesquieu, and Rousseau), and eventually found its most important expressions several centuries later, with the American Declaration of Independence (4 July 1776) and the French Revolution (1789–1799), which paved the floor to the modern states Constitutions.[27]

Interestingly, the 'Declaration of the Rights of Man and of the Citizen' (*Déclaration des droits de l'homme et du citoyen*) adopted on 26 August 1789 during the French Revolution, and the first ten amendments to the U.S. Constitution (later known as the 'United States Bill of Rights'[28]), adopted by the U.S. House of Representatives on 21 August 1789,[29] are both inspired by the principles deriving from the philosophical theories of the 'Enlightenment' and from the *ius naturalis* (natural law), and provide with the definitions of rights and freedoms, which are still the backbone of modern constitutions and international declarations of human rights (including the ECHR).

As of today 47 States have ratified the ECHR,[30] which has proven to be the most effective international instrument for the protection of human rights, particularly thanks to the activity of its judicial body.

---

26. Such translation can be found in L. Spooner, *An Essay on the Trial by Jury* (Boston: Cleveland, 1852). On the possible link between the right to a fair trial and clause 39 of the Magna Charta, see, among others, R. Clayton & H. Tomlinson, *Fair Trial Rights* (New York: Oxford University Press, 2010), 4.
27. See, among others, M.W. Janis, R.S. Kay & A.W. Bradley, *European Rights Law (Text and Materials)*, III edn (New York: Oxford University Press, 2008), 4–8; D.S. Mason, *A Concise History of Modern Europe: Liberty, Equality, Solidarity*, 2nd edn (Plymouth: Rowman & Littlefield Publishers, 2011), 18–19.
28. On the origin of the Bill of Rights see, among others, Richard E. Labunski, *James Madison and the Struggle for the Bill of Rights* (New York: Oxford University Press, 2006); David J. Bodenhamer & James W. Ely Jr. (eds), *The Bill of Rights in Modern America* (Bloomington: Indiana University Press, 2008); B. Schwartz, *The Great Rights of mankind. A History of the American Bill of Rights* (Lanham: Rowman & Littlefield, 2002); A. Reed Amar, *The Bill of Rights: Creation and Reconstruction* (Yale University Press: 1998); Leonard W. Levy, *Origin of the Bill of Rights* (Yale University Press, 2001).
29. The first ten amendments to the United States Constitution (known, collectively, as 'Bill of Rights') were passed by the Congress of the United States in New York, on 25 September 1789 and ratified on 15 December 1791, to protect individual rights and personal freedoms (in particular, related to liberty and property) and to limit governmental powers (in particular, with regard to judicial proceedings). In the Preamble to the Bill of Rights it can be read, *inter alia*, that:

    > THE Conventions of a number of the States, having at the time of their adopting the Constitution, expressed a desire, in order to prevent misconstruction or abuse of its powers, that further declaratory and restrictive clauses should be added: And as extending the ground of public confidence in the Government, will best ensure the beneficent ends of its institution (...).

30. As indicated in http://conventions.coe.int/treaty/Commun/ChercheSig.asp?NT=005&CM=&DF=&CL=ENG (accessed on 1 November 2013), as of 1 November 2013 the Member States were: Albania, Andorra, Armenia, Austria, Azerbaijan, Belgium, Bosnia and Herzegovina,

Actually, as it has been acutely noted, the European Convention was not, *per se*, exceptional and innovative, as it was in many aspects similar to other international instruments on human rights (such as, for instance, the above-mentioned United States Bill of Rights or the United Nations Universal Declaration on Human Rights), but what was 'extraordinary' was its 'enforcement machinery',[31] which allowed its effective implementation through the possibility, granted either to a State or an individual, to file a petition with the European Commission of Human Rights,[32] and with the subsequent establishment of an effective judicial authority of the European Court of Human Rights to adjudicate the cases brought before it.[33]

Bulgaria, Croatia, Cyprus, Czech Republic, Denmark, Estonia, Finland, France, Georgia, Germany, Greece, Hungary, Iceland, Ireland, Italy, Latvia, Liechtenstein, Lithuania, Luxembourg, Malta, Moldova, Monaco, Montenegro, Netherlands, Norway, Poland, Portugal, Romania, Russia, San Marino, Serbia, Slovak Republic, Slovenia, Spain, Sweden, Switzerland, the former Yugoslav Republic of Macedonia, Turkey, Ukraine and the United Kingdom.

31. See, in these terms, M.W. Janis, R.S. Kay & A.W. Bradley, *European Rights Law (Text and Materials)*, cited above, 19.
32. The Commission was given the right to hear complaints submitted by individuals in 1955, with the consent of the interested State.
33. With Protocol No. 11 to the Convention, a permanent European Court of Human Rights was established.

Chapter 2

Article 6 ECHR

Piero Leanza

Article 6 of the European Convention on Human Rights reads:

> (1) In the determination of his civil rights and obligations or of any criminal charge against him, everyone is entitled to a fair and public hearing within a reasonable time by an independent and impartial tribunal established by law. Judgment shall be pronounced publicly but the press and public may be excluded from all or part of the trial in the interests of morals, public order or national security in a democratic society, where the interests of juveniles or the protection of the private life of the parties so require, or to the extent strictly necessary in the opinion of the court in special circumstances where publicity would prejudice the interests of justice.
>
> (2) Everyone charged with a criminal offence shall be presumed innocent until proved guilty according to law.
>
> (3) Everyone charged with a criminal offence has the following minimum rights:
>
> (a) to be informed promptly, in a language which he understands and in detail, of the nature and cause of the accusations against him;
>
> (b) to have adequate time and facilities for the preparation of his defence;
>
> (c) to defend himself in person or through legal assistance of his own choosing or, if he has not sufficient means to pay for legal assistance, to be given it free when the interests of justice so require;
>
> (d) to examine or have examined witnesses against him and to obtain the attendance and examination of witnesses on his behalf under the same conditions as witnesses against him;
>
> (e) to have the free assistance of an interpreter if he cannot understand or speak the language used in court.

§2.01 PROCEEDINGS REGULATED BY ARTICLE 6 ECHR

Paragraph 1 of Article 6 ECHR explicitly states that 'everyone' is entitled to the right to a fair trial 'in the determination of his civil rights and obligations or of any criminal charge against him'.[1]

The field of application is thus clearly identified as either civil or criminal proceedings.[2] Article 6, however, does not provide a definition of 'criminal charge' and 'civil rights and obligations', nor of what is to be intended as 'determination'. It is then up to the interpretation of the European Court of Human Rights (ECtHR) to give a meaning to these terms and to expand the application of Article 6. Indeed, the orientation of the Court is that the right to a fair trial 'holds such a prominent a place that a restrictive interpretation of Article 6 would not correspond to the scope of the Convention'.[3]

Therefore, the ECtHR has interpreted the terms 'criminal charge' and 'civil rights and obligations' with an autonomous meaning, different from the one intended by national legislations.[4]

The Court's case law has further extended the application of Article 6 to other kinds of proceedings, such as proceedings before administrative courts, military courts, constitutional courts, etc.

It must be noted as well that, although the wording of the article explicitly refers to the 'trial', the guarantees provided by Article 6 also apply to the stages before the trial, such as the investigations (as far as criminal proceedings are concerned),[5] or the

1. On the scope of Article 6 ECHR see, *ex multis*, J. Charrier, *Code de la Convention Europenne des Droit de l'Homme*, 2nd edn (Paris: Litec, 2002); M. Chiavario (in Bartole, Conforti, Raimondi), *Commentario alla convenzione europea per al tutela dei diritti dell'uomo e delle libertà fondamentali* (Padova: Cedam, Padova, 2001); J.G. Merrills & A.H. Robertson, *Human Rights in Europe: A Study of the European Convention on Human Rights*, 4th edn (Manchester: Manchester University Press, 2001); J. Velu & R. Ergec, *La Convention europeenne des droits de l'homme* (Brussels: Brylant, 1990).
2. However, it must be noted that, although paragraphs 2 and 3 of Article 6 seem to refer only to criminal proceedings, the principles mentioned therein have been extended by the jurisprudence of the Court, under certain circumstances, also to civil and administrative proceedings.
3. See *Moreira de Azevedo v. Portugal*, Judgment of 23 October 1990, paragraph 66; and *Delcourt v. Belgium*, Judgment of 17 January 1970, paragraph 25.
4. On the autonomous meaning of the term 'civil' see, among others, *König v. Germany*, Judgment of 28 June 1987; *Ferrazzini v. Italy* (Grand Chamber), Judgment of 12 July 2001.
5. The issue related to the identification of the date when criminal proceedings start, for the purpose of the application of Article 6, will be examined more in detail *infra*, § 2.02 [B]. The question was examined mostly with regard to the right to have a trial within a reasonable time, where it is necessary to ascertain when the proceedings start. The basic principle applied by the Court is that, in criminal matters, the reasonable time begins to run as soon as a person is 'charged', which may also occur before the case is brought to trial (see, *ex multis*, *Deweer v. Belgium*, Judgment of 27 February 1980, paragraph 42), such as on the date of arrest, the date when the person concerned was officially notified that he would be prosecuted or the date when preliminary investigations were opened (*Wemhoff v. Germany*, Judgment of 27 June 1968, paragraph 19; *Ringeisen v. Austria*, Judgment of 16 July 1971, paragraph 110), the date when the investigating authorities request that the suspect produce evidence (*Funke v. France*, Judgment of 25 February 1993, paragraph 44), etc. Thus, the Court defined the term 'charge', for the purposes of Article 6(1), as 'the official notification given to an individual by the competent authority of an allegation that he has committed a criminal offence' or when 'the situation of the [suspect] has been substantially

administrative stages preceding the filing of a civil claim before a judicial authority,[6] and to the phases after the trial, such as the execution proceedings.[7] In other words, the provisions set forth in Article 6 apply not only to the proceedings before a court, but also to several other stages that precede or follow the judicial proceedings.

In this sense, for example, the ECtHR decided in *Johansen v. Norway*,[8] related to a complex procedure in the matter of deprivation of parental rights. The Court found that no unreasonable delay took place in the course of the procedure. However, the decision is quite interesting in the part where the Court considers the application of Article 6 not only to the judicial phase, but also to the previous phase before the national administrative body:

> The Court observes that the proceedings leading to the deprivation of parental rights and access commenced before the Committee on 13 December 1989 and ended when the Supreme Court refused leave to appeal on 19 September 1991 (see paragraphs 12 and 28 above). They thus lasted altogether one year and nine months.
>
> The Court shares the applicant's and the Commission's opinion that, in view of what was at stake for the applicant and the irreversible and definitive character of the measures concerned, the competent national authorities were required by Article 6 para. 1 (art. 6-1) to act with exceptional diligence in ensuring the progress of the proceedings. However, it does not find that they failed to discharge their obligations in this respect.
>
> (*Johansen v. Norway*, Judgment of 27 June 1996, paragraph 88)

The same principle has been affirmed in many Judgments of the Court related to the execution phase, among which *Burdov v. Russia*:[9]

> The Court reiterates that Article 6 § 1 secures to everyone the right to have any claim relating to his civil rights and obligations brought before a court or tribunal; in this way it embodies the 'right to a court', of which the right of access, that is the right to institute proceedings before courts in civil matters, constitutes one aspect. However, that right would be illusory if a Contracting State's domestic legal system allowed a final, binding judicial decision to remain inoperative to the detriment of one party. It would be inconceivable that Article 6 § 1 should describe in detail procedural guarantees afforded to litigants – proceedings that are fair, public and expeditious – without protecting the implementation of judicial decisions; to construe Article 6 as being concerned exclusively with access to a court and the conduct of proceedings would be likely to lead to situations incompatible with the principle of the rule of law which the Contracting States undertook to respect when they ratified the Convention. Execution of a judgment given by any

---

affected' (see, among others, *Eckle v. Germany*, Judgment of 15 July 1982, paragraph 74; *Deweer v. Belgium*, Judgment of 27 February 1980, paragraph 46).

6. See, for example, *W v. the United Kingdom*, Judgment of 8 July 1987, with regard to the administrative procedure preceding the judicial proceedings, in the matter of child care and parental 'right of access'.
7. See *Hornsby v. Greece*, Judgment of 19 March 1997, paragraph 40, wherein the Court states that the 'execution of a judgment given by any court must therefore be regarded as an integral part of the "trial" for the purposes of Article 6'.
8. *Johansen v. Norway*, Judgment of 27 June 1996.
9. See also, *ex multis*: *Di Pede v. Italy*, Judgment of 26 September 1996; *Hornsby v. Greece*, Judgment of 19 March 1997.

> court must therefore be regarded as an integral part of the 'trial' for the purposes of Article 6.
>
> (*Burdov v. Russia*, Judgment of 4 September 2002, paragraph 34)

Although Article 6 does not refer explicitly to the appellate stage, the jurisprudence of the Court has established the principle according to which appeals proceedings, too, under certain circumstances, are regulated by Article 6. The same reasoning can apply to the proceedings pending before a constitutional court, as the result of such proceedings has a direct effect on the civil rights of an individual.

Finally, in certain cases related to the enforcement of a foreign decision, the ECtHR has decided that, although the decision had been issued in another State, the State where the decision is to be ratified and/or enforced has to ascertain that the foreign Judgment was issued following a trial where the guarantees under Article 6 were granted to the parties. It is the case, for example, of the execution in Italy of the Judgments issued by the *Sacra Rota* (the Vatican court with jurisdiction on Catholic marriages).[10] The Vatican State did not ratify the European Convention on Human Rights; therefore, the task of verifying the respect, before that court, of the basic guarantees set forth in Article 6 is up to the State ratifying the decisions taken by the Vatican court:

> The Court notes at the outset that the applicant's marriage was annulled by a decision of the Vatican courts which was declared enforceable by the Italian courts. The Vatican has not ratified the Convention and, furthermore, the application was lodged against Italy. The Court's task therefore consists not in examining whether the proceedings before the ecclesiastical courts complied with Article 6 of the Convention, but whether the Italian courts, before authorising enforcement of the decision annulling the marriage, duly satisfied themselves that the relevant proceedings fulfilled the guarantees of Article 6. A review of that kind is required where a decision in respect of which enforcement is requested emanates from the courts of a country which does not apply the Convention. Such a review is especially necessary where the implications of a declaration of enforceability are of capital importance for the parties.
>
> (*Pellegrini v. Italy*, Judgment of 20 July 2001, paragraph 40)

§2.02 THE RIGHT TO A FAIR TRIAL IN CRIMINAL PROCEEDINGS

All the guarantees provided for in Article 6 (both the general ones listed under paragraph 1, and the more specific rights indicated in paragraphs 2 and 3) are applicable to criminal proceedings.[11]

10. P. Pirrone, *Il Caso Pellegrini dinanzi alla Corte europea dei diritti dell'uomo: efficacia in Italia delle sentenze ecclesiastiche ed equo processo*, in *Diritto pubblico comparato ed europeo*, IV, 2001, 2063.
11. For a comprehensive analysis of the right to a fair trial in criminal proceedings, see S. Trechsel & S.J. Summers, *Human Rights in Criminal Proceedings* (*Collected Courses in the Academy of European Law*), cited above; S. Stavros, *The Guarantees for Accused Persons under Article 6 of*

It is, however, necessary, that the 'determination of a criminal charge', which is the basis for the application of the rights granted by the article, be ascertained.

The established jurisprudence of the ECtHR holds that a criminal charge may be deemed effective only when the investigations have reached the point in which the defendant has been 'charged' with a criminal offence, i.e., clearly accused of it. It consequently follows that Article 6 shall not apply to other phases of the procedure, such as those related to legal aid,[12] preventive measures against crime,[13] or extradition proceedings,[14] all hypotheses in which no criminal charge has yet been brought against a person.

Is has, however, to be noted that some of Article 6 guarantees apply starting from the first investigation: for instance, in *Öcalan v. Turkey*, *Murray v. the United Kingdom*,[15] the Court observed that the right to defence exists also when there is not yet a clear charge against the suspect.[16]

---

the European Convention on Human Rights, cited above; P. van Dijk, *The Right of the Accused to a Fair Trial under International Law* (Utrecht: S.I.M., 1983).

12. See, among others, *Gutfreund v. France*, Judgment of 12 June 2003, paragraphs 32, 35 and 36.
13. See, for example, the Italian preventive measures legislation, the core of which is represented by the law of 31 May 1965, No. 575 (*Provisions against the Mafia* [translation by the Author]), which extended the application of preventive measures contained in the law of 27 December 1956, No. 1423 (*Preventive Measures against People Threatening Security and Public Morality* [translation by the Author]), also to persons suspected of belonging to mafia-type associations. A very important innovation - in order to fight the increasingly alarming Mafia phenomenon - was introduced by Law No. 646/1982 (the same law which introduced in the Italian criminal code Article 416-*bis*, punishing the criminal offence of the so called 'mafia-type association'). This same law, in the framework of the Law No. 575/1965, introduced preventive measures targeted to the assets of suspects of certain crimes. The legislative framework on the preventive measures was recently amended by the Legislative Decree 6 September 2011, n. 159.
14. See, *ex multis*, *Mamatkulov and Askarov v. Turkey*, Judgment of 4 February 2005, paragraphs 81-83.
15. In *John Murray v. the United Kingdom*, Judgment of 8 February 1996, paragraph 63, the Court observed:

> National laws may attach consequences to the attitude of an accused at the initial stages of police interrogation which are decisive for the prospects of the defence in any subsequent criminal proceedings. In such circumstances Article 6 will normally require that the accused be allowed to benefit from the assistance of a lawyer already at the initial stages of police interrogation. However, this right, which is not explicitly set out in the Convention, may be subject to restrictions *for good cause*. The question, in each case, is whether the restriction, in the light of the entirety of the proceedings, has deprived the accused of a fair hearing.

16. See, for example, *Öcalan v. Turkey*, Judgment of 12 March 2003, paragraphs 140 and 146, where the Court stated:

> The manner in which Article 6 §§ 1 and 3 (c) are applied during the investigation depends on the special features of the proceedings and the facts of the case. Article 6 will normally require that the accused be allowed to benefit from the assistance of a lawyer from the initial stages of police interrogation ...', and '... In these circumstances, the Court is of the view that to deny access to a lawyer for such a long period and in a situation where the rights of the defence might well be irretrievably prejudiced is detrimental to the rights of the defence to which the accused is entitled by virtue of Article 6'. The Court further observed that the right of the accused 'to communicate

With regard to the application of Article 6 to extradition proceedings, the Court has repeatedly affirmed that extradition proceedings fall neither in the notion of 'criminal charge' nor in the concept of 'civil rights and *obligations*'.[17] A paragraph may be quoted, *ex multis,* from the decision as to the admissibility of the application in *Sardinas Albo v. Italy,*[18] which also refers to previous relevant case law:

> As to the extradition proceedings, the Court recalls that the words 'determination ... of a criminal charge' in Article 6 § 1 of the Convention relate to the full process of the examination of an individual's guilt or innocence in relation to an offence, and not merely to the process of determining whether or not a person may be extradited to a foreign country (see *Raf v. Spain* (dec.), no. 53652/00, 21 November 2000, and *A.B. v. Poland* (dec.), no. 33878/96, 18 October 2001). Moreover, it has constantly been held that decisions regarding the entry, right to remain and deportation of aliens do not concern the determination of an applicant's civil rights or obligations or of a criminal charge against him within the meaning of Article 6 § 1 of the Convention (see *Maaouia v. France* [GC], no. 39652/98, §§ 33–41, ECHR 2000-X). This provision is therefore not applicable to the first and second set of proceedings concerning the extradition of the applicant to the United States.
>
> (*Sardinas Albo v. Italy,* Decision of 8 January 2004, paragraph 3[b])

Referring to the relevance of the procedure for granting legal aid, the Court has stated, *inter alia,* in *Gutfreund v. France,*[19] that:

> As regards the 'determination of [a] criminal charge', the Court notes that the procedure for applying for legal aid only concerned the provision of legal assistance to the applicant, and not the establishment of guilt or the determination of the amount of the penalty.
>
> (...) Despite the refusal of legal aid, the applicant therefore had a choice in the light of what was at stake and the nature of the proceedings between appearing in person or being represented by a lawyer. He opted for the latter alternative. It follows that the refusal of legal aid had no bearing on the determination of the charges against the applicant, and indeed he did not dispute that.

> with his legal representative out of hearing of a third person is part of the basic requirements of a fair trial in a democratic society and follows from Article 6 § 3 (c) of the Convention.

17. See, however, the case law of the ECtHR which requires that proceedings leading to the expulsion of aliens must respect some basic aspects of fairness (*inter alia, C.G and Others v. Bulgaria,* Judgment of 24 April 2008; *Nolan and K. v. Russia,* Judgment of 12 February 2009; *Saadi v. Italy,* (Grand Chamber), Judgment of 28 February 2008). Moreover, according to Article 1 of Protocol No. 7 ECHR:

    > 1. An alien lawfully resident in the territory of a State shall not be expelled therefrom except in pursuance of a decision reached in accordance with law and shall be allowed: (a) to submit reasons against his expulsion, (b) to have his case reviewed, and (c) to be represented for these purposes before the competent authority or a person or persons designated by that authority. 2. An alien may be expelled before the exercise of his rights under paragraph 1 (a), (b) and (c) of this Article, when such expulsion is necessary in the interests of public order or is grounded on reasons of national security.

18. *Sardinas Albo v. Italy,* Decision of 8 January 2004.
19. *Gutfreund v. France,* Judgment of 12 June 2003.

> The Court concludes from the foregoing that the refusal of legal aid was not a decisive factor in the determination of the criminal charge against the applicant.
>
> (*Gutfreund v. France*, Judgment of 12 June 2003, paragraphs 32, 35 and 36)

A few words must be spent on the applicability of Article 6 to the so-called 'preventive measures'. Such measures are peculiar legal instruments, typical of emergency legislation, which is very common in countries affected by the virulence of organized crime. They are, indeed, measures *ante delictum*, i.e., measures which are applied to suspects of crimes regardless of whether a crime has been committed or not (given certain conditions, strictly defined by the law). The preventive measures are 'personal' or 'asset-related'. The former are applied to the suspect of certain crimes and are directed to the 'person'; the latter are targeted to the goods belonging to the suspects.

With reference to the application of Article 6 to proceedings for the imposition of preventive measures (such as, for example, the 'special surveillance for public safety' or the 'seizure of assets'[20]), the orientation of the ECtHR is that such a procedure does not configure a 'criminal charge' in terms of Article 6.[21] See, for example, the Judgment in the case *Raimondo v. Italy*,[22] according to which:

> The Court shares the view taken by the Government and the Commission that special supervision is not comparable to a criminal sanction because it is designed to prevent the commission of offences. It follows that proceedings concerning it did not involve 'the determination ... of a criminal charge.'
>
> (*Raimondo v. Italy*, Judgment of 22 February 1994, paragraph 43)

In the same sense the Court had already expressed itself in *Guzzardi v. Italy*,[23] concluding that:

> In the Court's opinion, those proceedings did not involve the 'determination ... of a criminal charge', even when these words are construed within the meaning of the Convention.
>
> (*Guzzardi v. Italy*, Judgment of 6 September 1980, paragraph 108)

20. '*Sorveglianza speciale di pubblica sicurezza*' and '*sequestro di beni*', provided for in the Italian special legislation mentioned above, §2.02, footnote 13.
21. It has to be noted, however, that these measures can interfere with the right to a private life, protected by Article 8 ECHR, which reads:

> 1. Everyone has the right to respect for his private and family life, his home and his correspondence. 2. There shall be no interference by a public authority with the exercise of this right except such as is in accordance with the law and is necessary in a democratic society in the interests of national security, public safety or the economic well-being of the country, for the prevention of disorder or crime, for the protection of health or morals, or for the protection of the rights and freedom of others (see on the point, *ex multis*, *Kuznetsov v. Ukraine*, Judgment of 29 April 2003).

22. *Raimondo v. Italy*, Judgment of 22 February 1994.
23. *Guzzardi v. Italy*, Judgment of 6 September 1980.

[A] Notion of 'Criminal'

It is to be stressed once more that the expression 'criminal charge,' relevant for the application of Article 6, must necessarily carry an autonomous meaning, different from that adopted in national jurisdictions.[24]

The need to establish an autonomous meaning derives not only from the necessity to prevent differences in the application of Article 6 from one State to another, but also, considering the notions provided by diverse domestic legislation, the risk of allowing a Contracting State to waive the application of the Convention at its own discretion.

The meaning of 'criminal' has been clarified in many decisions of the Court, the first of which is the well-known *Engel and others v. The Netherlands*[25] (but see other subsequent Judgments, such as, for example, *Ozturk v. Germany*[26]), wherein the Court set out three criteria to this end: a) the classification of the offence in the domestic law; b) the nature of the offence; c) the possible punishment:[27]

> Having thus reaffirmed the 'autonomy' of the notion of 'criminal' as conceived of under Article 6 (art. 6), what the Court must determine is whether or not the 'regulatory offence' committed by the applicant was a 'criminal' one within the meaning of that Article (art. 6). For this purpose, the Court will rely on the criteria adopted in the above-mentioned Engel and others judgment (ibid., pp. 34-35, § 82). The first matter to be ascertained is whether or not the text defining the offence in issue belongs, according to the legal system of the respondent State, to criminal law; next, the nature of the offence and, finally, the nature and degree of severity of the penalty that the person concerned risked incurring must be examined, having regard to the object and purpose of Article 6 (art. 6), to the ordinary meaning of the terms of that Article (art. 6) and to the laws of the Contracting States.
>
> (*Ozturk v. Germany*, Judgment of 21 February 1984, paragraph 50)

[1] The Classification of the Offence in Domestic Law

In the above-mentioned case *Engel and others v. The Netherlands*, the Court had to decide, *inter alia*, whether an offence provided for by the Dutch legislation was of criminal or disciplinary nature:

> All the Contracting States make a distinction of long standing, albeit in different forms and degrees, between disciplinary proceedings and criminal proceedings. For the individuals affected, the former usually offer substantial advantages in comparison with the latter, for example as concerns the sentences passed.

24. See, *ex multis*, *Saunders v. UK*, Judgment of 29 November 1996 (Grand Chamber); *Funke v. France*, Judgment of 25 February 1993; *Neumeister v. Austria*, Judgment of 27 June 1968; *Ringeisen v. Austria*, Judgment of 16 July 1971.
25. *Engel and others v. The Netherlands*, Judgment of 8 June 1976.
26. *Ozturk v. Germany*, Judgment of 21 February 1984.
27. See also, on the determination of the three mentioned criteria, *Demicoli v. Malta*, Judgment of 27 August 1991, paragraphs 31-34; *Ravnsborg v. Sweden*, Judgment of 23 March 1994; *Schmautzer v. Austria*, Judgment of 23 October 1995; and many others.

> Disciplinary sentences, in general less severe, do not appear in the person's criminal record and entail more limited consequences. It may nevertheless be otherwise; moreover, criminal proceedings are ordinarily accompanied by fuller guarantees.
>
> It must thus be asked whether or not the solution adopted in this connection at the national level is decisive from the standpoint of the Convention. Does Article 6 (art. 6) cease to be applicable just because the competent organs of a Contracting State classify as disciplinary an act or omission and the proceedings it takes against the author, or does it, on the contrary, apply in certain cases notwithstanding this classification? This problem, the importance of which the Government acknowledge, was rightly raised by the Commission; it particularly occurs when an act or omission is treated by the domestic law of the respondent State as a mixed offence, that is both criminal and disciplinary, and where there thus exists a possibility of opting between, or even cumulating, criminal proceedings and disciplinary proceedings.
>
> (*Engel and others v. The Netherlands*, Judgment of 8 June 1976, paragraph 80)

It therefore follows from the reading of the Court's Judgment that the first criterion to adopt in ascertaining the presence of a 'criminal charge' is to verify if an offence is classified as 'criminal' by the domestic law of the respondent State. In particular, the Court found that, if a conduct is classified as criminal by the national legislation, Article 6 will automatically apply to the proceedings, with no need to verify whether the other two criteria are present or not:

> In the Neumeister Judgment of 27 June 1968, the Court has already held that the word 'charge' must be understood 'within the meaning of the Convention' (Series A no. 8, p. 41, para. 18, as compared with the second sub-paragraph on p. 28 and the first sub-paragraph on p. 35; see also the Wemhoff Judgment of 27 June 1968, Series A no. 7, pp. 26-27, para. 19, and the Ringeisen Judgment of 16 July 1971, Series A no. 13, p. 45, para. 110).
>
> The question of the 'autonomy' of the concept of 'criminal' does not call for exactly the same reply.
>
> The Convention without any doubt allows the States, in the performance of their function as guardians of the public interest, to maintain or establish a distinction between criminal law and disciplinary law, and to draw the dividing line, but only subject to certain conditions. The Convention leaves the States free to designate as a criminal offence an act or omission not constituting the normal exercise of one of the rights that it protects. This is made especially clear by Article 7 (art. 7). Such a choice, which has the effect of rendering applicable Articles 6 and 7 (art. 6, art. 7), in principle escapes supervision by the Court.
>
> The converse choice, for its part, is subject to stricter rules. If the Contracting States were able at their discretion to classify an offence as disciplinary instead of criminal, or to prosecute the author of a 'mixed' offence on the disciplinary rather than on the criminal plane, the operation of the fundamental clauses of Articles 6 and 7 (art. 6, art. 7) would be subordinated to their sovereign will. A latitude extending thus far might lead to results incompatible with the purpose and object of the Convention. The Court therefore has jurisdiction, under Article 6 (art. 6) and even without reference to Articles 17 and 18 (art. 17, art. 18), to satisfy itself that the disciplinary does not improperly encroach upon the criminal.

> In short, the 'autonomy' of the concept of 'criminal' operates, as it were, one way only.
>
> (*Engel and others v. The Netherlands*, Judgment of 8 June 1976, paragraph 81)

Only when the first criterion does not apply, need reference be made to the other two. The *ratio* of such interpretation lies basically in the fact that when a State already considers a certain conduct as a criminal offence, the need then arises to grant the accused the right to a fair trial in terms of Article 6.

[2] The Nature of the Offence

In identifying the second criterion – regarded by the ECtHR as the most important[28] – the Court has taken into consideration several features of the offence, among which, in particular: whether it applies to a restricted group of people or not;[29] whether the proceedings are 'brought by a public body under statutory powers of enforcement';[30] whether an offence is 'classified as part of the criminal law in the vast majority of the Contracting States';[31] and whether the penalty which derives has a deterrent and punitive purpose or a compensatory one.

The latter principle was applied by the Court, for example, in *Janosevic v. Sweden*, wherein, with reference to the Swedish legislation on penalties imposable by the Tax Authority and the County Administrative Court, the Court decided that 'the general character of the legal provisions on tax surcharges and the purpose of the penalties, which are both deterrent and punitive, suffice to show that for the purposes of Article 6 of the Convention the applicant was charged with a criminal offence', observing that:

> It is true that the tax surcharges were imposed on the applicant on objective grounds without the need to establish any criminal intent or negligence on his part. However, the lack of subjective elements does not necessarily deprive an offence of its criminal character; indeed, criminal offences based solely on objective elements may be found in the laws of the Contracting States (see *Salabiaku v. France*, Judgment of 7 October 1988, Series A no. 141-A, p. 15, § 27). In this connection, the Court notes that the present system of tax surcharges has replaced earlier purely criminal procedures. It appears that the change from the earlier system, which was one of penalties for intentional or negligent conduct, to the new system based on objective factors was prompted by the need for greater efficiency (...).
>
> Furthermore, the present tax surcharges are not intended as pecuniary compensation for any costs that may have been incurred as a result of the taxpayer's conduct. Rather, the main purpose of the relevant provisions on surcharges is to exert pressure on taxpayers to comply with their legal obligations and to punish breaches of those obligations. The penalties are thus both deterrent

28. See *Jussila v. Finland* (Grand Chamber), Judgment of 23 November 2006, paragraph 38.
29. See, *ex multis*, *Bendenoun v. France*, Judgment of 24 February 1994, paragraph 47.
30. *Benham v. the United Kingdom*, Judgment of 10 June 1996, paragraph 56.
31. *Ozturk v. Germany*, cited above, paragraph 53.

> and punitive. The latter character is the customary distinguishing feature of a criminal penalty (...).
>
> (*Janosevic v. Sweden*, Judgment of 23 July 2002, paragraph 68)

In the above-mentioned *Engel* case, the Court had already noted that 'the very nature of the offence is a factor of greater importance', specifying that:

> However, supervision by the Court does not stop there. Such supervision would generally prove to be illusory if it did not also take into consideration the degree of severity of the penalty that the person concerned risks incurring. In a society subscribing to the rule of law, there belong to the 'criminal' sphere deprivations of liberty liable to be imposed as a punishment, except those which by their nature, duration or manner of execution cannot be appreciably detrimental. The seriousness of what is at stake, the traditions of the Contracting States and the importance attached by the Convention to respect for the physical liberty of the person all require that this should be so (see, *mutatis mutandis*, the *De Wilde, Ooms and Versyp* Judgment of 18 June 1971, Series A no. 12, p. 36, last sub-paragraph, and p. 42 in fine).
>
> (*Engel and others v. The Netherlands*, Judgment of 8 June 1976, paragraph 82)

The criterion of the nature of the offence was also examined, among others, in *Weber v. Switzerland*, wherein the Court noted that when a provision applies only to a restricted group of people (such as, for example, persons belonging to a certain profession), it is generally of disciplinary nature and not a criminal offence. It is worth quoting a couple of paragraphs of the Judgment in this case:

> The second, weightier criterion is the nature of the offence.
>
> In the Government's submission, the impugned sentence was designed to punish a breach of a rule intended to protect defendants and ensure that proceedings were conducted objectively by shielding the judge in charge of them from any pressure, in particular by the media. The Commission considered that Article 185 applied to a limited number of people who shared the characteristic of taking part in a judicial investigation; although these people did not belong to the staff responsible for the administration of justice, they were in a 'special relationship of obligation' with the relevant authorities, which justified subjecting them to a special discipline.
>
> The Court does not accept this submission. Disciplinary sanctions are generally designed to ensure that the members of particular groups comply with the specific rules governing their conduct. Furthermore, in the great majority of the Contracting States disclosure of information about an investigation still pending constitutes an act incompatible with such rules and punishable under a variety of provisions. As persons who above all others are bound by the confidentiality of an investigation, judges, lawyers and all those closely associated with the functioning of the courts are liable in such an event, independently of any criminal sanctions, to disciplinary measures on account of their profession. The parties, on the other hand, only take part in the proceedings as people subject to the jurisdiction of the courts, and they therefore do not come within the disciplinary sphere of the judicial system. As Article 185, however, potentially affects the whole population, the offence it defines, and to which it attaches a punitive sanction, is a 'criminal' one for the purposes of the second criterion.
>
> (*Weber v. Switzerland*, Judgment of 22 May 1990, paragraphs 32-33)

Moreover, in *Ozturk v. Germany*, cited above, the Court held that, although a State may decriminalize certain offences, regarding them as administrative offences ('petty' crimes), nevertheless they shall be considered as 'criminal', for the purpose of the application of Article 6, with regard to their substantial nature:

> The Court does not underestimate the cogency of this argument. The Court recognises that the legislation in question marks an important stage in the history of the reform of German criminal law and that the innovations introduced in 1968/1975 represent more than a simple change of terminology.
>
> Nonetheless, the Court would firstly note that, according to the ordinary meaning of the terms, there generally come within the ambit of the criminal law offences that make their perpetrator liable to penalties intended, *inter alia*, to be deterrent and usually consisting of fines and of measures depriving the person of his liberty.
>
> In addition, misconduct of the kind committed by Mr. Öztürk continues to be classified as part of the criminal law in the vast majority of the Contracting States, as it was in the Federal Republic of Germany until the entry into force of the 1968/1975 legislation; in those other States, such misconduct, being regarded as illegal and reprehensible, is punishable by criminal penalties.
>
> (*Ozturk v. Germany*, Judgment of 21 February 1984, paragraph 53)

The Court specified, in the same Judgment, that it would be contrary to the object and purpose of Article 6, which guarantees to 'everyone charged with a criminal offence' the right to a court and to a fair trial, if a State were allowed to remove from the scope of this provision a whole category of offences merely on the grounds that they are regarded as less serious:

> The fact that it was admittedly a minor offence hardly likely to harm the reputation of the offender does not take it outside the ambit of Article 6 (art. 6). There is in fact nothing to suggest that the criminal offence referred to in the Convention necessarily implies a certain degree of seriousness. In this connection, a number of Contracting States still draw a distinction, as did the Federal Republic at the time when the Convention was opened for the signature of the Governments, between the most serious offences (crimes), lesser offences (*délits*) and petty offences (contraventions), whilst qualifying them all as criminal offences. Furthermore, it would be contrary to the object and purpose of Article 6 (art. 6), which guarantees to 'everyone charged with a criminal offence' the right to a court and to a fair trial, if the State were allowed to remove from the scope of this Article (art. 6) a whole category of offences merely on the ground of regarding them as petty. Nor does the Federal Republic deprive the presumed perpetrators of *Ordnungswidrigkeiten* of this right since it grants them the faculty - of which the applicant availed himself - of appealing to a court against the administrative decision.
>
> (*Ozturk v. Germany*, Judgment of 21 February 1984, paragraph 53)

Non-criminal conducts in several States, such as minor road traffic offences, have been dealt with in many other cases, where the ECtHR has concluded that, although the conduct may have been decriminalized by the domestic law, it nonetheless maintains its criminal classification for the purpose of Article 6. Further, in many States, minor traffic violations are still punished as criminal offences.

> Like the Commission, the Court notes that, although the offences in issue and the procedures followed in the case fall within the administrative sphere, they are

> nevertheless criminal in nature. This is moreover reflected in the terminology employed. Thus Austrian law refers to administrative offences (*Verwaltungsstraftaten*) and administrative criminal procedure (*Verwaltungsstrafverfahren*). In addition, the fine imposed on the applicant was accompanied by an order for his committal to prison in the event of his defaulting on payment (...).
>
> These considerations are sufficient to establish that the offence of which the applicant was accused may be classified as 'criminal' for the purposes of the Convention. It follows that Article 6 (art. 6) applies.
>
> (*Schmautzer v. Austria*, Judgment of 23 October 1995, paragraph 28)

However, in a case related to the withdrawal of a driving licence by the competent administrative authority, the Court decided that such a measure was not of criminal nature:

> As regards the nature of the measure, the Court observes that section 55 of the consolidated Acts does not presuppose any investigation or finding of guilt and that its application is totally independent of any criminal proceedings which may subsequently be brought. The immediate withdrawal of a driving licence appears to be a preventive measure for the safety of road-users, designed to take a driver who is potentially dangerous to other road-users temporarily off the roads. It should be compared with the procedure of issuing a licence, which is undoubtedly an administrative procedure and is aimed at ensuring that a driver is fit and qualified to drive on the public highway. The immediate withdrawal of a driving licence is a precautionary measure; the fact that it is an emergency measure justifies its being applied immediately and there is nothing to indicate that its purpose is punitive.
>
> (*Escoubet v. Belgium*, Judgment of 28 October 1999, paragraph 37)

Finally, the ECtHR affirmed the important principle according to which if it is ascertained that an offence can be regarded as criminal in the autonomous meaning for the purpose of the application of Article 6, there is no need to verify the recurrence of the third criterion (the severity of the punishment).

> As the contravention committed by Mr. Öztürk was criminal for the purposes of Article 6 (art. 6) of the Convention, there is no need to examine it also in the light of the final criterion stated above (at paragraph 50). The relative lack of seriousness of the penalty at stake (see paragraph 18 above) cannot divest an offence of its inherently criminal character.
>
> (*Ozturk v. Germany*, Judgment of 21 February 1984, paragraph 54)

The Grand Chamber also clarified that the degree of seriousness of the penalty is not relevant, for the purpose of the application of Article 6. A minor offence can be intended as a 'criminal charge' as well, and the inferior gravity of an offence can be relevant only when adopting the third criterion, i.e., the 'severity of the punishment':

> However, that does not conversely mean that the minor nature of an offence can, of itself, take it outside the ambit of Article 6, as there is nothing in the Convention to suggest that the criminal nature of an offence, within the meaning of the second of the *Engel* criteria, necessarily requires a certain degree of seriousness (see *Öztürk*, cited above, pp. 20-21, § 53). The reliance on the severity of the penalty in

> *Campbell and Fell* (pp. 37-38, § 72) was a matter relevant to the third of the *Engel* criteria as opposed to a factor defining the nature of the offence.
>
> (*Ezeh and Connors v. the United Kingdom*, [Grand Chamber], Judgment of 9 October 2003, paragraph 104)

[3] The Severity of the Punishment

With reference to the third criterion, the severity of the punishment, the Court has affirmed that 'according to the ordinary meaning of the terms, there generally come within the ambit of the criminal law offences that make their perpetrator liable to penalties intended, *inter alia*, to be deterrent and usually consisting of fines and of measures depriving the person of his liberty',[32] except 'those which by their nature, duration or manner of execution cannot be appreciably detrimental'.[33]

Thus, in a case where the penalty established by the domestic legislation was, alternatively, a pecuniary one and imprisonment for a period up to 60 days, the Court decided that the measure was to be intended as 'criminal', for the purpose of the application of Article 6:

> The third criterion is the degree of severity of the penalty that the person concerned risks incurring. The Court notes that in the present case, whilst the House imposed a fine of 250 Maltese liri on the applicant which has not yet been paid or enforced, the maximum penalty he risked was imprisonment for a period not exceeding sixty days or a fine not exceeding 500 Maltese liri or both. What was at stake was thus sufficiently important to warrant classifying the offence with which the applicant was charged as a criminal one under the Convention (. ...).
>
> (*Demicoli v. Malta*, Judgment of 27 August 1991, paragraph 34)

On the contrary, in the above-mentioned case *Escoubet v. Belgium*, related to the withdrawal of a driving licence, limited in time to no more than fifteen days, an overall consideration of such a measure, with regard to its scope and length, led the Court to exclude its criminal nature under the Convention:

> With regard to the degree of severity, the Court points out that the effect of immediate withdrawal of a driving licence is limited in time, since it cannot be withheld for more than fifteen days, unless there are special circumstances allowing it to be withheld for two further periods of fifteen days (see paragraph 19 above). The impact of such a measure, in scope and in length, is not sufficiently substantial to allow it to be classified as a 'criminal' penalty.
>
> In the instant case the Court observes that the withdrawal of the applicant's driving licence did not cause him significant prejudice, since he was able to get it back six days after he had handed it over to the police and two days after he had requested its return (see paragraphs 10 and 11 above).
>
> (*Escoubet v. Belgium*, Judgment of 28 October 1999, paragraph 38)

---

32. *Ibid.*, paragraph 53.
33. See *Engel and others*, cited above, paragraph 82.

However, in the case in which the penalty, provided as a pecuniary one, can be converted into a term of imprisonment under certain circumstances, the Court deemed the severity of such punishment as sufficient to classify the offence as a criminal one:

> As regards the third criterion – the nature and the degree of severity of the penalty incurred – the Court notes that the fine could amount to 500 Swiss francs (see paragraph 20 above) and be converted into a term of imprisonment in certain circumstances (see paragraph 22 above). What was at stake was thus sufficiently important to warrant classifying the offence with which the applicant was charged as a criminal one under the Convention.
>
> (*Weber v. Switzerland*, Judgment of 22 May 1990, paragraph 34)

[4] Alternative Nature of the Two Criteria

The Court of Strasbourg has decided in many cases that the criteria of the nature of the offence and the severity of the punishment are alternative and not cumulative, with the consequence that it is sufficient that only one of them be present to determine its classification as a criminal charge:[34]

> (...) it is the Court's established jurisprudence that the second and third criteria laid down in *Engel* are alternative and not necessarily cumulative: for Article 6 to be held applicable, it suffices that the offence in question is by its nature to be regarded as 'criminal' from the point of view of the Convention, or that the offence made the person liable to a sanction which, by its nature and degree of severity, belongs in general to the 'criminal' sphere.
>
> (*Ezeh and Connors v. the United Kingdom* [Grand Chamber], Judgment of 9 October 2003, paragraph 86)

However, the Court noted that 'a cumulative approach may be adopted where separate analysis of each criterion does not make it possible to reach a clear conclusion as to the existence of a criminal charge'.[35] This is what happened, for example, in *Campbell and Fell v. the United Kingdom*, wherein the Court observed that:

> Taking into account, therefore, both the 'especially grave' character of the offences with which Mr. Campbell was charged (see paragraph 27 above) and the nature and severity of the penalty that he risked incurring – and did in fact incur –, the Court finds that Article 6 (art. 6) is applicable to the Board of Visitors' adjudication in his case. It is accordingly not necessary to consider the sanctions, other than forfeiture of remission, which could have been or were imposed on him.
>
> (*Campbell and Fell v. the United Kingdom*, Judgment of 28 June 1984, paragraph 73)

---

34. See, *ex plurimis*, *Ezeh and Connors v. UK*, (Grand Chamber), Judgment of 9 October 2003; *Öztürk v. Germany*, Judgment of 21 February 1984; *Lutz v. Germany*, Judgment of 25 August 1987.
35. See *Ezeh and Connors v. the United Kingdom*, quoted above, and *Bendenoun v. France*, Judgment of 24 February 1994; *Benham v. the United Kingdom*, Judgment of 10 June 1996; *Garyfallou AEBE v. Greece*, Judgment of 24 September 1997; and *Lauko v. Slovakia*, Judgment of 2 September 1998.

[B] Autonomous Meaning of 'Criminal Charge' ('*accusation en matière pénale*')

The notion of 'charge' similarly has an autonomous meaning in the Convention.

The jurisprudence of the ECtHR has developed a copious case law related to this issue, in particular with reference to the right to have a trial within a reasonable time and to the right of access to a court.

A 'charge' is - in the autonomous meaning of the Convention - the official notification given by the competent authority to a person that he/she is accused of having committed a criminal offence (in the French text: '*accusation en matière pénale*'), or any act following which the situation of the suspect is 'substantially affected'.

In this sense the Court has decided, for example, in *Deweer v. Belgium* and *Neumeister v. Austria*:

> The 'charge' could, for the purposes of Article 6 par. 1 (art. 6-1), be defined as the official notification given to an individual by the competent authority of an allegation that he has committed a criminal offence. In several decisions and opinions the Commission has adopted a test that appears to be fairly closely related, namely whether 'the situation of the [suspect] has been substantially affected' (Neumeister case, Series B no. 6, p. 81; case of Huber v. Austria, Yearbook of the Convention, vol. 18, p. 356, 67; case of Hätti v. Federal Republic of Germany, ibid., vol. 19, p. 1064, 50, etc.).
>
> (*Deweer v. Belgium*, Judgment of 27 February 1980, paragraph 46)

> The terms 'criminal charge' and 'accusation' are in fact said to refer, in both the Continental and the Anglo-American systems, to the legal act of requesting the Court to rule on whether the allegation that an individual has committed a punishable offence is well-founded.
>
> (*Neumeister v. Austria*, Judgment of 27 June 1968, paragraph 28)

The Court further observed that the meaning of charge must be intended in a 'substantive' way and not in a 'formal' one,[36] thus investigating the concrete details of the procedure, beyond the formal appearance:

> However, the prominent place held in a democratic society by the right to a fair trial (see especially the above-mentioned *Airey* judgment, pp. 12-13, par. 24) prompts the Court to prefer a 'substantive', rather than a 'formal', conception of the 'charge' contemplated by Article 6 par. 1 (art. 6-1). The Court is compelled to look behind the appearances and investigate the realities of the procedure in question.
>
> (*Deweer v. Belgium*, Judgment of 27 February 1980, paragraph 44)

Logical corollary of the notion of 'criminal charge' is the identification of the moment in which a person is charged with a criminal offence, in order to establish when the guarantees of Article 6 become applicable.

---

36. See also *Eckle v. Germany*, Judgment of 15 July 1982, paragraph 73.

The concept is well expressed in the following sentences of *Corigliano v. Italy*, wherein the Court decided that a 'charge' in the meaning of Article 6 was present when the accused received the so-called 'judicial notification' issued by the Public Prosecutor:[37]

> In criminal matters, in order to assess whether the 'reasonable time' requirement contained in Article 6 § 1 (art. 6-1) has been complied with, one must begin by ascertaining from which moment the person was 'charged'; this may have occurred on a date prior to the case coming before the trial court (see, for example, the Deweer Judgment of 27 February 1980, Series A no. 35, p. 22, § 42), such as the date of arrest, the date when the person concerned was officially notified that he would be prosecuted or the date when the preliminary investigations were opened (see the Wemhoff Judgment of 27 June 1968, Series A no. 7, pp. 26-27, § 19, the Neumeister Judgment of the same date, Series A no. 8, p. 41, § 18, and the Ringeisen Judgment of 16 July 1971, Series A no. 13, p. 45, § 110). Whilst 'charge', for the purposes of Article 6 § 1 (art. 6-1), may in general be defined as 'the official notification given to an individual by the competent authority of an allegation that he has committed a criminal offence', it may in some instances take the form of other measures which carry the implication of such an allegation and which likewise substantially affect the situation of the suspect (see, inter alia, the above-mentioned Eckle judgment, Series A no. 51, p. 33, § 73).
>
> (*Corigliano v. Italy*, Judgment of 10 December 1982, paragraph 34)

Thus, pursuant to the above-mentioned general principles, in the case law of the Court, the following events, among others, have been considered as criminal charges: the arrest of the accused,[38] the notification to the accused that he is being investigated and that he will be prosecuted for the commission of a criminal offence,[39] the opening of the preliminary investigations,[40] the appointment of a defence lawyer, after the opening of a case file by the public prosecutor,[41] etc.

While the cases cited above are all related to civil law systems, it is worth noting that in common law systems the moment of the procedure identifiable as a 'charge' was found also in the accusation or the arrest of an individual by the police:

> In November 1977 the applicant was interviewed by the police and then charged with having used forged cattle feed vouchers which enable farmers to purchase cattle feed at a cheaper price.
>
> (...) The Commission first observes that the starting point of the period to be taken into consideration for assessing whether criminal proceedings have exceeded a reasonable time is the point at which the applicant becomes an 'accused'

37. The 'judicial notification' is an act of the criminal process, under the Italian law, intended to give the accused official notice of the commencement of criminal proceedings against him and of his entitlement to appoint a defending lawyer within a certain period of time (Article 369 of the Italian Criminal Procedure Code).
38. See *Foti v. Italy*, Judgment of 10 December 1982, paragraph 52; *Wemhoff v. Germany*, Judgment of 27 June 1968; *Neumeister v. Austria*, Judgment of 27 June 1968; and many others.
39. See *Corigliano v. Italy*, quoted above.
40. See *Wemhoff v. Germany*, and *Neumeister v. Austria*, quoted above.
41. See *Angelucci v. Italy*, Judgment of 19 February 1991.

> person. In the present case this period begins on 5 November 1977, the date on which the first charges were made against the applicant.
>
> (*X v. Ireland*, Decision No 9429/8 of the Commission on the admissibility of the application of 2 March 1983)

If it is of considerable importance to establish the moment in which a criminal charge is brought against the accused, it is also important to establish up to which point Article 6 continues to apply, i.e., when the criminal charge is finally determined:

> As regards the end of the 'time', in criminal matters the period governed by Article 6 par. 1 (art. 6-1) covers the whole of the proceedings in issue, including appeal proceedings (see the König Judgment of 28 June 1978, Series A no. 27, p. 33, par. 98).
>
> (*Eckle v. Germany*, Judgment of 15 July 1982, paragraph 76)

In the same sense the Court decided in *Konig v. Germany*,[42] wherein a parallelism is drawn between criminal and civil proceedings in the definition of the period covered by the guarantees of Article 6:

> As regards the period to which Article 6 (art. 6) is applicable, the Court has held that in criminal matters this period covers the whole of the proceedings in question, including appeal proceedings (above-mentioned Wemhoff judgment, pp. 26 and 27, paras. 18 and 20; above-mentioned Neumeister judgment, p. 41, para. 19; Delcourt Judgment of 17 January 1970, Series A no. 11, pp. 13-15, paras. 25 and 26). The position - as, moreover, the Government concede - is no different in the case of disputes ('contestations') over civil rights and obligations for which Article 6 para. 1 (art. 6-1) likewise requires that there be - at first instance, on appeal or in cassation - a determination.
>
> (*Konig v. Germany*, Judgment of 28 June 1978, paragraph 98)

Thus, although the ECHR does not provide for a right to an appeal,[43] when appeal proceedings are foreseen by the domestic legislation of a Signatory State, then Article 6 shall be applicable to such proceedings.[44] The Court has also held that Article 6 applies to the procedure for leave to appeal from a conviction, considering that appeals proceedings are normal steps in criminal proceedings.[45] On the contrary, the Commission has decided that Article 6 is not applicable to the proceedings for re-trial, when the criminal proceedings have been completed and the application of the convicted person is not to be considered as a 'normal step'.[46]

---

42. *Konig v. Germany*, Judgment of 28 June 1978.
43. See, however, Article 2 of Protocol 7 ECHR (*Right of appeal in criminal matters*) according to which: '1. Everyone convicted of a criminal offence by a tribunal shall have the right to have his conviction or sentence reviewed by a higher tribunal. The exercise of this right, including the grounds on which it may be exercised, shall be governed by law. 2. This right may be subject to exceptions in regard to offences of a minor character, as prescribed by law, or in cases in which the person concerned was tried in the first instance by the highest tribunal or was convicted following an appeal against acquittal.'
44. *Delcourt v. Belgium*, Judgment of 17 January 1970, paragraphs 25 and 26.
45. *Monnel and Morris*, Judgment of 2 March 1987, paragraph 54.
46. *Callaghan v. the United Kingdom*, Appl. No. 14739/89, Decision of 9 May 1989.

§2.03 THE RIGHT TO A FAIR TRIAL IN CIVIL PROCEEDINGS

Article 6 ECHR states that the guarantees provided therein shall apply, other than to criminal proceedings, also to proceedings related to the 'determination' of an individual's 'civil rights and obligations'.

It must be noted that the ECHR is the only international instrument of this kind which explicitly specifies that the guarantees provided for by Article 6, apply only to 'civil' rights and obligations. For example, Article 14(1) of the International Covenant on Civil and Political Rights (ICCPR) reads: 'In the determination of any criminal charge against him, or of *his rights and obligations in a suit at law* (...) (emphasis added)'. It is similarly provided for by Article 10 of the Universal Declaration of Human Rights (UDHR): 'Everyone is entitled in full equality to a fair and public hearing by an independent and impartial tribunal, in the determination of *his rights and obligations* and of any criminal charge against him' (emphasis added). Article 47(1) of the Charter of Fundamental Rights of the European Union (CRFEU) simply affirms that 'Everyone whose *rights and freedoms guaranteed by the law of the Union* are violated has the right to an effective remedy before a tribunal in compliance with the conditions laid down in this Article' (emphasis added), without any specification of the kind of 'rights' involved. Article 8(1) of the American Convention on Human Rights (ACHR) reads: 'Every person has the right to a hearing, with due guarantees and within a reasonable time, by a competent, independent, and impartial tribunal, previously established by law, in the substantiation of any accusation of a criminal nature made against him or *for the determination of his rights and obligations of a civil, labor, fiscal, or any other nature*' (emphasis added). Even more general is the African Charter on Human and People's Rights (ACHPR), which simply refers to 'the right to an appeal to competent national organs against acts of violating his fundamental rights as recognized and guaranteed by conventions, laws, regulations and customs in force' (Article 7(1), lit. a).

But when, exactly, does this 'determination' of civil rights and obligations occur? The answer to this question is offered by the vast case law of the ECtHR, by which – as will be explained in detail in the following sections – the core principles underlying the application of Article 6(1) to civil proceedings have been established. It can be first stated that, according to such case law, as a general rule civil rights and obligations are being determined when the proceedings before a domestic court have as their main object the recognition of a private law right (such as, in tort law or compensation claims). Further, the Court has held that Article 6 applies also to proceedings not directly related to the recognition of a civil right or obligations, when the proceedings may have a decisive influence on them. In other words, when any proceedings, even of an administrative nature, are directly 'decisive' for individual civil rights and obligation, they fall within the area of application of Article 6(1).

In this sense, the following observations contained in *Le Compte, Van Leuven and De Meyere v. Belgium*[47] are particularly interesting:

47. *Le Compte, Van Leuven and De Meyere v. Belgium*, Judgment of 23 June 1981.

> As regards the question whether the dispute related to the above-mentioned right, the Court considers that a tenuous connection or remote consequences do not suffice for Article 6 par. 1 (art. 6-1), in either of its official versions (*'contestation sur'*, 'determination of'): civil rights and obligations must be the object – or one of the objects – of the 'contestation' (dispute); the result of the proceedings must be directly decisive for such a right.
>
> (*Le Compte, Van Leuven and De Meyere v. Belgium*, Judgment of 23 June 1981, paragraph 47)

[A] The Existence of a 'Dispute' at National Level

The application of Article 6 requires the existence of a 'dispute' over rights and obligations at national level. In fact, the term 'contestation', present in the French text of the provision under examination (*'soit des contestations sur ses droits et obligations de caractère civil'*), does not have an equivalent in the English text ('in the determination of his civil rights and obligations'); however, in its case law, the Court of Strasbourg has provided for an interpretation of what is to be intended as 'dispute' in the autonomous meaning of the Convention.

Such interpretation is well summarized in *Pudas v. Sweden*[48] and *Benthem v. The Netherlands*,[49] wherein the Court lists the following principles, already expressed in previous decisions:[50]

> (a) Conformity with the spirit of the Convention requires that the word *'contestation'* (dispute) should not be construed too technically and should be given a substantive rather than a formal meaning.
> (b) The *'contestation'* (dispute) may relate not only to the actual existence of a right but also to its scope or the manner in which it may be exercised. It may concern both questions of fact and questions of law.
> (c) It must be genuine and of a serious nature.
> (d) The expression *'contestations sur (des) droits et obligations de caractère civil'* (disputes over civil rights and obligations) covers all proceedings the result of which is decisive for such rights and obligations. However, a tenuous connection or remote consequences do not suffice for Article 6 § 1 (art. 6-1): civil rights and obligations must be the object – or one of the objects – of the 'contestation' (dispute); the result of the proceedings must be directly decisive for such a right.
>
> (*Pudas v. Sweden*, Judgment of 27 October 1987, paragraph 31)

Therefore, in order to conclude that there is, in a specific case, a dispute over civil rights and obligations for the purpose of the application of Article 6, there must be a 'dispute' over a 'right' which is recognized by the domestic law. The dispute must be genuine and serious, it may relate not only to the actual existence of a right but to its scope or

48. *Pudas v. Sweden*, Judgment of 27 October 1987.
49. *Benthem v. the Netherlands*, Judgment of 23 October 1985.
50. See, for the principle listed: under point (a), *Le Compte, Van Leuven and De Meyere*, Judgment of 23 June 1981, paragraph 45; under point (b), *Albert and Le Compte*, Judgment of 10 February 1983, paragraphs 29 and 36; under point (c), *Sporrong and Lönnroth*, Judgment of 23 September 1982, paragraph 81; and, under point (d), *Ringeisen v. Austria*, Judgment of 16 July 1971, paragraph 94 and *Le Compte, Van Leuven and De Meyere*, cited above, paragraph 47.

the manner in which it can be exercised as well, and the outcome of the proceedings must be 'directly decisive' for the right in question.[51]

The Court furthermore clarified, in *Fayed v. the United Kingdom*,[52] that, in order to verify whether there is a dispute concerning civil rights and obligations at national level, not only the substantive content of the contested civil right, but also the possible existence of procedural limitations on the applicant's ability to undertake legal proceedings must be taken into consideration (see, on this point, *infra*, the Judgment issued in *Markovic v. Italy*[53]).

However, the Court specified that the dispute must be intended to lead to a judicial determination, and not merely to an administrative evaluation. This concept was affirmed, *inter alia*, in *San Juan v. France*,[54] in which the Court reasoned that proceedings for admission to a profession are not covered by Article 6 where they are related to the assessment of the knowledge and experience required for carrying on a certain profession.[55]

> In accordance with its case-law (see *Van Marle and Others*, cited above, p. 12, § 36), the Court considers that an assessment of that kind, evaluating knowledge and experience for carrying on a profession under a particular title, is akin to a school or university examination and is so far removed from the exercise of the normal judicial function that the safeguards in Article 6 cannot be taken to cover resultant disagreements.
>
> There was thus no '*contestation*' (dispute) within the meaning of Article 6, which accordingly was not applicable in the instant case.
>
> (*San Juan v. France*, Appl. No. 43956/98, Decision of 28 February 2001)

Similarly, the ECtHR excluded that certain proceedings may be considered as decisive for the determination of civil rights and obligations (and, therefore, excluded them from the application of Article 6), when their outcome is related to aspects not concerning the merits of the case.

To this effect, it is interesting to examine the decision of inadmissibility taken by the Commission in *Dassa Foundation and others v. Leichtenstein*,[56] related to a seizure order, wherein the Court, reaffirming the consolidated principles already expressed in previous decisions, stated that Article 6 does not apply to proceedings where only an interim measure is to be taken, before the decision on the merits:[57]

---

51. See, *Benthem v. the Netherlands*, cited above, paragraph 32; and, more recently, *Gutfreund v. France*, Judgment of 12 June 2003, paragraph 38.
52. *Fayed v. the United Kingdom*, Judgment of 21 September 1990, paragraph 68.
53. *Markovic and others v. Italy*, Judgment of 14 December 2006.
54. *San Juan v. France*, Appl. No. 43956/98, Decision of 28 February 2001. See also *Van Marle and Others v. the Netherlands*, Judgment of 26 June 1986, cited in the decision, and *Eisenberg v. France*, Appl. No. 52237/99, Decision of 2 September 2003.
55. See also, in the sense that the dispute needs to be 'justiciable' ('i.e., it must be one that inherently lends itself to judicial resolution'), D.J. Harris, M. O'Boyle, E. Bates, C. Buckley, *Harris, O'Boyle & Warbrick: Law of the European Convention on Human Rights*, 2nd edn (New York: Oxford University Press, 2009), 226.
56. *Dassa Foundation and others v. Liechtenstein*, Appl. No. 696/05, Decision of 10 July 2007.
57. See also, *ex multis*, *Kress v. France*, Appl. No. 39594/98, Decision of 29 February 2000; *Starikow v. Germany*, Appl. No. 23395/02, Decision of 10 April 2003; *Libert v. Belgium*, Appl. No. 44734/98, Decision of 8 July 2004.

> The Court must first determine whether or not Article 6 of the Convention is applicable to the seizure orders at issue. In order for an individual to be entitled to the guarantees laid down in that provision, the proceedings must concern 'the determination' of either his civil rights and obligations or of any criminal charge against him.
>
> According to the Court's case-law on the applicability of Article 6 under its civil head, proceedings before the domestic courts amount to 'the determination' of an applicant's civil rights and obligations if there is a real 'dispute' ('*contestation*') over these rights and obligations. The result of the proceedings in question must thus be directly decisive for such a right or obligation (see *Fayed v. the United Kingdom*, Judgment of 21 September 1994, Series A no. 294-B, pp. 45-46, § 56; *Zlínsat, spol. s r.o. v. Bulgaria*, no. 57785/00, § 72, 15 June 2006).
>
> Therefore, Article 6 does not apply to proceedings in which only interim or provisional measures are taken prior to the decision on the merits, as such proceedings do not, as a rule, affect the merits of the case and thus do not yet involve the determination of civil rights and obligations (...)
>
> (*Dassa Foundation and others v. Liechtenstein*, Appl. No. 696/05, Decision of 10 July 2007)

It must, however, be noted that exceptionally the Court has considered Article 6 to be applicable also to proceedings relating to interim orders or decisions. This happened, for example, where an interim decision was already able to determine the rights of the parties in relation to the final claim.[58] In particular, in *Markass Car Hire Ltd v. Cyprus*[59] the Commission reasoned that, although 'more recently, the Court held that Article 6 did not apply to proceedings relating to interim orders (...) adopted prior to the proceedings on the merits', such case law was not applicable to the case at hand (related to the breach of an agreement), where the interim measure taken by the national judicial body affected substantially the position of the applicant, causing to him irreversible prejudice:

> It follows that the interim decision of 31 March 1998 partly coincided with the main action and, unless reversed by the appeal court within a short time-limit, was to affect, as it did for a substantial period, the legal rights of the parties resulting from the purported contract (cf. *mutatis mutandis* Boca v. Belgium, no. 50615/99, decision of 12 June 2001). In this respect, the Court cannot overlook the drastic character of the interim decision which concerned, as the applicant maintains, almost the whole of the company's fleet of vehicles and disposed to a considerable degree of the other relevant civil action against the applicant. The combined effect of the measure and its duration caused irreversible prejudice to the applicant's interests and drained to a substantial extent the final outcome of the proceedings of its significance.
>
> In these circumstances, the Court considers that the interim decision in effect partially determined the rights of the parties in relation to the final claim against the applicant in civil action 3315/98, and thereby acquired the character of

58. See, in a case where an interim order immediately led to the institution of the main proceedings on the dispute in issue, *Air Canada v. the United Kingdom*, Judgment of 5 May 1995, paragraph 61.
59. *Markass Car Hire Ltd v. Cyprus*, Appl. No. 51591/99, Decision of 23 October 2001.

> a 'dispute' over a civil right and obligation to which Article 6 of the Convention was applicable.
>
> (*Markass Car Hire Ltd v. Cyprus*, Appl. No. 51591/99, Decision of 23 October 2001)

In cases related to the awarding of costs, one must differentiate between costs proceedings which are the continuation of the main proceedings on the merits, and proceedings initiated as 'subsidiary proceedings' on costs, after the decision on the merits has been taken.

In *Robins v. the United Kingdom*,[60] the Court, disagreeing with the assessment of the Commission, considered that the costs proceedings initiated by the applicants, even though separately decided, had to be 'seen as a continuation of the substantive litigation and accordingly as part of a determination of ... civil rights and obligations'.[61]

According to the interpretation of the Commission, applications for leave to appeal do not fall under the meaning of civil rights and obligations and are therefore excluded from the umbrella of Article 6. For example, in *Porter v. the United Kingdom*, with reference to the preliminary examination conducted by the House of Lords, in order to establish whether or not the conditions required for granting leave to appeal had been fulfilled, the Commission held that in such case the national court did not determine 'civil rights and obligations' within the meaning of Article 6(1):

> (...) Article 6 para. 1 (Art. 6-1) of the Convention does not apply to the preliminary proceedings on leave to appeal before the House of Lords and that, therefore, this aspect of the applicant's case must be rejected as being incompatible *ratione materiae* with the provisions of the Convention, in accordance with Article 27 para. 2 (Art. 27-2).
>
> (*Porter v. the United Kingdom*, Appl. No. 12972/87, Decision of 9 November 1987, paragraph 2)

It must be observed that Article 6 does not create any new substantive right which does not already exist within the national law; it rather grants an individual the procedural guarantees listed in the same provision (as interpreted by the case law of the European Court of Human Rights).

In particular, in *Markovic and others v. Italy*,[62] the Court, recalling the basic principle according to which 'Article 6 § 1 extends only to '*contestations*' (disputes) over (civil) 'rights and obligations' which can be said, at least on arguable grounds, to be recognized under domestic law', reaffirmed that 'it does not itself guarantee any particular content for (civil) 'rights and obligations' in the substantive law of the Contracting States'[63] and that 'the Court may not create by way of interpretation of Article 6(1) a substantive right which has no legal basis in the State concerned'.[64]

60. *Robins v. the United Kingdom*, Judgment of 23 September 1997, paragraph 29.
61. See also *Ziegler v. Switzerland*, Judgment of 21 February 2002, paragraphs 22-26.
62. *Markovic and others v. Italy*, cited above.
63. On this point, see also *James and others v. the United Kingdom*, Judgment of 21 February 1986, paragraph 81; *Lithgow and others v. the United Kingdom*, Judgment of 8 July 1986, paragraph 192; and *The Holy Monasteries v. Greece*, Judgment of 9 December 1994, paragraph 80; all quoted in *Markovic v. Italy*.
64. *Markovic and others v. Italy*, cited above, paragraph 93.

In the same Judgment, the Court emphasizes that 'the distinction between substantive limitations and procedural bars determines the applicability and, as the case may be, the scope of the guarantees under Article 6',[65] observing that:

> It would not be consistent with the rule of law in a democratic society or with the basic principle underlying Article 6 § 1 – namely that civil claims must be capable of being submitted to a judge for adjudication – if, for example, a State could, without restraint or control by the Convention enforcement bodies, remove from the jurisdiction of the courts a whole range of civil claims or confer immunities from civil liability on large groups or categories of persons (...).
>
> (*Markovic and others v. Italy*, Judgment of 14 December 2006, paragraph 97)

Finally, Article 6(1) is deemed applicable also in case of existing immunities or procedural bars which interfere with the possibility to act before a court for the protection of an individual's civil rights.[66] The Court concluded that 'where there is a serious and genuine dispute as to the lawfulness of such an interference, going either to the very existence or the scope of the asserted civil right, Article 6 § 1 entitles the individual 'to have this question of domestic law determined by a tribunal'.[67]

[B] The Autonomous Meaning of 'Civil Rights and Obligations'

The establishment of an autonomous meaning of the terms 'civil rights and obligations' is a key issue in the matter at hand, since – as it has been said with reference to the meaning of 'criminal charge' – the existence of different concepts of civil rights and obligations within the different legal systems of the Signatory States could cause a certain confusion and difficulty in the interpretation and application of Article 6. Indeed, simply accepting the meaning adopted by each national law would result in an unequal application of Article 6 in the different Signatory States.

However, the Court has also noted that it does not have to give an abstract definition of the concept of civil rights and obligations,[68] but, on the contrary, must assess case by case, according to the peculiar elements under evaluation, whether there is a 'civil right' which may fall under the protection of Article 6.

This is what happened, for example, with regard to social security-related claims, which are treated in some States as matters of public law, whereas they may fall within the category of civil rights, in the autonomous meaning of the Convention.

In *Feldbrugge v. The Netherlands*, related to a health insurance-related claim, the Court observed that:

---

65. *Markovic and others v. Italy*, cited above, paragraph 94.
66. See also, on this point, *Fayed v. the United Kingdom*, cited above, and *Le Compte, Van Leuven and De Meyere v. Belgium*, Judgment of 23 June 1981, paragraph 44.
67. *Markovic and others v. Italy*, cited above, paragraph 99, and the following, both quoted in the same Judgment: *Sporrong and Lönnroth v. Sweden*, Judgment of 23 September 1982, paragraph 81, and *Tre Traktörer AB v. Sweden*, Judgment of 7 July 1989, paragraph 40.
68. *Feldbrugge v. The Netherlands*, Judgment of 29 May 1986, paragraph 27.

> Under Netherlands legislation, the right in issue is treated as a public-law right (...). This classification, however, provides only a starting point (...); it cannot be conclusive of the matter unless corroborated by other factors.
>
> (*Feldbrugge v. The Netherlands*, Judgment of 29 May 1986, paragraph 28)

After having evaluated 'the relative cogency of the features of public law and private law' present in that case, the Court concluded that the latter were predominant:

> None of these various features of private law is decisive on its own, but taken together and cumulatively they confer on the asserted entitlement the character of a civil right within the meaning of Article 6 para. 1 (art. 6-1) of the Convention, which was thus applicable.
>
> (*Feldbrugge v. The Netherlands*, Judgment of 29 May 1986, paragraph 40)

Already in its Judgment delivered in the case *Konig v. Germany*[69] (which followed the path already laid out in *Ringeisen v. Austria*),[70] the Court had stressed that according to the Commission 'the concept of "civil rights and obligations" cannot be interpreted solely by reference to the domestic law of the respondent State':

> The Court confirms this case-law on the present occasion. Hence, it considers that the same principle of autonomy applies to the concept in question; any other solution might lead to results incompatible with the object and purpose of the Convention (see, *mutatis mutandis*, the above-mentioned *Engel and others* judgment, p. 34, para. 81).
>
> (*Konig v. Germany*, Judgment of 28 June 1978, paragraph 88)

In this regard, the jurisprudence of the ECtHR has played a significant role (just as it has with regard to the establishment of an autonomous meaning of 'criminal charge'[71]) and, after the first few years, in which some areas of uncertainty and confusion had existed for lack of a precise definition, there emerged a quite precise picture of what is intended as 'civil rights and obligations', for the purpose of the application of Article 6.

In the above-mentioned *Konig v. Germany*, for example, the Court affirmed the principle according to which, although it is necessary to establish an autonomous meaning of 'civil rights and obligations', the meaning ascribed to such terms by the domestic law cannot be disregarded, specifying, however, that the Court cannot limit its investigation to the legal classification and the literal wording of the national law, but must also refer to the 'substantive content and effects of the right' as provided for by the law of the State concerned. Furthermore, the Court must also 'take account of

69. *Konig v. Germany*, Judgment of 28 June 1978.
70. *Ringeisen v. Austria*, cited above.
71. The Court itself, in *Konig v. Germany* (Judgment of 28 June 1978, paragraph 88), recognized that 'the problem of the 'autonomy' of the meaning of the expressions used in the Convention, compared with their meaning in domestic law, has already been raised before the Court on several occasions', recalling that, with regard to criminal proceedings, the establishment of a 'meaning of the Convention' of the terms 'criminal' and 'charge' had been established by its vast jurisprudence (in particular by the *Neumeister* Judgment of 27 June 1968, paragraph 18, the *Wemhoff* Judgment of 27 June 1968, paragraph 19, the *Ringeisen* Judgment of 16 July 1971, paragraph 110, and the *Engel and others* Judgment of 8 June 1976, paragraph 81).

the object and purpose of the Convention and of the national legal systems of the other Contracting States':

> Whilst the Court thus concludes that the concept of 'civil rights and obligations' is autonomous, it nevertheless does not consider that, in this context, the legislation of the State concerned is without importance. Whether or not a right is to be regarded as civil within the meaning of this expression in the Convention must be determined by reference to the substantive content and effects of the right - and not its legal classification - under the domestic law of the State concerned. In the exercise of its supervisory functions, the Court must also take account of the object and purpose of the Convention and of the national legal systems of the other Contracting States (see, *mutatis mutandis*, the above-mentioned *Engel and others* judgment, p. 35, para. 82).
>
> (*Konig v. Germany*, Judgment of 28 June 1978, paragraph 89)

However, in this case, the Court did not deem it necessary to investigate further to determine an autonomous meaning of the rights and obligations involved. After having ascertained that the medical profession is counted, in the Federal Republic of Germany, among the traditional liberal professions, the Court held that the medical profession 'is not a public service: once authorized, the doctor is free to practise or not, and he provides treatment for his patients on the basis of a contract made with them', and that although the medical practitioner 'has the care of the health of the community as a whole', the responsibility that the medical profession bears towards the society, 'does not, however, alter the private character of the medical practitioner's activity'.[72] Therefore - the Court concluded - it is sufficient, for the purpose of its decision, to ascertain whether the object of the case at hand is or not of a 'private nature':

> In these conditions, it is of little consequence that here the cases concern administrative measures taken by the competent bodies in the exercise of public authority. Neither does it appear pertinent that, under the law of the State concerned, it is for administrative courts to give the decision on these cases and to do so in proceedings which leave to the court the responsibility for the investigation and for the conduct of the trial. All that is relevant under Article 6 para. 1 (art. 6-1) of the Convention is the fact that the object of the cases in question is the determination of rights of a private nature.
>
> Since it thus considers the rights affected by the withdrawal decisions and forming the object of the cases before the administrative courts to be private rights, the Court concludes that Article 6 para. 1 (art. 6-1) is applicable, without it being necessary in the present case to decide whether the concept of 'civil rights and obligations' within the meaning of that provision extends beyond those rights which have a private nature.
>
> (*Konig v. Germany*, Judgment of 28 June 1978, paragraphs 94-95)

This interpretation is apparently based on the main distinction between 'private law' and 'public law', so that rights and obligations which originate from relations between private individuals always fall within the meaning of 'civil rights and obligations' as

72. *Konig v. Germany*, cited above, paragraph 93.

intended by Article 6, whereas such a paradigm is not always valid for rights and obligations which arise from relations between private persons and the State.[73]

[C] The Meaning of 'Civil' Right

When the presence of a right has been established, it is important to verify whether it is a 'civil' right or not. This step is of great importance, considering that many Contracting States deny the existence of civil rights (and, therefore, the applicability of Article 6) in many cases where an individual right is the result of an administrative procedure.[74] Traditionally, the jurisprudence of the Court has been oriented in the sense of distinguishing between the main categories of 'private law' and 'public law', considering as 'civil rights' the ones which fall within the area of 'private law'. However, in recent years, the Court has extended the application of Article 6 also to cases previously considered as purely administrative.

In particular, the Court has held that it is not the classification of a certain right as made by the Contracting State that is of relevance, but the substantial content of such right. Therefore, what is decisive is not establishing whether the State has categorized a certain position as a civil right or not, or whether the State has acted as a private person or in the exercise of its public discretional powers: what is conclusive is that from the said proceedings a 'private' right or obligation arises (in other words, that the outcome of the proceedings is 'decisive for private rights and obligations'). Such concepts, already expressed in *Konig v. Germany*, can be found in many other cases examined by the Court,[75] such as, for example, in *H v. France*[76] and *Tre Traktörer Aktiebolag v. Sweden*:[77]

> Before the Court, however, the Government submitted that the applicability of Article 6 (art. 6) was a preliminary question which the Court had to consider if necessary of its own motion. They pointed out that while Mr H.'s action for damages had a pecuniary purpose, it was directed against a public body, Strasbourg Hospital, and was subject to the rules on the liability of such bodies in French law. For the rest, the Government left to the Court's discretion the question whether the dispute related to 'civil rights and obligations'. (...)
>
> It is clear from the Court's established case-law that the concept of 'civil rights and obligations' is not to be interpreted solely by reference to the respondent State's domestic law and that Article 6 para. 1 (art. 6-1) applies irrespective of the parties' status, be it public or private, and of the nature of the legislation which governs the manner in which the dispute is to be determined; it is sufficient that the outcome of the proceedings should be 'decisive for private rights and obligations' (...).
>
> (*H. v. France*, Judgment of 24 October 1989, paragraphs 46-47)

73. See, in this sense, D.J. Harris, M. O'Boyle, E. Bates, C. Buckley, *Harris, O'Boyle & Warbrick: Law of the European Convention on Human Rights*, cited above, 211.
74. See, among others, C. Ovey & R.C.A. White, *The European Convention on Human Rights*, 4th edn (New York: Oxford University Press, 2006), 168.
75. See, *ex multis*, *Benthem v. The Netherlands*, Judgment of 23 October 1985, paragraph 34; and *Pudas v. Sweden*, Judgment of 27 October 1987, paragraph 35.
76. *H. v. France*, Judgment of 24 October 1989.
77. *Tre Traktörer Aktiebolag v. Sweden*, Judgment of 7 July 1989.

> According to the Court's case-law, the concept of 'civil rights and obligations' is not to be interpreted solely by reference to the respondent State's domestic law. Article 6 para. 1 (art. 6-1) applies irrespective of the status of the parties, of the nature of the legislation which governs the manner in which the dispute is to be determined and of the character of the authority which has jurisdiction in the matter; it is enough that the outcome of the proceedings should be decisive for private rights and obligations (...).
>
> (*Tre Traktörer Aktiebolag v. Sweden*, Judgment of 7 July 1989, paragraph 41)

The concept under examination is notably expressed in the already-mentioned *Reingeisen v. Austria*, wherein the Court, analysing the wording of Article 6(1) both in the French ('*contestations sur ... droits et obligations de caractère civil*') and in the English text ('*determination of ... civil rights and obligations*'), remarked that the provision 'covers all proceedings the result of which is decisive for private rights and obligations':

> The character of the legislation which governs how the matter is to be determined (civil, commercial, administrative law, etc.) and that of the authority which is invested with jurisdiction in the matter (ordinary court, administrative body, etc.) are therefore of little consequence.
>
> In the present case, when Ringeisen purchased property from the Roth couple, he had a right to have the contract for sale which they had made with him approved if he fulfilled, as he claimed to do, the conditions laid down in the Act. Although it was applying rules of administrative law, the Regional Commission's decision was to be decisive for the relations in civil law ('*de caractère civil*') between Ringeisen and the Roth couple. This is enough to make it necessary for the Court to decide whether or not the proceedings in this case complied with the requirements of Article 6, paragraph (1) (art. 6-1), of the Convention.
>
> (*Ringeisen v. Austria*, Judgment of 16 July 1971, paragraph 94)

Thus, in *Veeber v. Estonia*, concerning a claim filed by an individual with an administrative court, for the alleged abuse of powers by the police in effecting the search and seizure of certain documents at his workplace, the ECtHR considered 'that the claim was covered by the civil limb of Article 6 § 1 of the Convention, seeing that it was designed to seek protection of individual rights from the interference by the executive authorities' and concluded for the application of Article 6(1).[78]

Similarly, in *Zlínsat, spol. s r.o. v. Bulgaria*,[79] although the 'dispute' before the national organs had developed exclusively before the various levels of the City Prosecutor's Office, the Court observed that the Order issued by the Prosecutor to suspend the performance of a privatization contract, had a decisive impact on the exercise of a 'civil right' of the applicant, and therefore considered Article 6(1) applicable:

78. *Veeber v. Estonia*, Judgment of 7 November 2001, paragraph 69.
79. *Zlínsat, spol. s r.o. v. Bulgaria*, Judgment of 15 June 2006.

> It remains to be established whether the measures taken by the Sofia City Prosecutor's Office against the applicant company concerned its civil rights and obligations, within the meaning of Article 6 § 1 (see, *mutatis mutandis, Allan Jacobsson v. Sweden (no. 1)*, Judgment of 25 October 1989, Series A no. 163, pp. 19-21, §§ 66-74). The Court observes on this point that the ordered suspension of the performance of the privatisation contract and the eviction of the applicant company from the hotel had a clear and decisive impact on its capability to use and operate it, which was undoubtedly an exercise of a civil right (see, *mutatis mutandis, Fredin v. Sweden (no. 1)*, Judgment of 18 February 1991, Series A no. 192, p. 20, § 63). The Court also finds that a real dispute existed, in particular with regard to the lawfulness of the Sofia City Prosecutor's Office's decisions: before the higher levels of the Prosecutor's Office, the applicant company – as well as the Sofia Municipality – claimed that these decisions were not in conformity with the relevant legal provisions (see paragraphs 10, 11, 26 and 28 above; see also *Skärby v. Sweden*, Judgment of 28 June 1990, Series A no. 180-B, p. 37, § 28 *in fine*). The outcome of this dispute, which was determined solely by the various levels of the Prosecutor's Office, was directly decisive for the company's exercise of the right to use and manage the hotel. It follows that Article 6 § 1, under its civil head, was applicable.
>
> (*Zlínsat, spol. s r.o. v. Bulgaria*, Judgment of 15 June 2006, paragraph 72)

Conclusively, proceedings involving 'civil rights and obligations' are not only proceedings pending before 'civil courts', but also proceedings before criminal and administrative courts, constitutional courts and even administrative bodies, as long as they are 'decisive' for private rights and obligations. In this sense, it has been correctly observed that 'the determining factor in delimiting the scope of Article 6 is whether or not the applicant's action has pecuniary implications (...). If it does, the proceedings are held to be a civil case'.[80]

This principle has been deemed valid by the Court also in cases between private persons and the State (on which see, *infra*, [F]), when the dispute in issue is pecuniary in nature:[81]

> The Court notes that the subject-matter of the applicant company's action was 'pecuniary' in nature and that the action was founded on an alleged infringement of rights which were likewise pecuniary rights. The right in question was therefore a 'civil right', notwithstanding the origin of the dispute and the fact that the administrative courts had jurisdiction.
>
> (*Editions Périscope v. France*, Judgment of 26 March 1992, paragraph 40)

A similar decision was issued in *Procola v. Luxembourg*,[82] where the Court, considering that in order to verify whether or not the proceedings are decisive for a civil right it is

80. Frédéric Edel, *The Length of Civil and Criminal Proceedings in the Case-Law of the European Court of Human Rights*, in Human Rights Files No. 16 (Council of Europe Publishing, 1996-2007), 8. In the same sense, see also D.J. Harris, M. O'Boyle, E. Bates, C. Buckley, *Harris, O'Boyle & Warbrick: Law of the European Convention on Human Rights*, cited above, 214.
81. See, *ex multis, Editions Périscope v. France*, Judgment of 26 March 1992. 45. In other judgments, the Court held Article 6(1) applicable in employment cases concerning a purely economic right (see *Lapalorcia v. Italy*, Judgment of 2 September 1997; *Nicodemo v. Italy*, Judgment of 2 September 1997; *Le Calvez v. France*, Judgment of 29 July 1998).
82. *Procola v. Luxembourg*, Judgment of 28 September 1995.

'necessary to look at the proceedings as whole',[83] reiterated the same principles already stated in the *Editions Périscope* Judgment:[84]

> The Court reiterates that Article 6 para. 1 (art. 6-1) is applicable where an action is 'pecuniary' in nature and is founded on an alleged infringement of rights which are likewise pecuniary rights, notwithstanding the origin of the dispute and the fact that the administrative courts have jurisdiction (...).
>
> (*Procola v. Luxembourg*, Judgment of 28 September 1995, paragraph 38)

[D] The Existence of a 'Right' in National Law

From the analysis contained in the above mentioned Judgments, it results that the first element to verify, in ascertaining whether Article 6 can be applied or not, is that a civil right exists in the national law of the Contracting State. Thus, if the national law does not provide for a civil right, the applicant cannot in any case apply to Strasbourg for the guarantees provided for by Article 6(1).

This principle was established, *inter alia*,[85] in *Rocher v. the United Kingdom*,[86] wherein the Court reaffirmed the principle that the Convention cannot create a civil right in favour of a party, if such a right does not exist in the national law of the applicant:

> Article 6 § 1 does not, however, guarantee any particular content for those (civil) 'rights' in the substantive law of the Contracting States: the Court may not create through the interpretation of Article 6 § 1 a substantive right which has no legal basis in the State concerned (see *Fayed*, cited above, pp. 49–50, § 65). Its guarantees extend only to rights which can be said, at least on arguable grounds, to be recognised under domestic law (...).
>
> (*Rocher v. the United Kingdom*, Judgment of 19 October 2005, paragraph 117)

In the judgment under examination, the Court disagreed with the submissions of the applicant and maintained that there is no inconsistency between the autonomous notion of 'civil right' (as explained in *König v. Germany* and in *Ferrazzini v. Italy*) and the requirement that the domestic law must recognize the existence of a 'right', concluding that:

> In assessing therefore whether there is a civil 'right' and in determining the substantive or procedural characterisation to be given to the impugned restriction, the starting-point must be the provisions of the relevant domestic law and their interpretation by the domestic courts (see *Masson and Van Zon v. the Netherlands*, Judgment of 28 September 1995, Series A no. 327-A, p. 19, § 49). Where,

83. *Procola v. Luxembourg*, cited above, paragraph 39.
84. See also, on the same point, *Beaumartin v. France*, Judgment of 24 November 1994, paragraph 28; *James and others v. the United Kingdom*, Judgment of 21 February 1986; *McElhinney v. Ireland* (Grand Chamber), Judgment of 21 November 2001, paragraph 23.
85. See also *James and others v. the United Kingdom*, Judgment of 21 February 1986; *Lithgow and others v. the United Kingdom*, Judgment of 8 July 1986; *The Holy Monasteries v. Greece*, Judgment of 9 December 1994.
86. *Rocher v. the United Kingdom*, Judgment of 19 October 2005.

> moreover, the superior national courts have analysed in a comprehensive and convincing manner the precise nature of the impugned restriction, on the basis of the relevant Convention case-law and principles drawn therefrom, this Court would need strong reasons to differ from the conclusion reached by those courts by substituting its own views for those of the national courts on a question of interpretation of domestic law (see *Z and others*, cited above, § 101) and by finding, contrary to their view, that there was arguably a right recognised by domestic law.
>
> (*Rocher v. the United Kingdom*, Judgment of 19 October 2005, paragraph 120)

Within the vast jurisprudence of the European Court on Human Rights, an interesting example of the application of such principles can be found in *Masson and Van Zon v. the Netherlands*[87] (indeed mentioned in *Rocher v. the United Kingdom*, examined above), in which the Court, with regard to the claim of an individual for the reimbursement of the costs incurred in the course of criminal proceedings (and the compensation for a lawful restriction of his liberty), excluded that such a right could derive from Article 6 or other provisions of the Convention or its Protocols:

> In view of the status of the Convention within the legal order of the Netherlands, the Court observes firstly that the Convention does not grant to a person 'charged with a criminal offence' but subsequently acquitted a right either to reimbursement of costs incurred in the course of criminal proceedings against him, however necessary these costs might have been, or to compensation for lawful restrictions on his liberty. Such a right can be derived neither from Article 6 para. 2 (art. 6-2) nor from any other provision of the Convention or its Protocols. It follows that the question whether such a right can be said in any particular case to exist must be answered solely with reference to domestic law.
>
> (*Masson and Van Zon v. the Netherlands*, Judgment of 28 September 1995, paragraph 49)

More in general, the jurisprudence of the ECtHR excludes the application of Article 6 in 'negligence' claims against public authorities, when a right to compensation is not provided by the national law and it is thus excluded by the national courts. An interesting application of this principle is to be found in the more recent *T.P. and K.M. v. the United Kingdom*,[88] wherein the Court stated that:

> The applicants may not claim therefore that they were deprived of any right to a determination on the merits of their negligence claims. Their claims were properly and fairly examined in light of the applicable domestic legal principles concerning the tort of negligence. Once the House of Lords had ruled on the arguable legal issues that brought into play the applicability of Article 6 § 1 of the Convention (see paragraphs 92 to 95 above), the applicants could no longer claim any entitlement under Article 6 § 1 to obtain any hearing concerning the facts. There was no denial of access to court and, accordingly, no violation of Article 6 of the Convention.
>
> (*T.P. and K.M. v. the United Kingdom*, Judgment of 10 May 2001, paragraph 103)

87. *Masson and Van Zon v. the Netherlands*, Judgment of 28 September 1995.
88. See *T.P. and K.M. v. the United Kingdom*, Judgment of 10 May 2001.

[E] Rights Deriving from Private Persons' Relations

Although the above-mentioned traditional distinction between private and public law is not decisive for determining whether or not a civil right falls within the autonomous meaning of 'civil rights and obligations' of Article 6, it is not contested that rights and obligations which traditionally belong to the private law, such as the ones deriving from private persons' relations, are covered by the umbrella of Article 6.

The ECtHR has decided in this sense, for example, in *Axen v. Germany*[89] and *Guincho v. Portugal*,[90] concerning claims for compensation related to car accidents, in the already- mentioned *Golder v. the United Kingdom*,[91] related to a case of defamation, and, more in general, in cases related to negligence.

Helmers v. Sweden[92] and *Tolstoy Miloslavsky v. the United Kingdom*[93] were related to the right to enjoy honour and a good reputation. In the latter, the Court also specified that the guarantees of Article 6 apply not only to the claimant (the person who claims to have been defamated and asks for the protection of his reputation before a Court), but also to the defendant in such proceedings, 'where the outcome is directly decisive for his or her "civil obligations" vis-à-vis the plaintiff'.[94]

The same principles have been applied in *Eriksson v. Sweden*,[95] related to the care of (and access to) children,[96] in *Keegan v. Ireland*,[97] concerning the adoption of children, and in *Airey v. Ireland*,[98] related to separation proceedings, wherein the Court stated that:

> There can be no doubt that the outcome of separation proceedings is 'decisive for private rights and obligations' and hence, *a fortiori*, for 'civil rights and obligations' within the meaning of Article 6 para. 1 (art. 6-1).
>
> (*Airey v. Ireland*, Judgment of 9 October 1979, paragraph 21)

Similarly, the Judges of Strasbourg have considered the existence of civil rights and obligations, for the purpose of the application of Article 6, in cases concerning contracts of sale (*Ringeisen v. Austria*),[99] property law (*Romaniak v. Poland*),[100] the right to run

89. *Axen v. Germany*, Judgment of 8 December 1983.
90. *Guincho v. Portugal*, Judgment of 10 July 1984.
91. *Golder v. the United Kingdom*, Judgment of 21 February 1975.
92. *Helmers v. Sweden*, Judgment of 29 October 1991.
93. *Tolstoy Miloslavsky v. the United Kingdom*, Judgment of 13 July 1995.
94. *Ibid.*, paragraph 58.
95. *Eriksson v. Sweden*, Judgment of 23 may 1989.
96. In the sense that the right of access to children is 'civil in character' see also *W. v. the United Kingdom*, Judgment of 8 July 1987; *Zander v. Sweden*, Judgment of 25 November 1993; *Olsson v. Sweden (no. 1)*, Judgment of 24 March 1988; *Johansen v. Norway*, Judgment of 7 August 1996.
97. *Keegan v. Ireland*, Judgment of 26 May 1994.
98. *Airey v. Ireland*, Judgment of 9 October 1979.
99. *Ringeisen v. Austria*, Judgment of 16 July 1971.
100. *Romaniak v. Poland*, Judgment of 24 October 2006.

a commercial activity (*Pudas v. Sweden*),[101] rights deriving from labour law (*Parashkevanova v. Bulgaria*),[102] and many other rights falling in the area of 'private law'.

[F] Rights Deriving from Relations between Private Persons and Public Authorities

As mentioned above (see, in particular, with reference to *König v. Germany*), according to the case law of the ECtHR, 'the notion of 'civil rights and obligations' cannot be interpreted solely by reference to the domestic law of the respondent State',[103] with the consequence that Article 6 ECHR covers not only 'private law disputes in the traditional sense',[104] but also disputes in which, regardless of whether the proceeding authority is an ordinary court or an administrative body,[105] the result of the proceedings is decisive for the determination of private rights and obligations.

A number of such cases concerns rights deriving from national social security and health insurance systems, as well as welfare benefits in general, where the domestic proceedings often are run by an administrative body or where anyway the respondent is a public authority.[106]

One of the leading cases in the subject matter is the already-mentioned *Feldbrugge v. The Netherlands*, related to a claim against the Netherlands health insurance system, where the Court, after evaluating the specific features of the national insurance system, concluded that Article 6 was applicable.

In particular, the Court acknowledged that under Dutch legislation, the right in issue is treated as a public-law right, observing, however, that such a circumstance 'cannot be conclusive of the matter unless corroborated by other factors'. The Court further noted that 'there exists great diversity in the legislation and case law of the member States of the Council of Europe as regards the juridical nature of the entitlement to health insurance benefits under social security schemes', so that 'some States - including the Netherlands - treat it as a public-law right, whereas others, on the contrary, treat it as a private-law right; others still would appear to operate a mixed system'.[107] Therefore, the ECtHR concluded that 'there exists no common standard pointing to a uniform European notion in this regard' and that 'an analysis of the

101. *Pudas v. Sweden*, Judgment of 27 October 1987.
102. *Parashkevanova v. Bulgaria*, Judgment of 3 May 2007.
103. *König v. Germany*, Judgment of 28 June 1978, paragraphs 88-89.
104. *Ibid.*, paragraph 90.
105. *Ringeisen v. Austria*, Judgment of 16 July 1971, paragraph 94.
106. See, among others, *Schouten and Meldrum v. The Netherlands*, Judgment of 9 December 1994 (related to the payment of social security contributions); *Obermeier v. Austria*, Judgment of 28 June 1990 (related to the contestation against dismissal from employment of a disabled person); *Lombardo v. Italy*, Judgment of 26 November 1992 (related to the 'difference in treatment with regard to pensions accorded to judges of the same grade and length of service, solely on the basis of the dates of their retirement'); *Salesi v. Italy*, Judgment of 26 February 1993 (related to the concession of a monthly disability allowance).
107. *Feldbrugge v. The Netherlands*, Judgment of 29 May 1986, paragraph 29.

characteristics of the Netherlands system of social health insurance discloses that the claimed entitlement comprises features of both public law and private law'.[108]

The Court listed, on the one hand, the features of public law which are present in the Dutch system: (1) Character of the legislation; (2) Compulsory nature of the insurance; (3) Assumption by the State of responsibility for social protection; and, on the other hand, the features of private law: (1) Personal and economic nature of the asserted right; (2) Connection with the contract of employment; (3) Affinities with insurance under the ordinary law. Finally, the Court drew attention to the fact that 'in the Netherlands, as in some other countries, the insured themselves participate in the financing of all or some of the social security schemes', and concluded as follows:

> Having evaluated the relative cogency of the features of public law and private law present in the instant case, the Court finds the latter to be predominant. None of these various features of private law is decisive on its own, but taken together and cumulatively they confer on the asserted entitlement the character of a civil right within the meaning of Article 6 para. 1 (art. 6-1) of the Convention, which was thus applicable.
>
> (*Feldbrugge v. The Netherlands*, Judgment of 29 May 1986, paragraph 40)

After the *Feldbrugge* Judgment, the jurisprudence of the ECtHR now recognizes that social security and welfare proceedings fall within the application of Article 6, whenever from such proceedings there derive statutory benefits to private persons. It is useful, in this regard, to cite *Schuler-Zgraggen v. Switzerland*, related to the entitlement to a pension on the grounds of incapacity for work due to illness, wherein the Court noted that:

> (...) despite the public-law features pointed out by the Government, the applicant was not only affected in her relations with the administrative authorities as such but also suffered an interference with her means of subsistence; she was claiming an individual, economic right flowing from specific rules laid down in a federal statute (...).
>
> (*Schuler-Zgraggen v. Switzerland*, Judgment of 24 June 1993, paragraph 46)

Many other cases related to claims against the State and other public institutions have been regarded by the ECtHR as private law rights covered by Article 6, be they of pecuniary or non-pecuniary nature.

For instance, the Court has recognized the application of Article 6 to cases concerning contracts for the sale of land,[109] expropriation of land,[110] permits to retain property acquired at a compulsory sale by auction,[111] compensation for the

108. *Feldbrugge v. The Netherlands*, cited above, paragraphs 29-30.
109. *Sramek v. Austria*, Judgment of 22 October 1984, wherein the Court decided for the applicability of the guarantees of Article 6 to administrative proceedings, related to the sale of agricultural land, before the Regional Real Property Transactions Authority (*Landesgrund-verkehrsbehörde*).
110. *Sporrong and Lönroth*, Judgment of 23 September 1982; *Bodén v. Sweden*, Judgment of 27 October 1987; *Zvolský and Zvolská v. the Czech Republic*, Judgment of 12 February 2003.
111. *Håkansson and Sturesson v. Sweden*, Judgment of 21 February 1990.

expropriation of shares, due to the nationalization of aircraft and shipbuilding companies,[112] compensation for damages caused to 'person and property' by the issuance of an unlawful arrest warrant,[113] or by unlawful detention followed by acquittal,[114] the withdrawal of an authorization to practise medicine,[115] the suspension of the right to practise medicine as result of disciplinary proceedings,[116] the right of a professional to be registered in a Bar Association,[117] the revocation of a taxi traffic licence,[118] the revocation of a restaurant licence to sell liquors,[119] the rejection of an application for a certificate of registration for a review in order to secure the tax concessions and preferential postal charges accorded to the press,[120] the right to the restitution of assets, although related to taxation issues,[121] the right to one's health, in the case of the activity of a polluting power plant,[122] etc.

---

112. *Lithgow and others v. the United Kingdom*, Judgment of 8 July 1986.
113. *Baraona v. Portugal*, Judgment of 8 July 1987. In this case the Court, in establishing whether the right claimed by the applicant was or not a 'civil right' under the autonomous meaning of the Conventions, reasoned as follows: 'The right to compensation asserted by the applicant is a private one, because it embodies a 'personal and property' interest and is founded on an infringement of rights of this kind, notably the right of property (...). The arrest warrant complained of caused Mr. Baraona to flee to Brazil with his family, abandoning his house, all his property and his business, which was eventually declared insolvent (...)'.
114. See, among others, *Georgiadis v. Greece*, Judgment of 29 May 1997, paragraph 35, where the Court noted that, although Article 533 of the (Greek) Code of Criminal Procedure (which grants the right to compensation when detention is followed by an acquittal) concerns public-law issues, 'the right to compensation created by that provision is, by its very nature, of a civil character ('*de caractère civil*')', observing that 'its typically private-law features ... confirm this conclusion as does the fact that it is for the civil courts to decide on the precise amount of the compensation to be granted'.
115. *König v. Germany*, cited above.
116. *Le Compte, Van Leuven and De Meyere v. Belgium*, Judgment of 23 June 1981; and *Albert and Le Compte v. Belgium*, Judgment of 10 February 1983.
117. *De Moor v. Belgium*, Judgment of 23 June 1994.
118. *Pudas v. Sweden*, Judgment of 27 October 1987.
119. *Tre Traktörer Aktiebolag v. Sweden*, Judgment of 7 July 1989.
120. *Editions Periscope v. France*, Judgment of 26 March 1992, paragraph 40.
121. See *National & Provincial Building Society and others v. the United Kingdom*, Judgment of 23 October 1997, paragraph 97:

> The Court considers that both sets of restitution proceedings (...) were private-law actions and were decisive for the determination of rights to quantifiable sums of money. This conclusion is not affected by the fact that the rights asserted in those proceedings had their background in tax legislation and the obligation of the applicant societies to account for tax under that legislation (...).

122. See, among others, *Okyay and others v. Turkey*, Judgment of 12 July 2005, related to the environmental pollution caused by the *Gökova, Yeniköy and Yatağan* (Turkey) thermal power plants and the consequent risk for the public health. In this case, the Court observed that such danger for the public health, deriving from the emissions of the plant, had been established by the *Aydın* Administrative Court, on the basis of an expert report, and reasoned that 'the applicants, as individuals entitled to live in a healthy and balanced environment and duty bound to protect the environment and prevent environmental pollution (...), had standing under Turkish law to ask the administrative courts to issue injunctions for the suspension of the power plants' environmentally hazardous activities, and to set aside the administrative authorities' decision to continue to operate them'. On these premises, the Court concluded that the case at hand was different from the previous *Balmer-Schafroth and others* and *Athanassoglou and others*, 'where the applicants had been unable to secure a

However, the ECtHR excluded the presence of 'civil rights and obligations' for the purpose of the application of Article 6(1) in a case related to claim for compensation for damages deriving from aircraft noise.[123]

[1] Disputes Related to the Right to Public Education

An important field of application of Article 6, as resulting from the more recent jurisprudence of the ECtHR, is that related to the right to public education.[124]

Traditionally, the right to public education has not been considered as a 'civil right' falling within the scope of Article 6(1). For example, in *Simpson v. the United Kingdom*,[125] the Commission declared inadmissible the application of a British citizen concerning the right to special education, considering that the relevant right (either under English domestic law or under Article 2 of Protocol No. 1) was not of a 'civil nature' for the purposes of Article 6(1) of the Convention, but belonged to the domain of public law:

> Although the notion of a civil right under this provision is autonomous of any domestic law definitions, the Commission considers that for the purposes of the domestic law in question and the Convention, the right not to be denied elementary education falls, in the circumstances of the present case, squarely within the domain of public law, having no private law analogy and no repercussions on private rights or obligations (cf. Eur. Court HR, *Deumeland* judgment of 29 May 1986, Series A no. 100 pp. 24-25 paras. 71-74). The Commission concludes, therefore, that there is no civil right at issue in the instant case and, accordingly, Article 6 para. 1 (Art. 6-1) of the Convention is not applicable to the administrative procedures before the domestic education authorities.

---

ruling by a tribunal on their objections to the extension of the operating permits of nuclear power plants', and from the *Ünver* case, 'where the right relied on by the applicant was a procedural right under administrative law and was not related to the defence of any specific right which he may have had under domestic law', and decided for the application of Article 6 (paragraphs 66-68).

123. *Powell and Rayner v. the United Kingdom*, Judgment of 21 February 1990. In this case, the applicants claimed that 'their access to the courts for the determination of their "civil rights and obligations" was unjustifiably denied by section 76(1) of the Civil Aviation Act 1982, which sets out a statutory bar to bringing an action in nuisance in respect of aircraft noise' (paragraph 34). The Court rejected the claim on the grounds of lack of jurisdiction under Article 6(1), accepting the assessment made by the Commission in its decision as to the admissibility of the application:

> As the Commission pointed out in its admissibility decisions, the effect of section 76(1) is to exclude liability in nuisance with regard to the flight of aircraft in certain circumstances, with the result that the applicants cannot claim to have a substantive right under English law to obtain relief for exposure to aircraft noise in those circumstances. To this extent there is no 'civil right' recognised under domestic law to attract the application of Article 6 § 1 (paragraph 36).

124. See, among others, *Oršuš and others v. Croatia*, (Grand Chamber), Judgment of 16 March 2010.

125. *Simpson v. the United Kingdom*, Appl. No. 14688/89, Decision of 4 December 1989.

> It follows that this aspect of the applicant's case must be rejected as being incompatible *ratione materiae* with the provisions of the Convention, pursuant to Article 27 para. 2 (Art. 27-2) of the Convention.
>
> (*Simpson v. the United Kingdom*, Appl. No. 14688/89, Decision of 4 December 1989)

The *revirement* in the ECtHR case law came with the Judgment in *Emine Araç v. Turkey*,[126] where the Court explicitly recognized, for the first time, the civil nature of the right of access to higher education.[127]

In this Judgment, the Court based its reasoning, *inter alia*, on the *Kök v. Turkey* Judgment,[128] according to which where a State confers a right that can be enforced through a judicial remedy, said right can be regarded as a civil one, in the autonomous meaning of the Convention and for the purpose of the application of Article 6(1).[129]

With specific regard to the right to public education, in the case at hand the ECtHR noted that the applicant could 'make an arguable claim' that the domestic law of her Country did in fact confer on her the right to enrol in the Faculty of Theology of Marmara University, provided that she satisfied the statutory conditions. The Court then pointed out that, although the regulation on enrolment in higher-education institutions fell within the sphere of public law, 'this public-law aspect does not suffice to exclude the right in question from the category of civil rights within the meaning of Article 6 § 1', concluding that 'proceedings which fall within the sphere of "public law" in the domestic legal order may come within the scope of Article 6 § 1 where their outcome is decisive for civil rights and obligations'.[130]

The same principles were reaffirmed, recently, in *Oršuš and others v. Croatia*,[131] wherein the Court observed that the same reasoning adopted in *Emine Araç v. Turkey* 'applies *a fortiori* in the context of primary education', following an *argumentum a maiore ad minus*, and concluded that:

> As to the present case, it seems clear that a 'dispute' arose in respect of the applicants' initial and then continuing placement in Roma-only classes during their schooling in primary schools. The proceedings before the domestic courts concerned the applicants' allegations of infringement of their right not to be discriminated against in the sphere of education, their right to education and their right not to be subjected to inhuman and degrading treatment. The applicants

126. *Emine Araç v. Turkey*, Judgment of 23 September 2008, paragraphs 14-25.
127. In this case, the applicant was a student seeking to enrol in the Faculty of Theology of Marmara University. However, when she provided an identity photograph which showed her wearing a headscarf, the Faculty informed her that the photograph she had supplied did not comply with the regulations in force and that, therefore, she could not be enrolled. Her attempts to recur to the competent judicial authorities (firstly, the Istanbul Administrative Court and, then, the Supreme Administrative Court) had no positive result, having the courts found the authorities' refusal had been in accordance with the law and regulations in force.
128. *Kök v. Turkey*, Judgment 19 October 2006, paragraph 36.
129. The Court mentioned also *Tinnelly & Sons Ltd and others and McElduff and others v. the United Kingdom*, Judgment of 10 July 1998, paragraph 61, stating the same principles.
130. The Court mentioned, in its reasoning, the well-known Judgments in *König* and *Le Compte, Van Leuven and De Meyere*, *Benthem v. the Netherlands*, and *Feldbrugge v. the Netherlands*, according to which 'State intervention by means of a statute or delegated legislation has not prevented the Court from finding the right in issue to have a private, and hence civil, character'.
131. *Oršuš and others v. Croatia*, cited above, paragraph 105.

> raised their complaints before the regular civil courts and in the Constitutional Court and their complaints were examined on the merits.
>
> (*Oršuš and others v. Croatia*, [Grand Chamber], Judgment of 16 March 2010, paragraph 106)

In the above Judgment, the Court also noted that the applicants' right not to be discriminated against on the basis of their race was guaranteed under Article 14(1) of the Constitution and, therefore, enforceable before the regular civil courts in their national legal system.[132]

[G] Rights which Do Not Fall under the Protection of Article 6

A number of rights and obligations do not fall within the umbrella of Article 6, mainly because they belong to the area of 'public law' rights. It has however to be noted that their number is more and more limited, due to the 'dynamic and evolutive approach' of the interpretation of the ECtHR.[133]

In this sense, the Court observed, in *Ferrazzini v. Italy*,[134] that since the Convention was adopted, relations between the individual and the State have significantly evolved and the State has increasingly intervened in regulating private law relations. As a consequence of that, procedures classified under national law as being part of 'public law' have been considered by the ECtHR in its jurisprudence as belonging to the area of civil law, in the autonomous meaning of the Convention, when their outcome is decisive for private rights and obligations (such as the already-mentioned examples of the sale of land, the running of a private clinic, the granting of an administrative license to serve alcoholic beverages, etc.).[135]

The Court, however, noted that there are individual rights which, despite a possible involvement of pecuniary interests of the parties, are not civil 'in nature' and are thus excluded from the application of Article 6 (such as political rights and obligations),[136] and there are disputes from which no civil right may arise in favour of an individual (such as disputes between administrative authorities and employees who occupy posts involving participation in the exercise of public powers,[137] disputes related to the expulsions of aliens,[138] proceedings concerning military service and

132. The Court in its reasoning recalled also, *mutatis mutandis*, *Tserkva Sela Sosulivka v. Ukraine*, Judgment of 28 February 2008, paragraph 42, and *Gülmez v. Turkey*, Judgment of 20 May 2008, paragraph 29.
133. See *Vilho Eskelinen and others v. Finland*, Judgment of 19 April 2007, paragraph 56.
134. *Ferrazzini v. Italy*, Judgment of 12 July 2001.
135. See, among others, the already-mentioned *Ringeisen v. Austria*, Judgment of 16 July 1971; *Sporrong and Lönnroth v. Sweden*, Judgment of 23 September 1982; *Benthem v. the Netherlands*, Judgment of 23 October 1985; *Tre Traktörer AB v. Sweden*, Judgment of 7 July 1989.
136. *Pierre-Bloch v. France*, Judgment of 21 October 1997.
137. *Pellegrin v. France*, Judgment of 8 December 1999.
138. *Maaouia v. France*, Judgment of 5 October 2000.

alternative service,[139] proceedings related to the refusal to issue a passport,[140] disputes concerning the right to report on court proceedings,[141] etc.).

[1] Disputes Concerning the Recruitment, Employment and Retirement of Public Servants

In *Vilho Eskelinen and others v. Finland* (concerning the entitlement of civil servants to a wage supplement) the ECtHR adopted a less restrictive interpretation in identifying a civil right for the purpose of the application of Article 6 in cases concerning the employment of civil servants, surpassing the previous orientation as expressed in *Pellegrin v. France*[142] and other cases:

> It is against this background and for these reasons that the Court finds that the functional criterion adopted in the case of *Pellegrin* must be further developed. While it is in the interests of legal certainty, foreseeability and equality before the law that the Court should not depart, without good reason, from precedents laid down in previous cases, a failure by the Court to maintain a dynamic and evolutive approach would risk rendering it a bar to reform or improvement (...).
>
> (*Vilho Eskelinen and others v. Finland*, Judgment of 19 April 2007, paragraph 56)

In previous cases, the ECtHR had held that disputes relating to the recruitment, careers and termination of employment of civil servants fell, as a general rule, outside the scope of Article 6.[143]

In *Pellegrin v. France*, the Court decided that Article 6 is not applicable in disputes between civil servants, employed in posts involving participation in the exercise of powers of the public authority, and the State, concerning their conditions of service, except disputes concerning pension rights which arise after the termination of the employment.

The criteria set forth by the ECtHR in the *Pellegrin* case were used in subsequent cases, such as, for example, *Pitkevic v. Russia*,[144] where the Court declared the inapplicability of Article 6(1) to a case regarding the dismissal of a judge, whose position was considered as involving the exercise of powers of the public authority (similarly to the armed forces and the police):

> As to the applicability of Article 6 § 1 of the Convention to the proceedings at issue, the Court recalls the *Pellegrin v. France* judgment (...) in which the Court stated that employment disputes between the authorities and public servants whose duties typified the specific activities of the public service, in so far as the latter was

139. *Nicolussi v. Austria*, Appl. No. 11734/95, Decision of 8 May 1987.
140. *Peltonen v. Finland*, Appl. No. 19583/92, Decision of 20 February 1995.
141. *Atkinson Crook and The Independent v. the United Kingdom*, Appl. No.13366/87, Decision of 3 December 1990.
142. *Pellegrin v. France*, cited above.
143. See, for example, *Neigel v. France*, Judgment of 17 March 1997. However, this general principle had been limited in several judgments, such as, for example, in *Francesco Lombardo v. Italy*, Judgment of 26 November 1992, and *Massa v. Italy*, Judgment of 24 August 1993, both having as their object purely pecuniary rights arising after the termination of the employment relation.
144. *Pitkevich v. Russia*, Appl. no. 47936/99, Decision of 8 February 2001.

> acting as the depositary of public authority responsible for protecting the general interests of the State, were not 'civil' and were excluded from the scope of Article 6 § 1 of the Convention. The Court noted that the manifest example of such activities was provided by the armed forces and the police.
>
> The Court observes that the judiciary, while not being part of ordinary civil service, is nonetheless part of typical public service. A judge has specific responsibilities in the field of administration of justice which is a sphere in which States exercise sovereign powers. Consequently, the judge participates directly in the exercise of powers conferred by public law and performs duties designed to safeguard the general interests of the State.
>
> It follows that the dispute concerning the applicant's dismissal from the judiciary did not concern her 'civil' rights or obligations within the meaning of Article 6 of the Convention. Accordingly, this provision is not applicable in the present case.
>
> (*Pitkevich v. Russia,* Appl. No. 47936/99, Decision of 8 February 2001)

However, in the above-mentioned *Vilho Eskelinen and others v. Finland* the Court noted that 'the application of the functional criterion may itself lead to anomalous results', since the applicants were employed by the Ministry of the Interior (some of them as police officers and one of them as an office assistant), and, therefore, 'on a strict application of the *Pellegrin* approach it would appear that the office assistant applicant in the present case would enjoy the guarantees of Article 6 § 1, whereas there is no doubt that the police officer applicants would not', which 'would be so irrespective of the fact that the dispute was identical for all the applicants'.[145]

The Court pointed out that, in order to exclude the protection embodied in Article 6, two conditions have to be fulfilled: 1) the State in its national law must have expressly excluded access to a court for the category of staff in question; 2) the exclusion must be justified on objective grounds in the State's interest:

> The mere fact that the applicant is in a sector or department which participates in the exercise of power conferred by public law is not in itself decisive. In order for the exclusion to be justified, it is not enough for the State to establish that the civil servant in question participates in the exercise of public power or that there exists, to use the words of the Court in the *Pellegrin* judgment, a 'special bond of trust and loyalty' between the civil servant and the State, as employer. It is also for the State to show that the subject matter of the dispute in issue is related to the exercise of State power or that it has called into question the special bond.
>
> (*Vilho Eskelinen and others v. Finland,* Judgment of 19 April 2007, paragraph 62)

According to the above arguments, the Court concluded that, in principle, there is no justification for the exclusion of ordinary employment disputes from the guarantees of Article 6 (for example, disputed concerning salaries, allowances or similar entitlements), on the sole basis of the peculiar nature of the relationship existing between a civil servant and the State. On the contrary, the Court explicitly stated that 'there will, in effect, be a presumption that Article 6 applies' and that 'it will be for the respondent Government to demonstrate, first, that a civil-servant applicant does not have a right of

145. *Vilho Eskelinen and others v. Finland,* cited above, paragraph 51.

access to a court under national law and, second, that the exclusion of the rights under Article 6 for the civil servant is justified'.[146]

[2] Disputes Related to Taxation

Another area of law that falls outside the category of 'civil rights and obligation' as interpreted by the ECtHR, is that related to taxes and other fiscal issues.

The Courts' case law is quite consistent in excluding taxation and other fiscal disputes from the applicability of Article 6, although they are 'pecuniary' in nature.

An important conclusion was reached by the Court in *Schouten and Meldrum v. The Netherlands,*[147] concerning a request for payment of contributions to the Occupational Association for Health and Mental and Social Well-being (*Bedrijfsvereniging voor de Gezondheid, Geestelijke en Maatschappelijke Belangen*) under the Health Insurance Act (*Ziektewet*), the Medical Assistance Fund Act (*Ziekenfondswet*), the Unemployment Insurance Act (*Werkloosheidswet*) and the Occupational Disability Insurance Act (*Wet op de arbeidsongeschiktheidsverzekering*). The ECtHR, after noting that 'this is the first time the Court has had to rule on the applicability of Article 6 para. 1 (art. 6-1) to a dispute concerning contributions under social-security schemes, as distinct from entitlement to benefits under such schemes', pointed out that 'approaches to benefits and to contributions are not necessarily the same' and concluded:

> Nor is it in itself sufficient to show that a dispute is 'pecuniary' in nature. There may exist 'pecuniary' obligations vis-à-vis the State or its subordinate authorities which, for the purpose of Article 6 para. 1 (art. 6-1), are to be considered as belonging exclusively to the realm of public law and are accordingly not covered by the notion of 'civil rights and obligations'. Apart from fines imposed by way of 'criminal sanction', this will be the case, in particular, where an obligation which is pecuniary in nature derives from tax legislation or is otherwise part of normal civic duties in a democratic society.
>
> (*Schouten and Meldrum v. The Netherlands,* Judgment of 9 December 1994, paragraph 50)

This principle has been reaffirmed in the already-mentioned *Ferrazini v. Italy,* where the Court held that 'pecuniary interests are clearly at stake in tax proceedings, but merely showing that a dispute is 'pecuniary' in nature is not in itself sufficient to attract the applicability of Article 6 § 1 under its 'civil' head'[148] and emphasized the public nature of the relation between the taxpayer and the tax authority,[149] thus excluding the application of Article 6(1) in such cases:

> In the tax field, developments which might have occurred in democratic societies do not, however, affect the fundamental nature of the obligation on individuals or companies to pay tax. In comparison with the position when the Convention was

146. *Vilho Eskelinen and others v. Finland,* cited above, paragraph 62.
147. *Schouten and Meldrum v. The Netherlands,* Judgment of 9 December 1994.
148. See also *Pierre-Bloch v. France,* Judgment of 21 October 1997; and *Editions Périscope v. France,* Judgment of 26 March 1992.
149. *Ferrazzini v. Italy,* Judgment of 12 July 2001.

> adopted, those developments have not entailed a further intervention by the State into the 'civil' sphere of the individual's life. The Court considers that tax matters still form part of the hard core of public-authority prerogatives, with the public nature of the relationship between the taxpayer and the community remaining predominant. Bearing in mind that the Convention and its Protocols must be interpreted as a whole, the Court also observes that Article 1 of Protocol No. 1, which concerns the protection of property, reserves the right of States to enact such laws as they deem necessary for the purpose of securing the payment of taxes (see, *mutatis mutandis*, *Gasus Dosier- und Fördertechnik GmbH v. the Netherlands*, Judgment of 23 February 1995, Series A no. 306-B, pp. 48–49, § 60). Although the Court does not attach decisive importance to that factor, it does take it into account. It considers that tax disputes fall outside the scope of civil rights and obligations, despite the pecuniary effects which they necessarily produce for the taxpayer.
>
> (*Ferrazzini v. Italy*, Grand Chamber, Judgment of 12 July 2001, paragraph 29)

However, the ECtHR has recognized the applicability of Article 6 to cases where taxation involves a punitive element as well, in which case it has considered the proceedings as having a criminal character and not a civil one.[150]

For example, in *Jussila v. Finland*,[151] a case concerning proceedings in which the applicant was found, as consequence of errors in his tax declaration, liable to pay VAT and an additional 10% surcharge, the Grand Chamber reaffirmed the general principle according to which 'the assessment of tax and the imposition of surcharges fall outside the scope of Article 6 under its civil head' and ruled that the case in question fell under the category of 'criminal' proceedings, thus attracting the application of Article 6.

The judgment under examination is particularly interesting in the part where the Court observes that 'no established or authoritative basis has therefore emerged in the case law for holding that the minor nature of the penalty, in taxation proceedings or otherwise, may be decisive in removing an offence, otherwise criminal by nature, from the scope of Article 6', noting that:

> Furthermore, the Court is not persuaded that the nature of tax-surcharge proceedings is such that they fall, or should fall, outside the protection of Article 6. Arguments to that effect have also failed in the context of prison disciplinary and minor traffic offences (see, among others, *Ezeh and Connors* and *Öztürk*, both cited above). While there is no doubt as to the importance of tax to the effective functioning of the State, the Court is not convinced that removing procedural safeguards in the imposition of punitive penalties in that sphere is necessary to maintain the efficacy of the fiscal system or indeed can be regarded as consonant with the spirit and purpose of the Convention. In this case the Court will therefore apply the *Engel* criteria as identified above.
>
> (*Jussila v. Finland*, [Grand Chamber], Judgment of 23 November 2006, paragraph 36)

150. See, among others, *Bendenoun v. France*, Judgment of 24 February 1994.
151. *Jussila v. Finland*, (Grand Chamber) Judgment of 23 November 2006. In this case the Häme Tax Office (*verotoimisto, skattebyrån*), after having requested that the applicant submit his observations concerning alleged errors in his value-added tax declarations (*arvonlisävero, mervärdesskatt*), made a reassessment of the payable taxes and ordered him to pay, among others, some tax surcharges. The applicant appealed to the Uusimaa County Administrative Court (*lääninoikeus, länsrätten*).

Then the Court, in applying the general criteria for the determination of a 'criminal charge', focused on the 'nature of the offence' and concluded that 'tax surcharges were imposed by general legal provisions applying to taxpayers generally' and that they 'were not intended as pecuniary compensation for damage but as a punishment to deter re-offending', thus establishing the criminal nature of the offence.[152]

Finally, the ECtHR deemed Article 6 applicable also to disputes concerning claims for the restitution of taxes already paid or for compensation deriving from an illegal refusal of a tax exemption, on the assumption that in such cases a claim of pecuniary nature is raised (and, therefore, that they are proceedings related to 'private law actions', and 'decisive for the determination of private law rights to quantifiable sums of money').[153]

[3] Disputes Related to Residence, Nationality, Asylum and Expulsion of Aliens

Cases concerning residence permits, requests for asylum, immigration, expulsion of aliens and, in general, immigration and nationality-related issues have been traditionally excluded by the ECtHR from the application of Article 6.[154]

One important such case is *Maaouia v. France*,[155] concerning an expulsion order against a Tunisian national (following sentencing to imprisonment), which was considered by the Court not as a criminal charge, but as a preventive measure for the purpose of the control of immigration. At the same time, the Court excluded that 'civil rights and obligations' could arise from the expulsion of an individual, and deemed Article 6 as inapplicable to such cases.[156]

In particular, the Court recalled the established orientation of the Commission in this subject matter,[157] stating that:

> The Court has not previously examined the issue of the applicability of Article 6 § 1 to procedures for the expulsion of aliens. The Commission has been called upon to do so, however, and has consistently expressed the opinion that the decision whether or not to authorise an alien to stay in a country of which he is not a

152. *Jussila v. Finland*, cited above, paragraphs 37-38.
153. See, for example, *The National & Provincial Building Society a.o. – United Kingdom*, Judgment of 23 October 1987, paragraph 97; *Éditions Périscope – France*, Judgment of 26 March 1992, paragraph 40; and others.
154. See, for example, *P. v. the United Kingdom*, Appl. no. 13162/87, Decision of 9 November 1987; *S.N. – Netherlands*, Appl. no. 13292/87, Decision of 13 November 1987; *X. v. the Federal Republic of Germany*, Appl. no. 6315/73, Decision of 30 September 1974; and many others.
155. *Maaouia v. France*, Judgment of 5 October 2000.
156. See, however, *C.G and Others v. Bulgaria*, *Nolan and K. v. Russia*, and *Saadi v. Italy*, cited above, *sub* 2.2, footnote 37, with reference to the jurisprudence of the ECtHR requiring that proceedings leading to the expulsion of aliens must respect some basic aspects of fairness.
157. *Uppal and Singh v. the United Kingdom*, Appl. no. 8244/78, Decision of 2 May 1979; *Bozano v. France*, Appl. no. 9990/82, Decision of 15 May 1984; *Urrutikoetxea v. France*, Appl. no. 31113/96, Decision of 5 December 1996; and *Kareem v. Sweden*, Appl. No. 32025/96, Decision of 25 October 1996.

> national does not entail any determination of his civil rights or obligations or of any criminal charge against him within the meaning of Article 6 § 1 of the Convention.
> (*Maaouia v. France*, Judgment of 5 October 2000, paragraph 35)

The Court then, on the assumption that 'by adopting Article 1 of Protocol No. 7 containing guarantees specifically concerning proceedings for the expulsion of aliens the States clearly intimated their intention not to include such proceedings within the scope of Article 6 § 1 of the Convention',[158] concluded that the proceedings of the case at hand did not concern 'civil rights and obligations', despite the possible repercussions of the exclusion order on the applicant's private and family life:

> In the light of the foregoing, the Court considers that the proceedings for the rescission of the exclusion order, which form the subject matter of the present case, do not concern the determination of a 'civil right' for the purposes of Article 6 § 1. The fact that the exclusion order incidentally had major repercussions on the applicant's private and family life or on his prospects of employment cannot suffice to bring those proceedings within the scope of civil rights protected by Article 6 § 1 of the Convention (...).
> (*Maaouia v. France*, Judgment of 5 October 2000, paragraph 38)

This conclusion is *ius receptum* by the subsequent case law of the ECtHR, which has often reiterated the principle according to which 'decisions regarding the entry, stay and deportation of aliens do not concern the determination of an applicant's civil rights or obligations or of a criminal charge against him, within the meaning of Article 6 § 1 of the Convention'.[159]

Interestingly, the ECtHR has however acknowledged that a conduct of the public administration or of a State organ may have, in some cases, 'repercussions' on private law rights, such as, for example, property rights, contracts, etc., whenever the outcome of the proceedings is 'directly decisive' for the determination of civil rights and obligations.[160] On this point, a certain criticism on a possible restrictive interpretation of the right of access to a court, with regard to the determination of civil rights and obligations, has been expressed by many Authors.[161]

---

158. *Maaouia v. France*, cited above, paragraph 37. The Court also recalled, *mutatis mutandis*, the *Neigel v. France* Judgment of 17 March 1997, paragraphs 43-44, and the *Maillard v. France* Judgment of 9 June 1998, paragraphs 39-41.
159. See, *ex multis*, *Penafiel Salgado v. Spain*, Appl. no. 65964/01, Decision of 16 April 2002; and, as far as extradition of aliens is concerned, *Mamatkulov and Askarov v. Turkey*, Judgment of 4 February 2005, paragraphs 81-83.
160. *Benthem v. The Netherlands*, Judgment of 23 October 1985, paragraph 34; *H. v. France*, Judgment of 24 October 1989, paragraph 46-47; *Tre Traktörer Aktiebolag v. Sweden*, Judgment of 7 July 1989, paragraph 41; *Pudas v. Sweden*, Judgment of 27 October 1987, paragraph 35.
161. See, among others, P. van Dijk & G.J.H. van Hoof, *Theory and Practice of the European Convention on Human Rights* (The Hague: Kluwer Law International, 1998), 392-393; D.J. Harris, M. O'Boyle, E. Bates, C. Buckley, *Harris, O'Boyle & Warbrick: Law of the European Convention on Human Rights*, cited above, 223; P. Lemmens, *Geschillen over burgerlijke rechten en verplichtingen* (Antwerpen: Kluwer, 1989); K.J. Partsch, *Die Rechte und Freiheiten der europäischen Menschenrechtskonvention* (Berlin: Dunker & Humblot, 1966), 143-145.

[4] Disputes Concerning Political Rights

The ECtHR, in its established jurisprudence, has also ruled that political rights, such as the right to stand for elections (and related electoral disputes) do not fall within the scope of Article 6.

The main argument for such exclusion lies in the consideration that the right to stand for election is not a 'civil right'. This principle has been reiterated by the Court in several decisions on the admissibility of applications as well as judgments on the merits.[162]

For instance, in *Guliyev v. Azerbaidjan*,[163] the Court pointed out that:

> (...) the proceedings in question involved the determination of the applicant's right to stand as a candidate in the presidential elections. The dispute in issue, therefore, concerned the applicant's political right and did not have any bearing on his 'civil rights and obligations' within the meaning of Article 6 § 1 of the Convention.
>
> (*Guliyev v. Azerbaidjan*, Appl. No. 35584/02, Decision of 27 May 2004)

Similarly, in the decision as to the admissibility of the application in *Hirst v. the United Kingdom*,[164] filed by a convicted prisoner in detention who had been subject to a ban on voting in parliamentary or local elections,[165] the Court declared the application inadmissible and reaffirmed that:

> (...) Article 6 § 1 of the Convention does not apply to electoral rights, such rights falling outside the scope of 'civil rights' (...). The applicant's complaints about the proceedings before the Court of Appeal which concerned the effect on his right to vote of the Representation of the People Act 1983 are incompatible *ratione materiae* and must be rejected pursuant to Article 35 §§ 3 and 4 of the Convention.
>
> (*Hirst v. the United Kingdom*, No. 74025/01, Decision of 8 July 2003)

See, however, the judgments in *Hirst v. the United Kingdom* [Grand Chamber],[166] and the recent *Scoppola v. Italy* [Grand Chamber],[167] with regard to the violation of Article 3 of Protocol No.1, when the domestic legislation hinders the right of vote of prisoners.

162. See, *ex multis*, *Mutalibov v. Azerbaijan*, Appl. No. 31799/03, Decision of 19 February 2004; *Cheminade v. France*, Appl. no. 31599/96, Decision of 26 January 1999; and *Pierre-Bloch v. France*, Judgment of 21 October 1997.
163. *Guliyev v. Azerbaidjan*, Appl. no. 35584/02, Decision of 27 May 2004. Similarly, in *Habsburgh-Lothringen v. Austria*, Appl. no. 15344/89, Decision of 14 December 1989, the Commission considered that 'a prohibition to run for the Office of Federal President does not concern 'civil rights' as envisaged by Article 6 para. 1 (art. 6-1) of the Convention'.
164. *Hirst v. the United Kingdom*, Appl. no. 74025/01, Decision of 8 July 2003.
165. The applicant relied on Article 3 of Protocol 1, alone and in conjunction with Article 14 ECHR, and on Article 10 ECHR.
166. In *Hirst v. the United Kingdom*, Judgment of 6 October 2005 the Grand Chamber confirmed the conclusion reached by the Chamber with the Judgment of 30 March 2004, that there had been a violation of Article 3 of Protocol No. 1.
167. In *Scoppola v. Italy*, Judgment of 22 May 2012, the Court decided that there was no violation of Article 3 of Protocol No. 1.

In the well-known *Pierre-Bloch v. France*,[168] the Court also specified that, despite the economic damage affecting the applicant as a consequence of the decision by which he was excluded from the right to stand for election (and condemned to pay a certain sum), the proceedings did not become civil in nature:[169]

> It is true that in the proceedings in question the applicant's pecuniary interests were also at stake. Where the Constitutional Council has found that the ceiling on election expenditure has been exceeded, the National Commission assesses a sum equal to the amount of the excess, which the candidate is required to pay the Treasury. The proceedings before the National Commission are not separable from those before the Constitutional Court since the National Commission has no discretion and is required to adopt the amount determined by the Constitutional Council (see paragraph 35 above). Furthermore, reimbursement in whole or in part of the expenditure recorded in campaign accounts, where provided for by law, is not possible until the accounts have been approved by the National Commission (see paragraph 33 above).
>
> This economic aspect of the proceedings in issue does not, however, make them 'civil' ones within the meaning of Article 6 § 1. The impossibility of securing reimbursement of campaign expenditure where the ceiling has been found to have been exceeded and the obligation to pay the Treasury a sum equivalent to the excess are corollaries of the obligation to limit election expenditure; like that obligation, they form part of the arrangements for the exercise of the right in question. Besides, proceedings do not become 'civil' merely because they also raise an economic issue (...).
>
> (*Pierre-Bloch v. France*, Judgment of 21 October 1997, paragraph 51)

§2.04 THE RIGHT TO A FAIR TRIAL IN ADMINISTRATIVE PROCEEDINGS

It has already been observed that the ECtHR has considered several types of administrative proceedings as *criminal* in nature, in the autonomous meaning of the Convention, thus deeming applicable in full the guarantees of Article 6 aimed at the protection of rights to individuals subject to a 'criminal charge'. That is the case, for instance, of proceedings leading to the imposition of fines for road traffic offences,[170] of tax surcharges,[171] and other proceedings related to minor offences in general.[172]

Administrative proceedings can be relevant to the application of Article 6 also when a decision taken by the competent administrative body or government organ produces certain effects on civil rights and obligations.

The possible application of Article 6 in administrative proceedings derives from the fact that in many States some decisions related to civil rights and obligations

168. *Pierre-Bloch v. France*, cited above.
169. The Court recalled in its judgment, on such principle, *Schouten and Meldrum v. the Netherlands*, Judgment of 9 December 1994, paragraph 50; and *Neigel v. France*, Judgment of 17 March 1997, paragraph 44.
170. See, among others, *Schmautzer v. Austria*, Judgment of 23 October 1995; *Malige v. France*, Judgment of 23 September 1998.
171. See *Jussila v. Finland*, Judgment of 23 November 2006.
172. See *Lauko v. Slovakia*, Judgment of 2 September 1998.

are taken not by a judicial body, but by an administrative institution or a State organ.[173] This may constitute, *inter alia*, a violation of the right of 'access to a court' and, therefore, it is necessary that the individuals affected have the right to appeal to a judicial body against an administrative decision, in order to fully enjoy the guarantees under Article 6 ECHR.

However, it must be noted that the possibility of appealing to a tribunal is not sufficient, since it is also necessary to verify that such a court have full power to decide both 'in fact' and 'in law'. In other words, it is necessary that the national court have full power to decide on the factual matters at stake, and not just the ability to verify the mere 'legitimacy' of the administrative act.

Such a conclusion has been reached by the ECtHR in several decisions. One of the first cases examined by the Court in this regard was *Le Compte, Van Leuven and De Meyere v. Belgium*,[174] where it was decided that, although Article 6(1) does not oblige the Contracting States to submit 'contestations' over 'civil rights and obligations' to a procedure conducted at each of its stages before a tribunal,[175] it is however necessary that after the issuance of an administrative decision the affected party have the right to appeal it – not only on questions of law, but also on questions of fact - before a judicial body.[176] Therefore, in the case in question, the Court observed that it was not sufficient that the complainant had the possibility to appeal the first instance administrative decision of the 'Provincial Council' to the 'Appeals Council' (another administrative body) and that then he had the possibility to appeal it also before the Court of Cassation, since the latter had only jurisdiction to examine errors 'in law', but not 'in fact':

> For civil cases, just as for criminal charges (...), Article 6 par. 1 (art. 6-1) draws no distinction between questions of fact and questions of law. Both categories of question are equally crucial for the outcome of proceedings relating to 'civil rights and obligations'. Hence, the 'right to a court' (see the above-mentioned Golder judgment, p. 18, par. 36) and the right to a judicial determination of the dispute (see the above-mentioned König judgment, p. 34, par. 98 in fine) cover questions of fact just as much as questions of law. Yet the Court of Cassation does not have jurisdiction to rectify factual errors or to examine whether the sanction is proportionate to the fault (see paragraph 33 above). It follows that Article 6 par. 1 (art. 6-1) was not satisfied unless its requirements were met by the Appeals Council itself.
>
> (*Le Compte, Van Leuven and De Meyere v. Belgium*, Judgment of 23 June 1981, paragraph 51)

The Court, in *Benthem v. The Netherlands*,[177] also stated that it is not sufficient that an administrative or governmental organ 'is empowered to determine the dispute', since

173. On the application of Article 6(1)ECHR to administrative law, see, among others, D.J. Harris 'The Application of Article 6 (1) of the European Convention on Human Rights to Administrative Law', in *British Yearbook of International Law* (Oxford, 1975), 47 (1), 157-200.
174. *Le Compte, Van Leuven and De Meyere v. Belgium*, Judgment of 23 June 1981.
175. In fact, in many Member States administrative bodies are traditionally competent to adjudicate such 'contestations'.
176. See also the *Deweer* Judgment of 27 February 1980, already cited, paragraph 48.
177. *Benthem v. The Netherlands*, Judgment of 23 October 1985.

'the Convention requires more than this: by the word "tribunal", it denotes "bodies which exhibit (...) common fundamental features", of which the most important are independence and impartiality, and "the guarantees of judicial procedure"'.[178] Such principles had already been expressed in the ECtHR established case law, among which the Judgment in *De Wilde, Ooms and Versyp*[179] deserves to be mentioned, as the Court noted that:

> It is true that the Convention uses the word 'court' (French 'tribunal') in several of its Articles. It does so to mark out one of the constitutive elements of the guarantee afforded to the individual by the provision in question (see, in addition to Article 5 (4), Articles 2 (1), 5 (1) (a) and (b), and 6 (1) (tribunal) (art. 5-4, art. 2-1, art. 5-1-a, art. 5-1-b, art. 6-1). In all these different cases it denotes bodies which exhibit not only common fundamental features, of which the most important is independence of the executive and of the parties to the case (see Neumeister Judgment of 27th June 1968, Series A, p. 44, paragraph 24), but also the guarantees of judicial procedure. The forms of the procedure required by the Convention need not, however, necessarily be identical in each of the cases where the intervention of a court is required. In order to determine whether a proceeding provides adequate guarantees, regard must be had to the particular nature of the circumstances in which such proceeding takes place.
>
> (*De Wilde, Ooms and Versyp*, Judgment of 18 June 1971, paragraph 78)

The orientation of the ECtHR is quite clear in the sense that when the power to adjudicate on administrative acts (such as disciplinary offence related ones) is conferred to administrative bodies (which can also be jurisdictional organs of professional associations), either such organs themselves comply with the requirements of Article 6(1), or they do not comply but are subject to a subsequent control by a judicial body with full jurisdiction, in order to grant the affected party the guarantees of Article 6(1). This is what was decided in the well-known case *Albert and Le Compte v. Belgium*:

> In many member States of the Council of Europe, the duty of adjudicating on disciplinary offences is conferred on jurisdictional organs of professional associations. Even in instances where Article 6 para. 1 (art. 6-1) is applicable, conferring powers in this manner does not in itself infringe the Convention (see the above-mentioned Le Compte, Van Leuven and De Meyere judgment, Series A no. 43, p. 23, first sub-paragraph). Nonetheless, in such circumstances the Convention calls at least for one of the two following systems: either the jurisdictional organs themselves comply with the requirements of Article 6 para. 1 (art. 6-1), or they do not so comply but are subject to subsequent control by a judicial body that has full jurisdiction and does provide the guarantees of Article 6 para. 1 (art. 6-1).
>
> (*Albert and Le Compte v. Belgium*, Judgment of 10 February 1983, paragraph 29)

The same principles were affirmed in a case related to an appeal against an administrative decision of dismissal from employment. In that case, although an appeal against the administrative act could have been submitted to the Austrian Administrative Court,

178. See *Benthem v. The Netherlands*, Judgment of 23 October 1985, paragraph 43.
179. *De Wilde, Ooms and Versyp*, Judgment of 18 June 1971.

the ECtHR decided that the power of such a body did not grant the affected person an appeal on the merits against the challenged decision, but only a limited review of the act:

> It follows that the conditions laid down in Article 6 § 1 (art. 6-1) are met only if the decisions of the administrative authorities binding the courts were delivered in conformity with the requirements of that provision.
>
> It is common ground that neither the Disabled Persons Board nor the Provincial Governor, who hears appeals against the decisions of the Board, can be regarded as independent tribunals within the meaning of Article 6 § 1 (art. 6-1).
>
> The Provincial Governor's decisions may, however, be the subject of an appeal to the Administrative Court. This appeal can be considered sufficient under Article 6 § 1 (art. 6-1) only if the Administrative Court could be described as 'a judicial body that has full jurisdiction' within the meaning of the Albert and Le Compte Judgment of 10 February 1983 (Series A no. 58, p. 16, § 29).
>
> In this respect it must be taken into account that the relevant legislation does not contain any substantial and precise provisions for the decisions to be taken by the Disabled Persons Board or the Provincial Governor. From this silence of the law, the Austrian Administrative Court has itself inferred that the Administrative Court can only determine whether the discretion enjoyed by the administrative authorities has been used in a manner compatible with the object and purpose of the law. This means, in the final result, that the decision taken by the administrative authorities, which declares the dismissal of a disabled person to be socially justified, remains in the majority of cases, including the present one, without any effective review exercised by the courts.
>
> In disputes concerning civil rights, such a limited review cannot be considered to be an effective judicial review under Article 6 § 1 (art. 6-1). There has therefore been a violation of Mr Obermeier's right of access to a court.
>
> (*Obermeier v. Austria*, Judgment of 28 June 1990, paragraph 70)

§2.05 APPLICABILITY OF ARTICLE 6 BEFORE MILITARY COURTS AND OTHER SPECIAL TRIBUNALS

Article 6 ECHR has been considered applicable to proceedings pending before military courts and other special tribunals, as well as to proceedings pending before ordinary courts, where one of the judges happened to be a military judge.[180]

For example, in *Hood v. the United Kingdom,*[181] *Findlay v. the United Kingdom,*[182] *Coyne v. the United Kingdom,*[183] *Cable and others v. the United Kingdom,*[184] *Cooper v. the United Kingdom,*[185] and many others, the Court considered Article 6 applicable to

180. See, among others, *Ocalan v. Turkey* (Grand Chamber), Judgment of 12 May 2005; and *Incal v. Turkey*, Judgment of 9 July 1998. In both cases the proceedings were pending before the National Security Court, composed of two ordinary judges and one military judge, replaced during the course of the proceedings by an ordinary judge.
181. *Hood v. the United Kingdom,* (Grand Chamber), Judgment 18 February 1999, where the Court found that there had been a violation of Article 6(1) because the court martial did not meet the requirements of independence and impartiality.
182. *Findlay v. the United Kingdom,* Judgment of 25 February 1997.
183. *Coyne v. the United Kingdom,* Judgment of 24 September 1997.
184. *Cable and others v. the United Kingdom* (Grand Chamber), Judgment of 18 February 1999.
185. *Cooper v. the United Kingdom,* Judgment of 16 December 2003.

proceedings pending before courts-martial, in *Nejdet Şahin and Perihan Şahin v. Turkey*[186] to proceedings pending before the Supreme Military Administrative Court, in *Mirilashvili v. Russia,*[187] *Kanayev v. Russia,*[188] *Sergey Schevchenko v. Ukraine,*[189] and many others, to proceedings pending before military courts, etc.

Most of the cases are related to the guarantee of an 'independent and impartial' tribunal 'established by law', and will therefore be examined more in detail *infra,* in Chapter 3.

§2.06 APPLICABILITY OF ARTICLE 6 BEFORE CONSTITUTIONAL COURTS

Although in the early jurisprudence of the ECtHR Article 6 was not considered applicable to proceedings before Constitutional courts, for the reason that such courts do not determine 'civil rights and obligations', nor 'criminal charges',[190] more recently the Court of Strasbourg has ruled that Article 6(1) applies also to proceedings before constitutional courts.

In particular, the ECtHR has recognized 'the special role played by constitutional courts in domestic legal systems',[191] reiterating the principle according to which Article 6(1) imposes on the Contracting States the duty to organize their judicial systems in such a way that their courts can meet each of its requirements,[192] concluding that:

> Although this obligation cannot be construed in the same way for a constitutional court as for an ordinary court, it is for the European Court in the last instance to verify that it has been complied with, having regard to the particular circumstances of each case and the criteria laid down in its case-law.
>
> (*Niederboster v. Germany*, Judgment of 27 February 2003, paragraph 43)

186. *Nejdet Şahin and Perihan Şahin v. Turkey,* (Grand Chamber), Judgment of 20 October 2011.
187. *Mirilashvili v. Russia,* Judgment of 11 December 2008.
188. *Kanayev v. Russia,* Judgment of 27 July 2006.
189. *Schevchenko v. Ukraine,* Judgment of 4 April 2006.
190. See, for all, *Buchholz v. Germany,* Judgment of 6 May 1981, paragraph 48, wherein the Court stated:

> For the purposes of arriving at a decision on the matters complained of, it suffices to point out that the Constitutional Court was not called on to determine the dispute ('contestation') between Mr. Buchholz and his employers which had been before the labour courts; its ruling was not concerned with the right claimed by the plaintiff against the defendants (see paragraph 36 above, as compared with paragraphs 13 and 15). The proceedings subsequent to the judgment by the Federal Labour Court thus fall outside the ambit of Article 6 par. 1 (art. 6-1). There is no need to decide whether it might be otherwise in different circumstances.

191. See *Niederboster v. Germany,* Judgment of 27 February 2003, paragraph 43; and *Tričković v. Slovenia,* Judgment of 12 June 2001, paragraphs 36 and 54.
192. See also *Pammel v. Germany,* Judgment of 1 July 1997, paragraph, and *Probstmeier v. Germany,* Judgment of 1 July 1997, paragraph 63 (both recalled by the Court in *Niederboster v. Germany*).

For example, in *Ruiz-Mateoz v. Spain*,[193] the Court observed that, although it was not 'called upon to give an abstract ruling on the applicability of Article 6 para. 1 (Article 6-1) to constitutional courts in general', with reference to the specific case there was a close link between the subject-matter and the proceedings before the Constitutional Court: indeed, only the annulment by the Constitutional Court of the contested provisions 'would have led the civil courts to allow the claims of the Ruiz-Mateos family'. The Court therefore concluded that:

> In the present case, the civil and the constitutional proceedings even appeared so interrelated that to deal with them separately would be artificial and would considerably weaken the protection afforded in respect of the applicants' rights. The Court notes that by raising questions of constitutionality, the applicants were using the sole – and indirect – means available to them of complaining of an interference with their right of property (...).
>
> (*Ruiz-Mateos v. Spain*, Judgment of 23 June 1993, paragraph 59)

In *Kraska v. Switzerland*, the Court declared the applicability of Article 6(1) to proceedings pending before the Federal Court (*Bundesgericht*), on the grounds that this Federal Court had the power to grant the applicant a civil right:

> As to whether Article 6 para. 1 (art. 6-1) also applied to the examination of Mr Kraska's public-law appeal, the Court reiterates that proceedings come within the scope of this provision, even if they are conducted before a constitutional court, where their outcome is decisive for civil rights and obligations (see, inter alia, the Ringeisen v. Austria Judgment of 16 July 1971, Series A no. 13, p. 39, para. 94, and the Le Compte, Van Leuven and De Meyere judgment, cited above, p. 20, para. 44); in order to determine whether this is so in a given case, it is necessary to have regard to all the circumstances (see, among other authorities, mutatis mutandis, the Bock v. Germany Judgment of 29 March 1989, Series A no. 150, p. 18, para. 37).
>
> The applicant complained that the Zurich Administrative Court had denied him the right to practise medicine independently. Moreover, it was open to the Federal Court not only to quash the contested judgment, but also – albeit exceptionally – to grant the authorisation which the applicant was seeking (see paragraph 14 above). Indeed he was able to obtain the authorisation on 8 December 1987 as a result of the Federal Court's decision to annul the waiting period imposed on 11 March 1987 (see paragraphs 12, 14 and 15 above). The direct effect of its Judgment of 22 October 1987 on the recognition of the right claimed is consequently beyond question.
>
> (*Kraska v. Switzerland*, Judgment of 19 April 1993, paragraph 26)

Similarly, the Court decided some years later in *Süßmann v. Germany*.[194]

In this case, the Respondent State argued that the Federal Constitutional Court is not an ordinary court, but it is comparable, as to its functions (supreme guardian of the Constitution), to the European Court of Human Rights itself, although only at a national level. For these reasons, according to the German Government, it does not rule on 'civil

193. *Ruiz-Mateos v. Spain*, Judgment of 23 June 1993.
194. *Süßmann v. Germany*, (Grand Chamber), Judgment of 16 September 1996.

rights and obligations' of individuals and, therefore, the requirements set forth in Article 6(1) cannot apply to it.

The Court, recalling its more recent jurisprudence on the subject matter,[195] remarked that:

> '... in determining whether Constitutional Court proceedings may be taken into account in assessing the reasonableness of the length of proceedings is whether the result of the Constitutional Court proceedings is capable of affecting the outcome of the dispute before the ordinary courts'[196] and reiterated that 'proceedings come within the scope of Article 6 para. 1 of the Convention (art. 6-1), even if they are conducted before a Constitutional Court, where their outcome is decisive for civil rights and obligations'.
>
> (*Süßmann v. Germany*, [Grand Chamber], Judgment of 16 September 1996, paragraph 41)

Then, noting that in the case under examination the proceedings before the Federal Court were decisive for the applicant's pension entitlements and therefore concerned his civil rights, decided for the applicability of Article 6(1).

This interpretation has been constantly reiterated by the ECtHR in its following decisions, such as *Pammel v. Germany,*[197] *Pierre-Bloch v. France,*[198] *Gast and Popp v. Germany,*[199] *Krčmář and others v. the Czech Republic,*[200] *Probstmeier v. Germany,*[201] and many others.

§2.07 APPLICABILITY OF ARTICLE 6 BEFORE ARBITRATION BOARDS

The question concerning the applicability of Article 6 in arbitration can be examined under two different aspects, e.g., the application of the guarantees under Article 6 to consensual arbitration and to statutory arbitration.[202]

The problem is easily solved in the latter hypothesis, where we are in presence of a compulsory arbitration (with the effect that the parties have no other option but to

195. *Deumeland v. Germany*, Judgment of 29 May 1986, paragraph 77; *Bock v. Germany*, Judgment of 29 March 1989, paragraph 37; and *Ruiz-Mateos v. Spain*, Judgment of 23 June 1993, paragraph 35.
196. *Süßmann v. Germany*, cited above, paragraph 39.
197. *Pammel v. Germany*, Judgment of 1 July 1997, paragraphs 46 et seq.
198. *Pierre-Bloch v. France*, Judgment of 21 October 1997, paragraphs 48 et seq.
199. *Gast and Popp v. Germany*, Judgment of 25 February 2000, paragraphs 62 et seq.
200. Judgment of 3 March 2000, paragraphs 29 et seq.
201. *Probstmeier v. Germany*, Judgment of 1 July 1997, paragraphs 48 et seq.
202. See, among others: R. Briner & F. von Schlabrendorff, *Article 6 of the European Convention on Human Rights and Its Bearing upon International Arbitration*, in *Law of International Business and Dispute Settlement in the 21st Century*, ed. R. Briner, L.Y. Fortier, K.P, Berger & J. Bredow (Carl Heymanns Verlag, 2001); *A. Jaksic, Arbitration and Human Rights* (Peter Lang, 2002); P. Lambert, *'L'arbitrage et l'article 6, 1° de la Convention européenne des droits de l'homme'*, in *L'arbitrage et la Convention européenne des droits de l'homme*, ed. Cambi Favre-Bulle - Dal - Flecheux - Lambert - Mourre, Droit et Justice No. 31 (Bruxelles: Nemesis, Bruylant, 2001), 9 et seq.

refer their case to the arbitrators), which can be considered, as to the applicability of Article 6(1), at the same level of ordinary civil proceedings.[203]

In cases of voluntary arbitration, the ECtHR observed in *Suovaniemi and others v. Finland*[204] that 'there is no doubt that a voluntary waiver of court proceedings in favour of arbitration is in principle acceptable from the point of view of Article 6',[205] remarking, however, that:

> Even so, such a waiver should not necessarily be considered to amount to a waiver of all the rights under Article 6. As indicated by the cases cited in the previous paragraph, an unequivocal waiver of Convention rights is valid only insofar as such waiver is 'permissible'. Waiver may be permissible with regard to certain rights but not with regard to certain others.
>
> (*Suovaniemi and Others v. Finland*, Appl. No. 31737/96, Decision of 23 February 1999)

Therefore, the Court reasoned, if on the one hand the parties can waive their right to have proceedings before an ordinary court or tribunal, remitting their dispute to a board of arbitrators, on the other hand this choice does not bring, as automatic consequence, a waiver to all the guarantees provided for by Article 6. For instance, the right to a public hearing can always be waived, even in court proceedings, but some doubts arises when it comes to the right to an impartial judge:

> A distinction may have to be made even between different rights guaranteed by Article 6. Thus, in the light of the case-law it is clear that the right to a public hearing can be validly waived even in court proceedings (see, Eur.Court H.R., Håkansson and Sturesson v. Sweden judgment of 21 February 1990, Series A no. 171, pp. 20–21, §§ 66–67). The same applies, *a fortiori,* to arbitration proceedings, one of the very purposes of which is often to avoid publicity. On the other hand, the question whether the fundamental right to an impartial judge can be waived at all, was left open in the Pfeifer and Plankl v. Austria case, as in any case in the circumstances of that case there was no unequivocal waiver.
>
> (*Suovaniemi and Others v. Finland*, Appl. No. 31737/96, Decision of 23 February 1999)

In the above-mentioned case, the Court considered the specific circumstances and reached the conclusion the also the waiver to the right to an impartial arbiter did not violate the Conventions, for a number of reasons: the parties were aware of such potential non-impartiality, they were represented by a counsel, and they had the opportunity, in the proceedings before the national courts, to raise their objections:

> In view of this the finding of the Finnish court based on Finnish law that by approving M. as an arbitrator despite the doubt, of which the applicants were aware, about his objective impartiality within the meaning of the relevant Finnish legislation does not appear arbitrary or unreasonable. Moreover, considering that

203. See, among others, *Bramelid and Malmström v. Sweden*, Appl. No. 8588/79, Decision of 12 December 1983, paragraph 38; and *Lithgow and Others v. the United Kingdom*, Judgment of 8 July 198, paragraphs 193 et seq.
204. *Suovaniemi and Others v. Finland*, Appl. no. 31737/96, Decision of 23 February 1999.
205. *Ibid.*, recalling *Bramelid and Malmström v. Sweden*, cited above.

> throughout the arbitration the applicants were represented by counsel, the waiver was accompanied by sufficient guarantees commensurate to its importance. The Court furthermore notes that in the proceedings before the national courts the applicants had ample opportunity to advance their arguments, inter alia, concerning the circumstances in which the waiver took place during the arbitration proceedings. Without having to decide whether a similar waiver would be valid in the context of purely judicial proceedings the Court comes to the conclusion that in the circumstances of the present case concerning arbitral proceedings the applicants' waiver of their right to an impartial judge should be regarded as effective for Convention purposes. Therefore the refusal of the Finnish courts to quash the arbitral award on the ground of M.'s participation in those proceedings does not disclose any appearance of a violation of Article 6 of the Convention.
>
> (*Suovaniemi and Others v. Finland*, Appl. No. 31737/96, Decision of 23 February 1999)

Similarly, the Commission decided in *Nordström-Janzon and Nordström-Lehtinen v. the Netherlands*, where it found no violation of Article 6(1):

> In the present case the arbitration was based on a joint-venture agreement and a subsequent Deed of Settlement concluded between the parties concerned. The arbitration was thus based on a voluntary agreement according to which disputes between the parties should not be settled by the ordinary courts but under a special arbitration system. Consequently, there was a renunciation by the parties of a procedure before the ordinary courts satisfying all the guarantees of Article 6 (Art. 6) of the Convention.
>
> (*Nordström-Janzon and Nordström-Lehtinen v. the Netherlands*, Appl. No. 28101/95, Decision of 27 November 1996)

But what happens when the arbitration board violates the basic rights guaranteed by Article 6(1)? Is the State responsible for the actions undertaken by the arbitrators? The answer, according to the literature[206] and the jurisprudence, is negative: the State does not have any direct responsibility for the arbitrators' actions, simply because they are not part of the judiciary of the concerned State.

Moreover, in *Nordström-Janzon and Nordström-Lehtinen v. the Netherlands*, cited above, the Commission reasoned that:

> ... [T]he grounds on which arbitral awards may be challenged before national courts differ among the Contracting States and considers that it cannot be required under the Convention that national courts must ensure that arbitral proceedings have been in conformity with Article 6 (Art. 6) of the Convention. In some respects – in particular as regards publicity – it is clear that arbitral proceedings are often not even intended to be in conformity with Article 6 (Art. 6), and the arbitration agreement entails a renunciation of the full application of that Article. The Commission therefore considers that an arbitral award does not necessarily have to be quashed because the parties have not enjoyed all the guarantees of Article 6 (Art. 6), but each Contracting State may in principle decide itself on which grounds an arbitral award should be quashed.
>
> (*Nordström-Janzon and Nordström-Lehtinen v. the Netherlands*, Appl. No. 28101/95, Decision of 27 November 1996)

---

206. See, among others, J.E.S. Fawcett, *The Application of the European Convention on Human Rights* (Oxford: Clarendon Press, 1987), 144-145.

However, the disputes concerning the validity of an arbitration award can fall within the jurisdiction of the ECtHR, when they involve the determination of 'civil rights and obligations' and therefore fall under the umbrella of Article 6(1).

In this sense the Court has decided, for example, in *Stran Greek Refineries and Stratis Andreadis v. Greece.*[207] In this case, the Respondent State argued that Article 6(1) was not applicable, because the subject of the 'contestation' before the national courts had not been a 'civil right', but 'the validity of the arbitration clause and consequently that of the arbitration award itself'.[208] The Court, however, considered that the outcome of the arbitration was 'pecuniary' in nature, since it was related to a claim for damages filed by the applicants, and therefore it involved 'civil rights and obligations':

> The Court notes that the applicants' right under the arbitration award was 'pecuniary' in nature, as had been their claim for damages allowed by the arbitration court. Their right to recover the sums awarded by the arbitration court was therefore a 'civil right' within the meaning of Article 6 (art. 6), whatever the nature, under Greek law, of the contract between the applicants and the Greek State (see, mutatis mutandis, the Editions Périscope v. France judgment of 26 March 1992, Series A no. 234-B, p. 66, para. 40). It follows that the outcome of the proceedings brought in the ordinary courts by the State to have the arbitration award set aside was decisive for a 'civil right'.
>
> (*Stran Greek Refineries and Stratis Andreadis v. Greece,* Judgment of 9 December 1994, paragraph 40)

§2.08 APPLICABILITY OF ARTICLE 6 BEFORE INTERNATIONAL TRIBUNALS AND 'HYBRID-COURTS'

Another interesting question is whether the guarantees under Article 6 ECHR apply also to proceedings before international tribunals and so-called 'hybrid-courts'.

International tribunals are a relatively recent creation. They are special criminal tribunals established by the United Nations (UN) with the specific aim to deal with cases concerning specific kind of crimes committed in period of war or, more in general, related to genocide.

The International Criminal Tribunal for former Yugoslavia (ICTY) was the first international tribunal, established by the UN in May 1993, for the purpose of trying those individuals responsible for serious violations of international humanitarian law in the territory of the former Yugoslavia, since the starting of the conflict in 1991 (recently, the ICTY has also dealt with cases related to violation of international humanitarian law in Kosovo).

Later on, the UN Security Council established the International Criminal Tribunal of Rwanda (ICTR), to prosecute those individuals responsible for the 1994 genocide occurred during the conflict between Hutus and Tutsis.

---

207. *Stran Greek Refineries and Stratis Andreadis v. Greece,* Judgment of 9 December 1994.
208. *Ibid.*, paragraph 38.

In 1998, with the Statute of Rome (which entered into force on 1 July 2002), the International Criminal Court (ICC) was established. According to Article 1 of the Statute, the ICC is 'a permanent institution and shall have the power to exercise its jurisdiction over persons for the most serious crimes of international concern', as referred to in the Statute itself, and 'shall be complementary to national criminal jurisdictions'. Article 5 of the Statute (*Crimes within the jurisdiction of the Court*) specifies: '1. The jurisdiction of the Court shall be limited to the most serious crimes of concern to the international community as a whole. The Court has jurisdiction in accordance with this Statute with respect to the following crimes: (a) The crime of genocide; (b) Crimes against humanity; (c) War crimes; (d) The crime of aggression.'

Hybrid-courts are different from international tribunals *stricto sensu* in that they work with mixed panels composed of local and international judges, and they apply both domestic and international law (which poses, sometimes, the issue of a possible conflict arising between the two). These courts have been established by the UN in post-conflict countries affected by a still weak judicial system, in the framework of peace-building operations and transitional justice measures.

In January 2002, it was established the Special Court for Sierra Leone (SCSL), which applies both international and domestic law, to try those individuals responsible for crimes committed during the civil war. Similarly, in 2003 the Extraordinary Cambers in the Courts of Cambodia (ECCC) were introduced to try the former Khmer Rouge leaders, and in 2007 the Special Tribunal for Lebanon (STL) saw the light.

The above examples of hybrid-courts are all operating in the field of criminal law. A rare example of a hybrid-court operating within the limbs of civil law was the Special Chamber of the Supreme Court of Kosovo on Kosovo Trust Agency Related Matters (SCSC), which will be described more in detail – due to its peculiar characteristics – at the end of this Section.

It is obvious that the guarantees under Article 6 of the Convention are not automatically applicable also to international tribunals, and that the ECHR cannot receive applications filed against such tribunals, but only against States.

The Commission, however, has expressed in a number of decisions the opinion that the guarantees provided by the Convention may apply also to international organizations. For example, in the leading-case *M. and Co. v. Germany*,[209] the Commission observed that 'the Convention does not prohibit a Member State from transferring powers to international organizations', clarifying that such transfer of powers does not exclude automatically the State's responsibility 'with regard to the exercise of the transferred powers', and that therefore such transfer of powers is not incompatible with the Convention when the fundamental rights are protected also within the international organization:

> Therefore the transfer of powers to an international organisation is not incompatible with the Convention provided that within that organisation fundamental rights will receive an equivalent protection.
>
> (*M. and Co. v. Germany*, Appl. No. 13258/87, Decision of 9 February 1990)

209. *M. and Co. v. Germany*, Appl. no. 13258/87, Decision of 9 February 1990.

The above view has become *ius receptum* in many judgments of the ECtHR, where the Court seems to have established the principle according to which in case of transfer of powers to international organizations the responsibility of the Member States continues to apply.[210]

Given that the international tribunals stem from international organizations (mainly, the UN), the above principle should be considered applicable also to them.

However, the ECtHR has stated in more than one occasion that the Convention does not apply to international tribunals, but has - at the same time - noted that before such tribunals the principles of independence and impartiality are already guaranteed by their Statute and Rules of Procedure.

For instance in the well-known *Naletilić v. Croatia*,[211] the applicant complained that the ICTY is not an impartial and independent tribunal established by law. The Court, dismissing the application as inadmissible, observed:

> The Court recalls that exceptionally, an issue might be raised under Article 6 of the Convention by an extradition decision in circumstances where the applicant risks suffering a flagrant denial of a fair trial. However, it is not an act in the nature of an extradition which is at stake here, as the applicant seems to think. Involved here is the surrender to an international court which, in view of the content of its Statute and Rules of Procedure, offers all the necessary guarantees including those of impartiality and independence.
>
> (*Naletilić v. Croatia*, Appl. No. 51891/99, Decision of 4 May 2000, paragraph 1[b])

The above reasoning should apply - *mutatis mutandis* - also to the already mentioned 'hybrid-courts'. However, in this case, the legal framework within which they operate is more complex, since these courts are characterized, as said above, by a mixed composition of international and local judges, and often by a mixed jurisdiction, with subsequent problems related to the applicable law.

A peculiar case study, mentioned above, is that of the SCSC,[212] a hybrid-court established by the United Nations Mission in Kosovo (UNMIK) in 2002[213] to deal mainly with cases related to the privatization of Socially Owned Enterprises (SOE),[214] and with cases concerning socially owned property.

Although neither this hybrid-court court nor the hosting country (Kosovo) are parties to the ECHR, there are several precedents in the SCSC's case law referring to

---

210. See, *ex multis*, *Matthews v. The United Kingdom*, Judgment of 18 February 1999; *Waite and Kennedy v. Germany*, Judgment of 18 February 1999; *Beer and Regan v. Germany*, Judgment of 18 February 1999. More recently, in the same sense, see *Nada v. Switzerland*, (Grand Chamber), Judgment of 12 September 2012, Separate (concurring) opinion of Judge Malinverni, paragraphs 25-26, according to which 'international organizations themselves are thus also bound by international human rights norms'.
211. *Naletilić v. Croatia*, Appl. no. 51891/99, Decision of 4 May 2000.
212. As of 1 January 2012, the former 'Special Chamber of the Supreme Court of Kosovo on Kosovo Trust Agency Related Matters' has been replaced by the 'Special Chamber of the Supreme Court of Kosovo on Privatization Agency of Kosovo Related Matters', established by the Law No. 04/L-033 of the Republic of Kosovo, thus becoming a domestic court (though still composed of both local and international judges).
213. With UNMIK Reg. 2002/13.
214. SOEs had already been set under the authority of the Kosovo Trust Agency, a body introduced by UNMIK.

Article 6 and other provisions of the ECHR, and directly applying the principles thereof.[215]

For example, in *Coca Cola Bottling Plant - Lipjan/Lipljan v. KTA*, the SCSC applied the general principles under Article 14 ECHR and noted:

> It is the established practice of the Chamber, while examining whether the Complainants had been subject to discrimination, to consider not only documentary evidence as required by Section 10.6 of UNMIK Regulation 2003/13, but all evidence in the proceeding. See SCEL 04-001, *Vahdet Kollari* in re *Thermosystem v. KTA* (2004). The restriction to only documentary evidence is discriminatory in itself in the light of the jurisprudence of the European Court of Human Rights under Article 14 of the European Convention of Human Rights. Further, the requirement that the complaint must be accompanied by documentary evidence is a virtual impossibility, and if applied as written would be a further discrimination.
>
> (*Coca Cola Bottling Plant - Lipjan/Lipljan employees v. KTA*, SCEL-05-0004, Judgment of 14 June 2006)

In a more recent case, concerning the claim of more than one thousand former employees of a SOE to be entitled to a share of the proceeds of the privatization of the enterprise, the SCSC referred expressly to the guarantees under Article 6 ECHR:

> (...) despite the structure of the UNMIK Regulation 2003/13, as amended, which does not provide any title to the employees who are included in the list by the Agency and who are contested by an aggrieved party to be a party in the proceedings before the Special Chamber, the Trial Panel holds the opinion that those persons are entitled to present their arguments and produce supporting evidence to the Court. Thus, during the hearing, the Court heard the employees whose inclusion in the list was contested, if they were present in the courtroom, on the basis of the 'contradictory principle' as well as of the right to be present at the trial (right to an oral hearing in person and to participate effectively) and of the principle of the 'equality of arms', which flows from Article 6 of the European Convention on Human Rights (...).
>
> (*Ramiz Sadiku employees v. PAK*, SCEL-09-0001, Judgment of 10 June 2011)

In other decisions, the SCSC referred to the principles laid down in Protocol 1, Article 1, ECHR, as to the protection of property rights, and to Article 6 ECHR, with reference to the reasonable length of proceedings and right of access to court, in cases where a

215. Kosovo is not among the signatory States to the ECHR. However, according to the Constitutional Framework for Provisional Self-Government in Kosovo, promulgated by UNMIK on 15 May 2001 (UNMIK/REG/2001/9), the ECHR had direct legal effect also in Kosovo: '3.2 The Provisional Institutions of Self-Government shall observe and ensure internationally recognized human rights and fundamental freedoms, including those rights and freedoms set forth in: ... The European Convention for the Protection of Human Rights and Fundamental Freedoms and its Protocols'. More recently, the Constitution of the Republic of Kosovo, which entered into force on 15 June 2008, in Article 22 provided that:

> Human rights and fundamental freedoms guaranteed by the following international agreements and instruments are guaranteed by this Constitution, are directly applicable in the Republic of Kosovo and, in the case of conflict, have priority over provisions of laws and other acts of public institutions: ... (2) European Convention for the Protection of Human Rights and Fundamental Freedoms.

suspension of the procedure, although expressly provided for by the law, was deemed to be in contrast with the above-mentioned principles.[216]

§2.09 STAGES OF PROCEEDINGS COVERED BY ARTICLE 6

Basically, the guarantees under Article 6 ECHR apply, as far as criminal proceedings are concerned, from the moment a person is subject to a criminal charge until such charge is finally determined;[217] and, as far as civil proceedings are concerned, from the moment civil proceedings are initiated (and, in some cases, even before[218]) until the moment they are brought to an end with a final decision and the time for an appeal has expired (and, as explained below, also in the execution phase).[219]

Although Article 6 does not explicitly grant an individual a right of appeal (which is, however, provided for by Article 2 of Protocol 7), the jurisprudence of the ECtHR has long since recognized that if a State provides the parties with a right of appeal, then Article 6 shall apply to the appeals procedure as well. In this sense the Court decided in *Delcourt v. Belgium*:

> Article 6 para. 1 (art. 6-1) of the Convention does not, it is true, compel the Contracting States to set up courts of appeal or of cassation. Nevertheless, a State which does institute such courts is required to ensure that persons amenable to the law shall enjoy before these courts the fundamental guarantees contained in Article 6 (art. 6) (see, *mutatis mutandis*, the Judgment of 23rd July 1968 on the merits of the case 'relating to certain aspects of the laws on the use of languages in education in Belgium', page 33, *in fine*). There would be a danger that serious consequences might ensue if the opposite view were adopted; the Principal Delegate of the Commission rightly pointed to those consequences and the Court cannot overlook them. In a democratic society within the meaning of the Convention, the right to a fair administration of justice holds such a prominent place that a restrictive interpretation of Article 6 para. 1 (art. 6-1) would not correspond to the aim and the purpose of that provision (see, mutatis mutandis, the Wemhoff Judgment of 27th June 1968, 'As to the Law' paragraph 8).
>
> (*Delcourt v. Belgium*, Judgment 17 January 1970, paragraph 25)

In particular, the Court examined the application of Article 6 to proceedings in appeal and before the Court of Cassation in criminal proceedings. The Court, in said decision, emphasized that 'judicial decisions always affect persons' and remarked that:

> In criminal matters, especially, accused persons do not disappear from the scene when the decision of the judges at first instance or appeal gives rise to an appeal in cassation. Although the Judgment of the Court of Cassation can only confirm or

216. See, *ex multis*, *Qamil (Daut) Bajrami v. Ramiz Sadiku*, ASC-10-0021, Decision of 31 October 2011.
217. See, among many others, the already-mentioned *Eckle v. Germany*, Judgment of 15 July 1982, paragraph 78.
218. See, for example, *W v. the United Kingdom*, Judgment of 8 July 1987, concerning the application of Article 6 (1) also to the administrative procedure (in the subject matter of 'child care') prior to the judicial proceedings concerning the determination of parental rights.
219. See, among others, *Lorenzi, Bernardini and Gritti v. Italy*, Judgment of 27 February 1992.

> quash such decision – and not reverse it or replace it – that judgment may rebound in different degrees on the position of the person concerned. He loses his status of a convicted person or, as the case may be, the benefit of his acquittal, at any rate provisionally, when a decision is set aside and the case is referred back to a trial court. A judgment in cassation sometimes has even more direct repercussions on the fate of an accused. If the highest court dismisses the appeal in cassation, the acquittal or conviction becomes final. If the Court of Cassation allows the appeal without ordering the case to be sent back, because, for example, the facts which led to the conviction do not constitute an offence known to the law (see Article 429 of the Code of Criminal Procedure and the judicial decisions given thereon), then by its own sole decision it puts an end to the prosecution.
>
> (*Delcourt v. Belgium*, Judgment 17 January 1970, paragraph 25)

The Court, with reference to criminal proceedings, observed also that a criminal charge is really 'determined' only when the verdict of acquittal or conviction has become final:

> Criminal proceedings form an entity and must, in the ordinary way terminate in an enforceable decision. Proceedings in cassation are one special stage of the criminal proceedings and their consequences may prove decisive for the accused. It would therefore be hard to imagine that proceedings in cassation fall outside the scope of Article 6 para. 1 (art. 6-1).
>
> (*Delcourt v. Belgium*, Judgment of 17 January 1970, paragraph 25)

In the case under examination, the Court concluded that Article 6 is therefore applicable also to proceedings in Cassation, specifying, however, that the way in which it applies depends 'on the special features of such proceedings'.[220]

Similarly, the ECtHR noted that Article 6 shall also apply to the phases preceding the process before a judicial body, both in civil and criminal proceedings: it is the case, for example, of the phase of the preliminary investigation preceding the trial before a court, or when the domestic law requires an individual to pass through an administrative procedure before being able to apply to a judical body for the protection of his civil rights.

An interesting case related to the application of Article 6 to administrative stages prior to the filing of a claim before a court is the already-mentioned *Schouten and Mendrum v. The Netherlands*.[221] The case concerned – *inter alia* – a demand for payment of contributions issued in March 1987 by the Occupational Association for Health and Mental and Social Well-being (*Bedrijfsvereniging voor de Gezondheid, Geestelijke en Maatschappelijke Belangen*, hereinafter 'BVG'). On 27 March 1987, Mr Schouten filed an objection to the BVG's demand and requested a formal 'confirmation' of its decision, with the intention to file an appeal at a later date. The appeal

---

220. See the already-examined *Delcourt v. Belgium*, Judgment of 17 January 1970, paragraph 26, wherein the Court concluded that:

> Thus, in order to determine whether Delcourt has been a victim of a violation of Article 6 (art. 6), it is necessary to examine what are, both in law and in practice, the functions exercised in a case of this kind by the Belgian Court of Cassation and by the *Procureur général*'s department attached to that Court.

221. *Schouten and Mendrum v. The Netherlands*, Judgment of 9 December 1994, paragraph 62.

was indeed filed on 21 December 1988 with the Rotterdam Appeals Tribunal (*Raad van Beroep*). The ECtHR, deciding on the issue of the reasonable time of the proceedings, with regard to the periods to be taken into consideration, in its decision held that:

> The formal confirmation by the BVG of its decision was an indispensable condition for the institution of proceedings before the Appeals Tribunal (see paragraph 38 above). Although, as the Government pointed out, the emergence of a dispute concerning civil rights and obligations is often not followed immediately by the institution of court proceedings, this is not decisive in the circumstances of the present case. A plaintiff is usually able to decide when to bring a civil action without having to wait for formalities affecting the admissibility of his claim to be completed by his opponent. The delay caused in each case by the BVG's failure, over a significant period, to provide formal confirmation of its decision is consequently relevant to assessing the reasonableness of the length of the proceedings.
>
> The Court therefore agrees with the Commission that in both cases the period to be taken into consideration began when the applicants requested formal confirmation.
>
> (*Schouten and Mendrum v. The Netherlands*, Judgment of 9 December 1994, paragraph 62)

With specific reference to civil proceedings, in *Robins v. the United Kingdom* the ECtHR held that stages subsequent to the decision on the merits, such as the decision on the awards of costs, can also be included in the meaning of 'legal proceedings for the determination of civil rights and obligations':

> The Court recalls that Article 6 § 1 of the Convention requires that all stages of legal proceedings for the 'determination of ... civil rights and obligations', not excluding stages subsequent to judgment on the merits, be resolved within a reasonable time (... .).
>
> (*Robins v. the United Kingdom*, Judgment of 23 September 1997, paragraph 28)

The ECtHR has also interpreted Article 6 as applicable in the execution proceedings following the decision on the merits, considering that the 'execution of a judgment given by any court must therefore be regarded as an integral part of the 'trial' for the purposes of Article 6':

> The Court reiterates that, according to its established case-law, Article 6 para. 1 (art. 6-1) secures to everyone the right to have any claim relating to his civil rights and obligations brought before a court or tribunal; in this way it embodies the 'right to a court', of which the right of access, that is the right to institute proceedings before courts in civil matters, constitutes one aspect (see the Philis v. Greece Judgment of 27 August 1991, Series A no. 209, p. 20, para. 59). However, that right would be illusory if a Contracting State's domestic legal system allowed a final, binding judicial decision to remain inoperative to the detriment of one party. It would be inconceivable that Article 6 para. 1 (art. 6-1) should describe in detail procedural guarantees afforded to litigants - proceedings that are fair, public and expeditious - without protecting the implementation of judicial decisions; to construe Article 6 (art. 6) as being concerned exclusively with access to a court and the conduct of proceedings would be likely to lead to situations incompatible with the principle of the rule of law which the Contracting States undertook to respect when they ratified the Convention (see, mutatis mutandis, the Golder v. the United

> Kingdom Judgment of 21 February 1975, Series A no. 18, pp. 16-18, paras. 34-36). Execution of a judgment given by any court must therefore be regarded as an integral part of the 'trial' for the purposes of Article 6 (art. 6); moreover, the Court has already accepted this principle in cases concerning the length of proceedings (see, most recently, the Di Pede v. Italy and Zappia v. Italy judgments of 26 September 1996, Reports of Judgments and Decisions 1996-IV, pp. 1383-1384, paras. 20-24, and pp. 1410-1411, paras. 16-20 respectively).
>
> (*Hornsby v. Greece*, Judgment of 19 March 1997, paragraph 40)

Similarly, in *Ruianu v. Romania*,[222] the ECtHR, with regard to the execution of final and binding judicial decisions, decided that the prevention or the excessive delay of the execution is a breach of Article 6.

The Court's interpretation went further: if, in the course of proceedings for the enforcement of a decision, the domestic court also takes an additional decision on compensation of damages, such proceedings have to be regarded as a 'second stage' of the main proceedings, and Article 6(1) shall be applicable to them. This is what was decided in *Silva Pontes v. Portugal*,[223] concerning a case in which the applicant had asked the domestic court to enforce the payment of part of the damages that had already been calculated, 'without prejudice to the remainder once the details necessary for its calculation have been established'.[224] The Court decided as follows:

> The Court accordingly takes the view, like the Commission, that the 'enforcement' proceedings were not intended solely to enforce an obligation to pay a fixed amount; they also served to determine important elements of the debt itself, as is moreover shown by the size of the out-of-court settlement on which the parties agreed (see paragraph 19 above). Those proceedings must therefore be regarded as the second stage of the proceedings which began on 20 December 1977 (see the Guincho v. Portugal Judgment of 10 July 1984, Series A no. 81, p. 13, para. 29, and the Martins Moreira v. Portugal Judgment of 26 October 1988, Series A no. 143, p. 16, para. 44). It follows that the dispute (contestation) over the applicant's right to damages would only have been resolved by the final decision in the enforcement proceedings.
>
> (*Silva Pontes v. Portugal*, Judgment of 23 March 1984, paragraph 33)

§2.10 ARTICLE 13 ECHR

Article 13 ECHR reads: 'Everyone whose rights and freedoms as set forth in this Convention are violated shall have an effective remedy before a national authority notwithstanding that the violation has been committed by persons acting in an official capacity'.

According to the consistent interpretation of the ECtHR, Article 13 'guarantees the availability at the national level of a remedy to enforce the substance of the Convention rights and freedoms in whatever form they might happen to be secured in

222. *Ruianu v. Romania*, Judgment of 17 June 2003.
223. *Silva Pontes v. Portugal*, Judgment of 23 March 1984.
224. Pursuant to Article 810 of the Portuguese Code of Civil Procedure: '*sem prejuizo de logo que recolhidos os necessários elementos, deduzirem liquidação da restante*'.

the domestic legal order'.[225] In other words, Article 13 requires the existence of a provision in the domestic legislation which grants a remedy for any 'arguable complaint' under the Convention, as well as for appropriate relief. The Court explained in its case law that 'the remedy required by Article 13 must be 'effective' in practice as well as in law'.[226]

Traditionally, the ECtHR has considered Article 13 as a general provision, in relation to Article 6, which has been considered as *lex specialis*. As a consequence of this, whenever the Court has deemed applicable Article 6, Article 13 has been considered to be 'absorbed' by the former.

Indeed, the Court has consistently affirmed[227] that 'the requirements of Article 13 are less strict than, and are here absorbed by, those of Article 6' and that 'the role of Article 6 § 1 in relation to Article 13 is that of a *lex specialis*'. See, for example, the Judgment in *Brualla Gómez de la Torre*, wherein the Court stated:

> The Court reiterates that where the right claimed is a civil right, the role of Article 6 § 1 in relation to Article 13 is that of a *lex specialis*, the requirements of Article 13 being absorbed by those of Article 6 § 1 (...). Consequently, it is unnecessary to rule on the complaint.
>
> (*Brualla Gómez de la Torre*, Judgment of 19 December 1997, paragraph 41)

More specifically, in the already mentioned *Golder v. the United Kingdom*,[228] the Court remarked the difference between Article 13, which concerns an effective remedy before a 'national authority', relating to the violation of a right guaranteed by the Convention, and Article 6(1), which covers claims relating to the existence of civil rights and obligations:

> Article 13 (art. 13) speaks of an effective remedy before a 'national authority' ('*instance nationale*') which may not be a 'tribunal' or 'court' within the meaning of Articles 6 para. 1 and 5 para. 4 (art. 6-1, art. 5-4). Furthermore, the effective remedy deals with the violation of a right guaranteed by the Convention, while Articles 6 para. 1 and 5 para. 4 (art. 6-1, art. 5-4) cover claims relating in the first case to the existence or scope of civil rights and in the second to the lawfulness of arrest or detention. What is more, the three provisions do not operate in the same field. The concept of 'civil rights and obligations' (Article 6 para. 1) (art. 6-1) is not co-extensive with that of 'rights and freedoms as set forth in this Convention' (Article 13) (art. 13), even if there may be some overlapping. As to the 'right to liberty' (Article 5) (art. 5), its 'civil' character is at any rate open to argument (Neumeister judgment of 27 June 1968, Series A no. 8, p. 43, para. 23; Matznetter judgment of 10 November 1969, Series A no. 10, p. 35, para. 13; De Wilde, Ooms and Versyp judgment of 18 June 1971, Series A no. 12, p. 44, para. 86). Besides, the requirements of Article 5 para. 4 (art. 5-4) in certain respects appear stricter than those of Article 6 para. 1 (art. 6-1), particularly as regards the element of 'time'.
>
> (*Golder v. the United Kingdom*, Judgment of 21 February 1975, paragraph 33)

225. *T.P. and K.M. v. the United Kingdom*, Judgment of 10 May 2001, paragraph 107.
226. *Ibid.*, paragraph 107; *Aydın v. Turkey*, Judgment of 25 September 1997, paragraph 103.
227. See, *ex multis*, *Kadubec v. Slovakia*, Judgment of 2 September 1998; *British-American Tobacco Company Ltd v. the Netherlands*, Judgment of 20 November 1995.
228. *Golder v. the United Kingdom*, Judgment of 21 February 1975.

More in particular, in cases related to the excessive length of proceedings,[229] the ECtHR, after finding a violation of the right to a 'hearing within a reasonable time', has decided that it is unnecessary to examine also the possible violation of Article 13, with regard to the lack of an effective remedy before the national authorities for the excessive length of the proceedings.

Recently, however, the Court had a partial *revirement*,[230] and opted for the possibility of a cumulative application of the two provisions, especially in cases concerning the breach of the right to a hearing within a reasonable time, which appears to be the most recurrent violation of Article 6 by the Contracting States.

In the Court's view, the time has come to review its case law in the light of the continuing accumulation of applications before it in which the only, or principal, allegation is that of a failure to ensure a hearing within a reasonable time in breach of Article 6 § 1:

> The growing frequency with which violations in this regard are being found has recently led the Court to draw attention to 'the important danger' that exists for the rule of law within national legal orders when 'excessive delays in the administration of justice' occur 'in respect of which litigants have no domestic remedy' (see, for example, Bottazzi v. Italy [GC], no. 34884/97, § 22, ECHR 1999-V; Di Mauro v. Italy [GC], no. 34256/96, § 23, ECHR 1999-V; A.P. v. Italy [GC], no. 35265/97, § 18, 28 July 1999, unreported; and Ferrari v. Italy [GC], no. 33440/96, § 21, 28 July 1999, unreported).
>
> Against this background, the Court now perceives the need to examine the applicant's complaint under Article 13 taken separately, notwithstanding its earlier finding of a violation of Article 6 § 1 for failure to try him within a reasonable time.
>
> (*Kudła v. Poland*, Judgment of 26 October 2000, paragraphs 148-149)

The Court reasoned that 'Article 13, giving direct expression to the States' obligation to protect human rights first and foremost within their own legal system, establishes an additional guarantee for an individual in order to ensure that he or she effectively enjoys those rights', and that 'the object of Article 13, as emerges from the *travaux préparatoires* (...), is to provide a means whereby individuals can obtain relief at national level for violations of their Convention rights before having to set in motion the international machinery of complaint before the Court'.[231] Therefore, the Court concluded that:

> From this perspective, the right of an individual to trial within a reasonable time will be less effective if there exists no opportunity to submit the Convention claim first to a national authority; and the requirements of Article 13 are to be seen as

229. See, among others, *Pizzetti v. Italy*, Judgment of 26 February 1993, paragraph 21: 'In view of its decision concerning Article 6 (art. 6), the Court does not consider it necessary also to examine the case under Article 13 (art. 13)'; and *Bouilly v. France*, Judgment of 7 December 1999, paragraph 27: '*Eu égard à sa décision relative à l'article 6, la Cour n'estime pas nécessaire de se placer de surcroît sur le terrain de l'article 13 de la Convention*'.
230. See the leading case *Kudła v. Poland*, Judgment of 26 October 2000; and *SCI Bounois v. France*, Judgment of 17 June 2003.
231. *Kudła v. Poland*, cited above, paragraph 152.

reinforcing those of Article 6 § 1, rather than being absorbed by the general obligation imposed by that Article not to subject individuals to inordinate delays in legal proceedings.

(*Kudla v. Poland*, Judgment of 26 October 2000, paragraph 152)

CHAPTER 3

Particular Aspects of the Right to a Fair Trial

Piero Leanza

§3.01 INTRODUCTION

As it has been said in the previous chapter, Article 6 ECHR guarantees the right to a fair trial in both civil and criminal matters.

The specific wording of Article 6 suggests that the guarantees under paragraph (1) apply to both criminal and civil proceedings, whilst the rights listed in paragraphs (2) and (3) are specifically intended for criminal proceedings.[1] However, the ECtHR case law indicates the extension of some of the guarantees provided for in paragraphs (2) and (3) to civil proceedings, where its principles are applicable by analogy.[2] Therefore, as the following paragraphs will explain, whenever an individual is charged with a criminal offence or is involved in proceedings concerning his civil rights and obligations, he is entitled to the right of access to court, to have a fair and public hearing before an independent and impartial tribunal established by law, and to have judgment pronounced publicly and within a reasonable time.

1. Indeed, while paragraph (1) of Article 6 begins with the sentence, 'In the determination of his civil rights and obligations or of any criminal charge against him ...', paragraphs (2) and (3) both begin with the words 'Everyone charged with a criminal offence ...'.
2. See – among others – *Dombo Beheer B. V. v. the Netherlands*, Judgment of 27 October 1993, paragraphs 32-33; *Albert and Le Compte v. Belgium*, Judgment of 10 February 1983, paragraph 39; *Feldbrugge v. the Netherlands*, Judgment of 26 May 1986, paragraph 44. In the literature see, among others, D.J. Harris, M.O. Boyle & C. Warbrick, *Law of the European Convention on Human Rights* (London: Butterworths, 1995), 202, wherein the Authors note that, however, such guarantees may apply with a different strength in civil and criminal proceedings.

§3.02 THE RIGHT OF ACCESS TO COURT

Although Article 6 does not explicitly provide for the right of 'access to a court,' it is widely accepted that such a right stems directly from paragraph (1), which grants everyone a 'fair and public hearing ... before an impartial tribunal established by law.'

The Court noted that the right of access is only one aspect of the broader 'right to a court,' embodied in Article 6(1):

> Article 6 § 1 embodies the 'right to a court', of which the right of access, that is, the right to institute proceedings before a court in civil matters, constitutes one aspect.
>
> (*Tinnelly & Sons Ltd and Others and McElduff and Others v. the United Kingdom*, Judgment of 10 July 1998, paragraph 72)

The right of access to a court outlined in the first paragraph of Article 6 applies to both civil and criminal proceedings, as clearly affirmed in *Deweer v. Belgium*: 'the "right to a court", which is a constituent element of the right to a fair trial, is no more absolute in criminal than in civil matters.'[3]

[A] *Golder* and Subsequent Rulings

From a historical perspective, the right of access to a court was firstly analysed by the ECtHR in *Golder v. the United Kingdom*,[4] where the Court, *inter alia*, noted that:

> Again, Article 6 para. 1 (art. 6-1) does not state a right of access to the courts or tribunals in express terms. It enunciates rights which are distinct but stem from the same basic idea and which, taken together, make up a single right not specifically defined in the narrower sense of the term. It is the duty of the Court to ascertain, by means of interpretation, whether access to the courts constitutes one factor or aspect of this right.
>
> (*Golder v. the United Kingdom*, Judgment of 21 February 1975, paragraph 28)

The Court, after a thorough analysis of the specific rights provided for by Article 6(1), concluded as follows:

> Taking all the preceding considerations together, it follows that the right of access constitutes an element which is inherent in the right stated by Article 6 para. 1 (art. 6-1). This is not an extensive interpretation forcing new obligations on the Contracting States: it is based on the very terms of the first sentence of Article 6 para. 1 (art. 6-1) read in its context and having regard to the object and purpose of the Convention, a lawmaking treaty (see the Wemhoff judgment of 27 June 1968, Series A no. 7, p. 23, para. 8), and to general principles of law.

3. *Deweer v. Belgium*, Judgment of 27 February 1980, paragraph 49. See also, in the same sense, *Le Compte, Van Leuven and De Meyere v. Belgium*, Judgment of 23 June 1981, paragraph 53.
4. *Golder v. the United Kingdom*, Judgment of 21 February 1975. In this case the applicant was a prisoner who complained that his right to access to court had been violated because he was refused permission by the Home Secretary to consult a solicitor in order to prepare a civil lawsuit against a prison officer.

> The Court thus reaches the conclusion, without needing to resort to 'supplementary means of interpretation' as envisaged at Article 32 of the Vienna Convention, that Article 6 para. 1 (art. 6-1) secures to everyone the right to have any claim relating to his civil rights and obligations brought before a court or tribunal. In this way the Article embodies the 'right to a court', of which the right of access, that is the right to institute proceedings before courts in civil matters, constitutes one aspect only. To this are added the guarantees laid down by Article 6 para. 1 (art. 6-1) as regards both the organisation and composition of the court, and the conduct of the proceedings. In sum, the whole makes up the right to a fair hearing. The Court has no need to ascertain in the present case whether and to what extent Article 6 para. 1 (art. 6-1) further requires a decision on the very substance of the dispute (English 'determination', French 'décidera').
>
> (*Golder v. the United Kingdom*, Judgment of 21 February 1975, paragraph 36)

In particular, the *Golder* court observed that Article 6(1) is not limited to proceedings that have already been initiated before a court, stating that it would be 'inconceivable' that the guarantees under Article 6(1) were only 'afforded to parties in a pending lawsuit and should not first protect that which alone makes it in fact possible to benefit from such guarantees, that is, access to court.' Under this untenable interpretation, the Court reasoned that any Contracting State could simply exclude from its jurisdiction certain classes of civil rights, taking away certain actions from courts and tribunals (leaving them, for example, under the authority of government organs).[5]

The ECtHR has repeatedly invoked the *Golder* Court's interpretation of Article 6(1) recognizing the access to court under a number of factual contexts, such as the right to legal aid, the presence of the parties in the proceedings, the interference between the right of access to court and immunities, limited jurisdiction, etc.

[B] *Ashingdane* and Limitations on the Right to Access a Court

Despite this wide application of the principles laid down in the *Golder* Judgment, the ECtHR has offered a caveat limiting the right of access to a court.

In *Ashingdane v. the United Kingdom,*[6] for example, the Court stated that the right of access to court might be subject to limitations set out in the laws and regulations of the Contracting States. The Court stated, however, that these limitations should not be interpreted to alter the essence of the right itself, in that any attempts to limit the right to a court under Article 6 (1) must be tailored so as to relate to a legitimate aim, and must bear a 'reasonable relationship of proportionality' with the aim sought to be achieved:[7]

5. The Court observed, *inter alia,* that: 'The fair, public and expeditious characteristics of judicial proceedings are of no value at all if there are no judicial proceedings' (*Golder v. the United Kingdom,* cited above, paragraph 35).
6. *Ashingdane v. the United Kingdom,* Judgment of 28 May 1985.
7. *Ex plurimis,* other than the judgment quoted in the text, see also *Fayed v. the United Kingdom,* Judgment of 21 September 1994, paragraph 65; *Tolstoy Miloslavsky v. the United Kingdom,* Judgment of 13 July 1995, paragraph 59; *Levages Prestations Services v. France,* Judgment of 23 October 1996, paragraph 40; *Bellet v. France,* Judgment of 4 December 1995, paragraph 31;

> Certainly, the right of access to the courts is not absolute but may be subject to limitations; these are permitted by implication since the right of access 'by its very nature calls for regulation by the State, regulation which may vary in time and in place according to the needs and resources of the community and of individuals' (see the above-mentioned *Golder* judgment, p. 19, paragraph 38, quoting the '*Belgian Linguistic*' judgment of 23 July 1968, Series A no. 6, p. 32, paragraph 5). In laying down such regulation, the Contracting States enjoy a certain margin of appreciation. Whilst the final decision as to observance of the Convention's requirements rests with the Court, it is no part of the Court's function to substitute for the assessment of the national authorities any other assessment of what might be the best policy in this field (see, *mutatis mutandis*, the *Klass and Others* judgment of 6 September 1978, Series A no. 28, p. 23, paragraph 49).
>
> Nonetheless, the limitations applied must not restrict or reduce the access left to the individual in such a way or to such an extent that the very essence of the right is impaired (see the above-mentioned *Golder* and '*Belgian Linguistic*' judgments, *ibid.*, and also the above-mentioned *Winterwerp* judgment, Series A no. 33, pp. 24 and 29, paragraphs 60 and 75). Furthermore, a limitation will not be compatible with Article 6 paragraph 1 (Article 6-1) if it does not pursue a legitimate aim and if there is not a reasonable relationship of proportionality between the means employed and the aim sought to be achieved.
>
> (*Ashingdane v. the United Kingdom*, Judgment of 28 May 1985, paragraph 57)

The same principles articulated in *Ashingdane* were further affirmed in *Tinnelly & Sons Ltd and Others and McElduff and Others v. the United Kingdom*,[8] where the Court remarked:

> However, this right is not absolute, but may be subject to limitations; these are permitted by implication since the right of access by its very nature calls for regulation by the State. In this respect, the Contracting States enjoy a certain margin of appreciation, although the final decision as to the observance of the Convention's requirements rests with the Court. It must be satisfied that the limitations applied do not restrict or reduce the access left to the individual in such a way or to such an extent that the very essence of the right is impaired. Furthermore, a limitation will not be compatible with Article 6 § 1 if it does not pursue a legitimate aim and if there is not a reasonable relationship of proportionality between the means employed and the aim sought to be achieved (see, among other authorities, the *Stubbings and Others v. the United Kingdom* judgment of 22 October 1996, *Reports* 1996-IV, p. 1502, § 50).
>
> (*Tinnelly & Sons Ltd and Others and McElduff and Others v. the United Kingdom*, Judgment of 10 July 1998, paragraph 72)

From the precedent outlined above, it is therefore a well-established principle that any limitation to the right of access to a court imposed by domestic legislation (such as,

---

Stubbings and Others v. the United Kingdom, Judgment of 22 October 1996, paragraphs 51-52; *Aït-Mouhoub v. France*, Judgment of 28 October 1998, paragraph 52.

8. *Tinnelly & Sons Ltd and Others and McElduff and Others v. the United Kingdom*, cited above.

inter alia, statutory limitation periods,[9] determination of a certain value of the claim as condition for the filing of an appeal,[10] obligations to pay in advance a certain sum as 'security' before filing an appeal,[11] immunity from liability,[12] limitation of presence of minors and other categories of people before a court,[13] etc.) must not impair the 'essence' of the right to a court.

[C] Domestic Procedural Requirements and Article 6(1)

With regard to time limits to file an appeal, the ECtHR has not clearly articulated whether Article 6(1) creates a right for a litigant to be apprised of the existence of time limits to file an appeal. In one case, the Court found that, when two different time limits are provided by the law (one for filing the appeal, and another to file a submission to substantiate the appeal), such a right might be recognized.

9. In *Stubbings and Others v. the United Kingdom*, Judgment of 22 October 2006, paragraphs 51-52, the Court held that the English relevant legislation providing for a statutory limitation period did not infringe the right of access to court under Article 6(1), reasoning as follows:

> It is noteworthy that limitation periods in personal injury cases are a common feature of the domestic legal systems of the Contracting States. They serve several important purposes, namely to ensure legal certainty and finality, protect potential defendants from stale claims which might be difficult to counter and prevent the injustice which might arise if courts were required to decide upon events which took place in the distant past on the basis of evidence which might have become unreliable and incomplete because of the passage of time. (...) In the instant case, the English law of limitation allowed the applicants six years from their eighteenth birthdays in which to initiate civil proceedings. In addition, subject to the need for sufficient evidence, a criminal prosecution could be brought at any time and, if successful, a compensation order could be made (see paragraphs 38–42 above). Thus, the very essence of the applicants' right of access to a court was not impaired.

10. See, for example, *Brualla Gómez de la Torre v. Spain*, Judgment of 19 December 1997, paragraphs 28-39, where the Court found that no violation of Article 6(1) had occurred, reasoning – *inter alia* – that 'The manner in which Article 6 § 1 applies to courts of appeal or of cassation depends on the special features of the proceedings concerned and account must be taken of the entirety of the proceedings conducted in the domestic legal order and the court of cassation's role in them; the conditions of admissibility of an appeal on points of law may be stricter than for an ordinary appeal' (paragraph 37).
11. See, for example, *Tolstoy Miloslavsky v. the United Kingdom*, where the applicant alleged that the requirement that he pay, as security, the sum of GBP 124,900 within fourteen days (failing which the appeal would be dismissed) had amounted to a total bar on his access to the Court of Appeal, since it had impaired the essence of his right of access to that court and was disproportionate. The Court, however, after carefully examining the applicable law in that context and the specific circumstances of the case, did not 'find that the national authorities overstepped their margin of appreciation in setting the conditions which they did for the applicant to pursue his appeal in the Court of Appeal' and therefore concluded that 'it cannot be said that those conditions impaired the essence of the applicant's right of access to court or were disproportionate for the purposes of Article 6 para. 1' (*Tolstoy Miloslavsky v. the United Kingdom*, cited above, paragraph 67).
12. See, among others, *T.P. and K.M. v. the United Kingdom*, Judgment of 10 May 2001, concerning a case of negligence liability of local authorities.
13. See, *ex multis*, *Ashingdane v. the United Kingdom*, cited above.

For example, in *Vecher v. France,*[14] the Court ruled that, since there was no fixed time to file a pleading to substantiate the already filed appeal, and since the French Court of Cassation, taking 'less time than usual to hear the appeal,' had decided the case (dismissing the appeal as untimely) eight days before the appellant actually submitted his written pleading, there was a violation of Article 6(1):

> In conclusion, since there was no fixed date for filing a pleading and the Court of Cassation took less than usual to hear the appeal, without Mr Vecher being either warned of the fact by the registry or able to foresee it, he was deprived of the possibility of putting his case in the Court of Cassation in a concrete and effective manner.
>
> (*Vecher v. France*, Judgment of 29 November 1996, paragraph 30)

In *Ganci v. Italy,*[15] the Court stated that the right to obtain a judicial decision can be inferred from the right to court. The applicant was a prisoner who had filed a number of appeals against decisions of the Ministry of Justice to impose on him a 'special regime.' In domestic law, the prisoner had ten days to appeal against the decree of the Ministry of Justice, and the competent court had ten days to issue a decision. The Court observed, *inter alia,* that the failure of the competent courts to issue a decision on the merits of this case in respect of four appeals filed by the prisoner, constituted a violation of Article 6(1).

> The Court notes at the outset that there is an essential feature in the instant case distinguishing it from *Messina (no. 2)*, cited above. In the present case the courts never ruled on the merits of the applicant's four appeals, whereas in the case of Mr Messina they did so out of time.
>
> The Court can only conclude that the lack of any decision on the merits of the appeals nullified the effect of the courts' review of the decrees issued by the Minister of Justice.
>
> In the Court's opinion, the applicable legislation lays down a time-limit of only ten days for adjudication partly because of the seriousness of the special regime's effects on prisoners' rights and partly because the impugned decision remains valid for only a limited time.
>
> In these circumstances, the Court considers that the lack of a decision by the court responsible for the execution of sentences on the appeals lodged against the decrees issued by the Minister of Justice breached the applicant's right to have his case heard by a court.
>
> Accordingly, there has been a violation of Article 6 of the Convention.
>
> (*Ganci v. Italy*, Judgment of 30 October 2003, paragraph 31)

In another case, judgment was not handed down on the merits because a domestic tribunal had lost the case file. The ECtHR held that this amounted to a violation of the right of access to court, stressing that such right would be illusory if it contemplated only the right to file a claim, without envisaging the right to a decision on such claim by the domestic judicial authorities:

---

14. *Vecher v. France*, Judgment of 29 November 1996.
15. *Ganci v. Italy*, Judgment of 30 October 2003.

> The Court recalls that the institution of proceedings does not, in itself, satisfy all the requirements of Article 6 § 1. The Convention is intended to guarantee not rights that are theoretical or illusory but rights that are practical and effective. The right of access to a court includes not only the right to institute proceedings but also the right to obtain a 'determination' of the dispute by a court. It would be illusory if a Contracting State's domestic legal system allowed an individual to bring a civil action before a court without ensuring that the case would be determined by a final decision in the judicial proceedings. It would be inconceivable for Article 6 § 1 to describe in detail procedural guarantees afforded to litigants – proceedings that are fair, public and expeditious – without guaranteeing the parties that their civil disputes will be finally determined (see *Multiplex v. Croatia*, no. 58112/00, § 45, 10 July 2003; *Kutić v. Croatia*, no. 48778/99, § 25, ECHR 2002-II). A litigant's right of access to a court would be illusory if he or she were to be kept in the dark about the developments in the proceedings and the court's decisions on the claim, especially when such decisions are of the nature to bar further examination (see *Sukhorubchenko*, cited above, § 53).
>
> (*Dubinskaya v. Russia*, Judgment of 13 July 2006, paragraph 41)

In *Lupaş and Others v. Romania*, a civil action involving the recovery of property held in undivided shares, the ECtHR ruled that the right of access to a court was violated when some of the co-owners of the property in question were prevented from initiating a lawsuit in the absence of the consent of all the co-owners (the so-called 'unanimity rule'). In *Lupaş*, the Court admitted that, in theory, the rule provided by the domestic civil code could be considered as conforming to Article 6(1) of the Convention; but it held that, in practice, the domestic civil code imposed an improper burden on the claimants, in effect hindering them from access to the court and ultimately obtaining a decision on their claim:

> Accordingly, reiterating that all the provisions of the Convention and its Protocols must be interpreted in such a way as to guarantee rights which are practical and effective as opposed to theoretical and illusory, the Court cannot accept the Government's argument that the dismissal of the applicants' actions placed only a temporary restriction on their right of access to a court. In this connection, it also notes that apart from a judgment given by the High Court of Cassation and Justice on 3 February 2005, the Government have not indicated any legal means whereby the applicants might be able to assert their inheritance rights. Lastly, the Court notes with interest that a bill to amend the Civil Code, expressly abandoning the unanimity rule, was recently tabled in Parliament.
>
> In the light of the foregoing considerations, the Court finds that the strict application of the unanimity rule imposed a disproportionate burden on the applicants, depriving them of any clear and practical opportunity to have the courts determine their applications for recovery of the land in issue and thereby impairing the very essence of their right of access to a court.
>
> (*Lupaş and Others v. Romania*, Judgment of 14 December 2006, paragraphs 75-76)

Regarding appeals proceedings, the ECtHR has consistently held that the right to a court implied by Article 6(1) does not compel the Contracting States to set up courts of appeal or of cassation. However, it has stated that where such courts do exist, the guarantees of Article 6(1), including the right of access to court, must be upheld.[16]

In light of this holding, in *Dunayev v. Russia* the Court held that the refusal by the domestic courts to accept an appeal constituted a violation of the right of access to court guaranteed by Article 6(1).[17] In other cases, the Court decided that where the right to an appeal is hindered by the fact that the appellant did not fully observe the appealed judgment, this will amount to a violation of the right of access to a court.

For example, in *Garcia Manibardo v. Spain*, an appeal was declared inadmissible by the domestic court (*Audiencia Provincial*) due to the failure of the appellant to make a deposit or a 'compensation award,' a precondition to file an appeal under Spanish law. The Court determined that the Spanish Court's denial of filing an appeal based on the claimant's failure to follow the compensation award requirements amounted to a violation of Article 6(1):

> In the instant case, the applicant's appeal was declared inadmissible owing to the statutory duty on persons other than those who are in receipt of legal aid to deposit with the *Audiencia Provincial* a specific amount (namely, the compensation award) as a condition precedent to their being permitted formally to lodge an appeal.
>
> The Court finds that by obliging her to pay the amount ordered, the *Audiencia Provincial* prevented the applicant from using an existing and available remedy, such that a disproportionate hindrance was put in the way of her right of access to a court. Consequently, there has been a violation of Article 6 § 1.
>
> (*Garcia Manibardo v. Spain*, Judgment of 15 February 2000, paragraphs 44-45)

Similarly, the ECtHR has found a violation of Article 6(1) in cases where under domestic law the admissibility of the appeal is subject to the surrender of the appellant to custody. For example, in *Papon v. France*[18] and in *Omar v. France*,[19] the Court – after stressing the crucial role of cassation proceedings, 'whose consequences may prove decisive for the accused' – observed that the requirement that the appellant surrender himself into custody in order to file an 'admissible' appeal constituted a disproportionate burden on the appellant and impaired the essence of the right of appeal:

> Noting that the applicant forfeited his right to appeal on points of law because he had failed to surrender to custody as required by Article 583 of the Code of Criminal Procedure as applicable at the time, it considers that, regard being had to all the circumstances of the case, he suffered disproportionate interference with his right of access to a court and, therefore, with his right to a fair trial (...).
>
> (*Papon v. France*, Judgment of 25 July 2002, paragraph 100)

16. See, *ex multis*, *Brualla Gómez de la Torre v. Spain*, cited above, paragraph 37; *Dunayev v. Russia*, Judgment of 24 May 2007, paragraph 34; *Kozlica v. Croatia*, Appl. No. 29182/03, Decision of 2 November 2006, paragraph 32.
17. *Dunayev v. Russia*, cited above, paragraphs 37-38.
18. *Papon v. France*, Judgment of 25 July 2002.
19. *Omar v. France*, (Grand Chamber), Judgment of 29 July 1998.

> The Court can only note that, where an appeal on points of law is declared inadmissible solely because, as in the present case, the appellant has not surrendered to custody pursuant to the judicial decision challenged in the appeal, this ruling compels the appellant to subject himself in advance to the deprivation of liberty resulting from the impugned decision, although that decision cannot be considered final until the appeal has been decided or the time-limit for lodging an appeal has expired.
>
> This impairs the very essence of the right of appeal, by imposing a disproportionate burden on the appellant, thus upsetting the fair balance that must be struck between the legitimate concern to ensure that judicial decisions are enforced, on the one hand, and the right of access to the Court of Cassation and exercise of the rights of the defence on the other.
>
> (*Omar v. France*, [Grand Chamber], Judgment of 29 July 1998, paragraph 40)

[D] Legal Aid

[1] Legal Aid Schemes and Article 6(1)

When an individual proceeds in a case without legal counsel, and is unable to properly defend himself or protect his rights, either in criminal or civil proceedings, Article 6(1) is invoked.

For example, in *Airey v. Ireland,*[20] the ECtHR held that Article 6(1) had been violated because the applicant was not able to bring an action for separation against her husband due to the fact that she did not have sufficient financial means to pay for a lawyer. The Court considered that due to their complexity, proceedings for separation in Ireland could not be brought in person by the applicant without assistance by a lawyer. Considering the generally high fees required for representation, the Court determined that in the absence of a legal aid scheme, or of a simplification of the procedure, the right of access to court was violated:

> (...) In addition, whilst Article 6 para. 1 (art. 6-1) guarantees to litigants an effective right of access to the courts for the determination of their 'civil rights and obligations', it leaves to the State a free choice of the means to be used towards this end. The institution of a legal aid scheme – which Ireland now envisages in family law matters (see paragraph 11 above) – constitutes one of those means but there are others such as, for example, a simplification of procedure. In any event, it is not the Court's function to indicate, let alone dictate, which measures should be taken; all that the Convention requires is that an individual should enjoy his effective right of access to the courts in conditions not at variance with Article 6 para. 1 (art. 6-1) (...).
>
> (*Airey v. Ireland*, Judgment of 9 October 1979, paragraph 26)

In its decision, the Court provided a limitation, in that the State need not 'provide free legal aid for every dispute relating to a 'civil right'' (indeed, a specific provision on legal aid [Article 6(3)] exists only with regard to criminal proceedings), but stressed that Article 6(1) may oblige the Signatory State to provide for the assistance of a lawyer,

20. *Airey v. Ireland*, Judgment of 9 October 1979.

where professional representation is necessary in law or due to the complexity of the procedure:

> To hold that so far-reaching an obligation exists would, the Court agrees, still with the fact that the Convention contains no provision on legal aid for those disputes, Article 6 para. 3 (c) (art. 6-3-c) dealing only with criminal proceedings. However, despite the absence of a similar clause for civil litigation, Article 6 para. 1 (art. 6-1) may sometimes compel the State to provide for the assistance of a lawyer when such assistance proves indispensable for an effective access to court either because legal representation is rendered compulsory, as is done by the domestic law of certain Contracting States for various types of litigation, or by reason of the complexity of the procedure or of the case.
>
> (*Airey v. Ireland*, Judgment of 9 October 1979, paragraph 26)

Where a legal-aid scheme does not exist under domestic law, the ECtHR has held that the State is obliged to provide alternative measures to ensure a litigant's right of access to court. This principle was articulated - among others - in *Andronicou and Constantinou v. Cyprus*.[21]

In *Andronicou*, the applicants alleged that the absence of a legal-aid system for civil litigants, coupled with the litigants' lack of adequate financial resources, in effect deprived them of the right of access to a court in that they were precluded from filing a lawsuit for damages based on their financial inability. However, the litigants were offered *ex gratia* legal aid from the Attorney General, but refused it. The Court held that based on the presence of an available legal-aid scheme, there was no violation of Article 6(1):

> The Court notes that whilst Article 6 § 1 of the Convention guarantees to litigants an effective right of access to the courts for the determination of their 'civil rights and obligations', it leaves to the State a free choice of the means to be used towards this end. The institution of a legal-aid scheme constitutes one of those means but there are others. It is not the Court's function to indicate, let alone stipulate, which measures should be taken. All that the Convention requires is that an individual should enjoy his effective right of access to the courts in conditions not at variance with Article 6 § 1 (see the *Airey v. Ireland* judgment of 9 October 1979, Series A no. 32, pp. 14-15, § 26).
>
> The Court, like the Commission, considers that the Attorney-General's *ex gratia* offer of 7 July 1995 provided a solution to help overcome the applicants' lack of resources. It is surprising that the applicants did not take up the offer immediately, given their need of financial assistance to institute proceedings and their determination to sue the authorities. It is significant in this respect that they had no hesitation in accepting the Government's earlier offer to cover the costs and expenses incurred through their participation in the proceedings of the commission of inquiry.
>
> In the circumstances therefore, the applicants cannot maintain that they did not have an effective access to a court within the meaning of Article 6 § 1 of the

21. *Andronicou and Constantinou v. Cyprus*, Judgment of 9 October 1997.

> Convention, it being recalled that this provision does not guarantee a litigant a favourable outcome. There has accordingly been no violation of Article 6 § 1.
>
> (*Andronicou and Constantinou v. Cyprus*, Judgment of 9 October 1997, paragraphs 199-201)

[E] Limitations to the Duty of Providing Legal Aid

Significantly, the ECtHR has ruled that domestic laws which allow the State to refuse to grant legal aid in limited, specific circumstances are compliant with Article 6(1).

For example, in cases where the applicant has substantial knowledge of the law and the subject matter of the case is not complex, limited access to legal aid does not violate Article 6(1). In *McVicar v. the United Kingdom*,[22] for instance, the Court, after reaffirming the principle set out in *Airey v. Ireland*, according to which 'Article 6 § 1 leaves to the State a free choice of the means to be used in guaranteeing litigants a right of effective access to a court,' remarked that:

> (...) the question whether or not that Article requires the provision of legal representation to an individual litigant will depend upon the specific circumstances of the case and, in particular, upon whether the individual would be able to present his case properly and satisfactorily without the assistance of a lawyer.
>
> (*McVicar v. the United Kingdom*, Judgment of 7 May 2002, paragraph 48)

However, in the similar case of *Steel and Morris v. UK*,[23] the ECtHR applied the following analysis when considering the complexity of the law(s) at issue, the nature of the case, and the legal education of the defendants. In *Steel*, the litigants were deemed unable to meet the criteria of providing adequate themselves *pro se* representation; therefore, the applicants were not able to represent themselves adequately. As such, Article 6(1) was violated. The facts before the *Steel* Court involved what was deemed complex litigation (the case file included around 40,000 pages of documentary evidence, and 130 witnesses were heard; the first instance trial lasted 313 court days and the appeal 28; the combined judgments of the trial court and the Court of Appeal extended to 1,100 pages), and the case had significant financial consequences for the appellants, who were low income. The Court reasoned that the appellants, given the complexity of the litigation and the gravity of the case, were not able to enjoy 'equality of arms' with the opposing side in the absence of legal aid.[24]

> In conclusion, therefore, the Court finds that the denial of legal aid to the applicants deprived them of the opportunity to present their case effectively before the court and contributed to an unacceptable inequality of arms with McDonald's. There has, therefore, been a violation of Article 6 § 1 of the Convention.
>
> (*Steel and Morris v. United Kingdom*, Judgment of 15 February 2005, paragraph 72)

---

22. *McVicar v. the United Kingdom*, Judgment of 7 May 2002.
23. *Steel and Morris v. United Kingdom*, Judgment of 15 February 2005.
24. See, on this principle, among many others, *De Haes and Gijsels v. Belgium*, Judgment of 24 February 1997, paragraph 53.

[F] Effectiveness of Legal Aid

The ECtHR has also considered the effectiveness of legal aid as it relates to the right to access a court. The jurisprudence of the Court of Strasbourg suggests that it is not sufficient for the State simply to grant legal aid to individuals (either in civil or criminal proceedings), but that State must also ensure that the assistance is of practical effect.

For example, in *Bertuzzi v. France*,[25] the applicant obtained legal aid but was not able to make use of it since the opposing party (the defendant) was a lawyer and because all three lawyers assigned to the applicant had personal connections to the defendant and obtained permission to withdraw. The applicant was not able to have another lawyer assigned to his case; therefore, he was unable to start the proceedings.[26] The Court observed that the principle of equality of arms articulated in *Steel* was violated:

> It considers that permitting the applicant to represent himself in proceedings against a legal practitioner did not afford him access to a court under conditions that would secure him the effective enjoyment of equality of arms that is inherent in the concept of a fair trial (...).
>
> (*Bertuzzi v. France*, Judgment of 13 February 2003, paragraph 31)

[G] Financial Burden

A number of rulings indicate that the right of access to a court is violated when litigation related filing fees under domestic law impose an excessive financial burden on the applicant.[27]

In *Kreuz v. Poland*,[28] the applicant alleged that the court fee of PLZ 100,000,000 was equivalent to his annual salary at that time and therefore constituted a de facto bar to his access to court. In light of these facts, the ECtHR held that there was a breach of Article 6(1):

> Assessing the facts of the case as a whole and having regard to the prominent place held by the right to a court in a democratic society, the Court considers that the judicial authorities failed to secure a proper balance between, on the one hand, the interest of the State in collecting court fees for dealing with claims and, on the other hand, the interest of the applicant in vindicating his claim through the courts.
>
> The fee required from the applicant for proceeding with his action was excessive. It resulted in his desisting from his claim and in his case never being heard by a court. That, in the Court's opinion, impaired the very essence of his right of access.

25. *Bertuzzi v. France*, Judgment of 13 February 2003.
26. See also *P., C. and S. v. The United Kingdom*, Judgment of 16 July 2002, where the applicants were initially granted legal aid, but after the withdrawal of their lawyer were not given the possibility to find another lawyer (paragraphs 92-100).
27. See, other than *Kreuz v. Poland*, quoted in the text, also *Weissman and Others v. Romania*, Judgment of 24 May 2006; *Teltronic-CATV v. Poland*, Judgment of 10 January 2006; *Stankov v. Bulgaria*, Judgment of 12 July 2007; and many others.
28. *Kreuz v. Poland*, Judgment of 19 June 2001.

> For the above reasons, the Court concludes that the imposition of the court fees on the applicant constituted a disproportionate restriction on his right of access to a court. It accordingly finds that there has been a breach of Article 6 § 1 of the Convention.
>
> (*Kreuz v. Poland*, Judgment of 19 June 2001, paragraphs 66-67)

[H] Limited Jurisdiction

Where a party is granted a civil 'right' under domestic law, the ECtHR has consistently protected the right of access to court. However, the Court has refused to widen the scope of this protection to cases where a civil 'right' is not at issue.

In *Boulois v. Luxembourg*,[29] the Grand Chamber did not recognize the existence of the right of access to court for a prisoner who was denied several requests for prison leave by the competent domestic authorities (the Attorney General and the Prison Board) and had consequently filed a complaint before the domestic Administrative Court and the Higher Administrative Court.

In *Boulois*, the domestic administrative courts had declined their jurisdiction. The applicant then applied to the ECtHR for relief, claiming that the domestic courts had violated Article 6(1). The Grand Chamber ruled that Article 6(1) was not applicable, since the issue did not concern a civil 'right' under (Luxembourg) domestic law.[30]

In its judgment, the Grand Chamber considered that Article 6(1) 'is not applicable under its criminal head, as the proceedings concerning the prison system did not relate in principle to a determination of a "criminal charge"'[31]. The Court further stated:

> The Court must therefore consider whether the applicant had a 'civil right', in order to assess whether the procedural safeguards afforded by Article 6 § 1 of the Convention were applicable to the proceedings concerning his requests for prison leave.
>
> (*Boulois v. Luxembourg*, [Grand Chamber], Judgment of 3 April 2012, paragraph 86)

Additionally, the Court noted that the 'dispute' present in the case centred around 'the actual existence of the right to prison leave claimed by the applicant.'[32] In deciding whether this amounted to a 'right' of the applicant, the Grand Chamber considered that permission to leave prison, within domestic law, existed as a 'privilege,' which 'may be granted' to prisoners in certain circumstances, but not as a civil 'right' granted to the prisoners (paragraphs 47, 49, and 96). The Court held that according to the relevant domestic law, 'the Prison Board enjoys a certain degree of discretion in deciding

29. *Boulois v. Luxembourg*, (Grand Chamber), Judgment of 3 April 2012.
30. In the judgment under examination, however, the Court reaffirmed the principles expressed in its settled case law, according to which prisoners continue to enjoy all the fundamental rights and freedoms guaranteed by the Convention, except the right to liberty, where the detention is lawfully imposed (see paragraph 84 and, among many others, *Dickson v. the United Kingdom*, [Grand Chamber], Appl. no. 44362/04, paragraph 67; and *Stummer v. Austria*, [Grand Chamber], Appl. no. 37452/02, paragraph 99, both quoted in the Judgment).
31. *Boulois v. Luxembourg*, cited above, paragraph 85.
32. *Ibid.*, paragraph 95.

whether the prisoner concerned merits the privilege in question'.[33] The Court then concluded that:

> In view of all the foregoing considerations, the Court cannot consider that the applicant's claims related to a 'right' recognised in Luxembourg law or in the Convention. Accordingly, it concludes, like the Government, that Article 6 of the Convention is not applicable.
>
> (*Boulois v. Luxembourg*, [Grand Chamber], Judgment of 3 April 2012, paragraph 104)

It its decision, the Grand Chamber almost completely reversed the Judgment of the Chamber (Second section) of 14 December 2010. In that case, it held that although Article 6 ECHR was not applicable to the specific case under its criminal head, it was applicable under its civil head.[34] The decision in *Boulois* can also be contrasted with the Judgment in *Enea v. Italy*,[35] where the Grand Chamber found the existence of a civil right of a prisoner in relation to family visits and correspondence. Although the court distinguished *Boulois v. Luxembourg* from the earlier case law, all the cases above concerned the nature of a civil right for the purposes of Article 6(1); they were not solely focused on the right of 'access' to court in its strictest sense.

The issue of limited jurisdiction came to the attention of the ECtHR in *Vasilescu v. Romania*.[36] This case concerned a claim for restitution of goods that had been confiscated by the public authorities during the Communist regime.

The applicant complained that in 1966, police officers from the Argeş *miliţia* had searched her house without a warrant, in connection with a police investigation carried on against her husband for unlawful possession of valuables, and had seized 327 gold coins. These coins were then deposited at the Argeş branch of the National Bank of Romania. After the criminal charges were dropped and the investigation discontinued, the applicant filed a lawsuit for the restitution of part of the gold coins and obtained favourable decisions at first instance and in appeals proceedings.

In 1994, however, the Procurator-General applied to the Supreme Court of Justice under Article 330 of the Code of Civil Procedure. The Supreme Court of Justice quashed all the earlier judgments in the applicant's favour. The Supreme Court of Justice held that under Article 275 of the Code of Civil Procedure, only the State Counsel for the county of Argeş had jurisdiction over the application of Mrs. Vasilescu. In her application to the Court of Strasbourg, Mrs. Vasilescu complained that her right of access to a court had been violated.

33. *Ibid.*, paragraph 99. The Court, in the same judgment, recalled its established case law, according to which 'the examination of requests for temporary release or of issues relating to the manner of execution of a custodial sentence do not fall within the scope of Article 6 § 1' (paragraph 87). In the same sense, see also *Neumeister v. Austria*, *Lorsé and Others v. the Netherlands* and *Montcornet de Caumont v. France*, all cited by the *Boulois* Court.
34. According to the Court (*Boulois v. Luxembourg*, Second section, Judgment of 14 December 2010), the applicant was entitled to be granted a certain period of prison leave since he met all the requirements laid down in the domestic legislation. In particular, the Chamber considered that the pecuniary implications of the reasons of his requests for prison leave were related to his resettling in the society and to his private life, and were therefore related to civil rights.
35. *Enea v. Italy*, (Grand Chamber), Judgment of 17 September 2009.
36. *Vasilescu v. Romania*, Judgment of 22 may 1998.

The Court observed that the Procurator-General's department 'consists of officials who carry out all their duties under the authority of the Procurator-General,'[37] under the supervision of the Minister of Justice. It concluded that even if the State Counsel exercised powers of a judicial nature, he exercised those powers as a member of the Procurator-General's department. The court therefore upheld the applicant's complaint that there was a violation of the right of access to court as guaranteed by Article 6(1):[38]

> The Court reiterates that only an institution that has full jurisdiction and satisfies a number of requirements, such as independence of the executive and also of the parties, merits the description 'tribunal' within the meaning of Article 6 § 1 (see, among other authorities, the *Beaumartin v. France* judgment of 24 November 1994, Series A no. 296-B, p. 63, § 38). Neither State Counsel for the county of Argeş nor the Procurator-General meets those requirements.
>
> There has therefore been a violation of Article 6 § 1.
>
> (*Vasilescu v. Romania*, Judgment of 22 may 1998, paragraph 41)

[I] Immunity

Immunity granted by international conventions or domestic law to special categories of persons such as states, embassies, international organizations, agents, employees, etc. may represent a bar to the power of domestic courts to adjudicate civil claims. This is relevant not only for litigation relating to employment, but also for claims for compensation and actions for damages in general. Where such immunity exists, the Court is required to determine not only whether a violation of the right of access to a court has occurred, but also whether Article 6(1) is applicable at all.

[1] Immunity for States and International Organizations

In *Al-Adsani v. the United Kingdom*,[39] the United Kingdom courts had ruled that the State of Kuwait was immune to a claim for damages for personal injuries suffered by an individual as a consequence of torture.[40] The applicant maintained that the English

37. *Ibid.*, paragraph 40.
38. In the sense that only an institution that has full jurisdiction and satisfies a number of requirements can be defined a 'tribunal', in the meaning of Article 6, see also, *ex plurimis*, *Ringeisen v. Austria*, Judgment of 16 July 1971, paragraph 95; *Le Compte, Van Leuven and De Meyere v. Belgium*, Judgment of 23 June 1981, paragraph 55; *Belilos v. Switzerland*, Judgment of 29 April 1988, paragraph 64; and *Beaumartin v. France*, Judgment of 24 November 1994, paragraph 38.
39. *Al-Adsani v. the United Kingdom*, (Grand Chamber), Judgment of 21 November 2001.
40. In particular, when the Court of Appeal examined the case, it found that the State of Kuwait was immune to the action filed by the claimant, on the basis of the State Immunity Act 1978, Section 1(1), which provides: 'A State is immune from the jurisdiction of the courts of the United Kingdom except as provided in the following provisions of this Part of this Act. ...', and Section 5, which reads:

    > A State is not immune as respects proceedings in respect of (a) death or personal injury; or

courts had failed to secure the enjoyment of his right not to be tortured and had denied him access to a court, contrary to Articles 3, 6(1) and 13 ECHR.

The ECtHR, noting that according to English law a civil action against a State is possible provided that the respondent State waives immunity, held that – in principle – Article 6(1) was applicable:

> The proceedings which the applicant intended to pursue were for damages for personal injury, a cause of action well known to English law. The Court does not accept the Government's submission that the applicant's claim had no legal basis in domestic law since any substantive right which might have existed was extinguished by operation of the doctrine of State immunity. It notes that an action against a State is not barred *in limine*: if the defendant State waives immunity, the action will proceed to a hearing and judgment. The grant of immunity is to be seen not as qualifying a substantive right but as a procedural bar on the national courts' power to determine the right.
>
> The Court is accordingly satisfied that there existed a serious and genuine dispute over civil rights. It follows that Article 6 § 1 was applicable to the proceedings in question.
>
> (*Al-Adsani v. the United Kingdom*, [Grand Chamber], Judgment of 21 November 2001, paragraphs 48-49)

However, following the principles set out in *Waite and Kennedy v. Germany*, the Court remarked that the right of access to a court is not absolute, but may be subject to limitation, provided that any limitations do not impair the essence of the right of access to court, and that they pursue a legitimate aim with 'a reasonable relationship of proportionality between the means employed and the aim sought to be achieved.'[41] The ECtHR held that the immunity granted to Kuwait by the 1978 Act pursued the legitimate aim of compliance with the principles of international law and was also proportionate to the aim pursued, in light of the rules set out in the Vienna Convention on the Law of Treaties of 23 May 1969:

> It follows that measures taken by a High Contracting Party which reflect generally recognised rules of public international law on State immunity cannot in principle be regarded as imposing a disproportionate restriction on the right of access to a court as embodied in Article 6 § 1. Just as the right of access to a court is an inherent part of the fair trial guarantee in that Article, so some restrictions on access must likewise be regarded as inherent, an example being those limitations generally accepted by the community of nations as part of the doctrine of State immunity.
>
> (*Al-Adsani v. the United Kingdom*, [Grand Chamber], Judgment of 21 November 2001, paragraph 56)

Finally, the Court concluded that although prohibition of torture is a peremptory norm in international law, the case under examination did not concern criminal liability for

---

(b) damage to or loss of tangible property, caused by an act or omission in the United Kingdom'. In that case, the Court observed, it was clear and uncontested that the torture occurred in Kuwait did not fall within the exception provided by Section 5.

41. *Waite and Kennedy v. Germany*, (Grand Chamber), Judgment of 18 February 1999, paragraph 59.

alleged acts of torture, but the immunity of a State sued for damages deriving from torture, which was legitimately covered by the State Immunity Act of 1978:

> In these circumstances, the application by the English courts of the provisions of the 1978 Act to uphold Kuwait's claim to immunity cannot be said to have amounted to an unjustified restriction on the applicant's access to a court.
>
> (*Al-Adsani v. the United Kingdom*, [Grand Chamber], Judgment of 21 November 2001, paragraph 67)

The ECtHR has reached similar conclusions in employment-related claims against a foreign State that enjoys immunity under international law. In *Fogarty v. the United Kingdom*,[42] the applicant was an employee of the United States Embassy in London, and the UK Courts afforded immunity to the employer under the 1978 act.

The Court, in deciding whether the restriction on the right to court pursued a legitimate aim, observed that 'sovereign immunity is a concept of international law, developed out of the principle *par in parem non habet imperium*, by virtue of which one State shall not be subject to the jurisdiction of another State' and that 'the grant of sovereign immunity to a State in civil proceedings pursues the legitimate aim of complying with international law to promote comity and good relations between States through the respect of another State's sovereignty.'[43]

The Court accepted the employer's argument that issues relating to the recruitment of staff for missions and embassies may involve sensitive and confidential aspects of the diplomatic and organizational policy of a foreign State. The Court noted that the International Law Commission did not exclude State immunity where the subject of the proceedings was related to the recruitment of staff, and concluded that the restriction was therefore proportionate to the pursued aim:

> In these circumstances, the Court considers that, in conferring immunity on the United States in the present case by virtue of the provisions of the 1978 Act, the United Kingdom cannot be said to have exceeded the margin of appreciation allowed to States in limiting an individual's access to court.
>
> (*Fogarty v. the United Kingdom*, Judgment of 21 November 2001, paragraph 39)

However, in *Sabeh El Leil v. France*,[44] the applicant alleged that he had been deprived of his right of access to a court in a lawsuit concerning the termination of his employment by the Kuwaiti Embassy in Paris as a result of the immunity from jurisdiction granted by the domestic courts to the State of Kuwait. The applicant had obtained judgment from the Employment Tribunal granting him compensation for the unjustified termination of his employment. However, the Court of Appeal had set aside the judgment, finding the claim inadmissible 'by virtue of the principle of jurisdictional immunity of foreign States.'[45]

42. *Fogarty v. the United Kingdom*, Judgment of 21 November 2001.
43. *Ibid.*, paragraph 34.
44. *Sabeh El Leil v. France*, (Grand Chamber), Judgment of 29 June 2011.
45. *Ibid.*, paragraph 15.

The ECtHR considered the established principles set out in *Cudak v. Lithuania*,[46] *Loizidou v. Turkey*,[47] and the above-mentioned *Fogarty v. the United Kingdom*, and remarked that 'in cases where the application of the rule of State immunity from jurisdiction restricts the exercise of the right of access to a court, the Court must ascertain whether the circumstances of the case justified such restriction.' The Court concluded that in the case at hand the French courts had failed to preserve a reasonable relationship of proportionality and had thus impaired the very essence of the applicant's right of access to a court:

> In conclusion, by upholding in the present case an objection based on State immunity and dismissing the applicant's claim without giving relevant and sufficient reasons, and notwithstanding the applicable provisions of international law, the French courts failed to preserve a reasonable relationship of proportionality. They thus impaired the very essence of the applicant's right of access to a court.
>
> (*Sabeh El Leil v. France*, [Grand Chamber], Judgment of 29 June 2011, paragraph 67)

In its judgment, the ECtHR applied the principles of international customary law as laid down in the International Law Commission's 1991 Draft Articles (now enshrined in the 2004 Convention). The Court noted that in the case at hand the applicant was neither a diplomatic or consular agent of Kuwait, nor a national of that State, and that his duties were not related to the sovereign interests of the State of Kuwait. The Court concluded that the French Court of Appeal and the Court of Cassation had therefore not provided a proper legal justification for limitation of his right of access to a court.

The ECtHR has adopted similar reasoning in respect of the immunity enjoyed by international organizations. In *Waite and Kennedy v. Germany*,[48] for example, the Court examined the aspect of the immunity granted to the European Space Agency (ESA).

The applicants had brought an action against the ESA before the Darmstadt Labour Court (*Arbeitsgericht*), maintaining that according to the German Provision of Labour (Temporary Staff) Act (*Arbeitnehmerüberlassungsgesetz*), they had acquired the status of employees of the ESA. The ESA argued that it was immune from jurisdiction under Article XV § 2 of the ESA Convention and its Annex I. The Darmstadt Labour Court accepted the ESA's argument and declared the applicants' actions inadmissible.

The ECtHR applied the test set out in the case law, examining the facts of the case with particular reference to the legitimacy of the aim pursued by the immunity granted to the ESA and to the proportion between the means adopted and the aim sought. The Court took into account the existence of an alternative means for protecting the applicants' interests and reached the conclusion that there had not been any violation of the right of access to court:

46. *Cudak v. Lithuania*, (Grand Chamber), Judgment of 23 March 2010.
47. *Loizidou v. Turkey*, Judgment of 18 December 1996.
48. *Waite and Kennedy v. Germany*, cited above.

> In view of all these circumstances, the Court finds that, in giving effect to the immunity from jurisdiction of ESA on the basis of section 20(2) of the Courts Act, the German courts did not exceed their margin of appreciation. Taking into account in particular the alternative means of legal process available to the applicants, it cannot be said that the limitation on their access to the German courts with regard to ESA impaired the essence of their 'right to a court' or was disproportionate for the purposes of Article 6 § 1 of the Convention.
>
> (*Waite and Kennedy v. Germany*, [Grand Chamber], Judgment of 18 February 1999, paragraph 73)

[2] Immunity for Certain Categories of State Servants

Where there is a public interest justification for doing so, a State can also grant immunity to certain categories of its own employees; for example, police officers or members of the judiciary.

The leading case in this area is *Osman v. the United Kingdom*.[49] The first applicant argued that in failing to adequately protect the second applicant and his father from a known danger, the police had failed to comply with their positive obligation under Article 2 ECHR; namely, 'Everyone's right to life shall be protected by law.' They also argued that the dismissal by the Court of Appeal of the negligence action on the grounds of State immunity constituted a restriction of their right of access to a court in violation of Article 6(1) ECHR.

The ECtHR held that, although Article 2 was violated, there was a breach of Article 6(1). The Court observed that although a rule protecting the police from actions in negligence might be justified on the basis that the constant risk of exposure to liability for their actions would hinder the police's ability to fight crime, 'a blanket immunity' would breach Article 6(1). To ensure compliance with Article 6(1), the Court stated that domestic courts should have regard to other public interest considerations in a particular case – 'considerations which must be examined on the merits and not automatically excluded by the application of a rule which amounts to the grant of an immunity to the police.'[50] Even where the immunity enjoyed by police agents is legitimate and in the wider public interest, the State must nevertheless grant individuals an alternative means of satisfaction if they suffer damages as a consequence of the negligent action of the police.

> The Court would observe that the application of the rule in this manner without further enquiry into the existence of competing public-interest considerations only serves to confer a blanket immunity on the police for their acts and omissions during the investigation and suppression of crime and amounts to an unjustifiable restriction on an applicant's right to have a determination on the merits of his or her claim against the police in deserving cases.
>
> (*Osman v. the United Kingdom*, [Grand Chamber], Judgment of 28 October 1998, paragraph 151)

---

49. *Osman v. the United Kingdom*, (Grand Chamber), Judgment of 28 October 1998.
50. *Ibid.*, paragraph 152.

The decision in *Osman* was undoubtedly controversial, and in similar cases (*Z. and Others v. the United Kingdom,*[51] and *T.P. and K.M. v. the United Kingdom*[52]) the ECtHR has found no violation of Article 6(1), notably upholding the application of an exclusionary rule by English law, which granted local authorities substantial immunity from the negligence actions filed against them for damage suffered by parents and their children. In *Z. and Others v. the United Kingdom,* the Court was cautious to state that the inability of the applicants to sue the local authorities was due to the lack of substantive right in the domestic law, and not because the local authorities were immune from suit, opting for the application of Article 13, instead of Article 6(1):[53]

> In the present case, the Court is led to the conclusion that the inability of the applicants to sue the local authority flowed not from an immunity but from the applicable principles governing the substantive right of action in domestic law.
>
> (*Z. and Others v. the United Kingdom,* [Grand Chamber], Judgment of 10 may 2001, paragraph 100)

In *Enrst v. Belgium,*[54] the Court found that the immunity granted to a magistrate with regard to civil claims for damages did not violate the right of access to justice, but only because the domestic jurisdiction provided the injured party with other means of protection of his interests.[55]

[3] Immunity for Parliamentary Members

Similar immunities are enjoyed by members of legislative assemblies. In *Syngelidis v. Greece,*[56] the case concerned a claim for compensation for non-pecuniary harm suffered by the applicant as a consequence of his ex-wife's alleged breach of a judicial decision

51. *Z. and Others v. the United Kingdom,* (Grand Chamber), Judgment of 10 May 2001.
52. *T.P. and K.M. v. the United Kingdom,* (Grand Chamber), Judgment of 10 May 2001.
53. *Z. and Others v. the United Kingdom,* cited above, paragraph 102, reads:

> It is nonetheless the case that the interpretation of domestic law by the House of Lords resulted in the applicants' case being struck out. The tort of negligence was held not to impose a duty of care on the local authority in the exercise of its statutory powers. Their experiences were described as 'horrific' by a psychiatrist (see paragraph 40 above) and the Court has found that they were victims of a violation of Article 3 (see paragraph 74 above). Yet the outcome of the domestic proceedings they brought is that they, and any children with complaints such as theirs, cannot sue the local authority in negligence for compensation, however foreseeable - and severe - the harm suffered and however unreasonable the conduct of the local authority in failing to take steps to prevent that harm. The applicants are correct in their assertions that the gap they have identified in domestic law is one that gives rise to an issue under the Convention, but in the Court's view it is an issue under Article 13, not Article 6 § 1.

54. *Ernst and Others v. Belgium,* Judgment of 15 July 2003.
55. *Ibid.*, paragraph 56, reads (official French version): '*Dans ces conditions, la Cour estime que, se limitant à reconnaître les spécificités liées au privilège de juridiction, les restrictions apportées au droit d'accès n'ont pas porté atteinte à la substance même de leur droit à un tribunal ou qu'elles aient été disproportionnées sous l'angle de l'article 6 § 1 de la Convention*'.
56. *Syngelidis v. Greece,* Judgment of 11 February 2010.

on the custody of their child. The applicant alleged that the parliamentary immunity of his ex-wife[57] violated his right of access to a court. The Court observed that when a State grants immunity to its members of parliament, the protection of individuals' civil rights may be hindered. However, following the principles set out in its earlier case law, according to which immunity must not impose a disproportionate restriction on the right of access to justice,[58] the Court remarked that:

> [I]n determining whether or not a particular measure was proportionate the Court examines whether the impugned acts were connected with the exercise of parliamentary functions in their strict sense.
>
> (*Syngelidis v. Greece*, Judgment of 11 February 2010, paragraph 44)

In that case, the Court held that the dispute between the couple was unrelated to the parliamentary activity. The refusal by the Greek Parliament to waive the M.P.'s immunity was unjustified and constituted a breach of the right of access to court embodied in Article 6(1):

> In this connection the Court notes that, if properly interpreted in the light of Article 6 § 1, Article 62 of the Greek Constitution entitles the Greek Parliament to refuse to grant leave for a prosecution only where the acts on which the prosecution is based are clearly connected with parliamentarian activity. In the context of the present case, there was no conceivable link between M.A.'s behaviour which formed the basis of the proposed criminal proceedings and her parliamentary functions. Her alleged failure to comply with the contact arrangements ordered by the domestic court was entirely unrelated to the performance of her functions as a member of parliament and to the functioning and reputation of Parliament in general. Such behaviour is more consistent with a personal quarrel between an ex-couple with regard to the regulation of their contact with their child.
>
> (*Syngelidis v. Greece*, Judgment of 11 February 2010, paragraph 46)

Similar reasoning had already been expressed by the ECtHR in *Cordova v. Italy*,[59] where the blanket immunity that protected a member of the Italian Parliament (and former President of the Italian Republic) from the claim for damages brought by an Italian public prosecutor was held to violate the right of access to justice guaranteed by Article 6(1).[60]

---

57. In the case under examination, the applicant had filed a criminal indictment in combination with a request for monetary compensation, pursuant to the Greek applicable law.
58. See also, on this point, *Kart v. Turkey*, (Grand Chamber), Judgment of 3 December 2009, paragraph 80; *Waite and Kennedy v. Germany*, cited above, paragraph 59; *T.P. and K.M. v. the United Kingdom*, cited above, paragraph 98.
59. *Cordova v. Italy*, (No. 1), Judgment of 30 January 2003.
60. The case is related to the claim for compensation for damage to his honour and reputation filed by a public prosecutor against a member of the Italian parliament. In the course of some investigations against a certain Mr C., the public prosecutor had found out, *inter alia*, that this Mr C. had had contact with the Senator and former Italian President Mr Francesco Cossiga. The latter, sent the prosecutor a fax, two letters and, later on, a small wooden horse and a tricycle, together with a detective game called '*Super Cluedo*', attaching to the parcel the following message: 'Have fun, dear Prosecutor! Best wishes, F. Cossiga' ('*Si prenda un po' di svago, gentile Procuratore! Cordialmente F. Cossiga*'). (See *Cordova v. Italy*, cited above, paragraph 11). In 1996 Mr Cossiga was brought to trial before the Messina District Court (where the public prosecutor

The Court held that the decision of the domestic court to apply the immunity provided for by Article 68(1) of the Italian Constitution, and the subsequent refusal of the same court to raise a conflict of State powers before the Constitutional Court (as requested by the applicant) amounted to an infringement of the right of access to a court.

> [...] In the present case, following the resolution of 2 July 1997 coupled with the Messina District Court's refusal to raise a conflict of State powers before the Constitutional Court, the prosecution of Mr Cossiga was abandoned and the applicant was deprived of the possibility of securing any form of reparation for his alleged damage.
>
> In these circumstances, the Court considers that there has been an interference with the applicant's right of access to a court.
>
> (*Cordova v. Italy*, (No. 1), Judgment of 30 January 2003, paragraphs 52-53)

Furthermore, the Court noted that the behaviour of the member of Parliament related to a personal dispute and was unrelated to the exercise of his parliamentary functions. Accordingly, it could not have been covered by parliamentary immunity:

> However the Court notes that, in the particular circumstances of this case, Mr Cossiga's behaviour was not connected with the exercise of parliamentary functions in their strict sense. Although it emerges from the decision of the Messina public prosecutor of 13 December 1997 (see paragraph 20 above) that Mr Cossiga had criticised the applicant's investigations in an earlier parliamentary question, the Court considers that ironic or derisive letters accompanied by toys personally addressed to a prosecutor cannot, by their very nature, be construed as falling within the scope of parliamentary functions. Such behaviour is more consistent with a personal quarrel. In such circumstances, it would not be right to deny someone access to a court purely on the basis that the quarrel might be political in nature or connected with political activities.
>
> (*Cordova v. Italy*, (No. 1), Judgment of 30 January 2003, paragraph 62)

The Court also observed that the resolution of the Italian Senate granting full immunity to the Parliament member left the applicant with no alternative means for the effective protection of his rights. The Court therefore considered that the immunity ran counter to the well-established principles laid down in its vast jurisprudence on the subject matter.[61]

The ECtHR reached a different conclusion in *A. v. the United Kingdom*,[62] a case involving the full immunity coverage afforded to an MP in respect of a civil action for damages brought by one of his neighbours. During the course of a speech in the House of Commons, the MP referred explicitly to the applicant, mentioning her name and address and referring to members of her family. The MP made allegations regarding her

---

intervened as civil party), but the Senate, by a resolution with a majority of votes, in 1997 decided that the acts of which Mr Cossiga was accused were covered by the immunity provided for in Article 68(1) of the Italian Constitution. With Judgment issued on 27 September 1997, the Messina District Court ruled that Mr Cossiga had no case to answer 'pursuant to Article 68 § 1 of the Constitution' (*ibid.*, paragraphs 12-14).

61. See, *ex multis*, *Waite and Kennedy v. Germany*, cited above.
62. *A. v. the United Kingdom*, Judgment of 17 December 2002.

way of living that the applicant considered to be defamatory. Because of the MP's speech, newspapers published articles containing extracts of the speech, including photographs of the applicant, and mentioning her name and address. (Headlines included '*MP Attacks 'Neighbours From Hell''* and '*MP names nightmare neighbour.'*) The applicant also suffered several racial attacks and harassment via letter and in person.

The applicant contended that the absolute privilege that covered the MP's statements about her in Parliament hindered her right of access to a court as guaranteed by Article 6(1).[63] The Court found that the applicant's right of access to a court under Article 6(1) had not been violated. The Court held that the immunity afforded to the MP pursued a legitimate aim, and the means employed were proportionate to interest pursued:

> The Court concludes that the parliamentary immunity enjoyed by the MP in the present case pursued the legitimate aims of protecting free speech in Parliament and maintaining the separation of powers between the legislature and the judiciary.
>
> (*A. v. the United Kingdom*, Judgment of 17 December 2002, paragraph 77)

> In light of the above, the Court believes that a rule of parliamentary immunity, which is consistent with and reflects generally recognised rules within signatory States, the Council of Europe and the European Union, cannot in principle be regarded as imposing a disproportionate restriction on the right of access to a court as embodied in Article 6 § 1 (see, *mutatis mutandis, Al-Adsani*, cited above, § 56). Just as the right of access to a court is an inherent part of the fair trial guarantee in that Article, so some restrictions on access must likewise be regarded as inherent, an example being those limitations generally accepted by signatory States as part of the doctrine of parliamentary immunity (*ibid.*).
>
> (*A. v. the United Kingdom*, Judgment of 17 December 2002, paragraph 83)

> It follows that, in all the circumstances of this case, the application of a rule of absolute Parliamentary immunity cannot be said to exceed the margin of appreciation allowed to States in limiting an individual's right of access to a court.
>
> (*A. v. the United Kingdom*, Judgment of 17 December 2002, paragraph 87)

[J] Presence of the Parties at the Proceedings

The parties generally have the right to be present during civil proceedings. Similarly, the accused has the right to be present in criminal proceedings. This is implied in the guarantees provided for by Article 6(1) and (3)(c),(d), and (e):[64]

---

63. Article 9 of the Bill of Rights 1689 ('... the freedom of speech and debates or proceedings in Parliament ought not to be impeached or questioned in a court or place out of Parliament.') does not refer to a substantive bar to civil claims, but rather to a procedural bar to the determination by a court of any claim which derives from words spoken in Parliament (see *A. v. the United Kingdom*, cited above, paragraphs 22 and 64).
64. See *Colozza v. Italy*, Judgment of 22 January 1985, paragraph 27.

> Although this is not expressly mentioned in paragraph 1 of Article 6, the object and purpose of the Article taken as a whole show that a person 'charged with a criminal offence' is entitled to take part in the hearing. Moreover, sub-paragraphs (c), (d) and (e) of paragraph 3 guarantee to 'everyone charged with a criminal offence' the right 'to defend himself in person', 'to examine or have examined witnesses' and 'to have the free assistance of an interpreter if he cannot understand or speak the language used in court', and it is difficult to see how he could exercise these rights without being present (...).
>
> (*Hermi v. Italy*, [Grand Chamber], Judgment of 18 October 2006, paragraph 59)

However, although this principle is generally accepted as being of universal application in criminal proceedings,[65] the presence of a party at the proceedings in civil cases is considered to be necessary only in certain circumstances. In other words, in criminal trials the absence of a party may be justified in exceptional cases and under certain circumstances, whereas in civil proceedings the presence of the parties is necessary only in exceptional cases; for example, when an assessment and evaluation of a party is needed for the adjudication of the case.

The Strasbourg case law suggests that unless a judical body finds it necessary to assess the party's personality, in the vast majority of civil cases the presence of a legal representative in court is sufficient. The Court has consistently affirmed that any right to be present during proceedings is not guaranteed *per se* by Article 6, but is derived indirectly from the right of equality of arms in adversarial proceedings'[66]

> (...) Article 6 of the Convention does not guarantee the right to attend a civil court in person, but rather a more general right to present one's case effectively before a court and to enjoy equality of arms with the opposing side.
>
> (*Pashayev v. Azerbaijan*, Judgment of 28 February 2012, paragraph 64).

This interpretation of Article 6(1) is consistent with decisions made by the ECtHR in several cases where an imprisoned applicant had not been given the possibility to appear in person to make oral submissions before a civil court in order to defend his claim. The corollary of this principle is that in civil litigation parties can always waive their right to be present at the proceedings, either implicitly or explicitly, without any restriction by the court.[67]

Conversely, the presence of the accused in a criminal trial is always necessary unless there are exceptional circumstances that make it impossible, notwithstanding all possible diligent efforts, to notify the accused of the day of the hearing, or unless there is an unequivocal waiver by the accused. The above interpretation can be drawn,

---

65. See, *ex plurimis*, *Hermi v. Italy*, (Grand Chamber), Judgment of 18 October 2006, paragraph 58; *Lala v. the Netherlands*, Judgment of 22 September 1994, paragraph 33; *Poitrimol v. France*, Judgment of 23 November 1993, paragraph 35; *De Lorenzo v. Italy*, Appl. No. 69264/01, Decision of 12 February 2004.
66. See, other than the Judgment quoted in the text, *McMichael v. the United Kingdom*, Judgment of 24 February 1995, paragraphs 17-27.
67. See, among others, *Kovalev v. Russia*, Judgment of 10 May 2007, paragraph 37; *Shilbergs v. Russia*, Judgment of 17 December 2009, paragraph 111; *Groshev v. Russia*, Judgment of 20 October 2005, paragraphs 27-31; *Håkansson and Sturesson v. Sweden*, Judgment of 21 February 1990, paragraph 66; *Schuler-Zgraggen v. Switzerland*, Judgment of 24 June 1993, paragraph 58.

inter alia, from the reasoning adopted in the well-known *Colozza v. Italy*.[68] In *Colozza*, the Court observed that there had been no waiver by the accused of his right to be present at the hearing, and that he did not have legal knowledge of the institution of criminal proceedings against him. Therefore, the Court held that Article 6 had been violated:

> In fact, the Court is not here concerned with an accused who had been notified in person and who, having thus been made aware of the reasons for the charge, had expressly waived exercise of his right to appear and to defend himself. The Italian authorities, relying on no more than a presumption (see paragraphs 12 and 20 above), inferred from the status of 'latitante' which they attributed to Mr. Colozza that there had been such a waiver.
>
> (*Colozza v. Italy*, Judgment of 22 January 1985, paragraph 28).

Similarly, in *F.C.B. v. Italy*,[69] the Court decided that a retrial in the absence of the accused, who was detained abroad, had violated his right to attend the trial alongside his defence counsel. In *F.C.B.*, the applicant alleged that he did not know when his trial before the Milan Assize Court of Appeal would take place, as he was in detention (under 'solitary confinement') in the Netherlands. He also maintained that the two attempts to notify him of the date of the trial were invalid.

The ECtHR held that the Italian Assize Court, which was aware that the applicant was detained abroad but did not adopt all the necessary measures in order to ensure his legal knowledge of the date of the trial and thus his attendance at the hearing, had violated Article 6(1) and (3), since the applicant had not waived his right to attend the hearing:

> The Court points out firstly that Mr F.C.B., who was not present at the hearing before the Milan Assize Court of Appeal despite the fact that he was charged with very serious crimes (see paragraph 10 above), had not expressed the wish to waive attendance. Moreover, that court had learnt from concurring sources (Mr F.C.B.'s counsel and two co-defendants) that apparently he was in custody in the Netherlands. Yet it did not adjourn the trial, nor did it investigate further to see whether the applicant had indeed consented to not being present; it merely stated that it had not been provided with proof that he was unable to attend.
>
> (*F.C.B. v. Italy*, Judgment of 28 August 1991, paragraph 33).

However, the Court noted that proceedings that are held in absence of the defendant are not, *per se*, contrary to Convention if the accused subsequently obtains a determination on the merits of the case from a court that has heard him.

> The Court has previously stated that it is of capital importance that a defendant should appear, both because of his right to a hearing and because of the need to verify the accuracy of his statements and compare them with those of the victim – whose interests need to be protected – and of the witnesses. The legislature must accordingly be able to discourage unjustified absences (see Poitrimol v. France, judgment of 23 November 1993, Series A no. 277-A, p. 15, § 35, and Krombach v.

68. *Colozza v. Italy*, cited above.
69. *F.C.B. v. Italy*, Judgment of 28 August 1991.

France, no. 29731/96, § 84, ECHR 2001-II). Proceedings that take place in the accused's absence will not of themselves be incompatible with the Convention if the accused may subsequently obtain, from a court which has heard him, a fresh determination of the merits of the charge (see Colozza v. Italy, judgment of 12 February 1985, Series A no. 89, p. 15, § 29, and Poitrimol, cited above, pp. 13-14, § 31).

(*Medenica v. Switzerland*, Judgment of 14 June 2001, paragraph 54).

Furthermore, the ECtHR has adopted a less absolute approach to the presence of the accused when it comes to appeal proceedings.[70] The Court has noted that while the presence of the accused is crucial in the trial hearing, it may not be vital in appeals proceedings, especially when the appeal court is called to deal only with points of law.

In *Kremzow v. Austria,*[71] the accused was not present at a hearing where the Court of Appeal had to decide on points of law. The Court found no violation of Article 6, stressing that in this case the presence of the lawyer had been sufficient.

In other cases, the Court has also suggested that complete non-participation in appeal or cassation proceedings may comply with the requirements of Article 6, provided that a public hearing was held at first instance.[72] Where a higher court is called to decide on the facts of the case, the presence of the accused is also not always considered necessary. The Court has observed that whether the presence of the accused is required will depend on the specific characteristics of the proceedings and the manner in which the applicant's interests were protected before the appellate court, as well as the nature of the issues in question and their importance to the appellant.[73]

However, when the appellate court has to examine both fact and law in order to make a full assessment on the guilt or innocence of the accused, and an assessment of the evidence given in person by the accused[74] is required, the Court has stated that the presence of the accused is an essential part of a fair trial.

[K] Amnesties

One of the few cases where the issue of amnesties has been considered involved is an admissibility decision in *Dujardin and others v. France.*[75]

70. See, for instance, *Monnell and Morris v. the United Kingdom*, Judgment of 2 March 1987, wherein the Court observes that 'The manner in which paragraph 1, as well as paragraph 3 (c), of Article 6 (art. 6-1, art. 6-3-c) is to be applied in relation to appellate or cassation courts depends upon the special features of the proceedings involved.'
71. *Kremzow v. Austria*, Judgment of 21 September 1993, paragraph 58.
72. See, among other authorities, *Monnell and Morris*, cited above, paragraph 58; and *Sutter v. Switzerland*, Judgment of 22 February 1984, paragraph 30.
73. See, for example, *Helmers v. Sweden*, Judgment of 29 October 1991, paragraphs 31-32; *Kamasinski v. Austria*, Judgment of 19 December 1989, paragraph 106; *Fejde v. Sweden*, Judgment of 29 October 1991, paragraph 31; and *Ekbatani v. Sweden*, Judgment of 26 May 1988, paragraphs 24-33.
74. *Ekbatani v. Sweden*, cited above, paragraph 32; *Dondarini v. San Marino*, Judgment of 6 July 2004, paragraph 27.
75. *Dujardin and others v. France*, Appl. No. 16734/90, Decision of 2 September 1991.

In this case the families of four unarmed gendarmes killed in a politically-motivated attack by insurgents in New Caledonia, a French colony, alleged the violation of Articles 2 and 6 ECHR when the French government granted a general amnesty, which covered also the offence of murder.[76] They complained, in particular, on the fact that the amnesty law put an end to the criminal investigation and trial.

In declaring that the application was inadmissible the Commission stated, with reference to the alleged violation of Article 2:

> The Commission observes in that connection that French legislation undoubtedly secures protection of life in so far as the crime of murder is a punishable offence in French criminal law. Admittedly, as with any criminal offence, the crime of murder may be covered by an amnesty. That in itself does not contravene the Convention unless it can be seen to form part of a general practice aimed at the systematic prevention of prosecution of the perpetrators of such crimes.
>
> (*Dujardin and others v. France*, Appl. No. 16734/90, Decision of 2 September 1991)

And, with reference to the alleged violation of Article 6(1):

> As for the complaints raised under Article 6 of the Convention, the Commission notes that the application is not very precise m that the applicants seem to be complaining that they did not have access to a court m order to contest the legislation in question However, the right of access to a court set forth in Article 6 para 1 of the Convention does not include the right to instigate criminal prosecutions (...).
>
> (*Dujardin and others v. France*, Appl. No. 16734/90, Decision of 2 September 1991)

The *Dujardin* decision emerged several years before the Court developed a full jurisprudence on Article 2. Subsequent cases involving State actors have revealed a considerable sense of reticence towards amnesty for State actors.

This sentiment was confirmed, for example, in *Abdülsamet Yaman v. Turkey*,[77] whose facts involved allegations of Article 3 violations arising from the torture inflicted on the applicant by the Turkish police.

The Court affirmed, *inter alia*, that when an agent of the State is accused of crimes that violate Article 3, the criminal proceedings and sentencing must not be time-barred, and the granting of an amnesty or pardon should not be permissible, and concluded that in the case at hand there was a violation of Article 13 ECHR:

> The Court further points out that where a State agent has been charged with crimes involving torture or ill-treatment, it is of the utmost importance for the purposes of an 'effective remedy' that criminal proceedings and sentencing are not time-barred and that the granting of an amnesty or pardon should not be permissible.
>
> (*Abdülsamet Yaman v. Turkey*, Judgment of 2 November 2004, paragraph 55)

76. With a law adopted by the National Assembly on 20 December 1989.
77. *Abdülsamet Yaman v. Turkey*, Judgment of 2 November 2004.

[L] Interference by Executive Authorities in the Execution of Judicial Decisions and the Principle of Legal Certainty

The logical corollary of the right of access to court is the right of the parties to obtain a final decision and to have that decision executed. Clearly, if after obtaining a decision by the competent judicial authority that decision is not given effect, the individual's substantive right will be meaningless. The right of access to a court, therefore, encompasses both the right to legal certainty and the right to effective court decisions.

This issue has been examined by the ECtHR in many judgments, with reference to both civil and criminal cases. In *Ryabykh v. Russia,*[78] the applicant alleged that Article 6(1) had been violated because the Presidium of the Belgorod Regional Court had set aside a final judgment issued in her favour by the Novooskolskiy District Court.

The Court reaffirmed that 'legal certainty presupposes respect for the principle of *res judicata* (...), that is the principle of the finality of judgments,' with the consequence that 'no party is entitled to seek a review of a final and binding judgment merely for the purpose of obtaining a rehearing and a fresh determination of the case.'[79] The Court noted that 'the right of a litigant to a court would be equally illusory if a Contracting State's legal system allowed a judicial decision which had become final and binding to be quashed by a higher court on an application made by a State official,'[80] concluding that:

> By using the supervisory review procedure to set aside the judgment of 8 June 1998, the Presidium of the Belgorod Regional Court infringed the principle of legal certainty and the applicant's 'right to a court' under Article 6 § 1 of the Convention.
>
> (*Ryabykh v. Russia*, Judgment of 24 July 2003, paragraph 57)

As noted in the above Judgment, these 'rights' stem directly from the general principle of *res judicata*, common to all the Member States of the Council of Europe. When a decision or a judgment is final, it cannot be undermined by any state authority, apart from in specific and exceptional cases, and the mechanism for doing so should be strictly limited by domestic procedural rules.

However, in many States there are procedural rules that allow public authorities (such as, for example, the prosecutor) to file an 'extraordinary' appeal at any time against a decision, even when it has become 'final.' In a number of cases, the ECtHR has held that such extraordinary appeals infringe the principle of *res judicata* in both civil and criminal proceedings and amount to a violation of Article 6(1).

For example, in the well-known case of *Brumărescu v. Romania,*[81] the Court held that allowing the Procurator-General of Romania to apply for a final judgment to be quashed violated the principle of legal certainty. In that case, the applicant alleged that in a judgment of 9 December 1993, the Court of First Instance had held that the nationalization of his parents' house had been unlawfully carried out, as his parents

78. *Ryabykh v. Russia*, Judgment of 24 July 2003.
79. *Ibid.*, paragraph 52.
80. *Ibid.*, paragraph 56.
81. *Brumărescu v. Romania*, Judgment of 28 October 1999.

fell into a category of persons whose property was exempted from nationalization. No appeal was brought against the judgment, which thus became final and irreversible.[82] However, after the judgment had been executed and the applicant had begun paying the land tax on the house, the Procurator-General of Romania filed an application (*recurs în anulare*) with the Supreme Court of Justice, requesting to quash the judgment of 9 December 1993 on the grounds that the Court of First Instance had exceeded its jurisdiction. The Supreme Court of Justice accepted the application and quashed the judgment. The Court of Strasbourg, following the principles set out above, concluded that Article 6(1) had been violated:

> In the present case the Court notes that at the material time the Procurator-General of Romania – who was not a party to the proceedings – had a power under Article 330 of the Code of Civil Procedure to apply for a final judgment to be quashed. The Court notes that the exercise of that power by the Procurator-General was not subject to any time-limit, so that judgments were liable to challenge indefinitely.
>
> The Court observes that, by allowing the application lodged under that power, the Supreme Court of Justice set at naught an entire judicial process which had ended in – to use the Supreme Court of Justice's words – a judicial decision that was 'irreversible' and thus *res judicata* – and which had, moreover, been executed.
>
> In applying the provisions of Article 330 in that manner, the Supreme Court of Justice infringed the principle of legal certainty. On the facts of the present case, that action breached the applicant's right to a fair hearing under Article 6 § 1 of the Convention.
>
> There has thus been a violation of that Article.
>
> (*Brumărescu v. Romania*, Judgment of 28 October 1999, paragraph 62)

Similarly, *Jasiūnienė v. Lithuania*[83] concerned the restitution of and compensation for nationalized property. The ECtHR held that 'by failing to take the necessary measures to comply with the judgment of 3 April 1996, the Lithuanian authorities deprived the provisions of Article 6 § 1 of the Convention of all useful effect.'[84] However, in *Užkurėlienė and Others v. Lithuania,*[85] where the execution of a judgment of the domestic court required a complex set of actions to be carried out by the national authorities under the domestic legislation on restitution of property rights, the Court found that a two-year delay in making the first offer for compensation in execution of the judgment, though 'regrettable,' did not violate Article 6(1):

> The Court notes that the first offer of compensation in execution of the judgment of 22 May 2000 was made to the applicants almost two years later, on 20 March 2002. Thereafter slightly more than two years passed until the last offer of compensation was made on 19 July 2004 (see §§ 20-26 above). While the Court

82. *Ibid.*, paragraphs 15-16.
83. *Jasiūnienė v. Lithuania*, Judgment of 6 March 2003.
84. *Ibid.*, paragraph 31.
85. *Užkurėlienė and Others v. Lithuania*, Judgment of 7 April 2005.

> finds such a lapse of time regrettable, it cannot be compared with the circumstances in the *Jasiūnienė* case cited above, where even at the time of the adoption of the Court's judgment in 2004 no appropriate executive decision had been taken regarding the court decision on restitution adopted as far back as 1996 (*loc. cit.*, §§ 27-32). In view of the above considerations, and in particular on account of the lack of activity established on the part of the applicants themselves, the Court considers that the delays in the execution of the judgment of 22 May 2000 were not such as to infringe upon the essence of the applicants' right to a court guaranteed by Article 6 of the Convention (...).
>
> (*Užkurėlienė and Others v. Lithuania*, Judgment of 7 April 2005, paragraph 36)

As far as criminal proceedings are concerned, the ECtHR found in *Bujniţa v. Moldova*[86] that the annulment of an acquittal, on request of the public prosecutor, violated the right of the applicant to a fair trial, pointing out that no new evidence had been submitted by the prosecutor. The Court, following the principles already laid down in its case law, stressed that any higher court's power of review should be limited to the correction of judicial errors and should not extend to carrying out a fresh examination. The Court held that 'a departure from that principle is justified only when made necessary by circumstances of a substantial and compelling character.'[87] In its judgment, the Court stated:

> However, although a mere possibility to re-open a criminal case is *prima facie* compatible with the Convention, including the guarantees of Article 6, certain special circumstances may reveal that the actual manner in which such a review was used impaired the very essence of the right to a fair trial. In particular, the Court has to assess whether, in a given case, the power to launch and conduct the request for annulment proceedings were exercised by the authorities so as to strike, as far as possible, a fair balance between the interests of the individual and the need to ensure the effectiveness of the system of criminal justice (...).
>
> (*Bujniţa v. Moldova*, Judgment of 16 January 2007, paragraph 22)

The Court concluded that these basic principles had not been respected, noting that the re-opening of the proceedings was requested not because new evidence had emerged or due to the discovery of serious procedural errors, but simply because the prosecutor's office disagreed with the court's assessment:

> The Court notes that the grounds for the re-opening of the proceedings were based neither on new facts nor on serious procedural defects, but rather on the disagreement of the Deputy Prosecutor General with the assessment of the facts and the classification of the applicant's actions by the lower instances. The Court observes that the latter had examined all the parties' statements and evidence and their original conclusions do not appear to have been manifestly unreasonable. In the Court's view, the grounds for the request for annulment given by the Deputy Prosecutor General in the present case were insufficient to justify challenging the finality of the judgment and using this extraordinary remedy to that end. The Court, therefore considers, as it has found in similar circumstances (see, for instance, *Savinskiy v. Ukraine*, no. 6965/02, § 25-27, 28 February 2006), that the

86. *Bujniţa v. Moldova*, Judgment of 16 January 2007.
87. *Ibid.*, paragraph 20.

> State authorities failed to strike a fair balance between the interests of the applicant and the need to ensure the effectiveness of the criminal justice system.
>
> (*Bujniţa v. Moldova*, Judgment of 16 January 2007, paragraph 23)

In *Assanidze v. Georgia*,[88] the ECtHR found that the failure of the State to release the defendant from detention following his acquittal breached Article 6(1). (The defendant was eventually released more than three years after his acquittal.) The Court, recalling the principles set out in *Hornsby v. Greece*,[89] stated that:

> Applying those principles to the instant case, the Court emphasises that it was impossible for the applicant to secure execution of the judgment of a court that had determined criminal charges against him, within the meaning of Article 6 § 1 of the Convention. It does not consider it necessary to establish which domestic authority or administration was responsible for the failure to execute the judgment, which was delivered more than three years ago. It merely observes that the administrative authorities taken as a whole form one element of a State subject to the rule of law and their interests accordingly coincide with the need for the proper administration of justice (see *Hornsby*, cited above, p. 511, § 41). If the State administrative authorities could refuse or fail to comply with a judgment acquitting a defendant, or even delay in doing so, the Article 6 guarantees the defendant previously enjoyed during the judicial phase of the proceedings would become partly illusory.
>
> Consequently, the fact that the judgment of 29 January 2001, which is a final and enforceable judicial decision, has still not been complied with more than three years later has deprived the provisions of Article 6 § 1 of the Convention of all useful effect.
>
> (*Assanidze v. Georgia*, Judgment of 8 April 2004, paragraphs 183-184)

The Court has ruled that the principles outlined above also apply to proceedings before administrative courts. In *Hornsby v. Greece*, the Court remarked that the right to a fair trial would be illusory if a contracting State allowed a final and binding judicial decision to remain 'inoperative' and that proper execution of judgments must be regarded as an integral part of the right to a fair trial for the purposes of Article 6.[90]

§3.03 THE RIGHT TO A FAIR AND PUBLIC HEARING

The right to a fair and public hearing constitutes an aspect of the wider concept of the 'access to a court.' It applies to both criminal and civil proceedings in a way similar to the other guarantees provided by Article 6(1).

The right to a public hearing is not absolute; the ECtHR has affirmed in its case law that even in criminal proceedings where there is a high expectation of publicity, it might be necessary to limit the open and public nature of proceedings. Ensuring the

---

88. *Assanidze v. Georgia*, Judgment of 8 April 2004.
89. *Hornsby v. Greece*, Judgment of 19 March 1997.
90. *Ibid.*, paragraph 40. In the same sense see, *ex multis*, *Immobiliare Saffi v. Italy*, Judgment of 28 July 1999, paragraphs 63 and 66, wherein the Court examined the issue also under the aspect of undue delay of execution proceedings (around thirteen years in that case).

safety and privacy of witnesses and protecting justice and the public are further examples given in the case law where this might prove necessary.[91]

In *De Bombo Beheer B.V. v. The Netherlands*, the Court observed that in civil proceedings the Contracting States have a wider discretion than in criminal cases when establishing procedural rules concerning the right to a fair hearing. This is a direct consequence of the lack, for civil proceedings, of specific provisions, such as paragraphs 2 and 3 of Article 6:

> The requirements inherent in the concept of 'fair hearing' are not necessarily the same in cases concerning the determination of civil rights and obligations as they are in cases concerning the determination of a criminal charge. This is borne out by the absence of detailed provisions such as paragraphs 2 and 3 of Article 6 (art. 6-2, art. 6-3) applying to cases of the former category. Thus, although these provisions have a certain relevance outside the strict confines of criminal law (see, mutatis mutandis, the Albert and Le Compte v. Belgium judgment of 10 February 1983, Series A no. 58, p. 20, para. 39), the Contracting States have greater latitude when dealing with civil cases concerning civil rights and obligations than they have when dealing with criminal cases.
>
> (*De Bombo Beheer B.V. v. The Netherlands*, Judgment of 27 October 1993, paragraph 32)

[A] The Right to a Public and Oral Hearing

The interpretation given by the Court of Strasbourg on the 'right to an oral hearing' is consolidated in its vast jurisprudence. The Court has consistently stated that in proceedings before a court of first instance where there is no opportunity to appeal, the right to a 'public hearing' implies a right to an 'oral hearing,' except when special and exceptional circumstances justify such a hearing not being held:[92]

> The Court first finds that the entitlement to a 'public hearing' in Article 6 § 1 necessarily implies a right to an 'oral hearing'. However, the obligation under Article 6 § 1 to hold a public hearing is not an absolute one. Thus, a hearing may be dispensed with if a party unequivocally waives his or her right thereto and there are no questions of public interest making a hearing necessary. A waiver can be done explicitly or tacitly, in the latter case for example by refraining from submitting or maintaining a request for a hearing (see, among other authorities, Håkansson and Sturesson v. Sweden, judgment of 21 February 1990, Series A no. 171-A, p. 20, § 66; and Schuler-Zgraggen v. Switzerland, judgment of 24 June 1993, Series A no. 263, pp. 19-20, § 58).
>
> Furthermore, a hearing may not be necessary due to exceptional circumstances of the case, for example when it raises no questions of fact or law which cannot be adequately resolved on the basis of the case-file and the parties' written observations (see, mutatis mutandis, Fredin v. Sweden (no. 2), judgment of

91. See, among others, *Doorson v. The Netherlands*, Judgment of 26 March 1996, paragraph 70; *Jasper v. The United Kingdom* (Grand Chamber), Judgment of 16 February 2000, paragraph 52; *T. v. The United Kingdom* (Grand Chamber), Judgment of 16 December 1999, paragraphs 83 et seq.
92. In the same sense, see also *Fischer v. Austria*, Judgment of 26 April 1995, paragraph 44; *Allan Jacobsson v. Sweden*, Judgment of 19 February 1998, paragraph 46; and many others.

> 23 February 1994, Series A no. 283-A, pp. 10-11, §§ 21-22; and Fischer v. Austria, judgment of 26 April 1995, Series A no. 312, pp. 20-21, § 44).
>
> (*Salomonsson v. Sweden*, Judgment of 12 November 2002, paragraph 34)

These circumstances are related to the nature of the subject matter to be decided by the domestic court. For example, in cases concerning social security schemes, where the issues in dispute are technical,[93] the Court has held that that the dispute may be better decided by written proceedings, and that regularly holding oral hearings could even represent an obstacle to the efficacy of justice in such cases:

> The exceptional character of the circumstances that may justify dispensing with an oral hearing essentially comes down to the nature of the issues to be decided by the competent national court, not to the frequency of such situations. It does not mean that refusing to hold an oral hearing may be justified only in rare cases. For example, the Court has recognised that disputes concerning benefits under social-security schemes are generally rather technical, often involving numerous figures, and their outcome usually depends on the written opinions given by medical doctors. Many such disputes may accordingly be better dealt with in writing than in oral argument. Moreover, it is understandable that in this sphere the national authorities should have regard to the demands of efficiency and economy. Systematically holding hearings could be an obstacle to the particular diligence required in social-security cases (...).
>
> (*Fexler v. Sweden*, Judgment of 13 October 2011, paragraph 57)

When a public hearing has been held at first instance, the lack of a hearing at the appellate instance may be justified and does not necessarily lead to a violation of Article 6(1). Most commonly, this circumstance arises in proceedings concerning 'leave-to-appeal,' which involve only questions of law, and not questions of fact:

> Provided a public hearing has been held at first instance, the absence of such a hearing before a second or third instance may accordingly be justified by the special features of the proceedings at issue. Thus, leave-to-appeal proceedings and proceedings involving only questions of law, as opposed to questions of fact, may comply with the requirements of Article 6 (art. 6), although the appellant was not given an opportunity of being heard in person by the appeal or cassation court (...).
>
> (*Helmers v. Sweden*, 29 October 1991, paragraph 36)

In *Piekara v. Poland*,[94] the applicant had applied to the 'Veterans and Persecuted Persons' Office' (*Urząd do Spraw Kombatantów i Osób Represjonowanych*) to be granted 'veteran status.' Before the ECtHR he claimed that as he was not heard in person, he did not have a 'fair trial' for the purposes of Article 6(1) before that administrative body. The Court reiterated that the absence of a public hearing before an administrative body does not lead to a violation of Article 6(1) when the case is, after the administrative proceedings, examined on appeal by a court before which the

93. See, *ex multis*, *Schuler-Zgraggen v. Switzerland*, 24 June 1993, paragraph 58.
94. *Piekara v. Poland*, Judgment of 15 June 2004.

requirement of a public hearing is satisfied. Recalling *Le Compte, Van Leuven and De Meyere v. Belgium*, the Court noted:

> In the present case the applicant appealed twice to the Supreme Administrative Court against the decisions given by the President of the Veterans and Persecuted Persons' Office. On 4 April 2000 the Supreme Administrative Court, having examined the applicant's complaint at the public hearing, gave a final decision dismissing his claim for 'veteran status.' Finally, the Court observes that the scope of review of the Supreme Administrative Court is sufficient to comply with Article 6 § 1 (...).
>
> (*Piekara v. Poland*, Judgment of 15 June 2004, paragraph 35)

In *Eriksson v. Sweden*,[95] the case concerned a request for a life annuity (*livränta*) filed by a worker at the Social Insurance Office (*Försäkringskassan*) of the County of Södermanland. The applicant alleged that the lack of an oral hearing before the Administrative Court of Appeal and the Supreme Administrative Court had violated his rights under Article 6(1) of the Convention.

The ECtHR, following its consolidated case law on the right to a public hearing, observed that no oral hearing had been held at any stage of the domestic proceedings. However, the applicant had never requested an oral hearing before the County Administrative Court (before which the proceedings were normally in writing), and the ECtHR therefore considered that the applicant, who was represented by a lawyer, had waived his right to an oral hearing. However, the applicant had requested an oral hearing before the Administrative Court of Appeal, and had made another such request before the Supreme Administrative Court. Both domestic courts refused his request, and the ECtHR – recalling the principle that 'provided a public hearing has been held at first instance, a less strict standard applies to the appellate level' – held that 'this less strict standard should also apply if an oral hearing has been waived at first instance and requested only on appeal.' The Court further noted that in the case at hand the domestic courts had not made a full examination of the case but had limited their consideration to questions of law, concluding that:

> Having regard to all of the above, the Court is satisfied that the question of whether or not to grant leave to appeal could be adequately resolved on the basis of the case-file and the written submissions, and that, accordingly, the absence of an oral hearing before the Administrative Court of Appeal and the Supreme Administrative Court was justified and did not therefore amount to a violation of Article 6 § 1 of the Convention.
>
> (*Eriksson v. Sweden*, Judgment of 12 April 2012, paragraph 72)

The right to a public and oral hearing can also be waived by the concerned party, provided that the waiver is unequivocal. This principle has been repeated by the ECtHR in several decisions, including *Schuler-Zgraggen v. Switzerland*, where the Court affirmed:

95. *Eriksson v. Sweden*, Judgment of 12 April 2012.

> The Court reiterates that the public character of court hearings constitutes a fundamental principle enshrined in paragraph 1 of Article 6 (art. 6-1). Admittedly, neither the letter nor the spirit of this provision prevents a person from waiving of his own free will, either expressly or tacitly, the entitlement to have his case heard in public, but any such waiver must be made in an unequivocal manner and must not run counter to any important public interest (see, among other authorities, the Håkansson and Sturesson v. Sweden judgment of 21 February 1990, Series A no. 171-A, p. 20, para. 66).
>
> (*Schuler-Zgraggen v. Switzerland*, 24 June 1993, paragraph 58)

In *Werner v. Austria*,[96] the applicant complained that he should have had a public hearing in the domestic criminal courts, where his compensation claim for unlawful detention was pending. The applicant had made no request to have a hearing; however, he maintained that his behaviour could not amount to a waiver of his rights, because the relevant provisions of the Austrian legislation did not provide for a hearing.

In its decision, the Court reiterated that the right to a public hearing is a fundamental principle enshrined in Article 6(1), aiming to protect litigants against the 'administration of justice in secret with no public scrutiny.'[97] The Court held that no public hearing was provided for by the relevant domestic legislation, deciding that 'the applicant cannot be blamed for not having made an application which had no prospect of success'.[98]

The right to an oral hearing has been deemed to exist also in proceedings before administrative courts.[99] For example, in *L. v. Finland*,[100] concerning proceedings relating to childcare, following a claim filed by the social welfare authorities before the County Administrative Court, the applicants complained that the County Administrative Court rejected their request to hold an oral hearing. The ECtHR, after examining the specific circumstances of the case, found that there had been a breach of Article 6(1), reasoning that:

> In this respect the Court notes that at no stage of the previous proceedings had there been an oral hearing. In view of this, the nature of the issues and of what was at stake for the applicants, the Court is not satisfied that there were exceptional circumstances which, in the light of the case-law referred to by the Government, would have justified dispensing with a hearing.
>
> (*L. v. Finland*, Judgment of 27 April 2000, paragraph 132)

A violation of the right to an oral hearing was also found by the ECtHR in a case regarding proceedings for restitution of expropriated property. In *Bakova v. Slovakia*,[101] the Court observed that the applicant was in principle entitled to a public

96. *Werner v. Austria*, Judgment of 24 November 1997.
97. *Ibid.*, paragraph 45.
98. *Ibid.*, paragraph 48.
99. *Lundevall v. Sweden*, Judgment of 12 November 2002; *Håkansson and Sturesson v. Sweden*, Judgment of 21 February 1990; and many others.
100. *L. v. Finland*, Judgment of 27 April 2000.
101. *Bakova v. Slovakia*, Judgment of 12 November 2002. See, in the same terms, also *Malhous v. The Czech Republic*, Judgment of 12 July 2001.

hearing as none of the exceptions laid down in the second sentence of Article 6(1) applied, and, in any case, none of these exceptions had been invoked in the domestic proceedings. Then, after assessing that the administrative office which had dealt with the applicant's claim could not be considered an independent and impartial tribunal, the Court concluded that the right of the applicant to a public hearing had been undermined:

> After the dismissal of her claim by the administrative authority, the applicant sought redress before the Košice Regional Court. She alleged, inter alia, that the District Office had failed to establish the relevant facts correctly and that there had been no hearing in the case. The Regional Court, however, dispensed with a hearing with reference to Article 250f of the Code of Civil Procedure. Thus the failure to hold a hearing before the Regional Court was not based on the applicant's failure to request one.
>
> (*Bakova v. Slovakia*, Judgment of 12 November 2002, paragraph 33)

[B] The Rules of Evidence

The possible infringement of the principles and rights provided by Article 6 ECHR with regard to rules of evidence has been examined by the Strasbourg organs mainly with regard to criminal cases, where the subject matter also shows links and interferences with the principle of 'equality of arms.'

However, there are also a number of decisions and judgments specifically focused on civil cases, where the position of the ECtHR is the same as the one expressed with regard to criminal cases: the national legislation can provide for specific procedural rules to be followed by domestic courts, provided that such rules do not violate the fundamental principles set forth in Article 6.

[1] Admissibility and Assessment of Evidence

As mentioned above, regulating the admissibility of evidence is a matter left to national law, and it is up to the domestic courts to assess the evidence collected before them. A logical corollary of this principle is that the ECtHR does not rule as to whether evidence is correctly admitted in domestic proceedings, but it may assess whether or not the proceedings as a whole have respected the right to a fair trial:

> The Court reiterates that the admissibility of evidence is primarily a matter for regulation by national law and as a general rule it is for the national courts to assess the evidence before them. The Court's task under the Convention is not to give a ruling as to whether statements of witnesses were properly admitted as evidence, but rather to ascertain whether the proceedings as a whole, including the way in which evidence was taken, were fair (...).
>
> (*Van Mechelen and Others v. The Netherlands*, Judgment of 23 April 1997, paragraph 50)

> (...) while Article 6 of the Convention guarantees the right to a fair hearing, it does not lay down any rules on the admissibility of evidence or the way it should be

> assessed, which are therefore primarily matters for regulation by national law and the national courts.
>
> (*García Ruiz v. Spain*, Judgment of 21 January 1999, paragraph 28)

This interpretation has been frequently reiterated, as for example in *Mantovanelli v. France,*[102] where the Court, *inter alia*, observed that:

> It is for the national courts to assess the evidence they have obtained and the relevance of any evidence that a party wishes to have produced. The Court has nevertheless to ascertain whether the proceedings considered as a whole, including the way in which the evidence was taken, were fair as required by Article 6 para. 1 (...).
>
> (*Mantovanelli v. France*, Judgment of 18 March 1997, paragraph 34)

[2] Illegally Obtained Evidence

In the well-known *Schenk v. Switzerland,*[103] the applicant complained that his right to respect for his private life and his correspondence had been violated by collecting unlawful (not authorized according to the law) recordings of his telephone communications (Article 8 ECHR), and maintained that his right to a fair trial had been infringed by the use of such recordings as evidence in the criminal proceedings instated against him [Article 6(1) and (3) ECHR].

The Commission, by decision of 6 March 1986, declared the application admissible with regard to the use of the recording, stating that the complaint actually fell within the principle of the right to a fair trial, but dismissed the complaint based on Article 8, for the reason that domestic remedies had not been exhausted.

Interestingly, the Swiss authorities had already recognized the unlawfulness of the unauthorized telephone recordings; nevertheless, they had declared them admissible as evidence in the trial against the applicant.

The Court observed that Article 6 ECHR leaves it to the national law to lay down the specific rules of evidence, and that, therefore, the task of the Court is only to assess whether the applicant's trial as a whole was fair or not:

> While Article 6 (art. 6) of the Convention guarantees the right to a fair trial, it does not lay down any rules on the admissibility of evidence as such, which is therefore primarily a matter for regulation under national law.
>
> The Court therefore cannot exclude as a matter of principle and in the abstract that unlawfully obtained evidence of the present kind may be admissible. It has only to ascertain whether Mr. Schenk's trial as a whole was fair.
>
> (*Schenk v. Switzerland*, Judgment of 12 July 1988, paragraph 46)

The Court, considering the specific circumstances recurring in the case at hand, concluded that Article 6(1) was not violated: first of all, because the applicant's rights

---

102. *Mantovanelli v. France*, Judgment of 18 March 1997. See also, in the same sense, *Doorson v. The Netherlands*, Judgment of 26 March 1996, paragraph 67; and many others.
103. *Schenk v. Switzerland*, Judgment of 12 July 1988.

of defence had not been disregarded; secondly, because the applicant was aware that the recording was unlawful and had actually challenged its authenticity (the fact that his attempts were unsuccessful made no difference in the opinion of the Court); then, also because the recording of the telephone conversation was not the only evidence on which his conviction had been based.

> (...) It emerges clearly from this passage that the criminal court took account of a combination of evidential elements before reaching its opinion.
>
> In conclusion, the use of the disputed recording in evidence did not deprive the applicant of a fair trial and therefore did not contravene Article 6 para. 1 (...).
>
> (*Schenk v. Switzerland*, Judgment of 12 July 1988, paragraphs 48-49)

An interesting case is the recent *Jalloh v. Germany*,[104] where the applicant complained that the forceful administration of emetics to which he had been subjected by the proceeding authorities in order to obtain evidence (a tiny plastic bag containing drugs, which the suspect had swallowed) was illegal and violated Articles 3 and 8 ECHR.[105] As a consequence, given that the evidence thereby obtained had formed the only basis for his conviction, he alleged that the entire criminal proceeding against him had been unfair and in breach of Article 6 ECHR.

In particular, the applicant maintained that by forcing him against his will to produce evidence of an offence by use of the emetics, the proceeding authorities had violated his right not to incriminate himself and, therefore, his right to a fair trial. According to the applicant, the principle against self-incrimination is not limited to statements obtained by force, but applies also to objects (and, thus, material evidence) obtained by such means. He concluded that the administration of emetics equalled the administration of a truth serum to obtain a confession, which was expressly forbidden by Article 136a of the German Code of Criminal Procedure.[106]

The ECtHR observed that 'public interest concerns cannot justify measures which extinguish the very essence of an applicant's defence rights, including the privilege against self-incrimination guaranteed by Article 6,'[107] and remarked that:

> As regards the use of evidence obtained in breach of the right to silence and the privilege against self-incrimination, the Court observes that these are generally recognised international standards which lie at the heart of the notion of a fair procedure under Article 6. Their rationale lies, inter alia, in the protection of the accused against improper compulsion by the authorities, thereby contributing to the avoidance of miscarriages of justice and to the fulfilment of the aims of Article 6. The right not to incriminate oneself, in particular, presupposes that the prosecution in a criminal case seek to prove their case against the accused without

104. *Jalloh v. Germany*, Judgment of 11 July 2006.
105. The applicant had refused to take the emetics (*Brechmittel*) necessary to provoke vomiting, and was therefore immobilized by the police, while the doctor forcibly administered the medication to him via a tube introduced into his stomach through the nose, and also injected him with 'apomorphine', after which the applicant regurgitated one bubble containing 0.2182 grams of cocaine (*ibid.*, paragraph 13).
106. *Ibid.*, paragraphs 89-90.
107. *Ibid.*, paragraph 97.

> resort to evidence obtained through methods of coercion or oppression in defiance of the will of the accused (...).
>
> (*Jalloh v. Germany*, Judgment of 11 July 2006, paragraph 100)

The Court further noted that in order to ascertain whether or not a certain procedure has been carried out in breach of the privilege against self-incrimination, the following elements have to be examined: 'the nature and degree of the compulsion, the existence of any relevant safeguards in the procedures and the use to which any material so obtained is put.'[108]

The ECtHR case law, however, tends to exclude from the above-mentioned limits certain forms of compulsory acquisition of bodily samples, such as blood, DNA, breath, and urine, as well as documents acquired through a warrant:[109]

> The right not to incriminate oneself is primarily concerned, however, with respecting the will of an accused person to remain silent. As commonly understood in the legal systems of the Contracting Parties to the Convention and elsewhere, it does not extend to the use in criminal proceedings of material which may be obtained from the accused through the use of compulsory powers but which has an existence independent of the will of the suspect such as, inter alia, documents acquired pursuant to a warrant, breath, blood and urine samples and bodily tissue for the purpose of DNA testing.
>
> (*Saunders v. The United Kingdom*, [Grand Chamber], Judgment of 17 December 1996, paragraph 69)

In the above-mentioned *Jolloh v. Germany*, the Court, after excluding that in the instant case the conduct of the authorities in acquiring by force evidence from the applicant constituted a form of torture, ruled that the treatment to which the applicant was subjected nevertheless fell within the ambit of conducts prohibited by Article 3 ECHR as inhuman and degrading treatment,[110] and concluded – after weighing all the circumstances of the case – for the illegality of the evidence so acquired and the

---

108. In these terms see *ibid.*, paragraph 101; *Tirado Ortiz and Lozano Martin v. Spain*, Appl. No. 43486/98, Decision of 15 June 1999; *Heaney and McGuinness v. Ireland*, Judgment of 21 December 2000, paragraphs 51-55.
109. *Jalloh v. Germany*, cited above, paragraph 102.
110. In particular, the Court noted that:

> The authorities subjected the applicant to a grave interference with his physical and mental integrity against his will. They forced him to regurgitate, not for therapeutic reasons, but in order to retrieve evidence they could equally have obtained by less intrusive methods. The manner in which the impugned measure was carried out was liable to arouse in the applicant feelings of fear, anguish and inferiority that were capable of humiliating and debasing him. Furthermore, the procedure entailed risks to the applicant's health, not least because of the failure to obtain a proper anamnesis beforehand. Although this was not the intention, the measure was implemented in a way which caused the applicant both physical pain and mental suffering. He has therefore been subjected to inhuman and degrading treatment contrary to Article 3 (*Jalloh v. Germany*, cited above, paragraph 82).

unfairness of the whole proceedings.[111] In doing so, the Court left open the general question whether the use of evidence obtained by an act qualified as inhuman and degrading treatment automatically renders a trial unfair, but decided for the unfairness of the specific procedure used in that specific case:

> The Court notes that, even if it was not the intention of the authorities to inflict pain and suffering on the applicant, the evidence was obtained by a measure which breached one of the core rights guaranteed by the Convention. Furthermore, it was common ground between the parties that the drugs obtained by the impugned measure were the decisive element in securing the applicant's conviction. It is true that, as was equally uncontested, the applicant was given the opportunity, which he took, of challenging the use of the drugs obtained by the impugned measure. However, any discretion on the part of the national courts to exclude that evidence could not come into play as they considered the administration of emetics to be authorised by domestic law. Moreover, the public interest in securing the applicant's conviction cannot be considered to have been of such weight as to warrant allowing that evidence to be used at the trial. As noted above, the measure targeted a street dealer selling drugs on a relatively small scale who was eventually given a six-month suspended prison sentence and probation.
>
> In these circumstances, the Court finds that the use in evidence of the drugs obtained by the forcible administration of emetics to the applicant rendered his trial as a whole unfair.
>
> (*Jalloh v. Germany*, Judgment of 11 July 2006, paragraphs 107-108)

[3] Access to Evidence by the Parties

The right of access to evidence has a key importance in criminal proceedings, but it is also relevant to civil and administrative proceedings. In all of them, it is strongly connected with the principles of equality of arms and adversarial proceedings.

As far as criminal proceedings are concerned, the Court has in many occasions stressed that 'it is a fundamental aspect of the right to a fair trial that criminal proceedings should be adversarial and that there should be equality of arms between the prosecution and defence.'[112] It has clarified, however, that this does not imply that the parties must be exactly in the same position, and that the national law can provide

111. The decision was not unanimous. Among the several dissenting opinions expressed by a number of judges, it is worth mentioning the opinion of Judges Ress, Pellonpaa, Baka and Sikuta, who found that no violation of Article 3 ECHR (and, consequently, of Article 6) occurred in the case at hand. In particular, they considered as determinant elements the gravity of the crime, and the fact that possible alternative measures (such as waiting for the suspect to expel naturally the drugs) would have deprived the suspect of 'a part of the minimum rights to which detainees should be entitled' (privacy when using the toilet), 'so much so that its deprivation has been regarded as an important element justifying the conclusion that conditions of detention amount to degrading treatment in violation of Article 3'). A final consideration of the dissenting judges was that, 'however, anyone engaging in drug trafficking must take into account the possibility of being subjected to law-enforcement measures which are far from pleasant' (see *Jalloh v. Germany*, cited above, joint dissenting opinion of Judges Ress, Pellonpaa, Baka and Sikuta).
112. See, *ex multis*, *Owen Oyston v. The United Kingdom*, Appl. No. 42011/98, Decision of 22 January 2002; *Van Mechelen and Others v. The Netherlands*, Judgment of 23 April 1997.

for specific circumstances where restrictions on the right of access to evidence are necessary and, therefore, legitimate:

> While both prosecution and defence must be given an opportunity to have knowledge of and comment on the observations filed and the evidence adduced by the other party and a defendant be given an adequate and proper opportunity to challenge and question a witness against him, there may be circumstances where restrictions on access to evidence or to a witness may be necessary or unavoidable. The Court has recognised that in such cases Article 6 § 1 taken together with Article 6 § 3(d) requires that the handicaps under which the defence labours be sufficiently counterbalanced by the procedures followed by the judicial authorities (...)
>
> (*Owen Oyston v. The United Kingdom*, Appl. No. 42011/98, Decision of 22 January 2002)

But the validity of the principle has been equally affirmed with regard to civil and administrative proceedings.

For instance, in the already mentioned *Mantovanelli v. France*, the ECtHR dealt with the right of the parties to attend the interviews held by an expert appointed by the Nancy Administrative Court and to have access to the documents used by the expert.

The Court, after reaffirming that the right to adversarial proceedings entails that 'each party must in principle have the opportunity not only to make known any evidence needed for his claims to succeed, but also to have knowledge of and comment on all evidence adduced or observations filed with a view to influencing the court's decision,'[113] stressed that the adversarial principle applies to proceedings in a tribunal; therefore, from the provision laid down in Article 6(1), no general principle may be inferred relating to the activity of experts appointed by a court. In other words, the Court explained, 'what is essential is that the parties should be able to participate properly in the proceedings before the 'tribunal.''[114]

In the case at hand, however, the Court concluded that there was a violation of the right to a fair hearing, because the applicants – as a consequence of not having had the possibility to cross examine five people interviewed by the expert, and of having examined the documents used by the expert only after the report had been transmitted – were not able 'to comment effectively on the main piece of evidence':

> However, while Mr and Mrs Mantovanelli could have made submissions to the administrative court on the content and findings of the report after receiving it, the Court is not convinced that this afforded them a real opportunity to comment effectively on it. The question the expert was instructed to answer was identical with the one that the court had to determine, namely whether the circumstances in which halothane had been administered to the applicants' daughter disclosed negligence on the part of the CHRN. It pertained to a technical field that was not within the judges' knowledge. Thus although the administrative court was not in law bound by the expert's findings, his report was likely to have a preponderant influence on the assessment of the facts by that court.

113. *Mantovanelli v. France*, cited above, paragraph 33.
114. *Ibid.*

> Under such circumstances, and in the light also of the administrative courts' refusal of their application for a fresh expert report at first instance and on appeal (see paragraphs 19-22 above), Mr and Mrs Mantovanelli could only have expressed their views effectively before the expert report was lodged. No practical difficulty stood in the way of their being associated in the process of producing the report, as it consisted in interviewing witnesses and examining documents. Yet they were prevented from participating in the interviews, although the five people interviewed by the expert were employed by the CHRN and included the surgeon who had performed the last operation on Miss Mantovanelli, and the anaesthetist. The applicants were therefore not able to cross-examine these five people who could reasonably have been expected to give evidence along the same lines as the CHRN, the opposing side in the proceedings. As to the documents taken into consideration by the expert, the applicants only became aware of them once the report had been completed and transmitted.
>
> Mr and Mrs Mantovanelli were thus not able to comment effectively on the main piece of evidence. The proceedings were therefore not fair as required by Article 6 para. 1 of the Convention (art. 6-1). There has accordingly been a breach of that provision (art. 6-1).
>
> (*Mantovanelli v. France*, Judgment of 18 March 1997, paragraph 36)

Similarly, in *Kerojärvi v. Finland,*[115] concerning a request by the applicant for compensation for certain injuries allegedly resulting from his military service during the wars between Finland and the Soviet Union in the period 1939-1945, the Court found that Article 6(1) had been violated because the applicant had not been given the possibility to examine certain documents in the case file.

[C] The Right to a Judgment Pronounced Publicly

Unlike the right to an oral hearing, which may be subject to some exceptions, the right to a judgment pronounced publicly has - according to the ECtHR, no exception.

In *Campbell and Fell v. The United Kingdom,*[116] the Court pointed out that if it is true that the right of access to court - under the specific aspect of the right to a public hearing - may be subject to limitations, this possibility results from the fact that the right in question derives from the first sentence of Article 6(1) but is not defined therein. On the contrary, the second sentence of the same Article contains a detailed list of exceptions; therefore, such principle cannot be regarded as subject to implied limitations.[117]

In any case, according to the Court, 'pronounced publicly' does not necessarily imply that a judgment must be 'read aloud' and delivered in a courtroom. Indeed, the principle of 'publicity' is meant to protect litigants against the administration of justice in secret, with no public scrutiny, with the logical consequence that in some cases,

115. *Kerojärvi v. Finland*, Judgment of 19 July 1995, paragraphs 38-43.
116. *Campbell and Fell v. The United Kingdom*, Judgment of 28 June 1984.
117. In this case, the Court, on the premise that no step had been taken to make public the decision, found a violation of Article 6(1) (*Campbell and Fell v. The United Kingdom*, cited above, paragraph 91).

depending on the specific characteristics of the proceedings, it is sufficient to respect the principle of publicity that courts' decisions are made available to the public by any other means; for example, by depositing them in the court registry.

For instance, in the well-known case of *Pretto v. Italy*,[118] the applicants complained that the judgment of 19 October 1976 of the Italian Court of Cassation had not been pronounced publicly.[119] The ECtHR reiterated the general principle according to which:

> The public character of proceedings before the judicial bodies referred to in Article 6 § 1 (art. 6-1) protects litigants against the administration of justice in secret with no public scrutiny; it is also one of the means whereby confidence in the courts, superior and inferior, can be maintained. By rendering the administration of justice visible, publicity contributes to the achievement of the aim of Article 6 § 1 (art. 6-1), namely a fair trial, the guarantee of which is one of the fundamental principles of any democratic society, within the meaning of the Convention (...).
>
> (*Pretto v. Italy*, Judgment of 8 December 1983, paragraph 21)

The Court observed that, although the legal systems and judicial practice of the States of the Council of Europe present some diversity, all of them subscribe to the 'principle of publicity,' and in order to ascertain the meaning of 'publicity' under the Convention, proceeded to an analysis of the literal wording of Article 6(1):

> The terms used in the second sentence of Article 6 § 1 (art. 6-1) – 'judgment shall be pronounced publicly', '*le jugement sera rendu publiquement*' – might suggest that a reading out aloud of the judgment is required. Admittedly the French text employs the participle '*rendu*' (given), whereas the corresponding word in the English version is 'pronounced' (*prononcé*), but this slight difference is not sufficient to dispel the impression left by the language of the provision in question: in French, '*rendu publiquement*' – as opposed to '*rendu public*' (made public) – can very well be regarded as the equivalent of '*prononcé publiquement*'.
>
> At first sight, Article 6 § 1 (art. 6-1) of the European Convention would thus appear to be stricter in this respect than Article 14 § 1 of the 1966 International Covenant on Civil and Political Rights, which provides that the judgment 'shall be made public', '*sera public*'.
>
> (*Pretto v. Italy*, Judgment of 8 December 1983, paragraph 25)

Nevertheless, since different legal traditions of the States of the Council of Europe entail that different means of publicity may be adopted besides reading the decision in a public hearing (e.g., simply depositing such decision in a registry accessible to the public), the ECtHR did not adopt a literal interpretation of Article 6(1):

> The Court therefore does not feel bound to adopt a literal interpretation. It considers that in each case the form of publicity to be given to the 'judgment' under the domestic law of the respondent State must be assessed in the light of the

118. *Pretto v. Italy, Judgment of* 8 December 1983.
119. In accordance with Article 133 of the Code of Civil Procedure, the Judgment issued on 19 October 1976 by the Court of Cassation was deposited in the court registry, but not pronounced in public.

> special features of the proceedings in question and by reference to the object and purpose of Article 6 § 1 (art. 6-1).
>
> (*Pretto v. Italy*, Judgment of 8 December 1983, paragraph 26)

Conclusively, after considering the entirety of the proceedings before the Italian courts and the specific role of the Court of Cassation (which judges in law and not on the facts), the ECtHR decided that the principle of publicity under Article 6 had not been violated by the judgment having been 'made public by being deposited ... in the court registry':

> Furthermore, the Court of Cassation took its decision after holding public hearings and, although the judgment dismissing the appeal on points of law was not delivered in open court, anyone may consult or obtain a copy of it on application to the court registry (see paragraph 15 above).
>
> In the opinion of the Court, the object pursued by Article 6 § 1 (art. 6-1) in this context – namely, to ensure scrutiny of the judiciary by the public with a view to safeguarding the right to a fair trial – is, at any rate as regards cassation proceedings, no less achieved by a deposit in the court registry, making the full text of the judgment available to everyone, than by a reading in open court of a decision dismissing an appeal or quashing a previous judgment, such reading sometimes being limited to the operative provisions.
>
> The absence of public pronouncement of the Court of Cassation's judgment therefore did not contravene the Convention in the present case.
>
> (*Pretto v. Italy*, Judgment of 8 December 1983, paragraphs 27-28)

Similarly, in *Axen v. Germany*,[120] the Court held that a public pronouncement of the decision (in that case, of a Supreme Court) was not necessary, given that the judgments of the lower courts had been pronounced publicly. Additionally, in *Sutter v. Switzerland*,[121] it stated that a public delivery of a decision of the Military Court of Cassation was not necessary, considering that the requirement of public scrutiny had been met by granting the possibility of requesting a copy of the judgment from the court registry and by publication of the same in an official case law collection.

Nevertheless, in the already mentioned *Werner v. Austria*,[122] the Court specified that if the court registry is not accessible to everyone (i.e., to the 'public'), simply putting a court decision in such registry does not comply with the requirement of publicity enshrined in Article 6.

In this case, the applicant complained that the Vienna Regional Court and Court of Appeal, when deciding on his claim for compensation for his detention, had neither held a public hearing nor pronounced their judgments publicly, but had only served on him their decisions.[123]

The Court, after recalling the principle already stated in *Pretto v. Italy*, according to which 'in each case the form of publicity to be given to the 'judgment' under the

120. *Axen v. Germany*, Judgment of 8 December 1983, paragraph 32.
121. *Sutter v. Switzerland*, Judgment of 22 February 1984, paragraph 34.
122. *Werner v. Austria*, Judgment of 24 November 1997.
123. *Ibid.*, paragraph 29.

domestic law of the respondent State must be assessed in the light of the special features of the proceedings,' concluded that there had been a breach of Article 6(1).

In particular, the Court observed that according to the relevant Austrian law, a third party can be given leave to examine the files and obtain copies of judgments if he shows a legitimate interest, but such right is granted only upon discretion of the court, so that judgments are normally not made available to everyone.[124]

On the other hand, the Court noted that 'it may be of importance to the person concerned that the fact that suspicion concerning him has been dispelled should be brought to the knowledge of the public,'[125] and concluded that:

> That being so, in view of the fact that no judicial decision was pronounced publicly and that publicity was not sufficiently ensured by other means, the Court, like the Commission, concludes that there has been a breach of Article 6 § 1 in this respect.
>
> (*Werner v. Austria*, Judgment of 24 November 1997, paragraph 60)

In *B. and P. v. the United Kingdom,*[126] concerning a decision on the residence of children, the Court, however, decided that by holding a private hearing and not pronouncing the decision publicly, Article 6(1) was not violated.

In particular, the Court held that the national authorities were justified in conducting the proceedings in chambers in order to protect the privacy of the children and the parties, as well as in the interest of justice, and found that pronouncing the judgment in public 'would, to a large extent, frustrate these aims.'

The Court then noted that anyone who could establish an interest might have consulted or obtained a copy of the decisions of the first-instance courts, and that the judgments of the Court of Appeal and of first-instance courts in cases of special interest are also routinely published, thus allowing the public to have knowledge of the relevant case law. It therefore concluded that in the case at hand, Article 6(1) of the Convention did not require that residence judgments were made available to the public.

> Having regard to the nature of the proceedings and the form of publicity applied by the national law, the Court considers that a literal interpretation of the terms of Article 6 § 1 concerning the pronouncement of judgments would not only be unnecessary for the purposes of public scrutiny but might even frustrate the primary aim of Article 6 § 1, which is to secure a fair hearing (see, *mutatis mutandis, Sutter*, cited above, p. 14, § 34).
>
> The Court thus concludes that the Convention did not require making available to the general public the residence judgments in the present cases, and that there has been no violation of Article 6 § 1 in this respect.
>
> (*B. and P. v. The United Kingdom*, Judgment of 24 April 2001, paragraphs 48-49)

---

124. The Court noted that 'in Austria the possibility of obtaining the full texts of judgments from the court registry in fact exists only in respect of judgments of the Supreme Court, the Administrative Court and the Constitutional Court (...) and not in respect of the judgments and decisions of courts of appeal or first instance' (*Werner v. Austria*, cited above, paragraph 58).
125. *Werner v. Austria*, cited above, paragraph 59.
126. *B. and P. v. The United Kingdom*, Judgment of 24 April 2001.

§3.04 THE PRINCIPLE OF EQUALITY OF ARMS

The notion of 'equality of arms' has been extensively interpreted by the ECtHR with reference to both civil and criminal proceedings.

The basic principle, as stressed by the Court in its rich case law, is that every party to the proceedings 'shall have a reasonable opportunity of presenting his case to the Court under conditions which do not place him at substantial disadvantage *vis-à-vis* his opponent.'[127]

The principle of equality of arms is, therefore, strongly connected with the right to adversarial proceedings, according to which each party must be granted the possibility to have knowledge and comment on the evidence adduced and on the observation filed by the other party.

While the above-mentioned principles apply to both civil and criminal proceedings, with regard to criminal proceedings they partially interfere with the guarantee under Article 6(3)(b). As consequence, the principle of equality of arms between the prosecution and the defence not only implies that each party has the right to have knowledge of the evidence adduced by the other party, but also entails an obligation on the prosecuting and investigating authorities to disclose any evidence in its possession which may play in favour of the defendant.

The existence of this obligation has been emphasized by the ECtHR, among others, in a number of cases against the United Kingdom, where the Court has stressed that the principle in question is also recognized by English law:

> The Court considers that it is a requirement of fairness under paragraph 1 of Article 6 (art. 6-1), indeed one which is recognised under English law, that the prosecution authorities disclose to the defence all material evidence for or against the accused and that the failure to do so in the present case gave rise to a defect in the trial proceedings.
>
> (*Edwards v. The United Kingdom*, Judgment of 16 December 1992, paragraph 32)

In *Rowe and Davis v. The United Kingdom*,[128] the Court found that Article 6 was violated because during the trial at first instance the prosecution decided, without informing the judge, to withhold relevant evidence on the grounds of public interest. The Court, though, recalling that the party's right to disclosure of relevant evidence is not an absolute right and that such right can be limited in case of predominant national security or the need to protect witnesses,[129] remarked on the importance that any limitation on the accused's rights 'must be sufficiently counterbalanced by the procedures followed by the judicial authorities.'[130]

Then, recalling the established principle according to which it is not the role of the ECtHR to decide whether or not the non-disclosure of evidence is strictly necessary

127. See, *ex multis*, *Kaufman v. Belgium*, Appl. No. 10938/84, Decision of 9 December 1986; *Ankerl v. Switzerland*, Judgment of 23 October 1996, paragraph 38.
128. *Rowe and Davis v. The United Kingdom*, Judgment of 16 February 2000.
129. See, on this point, also *Doorson v. The Netherlands*, Judgment of 26 March 1996, paragraph 70, recalled by the Court in *Rowe and Davis v. The United Kingdom*.
130. *Rowe and Davis v. The United Kingdom*, cited above, paragraph 61.

in a specific case (which falls in the competence of national courts), the Court affirmed that:

> (...) the European Court's task is to ascertain whether the decision-making procedure applied in each case complied, as far as possible, with the requirements of adversarial proceedings and equality of arms and incorporated adequate safeguards to protect the interests of the accused.
>
> (*Rowe and Davis v. The United Kingdom*, Judgment of 16 February 2000, paragraph 63)

The Court concluded that the conduct of the prosecution office described above deprived the applicants of a fair trial:

> In conclusion, therefore, the prosecution's failure to lay the evidence in question before the trial judge and to permit him to rule on the question of disclosure deprived the applicants of a fair trial.
>
> (*Rowe and Davis v. The United Kingdom*, Judgment of 16 February 2000, paragraph 66)

As far as civil matters are concerned, the reasoning followed by the Court of Strasbourg in *Dombo Beheer v. The Netherlands* is quite interesting.[131] The Court, on the one hand, pointed out that the requirements of a fair hearing are not necessarily the same in civil cases as they are in criminal cases, due to the absence of specific provisions for civil cases, such as paragraphs 2 and 3 of Article 6; on the other hand, it recalled its established case law on the applicability of the principle of equality of arms to civil proceedings.[132]

In the instant case, the applicant complained that his right to a fair trial had been impaired by the domestic court not allowing him to call as witness in a civil case his former managing director (on the grounds that he could be identified with the applicant itself), while the other party was permitted to call as witness the branch manager of the bank. The Court, observing that the two witnesses were substantially in the same position and that there was, therefore, no reason to admit one and reject the other, concluded as follows:

> In the instant case, it was incumbent upon the applicant company to prove that there was an oral agreement between it and the Bank to extend certain credit facilities. Only two persons had been present at the meeting at which this agreement had allegedly been reached, namely Mr van Reijendam representing the applicant company and Mr van W. representing the Bank. Yet only one of these two key persons was permitted to be heard, namely the person who had represented the Bank. The applicant company was denied the possibility of calling the person who had represented it, because the Court of Appeal identified him with the applicant company itself.

131. *Dombo Beheer v. The Netherlands*, Judgment of 27 October 1993, paragraph 32. See, for the application of the principles laid down in *Dombo Beheer* to the Italian legal system, A. Battistuzzi, *La Prova testimoniale*, in *Le prove civili*, ed. P. Leanza (Torino: Giappichelli, 2012), 182–188.
132. *Feldbrugge v. The Netherlands*, Judgment of 26 May 1986, paragraph 44. See also *Ankerl v. Switzerland*, Judgment of 23 October 1996, paragraph 38.

> During the relevant negotiations Mr van Reijendam and Mr van W. acted on an equal footing, both being empowered to negotiate on behalf of their respective parties. It is therefore difficult to see why they should not both have been allowed to give evidence.
>
> (*Dombo Beheer v. The Netherlands*, Judgment of 27 October 1993, paragraphs 34-35)

In the well-known *Steel and Morris v. The United Kingdom,*[133] the Court examined the principle of equality of arms under the aspect of a party's right to legal aid. In this case, though, confirming the established jurisprudence according to which there is no general obligation on States to grant legal aid, the Court affirmed that in some cases its lack can lead to the infringement of the principle of equality of arms. In particular, the Court observed that:

> (...) the disparity between the respective levels of legal assistance enjoyed by the applicants and McDonald's (...) was of such a degree that it could not have failed, in this exceptionally demanding case, to have given rise to unfairness, despite the best efforts of the judges at first instance and on appeal.
>
> (*Steel and Morris v. The United Kingdom*, Judgment of 15 February 2005, paragraph 69)

The Court concluded that there was, in the specific case, a violation of Article 6:

> (...) the denial of legal aid to the applicants deprived them of the opportunity to present their case effectively before the court and contributed to an unacceptable inequality of arms with McDonald's.
>
> (*Steel and Morris v. The United Kingdom*, Judgment of 15 February 2005, paragraph 72)

§3.05 ADVERSARIAL PROCEEDINGS

As noted above, the principle of equality of arms is linked to the right to adversarial proceedings, according to which each party shall have the opportunity to have knowledge and comment on the evidence adduced and on the observation filed by the other party.[134] This link was affirmed, among many others, in the above-mentioned *Rowe and Davis v. The United Kingdom:*[135]

> It is a fundamental aspect of the right to a fair trial that criminal proceedings, including the elements of such proceedings which relate to procedure, should be adversarial and that there should be equality of arms between the prosecution and defence. The right to an adversarial trial means, in a criminal case, that both

133. *Steel and Morris v. The United Kingdom*, Judgment of 15 February 2005.

134. See, *ex multis*, *Vermeulen v. Belgium*, Judgment of 20 February 1996, paragraph 33; *Nideröst-Huber v. Switzerland*, Judgment of 18 February 1997, paragraph 24; *McMichael v. The United Kingdom*, Judgment of 24 February 1995, paragraph 80; *Kerojärvi v. Finland*, Judgment of 19 July 1995, paragraph 42.

135. *Rowe and Davis v. The United Kingdom*, Judgment of 16 February 2000. See also, in the same terms, *Brandstetter v. Austria*, Judgment of 28 August 1991, paragraphs 66-67.

prosecution and defence must be given the opportunity to have knowledge of and comment on the observations filed and the evidence adduced by the other party (...).

(*Rowe and Davis v. The United Kingdom*, Judgment of 16 February 2000, paragraph 60)

In *Werner v. Austria*,[136] the ECtHR took into consideration the fact that the observations submitted to the Court of Appeal by the principal public prosecutor had not been communicated to the defendant, who therefore did not have the opportunity to file a reply.

The Court, after recalling its established case law according to which the right to adversarial proceedings applies also to civil proceedings,[137] concluded that there had been a breach of Article 6(1), on account of the Court of Appeal's failure to communicate the principal public prosecutor's observations to the applicant.[138]

An interesting case where the ECtHR examined the link and possible interferences between the principle of equality of arms and the right to adversarial proceedings is *Krcmar and Others v. The Czech Republic*,[139] concerning a lawsuit filed against the State for restitution of nationalized property.

It is worth examining the case in more detail. In November 1991, pursuant to the Extra-Judicial Rehabilitations Act no. 87/1991 (*zákon o mimosoudních rehabilitacích*) and the Transfer of the State's Property to Other Persons Act no. 92/1991 (*zákon o převodu majetku státu na jiné osoby*), the applicants filed a claim against the Ministry for Administration of National Property and its Privatization (*Ministerstvo pro správu národního majetku a jeho privatizaci*) for the restitution of a Company. They alleged to be entitled to the restitution since they were Czech nationals and successors in title to the original owners of the Company, and maintained that the Company had been nationalized in violation of generally recognized human rights and freedoms within the meaning of section 2(3) of the Act. no. 87/1991.

By decision of 29 June 1993, the Prague 1 District Court (*obvodní soud*) rejected the applicants' claim. The applicants appealed to the Prague Municipal Court (městský soud). The appeals subsequently filed by the applicants were dismissed respectively by the Prague Municipal Court (*městský soud*) and the High Court (*Vrchní soud*).

Then the applicants filed a constitutional appeal (*ústavní stížnost*), alleging the violation of Articles 11(1) and 36(1) of the Charter of Fundamental Rights and Freedoms (*Listina základních práv a svobod*) and challenging the decision of the ordinary courts.

On 2 October 1996, the Constitutional Court, after a public hearing, dismissed the applicants' appeal, on the basis of documentary evidence collected during the proceedings and never shown during the hearing.

136. *Werner v. Austria*, cited above.
137. See, among others, *Lobo Machado v. Portugal*, Judgments of 20 February 1996, paragraph 31, and *Nideröst-Huber v. Switzerland*, Judgment of 18 February 1997, paragraph 28, both cited by the Court.
138. *Werner v. Austria*, cited above, paragraphs 66-69.
139. *Krcmar and Others v. The Czech Republic*, Judgment of 3 March 2000.

The applicants complained that they did not have a fair hearing in the proceedings before the Constitutional Court, since the decision was issued on the basis of documents which had not been produced or shown at the hearing, nor discussed by the parties.

The ECtHR considered that the acquisition of additional evidence by the Constitutional Court on its own motion did not violate, *per se*, the right to a fair hearing. In particular, the Court found that the principle of equality of arms, which requires that each party be given a reasonable opportunity to present its case under conditions that do not place it at a substantial disadvantage vis-à-vis its opponent, was not violated, because the documentary evidence in question was not communicated to either of the parties to the dispute before the Constitutional Court.

However, the Court found a violation of the right to adversarial proceedings, because none of the parties had the opportunity to have knowledge of, and comment on, all evidence adduced or observations filed in the proceedings.[140]

> The Court further considers that granting the applicants the possibility to discuss all the documentary evidence submitted to the Constitutional Court was all the more necessary because the evidence which was reiterated by the Constitutional Court at the oral hearing had formed part of the basis on which the Prague 1 District Court had found that the nationalization of the Company had been carried out contra legem. In addition, the documents did not contain facts which were generally known or known to the Constitutional Court through the exercise of its functions, nor did they constitute generally binding legislative or regulatory instruments published or announced in the Official Gazette, none of which, according to Article 121 of the Code of Civil Procedure, would have been necessary to prove.
>
> The Court finds therefore that, in the present case, respect for the right to a fair hearing, guaranteed by Article 6 § 1, required that the applicants be given the opportunity to comment on the documentary evidence produced at the request of the Constitutional Court by the national authorities.
>
> There has accordingly been a breach of Article 6 § 1 of the Convention.
>
> (*Krcmar and Others v. The Czech Republic*, Judgment of 3 March 2000, paragraphs 44-46)

§3.06 THE RIGHT TO AN INDEPENDENT AND IMPARTIAL TRIBUNAL ESTABLISHED BY LAW

Another key guarantee under Article 6(1) is the right to an independent and impartial tribunal established by law.

In the following sections, we will examine separately the principles of independence and impartiality, as addressed by the ECtHR in its case law, with specific reference to the appointment of judges and composition of 'tribunals,' the appearance of independence and impartiality, and the existence of safeguards against undue external pressures. However, it has to be noted that the requirement of independency of judges is so strictly connected with their impartiality that the ECtHR has almost

140. See also, on this point, *Nideröst-Huber v. Switzerland*, cited above, and *Mantovanelli v. France*, Judgment of 18 March 1997, paragraph 33, both quoted by the Court in the *Krcmar* Judgment.

always examined the two aspects together. Prominence will, therefore, be given to some cases in which the Court examined the two aspects jointly.

[A] Independence

The ECtHR has on many occasions affirmed that in order to establish whether a tribunal can be considered 'independent' or not, for the purposes of Article 6(1), 'regard must be had, inter alia, to the existence of safeguards against outside pressures and the question whether it presents an appearance of independence.'[141]

To these two main aspects it must be added the composition of a tribunal, the appointment procedure of its members, and the duration of their office.

Indeed, the Court has noted that to have a 'tribunal' in the meaning of the Convention, it is not sufficient that it exercises judicial functions, but it is also necessary that it satisfies a series of further requirements, such as independence from the executive and from the parties to the case, duration of its members' terms of office, existence of guarantees afforded by its procedure, and 'appearance of independence.'[142]

In *Campbell and Fell v. The United Kingdom*, concerning certain proceedings before the Prison Board of Visitors, the Court reaffirmed that such body – when carrying out its adjudicatory tasks – can be considered a 'tribunal established by law,' since it has, according to English law, the power to issue binding decisions.

The Court remarked that the word 'tribunal' in Article 6(1) need not necessarily be associated with a 'traditional' court,[143] but can be used to identify any body which is independent from the parties and the executive power, and which also offers guarantees of a judicial procedure.[144]

In the *Campbell and Fell* case, the applicant had alleged that the Board of Visitors was not an 'independent' tribunal, for the main reasons that it was not seen by prisoners as independent and was, in practice, 'an arm of the executive,' since its members were under the control of the prison authorities and had to accept the Home Secretary's directions.

The Court, recalling the principles stated in its established case law on the subject matter (among others, in *Le Compte, Van Leuven and De Meyere v. Belgium*,[145] *Piersack v. Belgium*,[146] and *Delcourt v. Belgium*[147]), examined the specific characteristics of the Board of Visitors and concluded that the guarantee of independence had not been

141. See, among many other authorities, *Findlay v. The United Kingdom*, Judgment of 25 February 1997, paragraph 73; *Incal v. Turkey*, Judgment of 9 June 1998, paragraph 65; *Coëme and Others v. Belgium*, Judgment of 22 June 2000, paragraph 120.
142. See, among many others, *Ringeisen v. Austria*, Judgment of 16 July 1971, paragraph 95; *Bryan v. The United Kingdom*, Judgment of 22 November 1995, paragraph 37; *Findlay v. The United Kingdom*, Judgment of 25 February 1997, paragraph 73.
143. *Campbell and Fell v. The United Kingdom*, cited above, paragraph 76.
144. See, *mutatis mutandis*, with regard to Article 5(4) ECHR, *X v. The United Kingdom*, Judgment of 5 November 1981, paragraph 53.
145. *Le Compte, Van Leuven and De Meyere*, Judgment of 23 June 1981, paragraph 55.
146. *Piersack v. Belgium*, Judgment of 1 October 1982, paragraph 27.
147. *Delcourt v. Belgium*, Judgment of 17 January 1970, paragraphs 31-38.

violated in that case.[148] In particular, taking into account that it was not subject to instructions by the executive in its adjudicatory functions, it found that the Board of Visitors was an independent body.

As far as the 'appearance' of independence, already in the *Delcourt* case the Court had stressed the importance of the dictum 'justice must not only be done; it must also be seen to be done.'[149]

Also following this assumption in *Sramek v. Austria,*[150] the Court considered that Article 6(1) was violated because one of the members of the Regional Authority, which decided in the appeals proceedings on the case of the applicant, was a civil servant in a subordinate position to one of the parties to the proceedings (i.e., the Land Government). This circumstance alone, regardless of whether or not the member was in practice influenced in its decision, altered the confidence that the public must have in a tribunal. In this case, the ECtHR gave considerable importance to the 'appearance' of independence in order to establish that Article 6 had been violated.

> As was pointed out by the Government, the Transactions Officer could not take advantage of his hierarchical position to give to the rapporteur instructions to be followed in the handling of cases (see paragraph 26 above), and there is nothing to indicate that he did so on the present occasion.
>
> Nonetheless, the Court cannot confine itself to looking at the consequences which the subordinate status of the rapporteur vis-à-vis the Transactions Officer might have had as a matter of fact. In order to determine whether a tribunal can be considered to be independent as required by Article 6, appearances may also be of importance (see, mutatis mutandis, the above-mentioned Campbell and Fell judgment, Series A no. 80, pp. 39-40, paragraph 78, and the Piersack judgment of 1 October 1982, Series A no. 53, pp. 14-15, paragraph 30).
>
> Where, as in the present case, a tribunal's members include a person who is in a subordinate position, in terms of his duties and the organization of his service, vis-à-vis one of the parties, litigants may entertain a legitimate doubt about that person's independence. Such a situation seriously affects the confidence which the courts must inspire in a democratic society (see, mutatis mutandis, the above-mentioned Piersack judgment, Series A no. 53, pp. 14-15, paragraph 30).
>
> (*Sramek v. Austria*, Judgment of 22 October 1984, paragraphs 41-42)

However, the fact that judges are appointed by the executive does not violate, *per se*, the guarantee of independence, as stated by the Court, among others, in the above-mentioned *Campbell and Fell v. The United Kingdom*:

> Members of Boards are appointed by the Home Secretary, who is himself responsible for the administration of prisons in England and Wales (...).
>
> The Court does not consider that this establishes that the members are not independent of the executive: to hold otherwise would mean that judges appointed by or on the advice of a Minister having responsibilities in the field of the administration of the courts were also not 'independent'. Moreover, although it is true that the Home Office may issue Boards with guidelines as to the performance

148. *Campbell and Fell v. The United Kingdom*, cited above, paragraphs 78-82.
149. *Delcourt v. Belgium*, cited above, paragraph 31; see also *Piersack v. Belgium*, cited above, paragraphs 27 et seq.
150. *Sramek v. Austria*, Judgment of 22 October 1984.

> of their functions (...), they are not subject to its instructions in their adjudicatory role.
>
> (*Campbelland Fell v. The United Kingdom*, Judgment of 28 June 1984, paragraph 79)

Similarly, the circumstance that the duty term of tribunals' members is limited or particularly short (as in the *Campbell and Fell* case – three years) does not itself constitute a lack of independence when it is fixed and predetermined:

> Members of Boards hold office for a term of three years or such less period as the Home Secretary may appoint (...).
>
> The term of office is admittedly relatively short but the Court notes that there is a very understandable reason: the members are unpaid (...) and it might well prove difficult to find individuals willing and suitable to undertake the onerous and important tasks involved if the period were longer.
>
> (*Campbell and Fell v. The United Kingdom*, Judgment of 28 June 1984, paragraph 79)

In *Beaumartin v. France*,[151] the Court instead focused on the fact that if a tribunal can refer a question of interpretation of the law to the executive (which, in the case at hand, was also one of the parties), the guarantee of independence is not satisfied:

> (...) It observes, however, that in the instant case the Conseil d'Etat referred to a representative of the executive for a solution to the legal problem before it. It dismissed the application filed by Mr Beaumartin and his sisters because the minister had confirmed the interpretation adopted by the compensation committee. The Court points out, in addition, that the minister's involvement, which was decisive for the outcome of the legal proceedings, was not open to challenge by the applicants, who had moreover not been afforded any possibility of giving their opinion on the use of the referral procedure and the wording of the question.
>
> Only an institution that has full jurisdiction and satisfies a number of requirements, such as independence of the executive and also of the parties, merits the designation 'tribunal' within the meaning of Article 6 para. 1 (art. 6-1) (see, inter alia, the Ringeisen v. Austria judgment of 16 July 1971, Series A no. 13, p. 39, para. 95; the Le Compte, Van Leuven and De Meyere v. Belgium judgment of 23 June 1981, Series A no. 43, p. 24, para. 55; and the Belilos v. Switzerland judgment of 29 April 1988, Series A no. 132, p. 29, para. 64). The Conseil d'Etat did not meet these requirements in the instant case.
>
> In sum, the applicants' case was not heard by an independent tribunal with full jurisdiction. There has accordingly been a violation of Article 6 para. 1 (art. 6-1) in this respect also.
>
> (*Beaumartin v. France*, Judgment of 24 November 1994, paragraphs 38-39)

Similarly, in *Van de Hurk v. The Netherlands*,[152] the ECtHR remarked that the requirement of independence is not fulfilled when the executive (in that case, the Crown) can decide whether or not to implement a judgment of a tribunal.

151. *Beaumartin v. France*, Judgment of 24 November 1994. See also, for a similar approach, *Benthem v. The Netherlands*, Judgment of 23 October 1985, paragraphs 38-43.
152. *Van de Hurtk v. The Netherlands*, Judgment of 19 April 1994.

The applicant alleged that his case had not been determined by an 'independent tribunal,' since the domestic law (section 74 of the 1954 Act) allowed the Crown to decide that judgments of the tribunal could not be implemented (though in his case the Government never took advantage of such power). In its decision, the Court examined conjointly the question of when it can be said that a body is a 'tribunal' in the meaning of the Convention, and the question of its independence.

As to the first point, the Court recalled its established case law, wherein it is clearly affirmed that the power to issue binding decisions, which cannot be altered by non-judicial authorities to the detriment of an individual party, is an essential component of the notion itself of a 'tribunal.'[153] On the second aspect, it emphasized that the above-mentioned power is also a component of the requirement of 'independence' of a tribunal.

The Court finally considered of no influence the fact that the Crown had never exercised its powers under section 74 of the 1954 Act: this law was indeed still in force, which meant that there was nothing that would prevent the Crown from recourse to its powers in case it was considered necessary.[154]

[B] Impartiality

The ECtHR has repeatedly stated that the personal impartiality of members of a 'tribunal' (in the meaning of Article 6 of the Convention) must be presumed until there is proof to the contrary.[155]

The Court has also stressed the relevance of the above-mentioned principle of 'appearance' of impartiality. This does not mean, however, that appearance of lack of impartiality can suffice to assess that the guarantees under Article 6(1) have been violated. For example, in the already mentioned *Campbell and Fell*, the Court stated:

> However, it is not possible to confine oneself to a purely subjective test: in this area, appearances may be of a certain importance and account must be taken of questions of internal organisation (see the above-mentioned Piersack judgment, Series A no. 53, pp. 14-15, para. 30).
>
> Prior to 6 October 1976, the Albany Prison Board of Visitors played no role whatsoever in the disciplinary proceedings against the applicant; when it sat on that date, it came fresh to his case (see paragraphs 12-14 above). The Court, therefore, perceives nothing in the actual organisation of the adjudication that would reflect adversely on the Board's objective 'impartiality'.
>
> There remains the fact that Mr. Campbell might not have seen the Board as being totally free from bias. However, for reasons similar to those given in paragraph 81 above, the Court does not consider that, in the particular context, this suffices to establish that this requirement of Article 6 (art. 6) was not satisfied.
>
> (*Campbell and Fell v. The United Kingdom*, Judgment of 28 June 1984, paragraph 85)

153. *Benthem v. The Netherlands*, Judgment of 23 October 1985, paragraph 40; *H. v. Belgium*, Judgment of 30 November 1987, paragraph 50; and *Belilos v. Switzerland*, Judgment of 29 April 1988, paragraph 64.
154. *Van de Hurtk v. The Netherlands*, cited above, paragraph 50.
155. See, *ex multis*, *Campbell and Fell v. The United Kingdom*, cited above, paragraph 83; *Le Compte, Van Leuven and De Meyere*, cited above, paragraph 58.

In *Piersack v. Belgium*, the ECtHR made an interesting analysis of the method of assessing the 'impartiality' of a tribunal, making a distinction between a subjective and an objective approach.

As often remarked in its case law, there are two aspects to impartiality: the first implies that a 'tribunal' must be 'subjectively free of personal prejudice or bias,' whereas the second indicates that it must offer 'sufficient guarantees to exclude any legitimate doubt in this respect':[156]

> Whilst impartiality normally denotes absence of prejudice or bias, its existence or otherwise can, notably under Article 6 § 1 (art. 6-1) of the Convention, be tested in various ways. A distinction can be drawn in this context between a subjective approach, that is endeavouring to ascertain the personal conviction of a given judge in a given case, and an objective approach, that is determining whether he offered guarantees sufficient to exclude any legitimate doubt in this respect.
>
> (*Piersack v. Belgium*, Judgment of 1 October 1982, paragraph 30)

In particular, with regard to the subjective approach, the Court noted that in the case at hand the applicant was confident and did not show any doubt on the personal impartiality of a judge who had previously served in the public prosecutor's department (though not dealing personally with the case at stake). It remarked, however, that a subjective test is not sufficient, since also the public appearance of independence and impartiality of the judges has its importance. On the other hand - continued the Court - the objective approach cannot be given so much importance that all former judicial officers in the public prosecutor's department should be considered unable to serve as judges in every case examined by that department:

> It would be going too far to the opposite extreme to maintain that former judicial officers in the public prosecutor's department were unable to sit on the bench in every case that had been examined initially by that department, even though they had never had to deal with the case themselves. So radical a solution, based on an inflexible and formalistic conception of the unity and indivisibility of the public prosecutor's department, would erect a virtually impenetrable barrier between that department and the bench. It would lead to an upheaval in the judicial system of several Contracting States where transfers from one of those offices to the other are a frequent occurrence. Above all, the mere fact that a judge was once a member of the public prosecutor's department is not a reason for fearing that he lacks impartiality; the Court concurs with the Government on this point.
>
> (*Piersack v. Belgium*, Judgment of 1 October 1982, paragraph 30)

In the specific case, however, the Court found that Article 6(1) had been violated, in view of the specific and concrete circumstances, among which was the fact that the judge who presided over the Brabant Assize Court before which the Indictments Chamber of the Brussels Court of Appeal had remitted the applicant for trial, had previously been the head of the public prosecutor's department that was responsible

156. See, in these terms, *Pullar v. the United Kingdom*, Judgment of 10 June 1996, paragraph 30; *Findlay v. The United Kingdom*, cited above, paragraph 73; and, mutatis mutandis, *Gautrin and Others v. France*, Judgment of 20 May 1998, paragraph 58; *Thomann v. Switzerland*, Judgment of 10 June 1996, paragraph 30; *Bulut v. Austria*, Judgment of 22 February 1996, paragraph 31.

for the prosecution instituted against the applicant. The Court, with specific regard to this point, observed that as head of that department, the judge 'had been entitled to revise any written submissions by them to the courts, to discuss with them the approach to be adopted in the case and to give them advice on points of law' and that 'the information obtained by the Commission and the Court' tended to confirm that he had in fact played 'a certain part in the proceedings.'[157]

According to the Court, the above-mentioned circumstances were sufficient, with no need to investigate further the concrete role played by the judge in the specific case, to find that the impartiality of the 'tribunal' which had to determine the merits of the charge was 'capable of appearing open to doubt.'[158]

The adoption of the subjective and objective approach is established in the rich jurisprudence of the ECtHR on the subject matter:

> As for impartiality within the meaning of Article 6 § 1, there are two tests for assessing whether a tribunal is impartial: the first consists in seeking to determine the personal conviction of a particular judge in a given case and the second in ascertaining whether the judge offered guarantees sufficient to exclude any legitimate doubt in this respect (...).
>
> (*Coëme and Others v. Belgium*, Judgment of 22 June 2000, paragraph 121)

Similarly, in *Noriter v. The Netherlands,*[159] the applicant complained that his case had been dealt with by just one judge, who had made all the relevant decisions, during the pre-trial phase as well as at the trial. Though the applicant stated that he did not have any doubt about the personal impartiality of the judge, he pointed out that since the said judge had decided on four occasions on his detention on remand, he had already reached the conclusion at that stage that there had been 'serious indications' that the applicant had committed the crime of which he was accused. These circumstances led the applicant to raise legitimate doubt that when the judge tried his case as a single judge, he lacked the necessary impartiality.

The Court considered the specific circumstances of the case, and – notwithstanding the fact that the judge had already acted as investigating judge – ruled that there had been no violation of the impartiality requirement under Article 6(1):

> The mere fact that Juvenile Judge Meulenbroek also made pre-trial decisions, including decisions relating to detention on remand, cannot be taken as in itself justifying fears as to his impartiality; what matters is the scope and nature of these decisions.
>
> Apart from his decisions relating to the applicant's detention on remand, Juvenile Judge Meulenbroek made no other pre-trial decisions than the one allowing the application made by the prosecution for a psychiatric examination of the applicant, which was not contested by the latter. He made no other use of his powers as investigating judge.
>
> As for his decisions on the applicant's detention on remand, they could justify fears as to the judge's impartiality only under special circumstances such as

157. *Piersack v. Belgium*, cited above, paragraph 31.
158. *Ibid.*, paragraph 31.
159. *Nortier v. The Netherlands*, Judgment of 24 August 1993.

> those which obtained in the Hauschildt case (see the Hauschildt v. Denmark judgment of 24 May 1989, Series A no. 154, p. 22, para. 51, and the Sainte-Marie v. France judgment of 16 December 1992, Series A no. 253-A, p. 16, para. 32).
>
> There was nothing of that nature in the present case. Contrary to the applicant's arguments, the questions which Juvenile Judge Meulenbroek had to answer when taking these decisions were not the same as those which were decisive for his final judgment. In finding that there were 'serious indications' against the applicant his task was only to ascertain summarily that the prosecution had prima facie grounds for the charge against the applicant (see paragraph 27 above). The charge had, moreover, been admitted by the applicant and had already at that stage been supported by further evidence.
>
> (*Nortier v. The Netherlands*, Judgment of 24 August 1993, paragraphs 33-35)

Another case where the requirements of independence and impartiality have been examined conjointly is *Procola v. Luxembourg,*[160] concerning a complaint related to the introduction of the 'milk quota' system in the Member States of the European Community by EEC Regulations 856/84 and 857/84 of 31 March 1984.

The applicant (an agricultural association under Luxembourg law) complained of an infringement of their right to an independent and impartial tribunal, on the ground that some of the members of the Judicial Committee of the *Conseil d'Etat* who ruled on its application for judicial review had previously given their opinion on the lawfulness of the impugned provisions.

The ECtHR found that it was not necessary to determine whether the Judicial Committee was an independent tribunal, because the applicant had not questioned the method of appointment of the members of the *Conseil d'Etat* and the length of their terms of office, nor had he put in doubt that there were sufficient safeguards against extraneous pressure. The Court rather considered that the only issue to be decided was whether the Judicial Committee satisfied the impartiality requirement of Article 6 ECHR, in view of the fact that four of its five members had had to rule on the lawfulness of a regulation which they had previously examined in their advisory capacity. The Court concluded that the doubt of impartiality in this case was sufficient to determine a breach of Article 6(1).

> The Court notes that four members of the *Conseil d'Etat* carried out both advisory and judicial functions in the same case. In the context of an institution such as Luxembourg's *Conseil d'Etat* the mere fact that certain persons successively performed these two types of function in respect of the same decisions is capable of casting doubt on the institution's structural impartiality. In the instant case, Procola had legitimate grounds for fearing that the members of the Judicial Committee had felt bound by the opinion previously given. That doubt in itself, however slight its justification, is sufficient to vitiate the impartiality of the tribunal in question, and this makes it unnecessary for the Court to look into the other aspects of the complaint.
>
> (*Procola v. Luxembourg*, Judgment of 18 September 1995, paragraphs 45-46)

Finally, according to the established jurisprudence of the ECtHR, whenever a judge is under legitimate suspicion of lack of impartiality, he must withdraw:

---

160. *Procola v. Luxembourg*, Judgment of 18 September 1995.

> Under the objective test, it must be determined whether, quite apart from the judge's personal conduct, there are ascertainable facts which may raise doubts as to his impartiality. In this respect even appearances may be of a certain importance. What is at stake is the confidence which the courts in a democratic society must inspire in the public and above all, as far as criminal proceedings are concerned, in the accused. Accordingly, any judge in respect of whom there is a legitimate reason to fear a lack of impartiality must withdraw (...).
>
> (*Hauschildt v. Denmark*, Judgment of 24 May 1989, paragraph 44)

[C] Absence of Bias of Judges

The question of bias of judges is a key issue with regard to the right to an independent and impartial tribunal.

Among the numerous cases addressed by the ECtHR, a number of cases concerned possible bias of judges or members of a jury because of their racial prejudices.

In *Gregory v. The United Kingdom,*[161] the applicant – who had been tried for robbery at the Manchester Crown Court – alleged that on the final day of the trial, before the jury reached their verdict, a note was passed by the jury to the judge, reading: '*Jury showing racial overtones. 1 member to be excused.*' Then the trial judge, in absence of the jury, showed the note to the counsel for the prosecution and the defence, and after having consulted them on the appropriate action, called back the jury and warned them to decide only on the basis of evidence, putting aside any personal prejudice.[162]

The verdict found the applicant guilty, and he was sentenced to six years of prison.

The Court recalled the established principles affirmed in its case law, according to which 'it is of fundamental importance in a democratic society that the courts inspire

161. *Gregory v. The United Kingdom*, Judgment of 25 February 1997.

162. The trial judge addressed the jury in the following terms:

> You are brought here as twelve people from your various walks of life, your various backgrounds. Everybody has preconceived ideas and thoughts but you are brought here from twelve different backgrounds expecting to apply your twelve different minds to the problems that are put before you ... you decide this case according to the evidence and nothing else in the case. Any thoughts or prejudice of one form or another, for or against anybody, must be put out of your minds. You decide this case on evidence. It is the evidence alone which decides the case. Do you understand that, members of the jury? You are the judges and you decide it on the evidence, and weighing the individuals as you saw them and allowing no other factor to influence your decision, but your decision about the quality of the evidence and the way in which a particular individual you are considering, treating them all alike and making no distinction whether a person is a defendant or otherwise, where he lives, where he comes from. Do you understand that? I am certainly not going to discharge any member of the jury because he or she may wish [me] to do so because they dislike certain overtones in the conversation. Decide this case according to the evidence. Members of the jury, I am not saying you should be biased in favour or against it. Look at the way it was given. Decide the case that way and no other. That is your sworn duty. I expect you to abide by your sworn duty.
>
> (See *Gregory v. The United Kingdom*, cited above, paragraph 13)

confidence in the public and above all, as far as criminal proceedings are concerned, in the accused,'[163] and that a tribunal, including a jury, must be impartial from a subjective as well as an objective point of view.[164]

The Court noted that in the case at hand there had been no evidence of actual or subjective bias of one or more jurors, and that the members of the jury were committed by oath or affirmation to faithfully try the applicant and to give a true verdict only according to the evidence. Therefore, it examined only whether, considering all the specific circumstances, there had been sufficient guarantees of the impartiality of the jury.

The Court concluded that, although the trial judge had not discharged the jury, he had taken all the necessary steps in ensuring that they would decide according to evidence and without being biased by any personal prejudice, and that was sufficient to safeguard the guarantees of impartiality under Article 6(1):

> The trial judge chose to deal with the allegation by means of a firmly worded redirection to the jury having had the benefit of submissions from both counsel. His statement was clear, detailed and forceful. He was anxious to ensure that his words were understood, and he deliberately broke off on occasions to satisfy himself that such was the case. He sought to impress on the jury that their sworn duty was to try the case on the evidence alone and that they must not allow any other factor to influence their decision.
>
> Admittedly the judge did not make any reference in his direction to the words 'racial prejudice'. However, it is to be noted that he instructed the jury to put out of their minds 'any thoughts or prejudice of one form or another'. The meaning of such words must have been clear, in particular to any juror whose conduct may have given rise to the allegation of racial overtones. It is significant that on no subsequent occasion was there any further suggestion of racial comment. The judge could reasonably consider therefore that the jury had complied with the terms of his redirection and that any risk of prejudice had been effectively neutralised.
>
> The Court's assessment of the facts leads it to conclude therefore that, in the instant case, no more was required under Article 6 (art. 6) to dispel any objectively held fears or misgivings about the impartiality of the jury than was done by the judge. While the guarantee of a fair trial may in certain circumstances require a judge to discharge a jury it must also be acknowledged that this may not always be the only means to achieve this aim. In circumstances such as those in issue, other safeguards, including a carefully worded redirection to the jury, may be sufficient. The Court considers that it is confirmed in this conclusion by the view taken of the judge's handling of the note by the judges on appeal in application of legal principles which corresponded closely to its own case-law on the objective requirements of impartiality (...).
>
> (*Gregory v. The United Kingdom*, Judgment of 25 February 1997, paragraphs 47-48)

The Court also remarked that the *Gregory* case was different from *Remli v. France*,[165] where it had found a violation of Article 6(1) on the grounds that the trial judges 'failed

163. *Gregory v. The United Kingdom*, cited above, paragraph 43; see also *Padovani v. Italy*, Judgment of 26 February 1993, paragraph 27, quoted by the Court.
164. See, *ex multis*, *Pullar v. The United Kingdom*, Judgment of 10 June 1996, paragraph 30.
165. *Remli v. France*, Judgment of 24 April 1996.

to react to an allegation that an identifiable juror had been overheard to say that he was a racist.'[166]

In the *Remli* case, the Rhône Assize Court had to try the applicant and his co-defendant, both of North African origin. A third person, Mrs. M., had certified in writing that she had heard one of the jurors say: '*What's more, I'm a racist.*' The ECtHR noted that Mrs. M.'s statement, containing a serious allegation, had been filed with the Assize Court by the applicant's lawyers, but the court had dismissed the application without even examining the submitted evidence, on the ground that it was 'not able to take formal note of events alleged to have occurred out of its presence.'

The ECtHR found that in this case Article 6(1) had been violated:

> Like the Commission, the Court considers that Article 6 para. 1 (art. 6-1) of the Convention imposes an obligation on every national court to check whether, as constituted, it is 'an impartial tribunal' within the meaning of that provision (art. 6-1) where, as in the instant case, this is disputed on a ground that does not immediately appear to be manifestly devoid of merit.
>
> In the instant case, however, the Rhône Assize Court did not make any such check, thereby depriving Mr Remli of the possibility of remedying, if it proved necessary, a situation contrary to the requirements of the Convention. This finding, regard being had to the confidence which the courts must inspire in those subject to their jurisdiction, suffices for the Court to hold that there has been a breach of Article 6 para. 1 (art. 6-1).
>
> (*Remli v. France*, Judgment of 23 April 1996, paragraph 48)

Similarly, in *Sander v. The United Kingdom*,[167] the ECtHR held that the trial judge had not responded appropriately to a detailed report (submitted by a member of the jury itself) alleging that one of the jury's members was seriously biased due to racist beliefs, and found a breach of Article 6(1).

> In this connection, the Court observes that the facts of the applicant's case can be distinguished from the Gregory case cited above, in which the Court found no violation of the Convention. In the latter case there was no admission by a juror that he had made racist comments, in the form of a joke or otherwise; there was no indication as to who had made the complaint and the complaint was vague and imprecise. Moreover, as opposed to the Gregory case, in the present case the applicant's counsel insisted throughout the proceedings that dismissing the jury was the only viable course of action.
>
> The Court has accepted that, although discharging the jury may not always be the only means to achieve a fair trial, there are certain circumstances where this is required by Article 6 § 1 of the Convention (see the Gregory judgment cited above, p. 310, § 48). In the present case the judge was faced with a serious allegation that the applicant risked being condemned because of his ethnic origin. Moreover, one of the jurors indirectly admitted to making racist comments. Given the importance attached by all Contracting States to the need to combat racism (see paragraph 23 above), the Court considers that the judge should have reacted in a more robust manner than merely seeking vague assurances that the jurors could set aside their prejudices and try the case solely on the evidence. By failing to do

166. *Gregory v. The United Kingdom*, cited above, paragraph 49.
167. *Sander v. The United Kindgom*, Judgment of 9 May 2000.

> so, the judge did not provide sufficient guarantees to exclude any objectively justified or legitimate doubts as to the impartiality of the court. It follows that the court that condemned the applicant was not impartial from an objective point of view.
>
> (*Sander v. The United Kingdom*, Judgment of 9 May 2000, paragraphs 33-34)

In *Popescu Nasta v. Romania,*[168] the ECtHR found that no bias to the independence of judges derived from a speech (containing critiques to the judiciary) made in public by the President of Romania, on the grounds that such comments were addressed to the executive power and not to the judiciary.[169]

[D] Tribunal Established by Law and Lawful Judge

'Established by law' in the meaning of the Convention implies that both the court system of a State and the specific judicial body are regulated by law and not left to discretional acts of the executive or of the judicial authorities:[170]

> According to the case-law, the object of the term 'established by law' in Article 6 of the Convention is to ensure 'that the judicial organisation in a democratic society [does] not depend on the discretion of the Executive, but that it [is] regulated by law emanating from Parliament' (see Zand v. Austria, application no. 7360/76, Commission's report of 12 October 1978, Decisions and Reports (DR) 15, pp. 70 and 80). Nor, in countries where the law is codified, can organization of the judicial system be left to the discretion of the judicial authorities, although this does not mean that the courts do not have some latitude to interpret the relevant national legislation.
>
> (*Coëme and Others v. Belgium*, Judgment of 22 June 2000, paragraph 98)

With regard to the first aspect - i.e., that the judicial system does not depend on the discretion of the Executive, but that it is regulated by law emanating from the Parliament - this does not imply that the law must regulate each aspect of the judiciary, rather that the Parliament establishes the organizational framework for the judicial organization, leaving to the delegated legislation the regulation of specific details.[171]

---

168. *Popescu Nasta v. Romania*, Judgment of 7 January 2003.
169. '*La Cour note que les déclarations du Président de la Roumanie, sans doute critiques à l'égard du pouvoir judiciaire, s'adressaient en premier lieu à l'administration chargée d'exécuter les décisions de justice et non pas aux tribunaux. Or, rien ne permet à la Cour de conclure qu'en l'espèce, ses déclarations auraient influencé les juges de la Cour suprême qui ont statué dans l'affaire du requérant*' (*Popescu Nasta v. Romania*, cited above, paragraph 44; from the original in French).
170. *Buscarini v. San Marino*, Appl. No. 31657/96, Decision of 4 May 2000.
171. *Fruni v. Slovakia*, Judgment of 21 June 2011, paragraphs 134-136. See also *Savino and Others v. Italy*, Judgment of 28 July 2009, paragraph 94. ('... *D'ailleurs, la Cour rappelle que la délégation de pouvoirs dans des questions touchant à l'organisation judiciaire est acceptable dans la mesure où cette possibilité s'inscrit dans le cadre du droit interne de l'Etat en question, y compris les dispositions pertinentes de la Constitution (Zand c. Autriche, précité, §§ 69 et 71*; from the original in French.')

The second aspect implies that also the composition of the specific court must be set in accordance to the law. However, courts have some margin of discretion in interpreting the relevant national legislation.[172]

Accordingly, the ECtHR found in a number of decisions that a court composed of judges in violation of the rules set by the national law violates the above-mentioned principle.

For example, in *Posokhov v. Russia,*[173] the applicant complained that the court that had convicted him could not be considered a 'tribunal established by law,' since it had been composed in breach of the relevant domestic rules: (i) neither the president of the court nor the presiding judge had drawn lots for the lay judges as required by the Lay Judges Act; (ii) the lay judges had been acting in this capacity before the applicant's trial for at least eighty-eight days instead of the maximum fourteen days permitted by law; and (iii) there was no evidence that any judicial authority had been conferred on them before the trial.[174]

The Court, recalling the general principle according to which 'the phrase "established by law" covers not only the legal basis for the very existence of a "tribunal" but also the composition of the bench in each case',[175] found that there was a violation of Article 6(1) in this case:

> The parties' dispute focuses on the extent to which the participation of the lay judges Ms Streblyanskaya and Ms Khovyakova in the hearing of 22 May 2000 complied with the domestic legislation, notably the Lay Judges Act.
>
> The applicant's initial claim was that the two women had, contrary to section 9 of the Act, been acting as lay judges before the applicant's trial for at least eighty-eight days, instead of the maximum fourteen days per year. Moreover, their names had not been drawn by lot, in breach of section 5 of the Act.
>
> The applicant subsequently supplemented that complaint. On the basis of the Neklinovskiy District Authority's reply of 4 October 2002 that there was no record of any adoption of lay judges' lists before 4 February 2000, the applicant concluded that there was no proof that Ms Streblyanskaya and Ms Khovyakova had ever been appointed as lay judges, even before the enactment of the Lay Judges Act.
>
> In their defence, the Government referred to the Presidential Decree of 25 January 2000 which extended the statutory term of office of the current lay judges until new lists had been established under the Lay Judges Act. The Government did not contest the fact that Ms Streblyanskaya and Ms Khovyakova had served for more than fourteen days before the applicant's trial. But the Government could not accept the notion that a lengthier period of service would automatically entail a violation of the Act, since the lay judges' statutory term was for five years and they preserved their judicial authority during the whole of that period.
>
> However, apart from the apparent failure to observe the requirements of the Lay Judges Act regarding the drawing of random lots and two weeks' service per year, the Court is particularly struck by the fact that the Neklinovskiy District Authority – the body responsible for the appointment of lay judges – has confirmed

172. See, among others, the reasoning made by the Court in *Piersack v. Belgium*, cited above, paragraph 33.
173. *Posokhov v. Russia*, Judgment of 4 March 2003.
174. *Ibid.*, paragraphs 29-30.
175. *Ibid.*, paragraph 39.

> that it had no list of lay judges appointed before 4 February 2000. The authority thus failed to present any legal grounds for the participation of Ms Streblyanskaya and Ms Khovyakova in the administration of justice on the day of the applicant's trial, bearing in mind that the list adopted on 4 February 2000 only took effect on 15 June 2000 after its approval by the Rostov Regional Legislature.
>
> These circumstances, cumulatively, do not permit the Court to conclude that the Neklinovskiy District Court which heard the applicant's case on 22 May 2000 could be regarded as a 'tribunal established by law'.
>
> (*Posokhov v. Russia, Judgment of* 4 March 2003, paragraphs 41-43)

In *Zeynalov v. Azerbaijan*,[176] the applicant complained that a judge had been a member of both Supreme Court panels that had examined his two appeals, and alleged a breach of Article 6 on the grounds that the participation of the judge in the examination of the same case for the second time had violated the requirements of the domestic procedural law. The ECtHR reiterated that the requirement that a tribunal is 'established by law' concerns not only the legal basis for the existence of a tribunal but also that the bench in each case is composed according to the rules set forth in the domestic law,[177] and found that in the case at hand Article 6 had been violated.

> In the present case, the Court notes that, as admitted by the Government, Article 109 of the CCrP provided that a judge should be disqualified from hearing any case which he or she had already heard previously in any of the three levels of ordinary jurisdiction (see paragraph 12 above). The relevant domestic case-law also provided a clear interpretation of this rule, which provided that a judge in such a position should automatically disqualify himself or herself even in the absence of an objection from the parties (see paragraph 14 above). As judge N.H. was in the exact same position in the present case, the Court concludes – and, as noted above, the Government accepted – that the composition of the Supreme Court's panel examining the applicant's second appeal on points of law concerning the same criminal case was in breach of the relevant domestic rules. Therefore, it was not a 'tribunal established by law' within the meaning of Article 6 § 1 of the Convention.
>
> (*Zeynalov v. Azerbaijan*, Judgment of 30 May 2013, paragraph 31)

§3.07 THE RIGHT TO A DECISION WITHIN A REASONABLE TIME

The right to a decision within a reasonable time serves the function of protecting civil litigants and criminal defendants against excessive delays in legal proceedings, and to underline the importance of rendering justice without delays.

The calculation of the period differs between criminal and civil proceedings.

Pursuant to Article 6(1) everyone charged with a criminal offence is entitled to a fair hearing in a reasonable time. The wording of Article 6(1) suggests that the time period for the reasonable length of proceedings commences on the day the person is charged:

176. *Zeynalov v. Azerbaijan*, Judgment of 30 May 2013.
177. The Court recalled, among others, *Buscarini v. San Marino*, Appl. No. 31657/96, Decision of 4 May 2000; *Lavents v. Latvia*, Judgment of 28 November 2002, paragraph 144; and *Sokurenko and Strygun v. Ukraine*, Judgment of 20 July 2006, paragraph 24.

> In criminal matters, the 'reasonable time' referred to in Article 6 par. 1 (art. 6-1) begins to run as soon as a person is 'charged'; this may occur on a date prior to the case coming before the trial court (see, for example, the Deweer judgment of 27 February 1980, Series A no. 35, p. 22, par. 42), such as the date of arrest, the date when the person concerned was officially notified that he would be prosecuted or the date when preliminary investigations were opened (see the Wemhoff judgment of 27 June 1968, Series A no. 7, pp. 26-27, par. 19, the Neumeister judgment of the same date, Series A no. 8, p. 41, par. 18, and the Ringeisen judgment of 16 July 1971, Series A no. 13, p. 45, par. 110). 'Charge', for the purposes of Article 6 par. 1 (art. 6-1), may be defined as 'the official notification given to an individual by the competent authority of an allegation that he has committed a criminal offence', a definition that also corresponds to the test whether 'the situation of the [suspect] has been substantially affected' (see the above-mentioned Deweer judgment, p. 24, par. 46).
>
> (*Eckle v. Germany*, Judgment of 15 July 1982, paragraph 73)

Thus, a charge in the meaning of Article 6 ECHR usually involves an 'official notification given to an individual by the competent authority of an allegation that he has committed a criminal offence'.[178] However, some decisions have set the time of commencement at the search of a suspect's home[179] or when a suspect is placed under arrest.[180]

In civil proceedings the time of commencement 'begins to run from the moment the action was instituted before the tribunal'.[181] However, as in criminal cases, the standard has been interpreted also in a way to include the period preceding the issuance of the writ commencing proceedings before the court.[182]

[A] The Length of the Proceedings and the Length of Delays

The majority of the ECtHR case law is related to the reasonableness of the length of judicial proceedings.

While this issue is common to most States (save a few 'virtuous' exceptions), a high number of applications have been filed against Italy, where delays in judicial proceedings, either civil or criminal, have been for years one of the biggest concern for a proper functioning of the judicial system.

Among many others, in *E.P. v. Italy*,[183] the ECtHR observed that the continuous and generalized delays in proceedings was a serious violation of the Convention, and invited the Italian authorities to take concrete steps in order to solve the problem. In the case at hand, related to placement of minors, the period to be taken into consideration

178. *Deweer v. Belgium*, Judgment of 27 February 1980, paragraph 44.
179. See, *ex multis*, *Ommer v. Germany*, Judgment (no. 1) of 13 November 2008, paragraph 54.
180. See, *ex multis*, *Wemhoff v. Germany*, Judgment of 27 June 1968, paragraph 19.
181. See, among others, *Erkner and Hofauer v. Austria*, Judgment of 24 March 1987, paragraph 64.
182. *Golder v. The United Kingdom*, Judgment of 21 February 1975, paragraph 32: 'It is conceivable also that in civil matters the reasonable time may begin to run, in certain circumstances, even before the issue of the writ commencing proceedings before the court to which the plaintiff submits the dispute.'
183. *E.P. v. Italy*, Judgment of 16 November 1999.

started on 26 October 1988, when the Rome Youth Court intervened for the first time by ordering the temporary placement of a minor with the applicant's brother's family, and ended on 24 October 1995 when the Court of Cassation's Judgment of 7 June 1995 was deposited with the registry. The Court recalled the observations already made, *inter alia*, in the judgments issued the same year in the case *Bottazzi v. Italy*, stressing that 'there was in Italy an accumulation of breaches of the "reasonable time" requirement constituting a practice contrary to the Convention'.[184] It also recalled that in proceedings concerning the custody of a child, particular celerity is required,[185] and concluded that:

> Having examined the facts of the case in the light of the arguments put forward by the parties and having regard to its case-law in this field, the Court considers that the length of the proceedings failed to meet the 'reasonable time' requirement and constitutes a further example of the practice referred to above.
>
> (*E.P. v. Italy*, Judgment of 16 November 1999, paragraphs 54-55)

But the attention of the ECtHR towards the situation of the Italian judicial system had started much before, since the *Capuano v. Italy* case (1987), as recalled in the above mentioned *Bottazzi v. Italy*:

> The Court next draws attention to the fact that since 25 June 1987, the date of the Capuano v. Italy judgment (Series A no. 119), it has already delivered 65 judgments in which it has found violations of Article 6 § 1 in proceedings exceeding a 'reasonable time' in the civil courts of the various regions of Italy. Similarly, under former Articles 31 and 32 of the Convention, more than 1,400 reports of the Commission resulted in resolutions by the Committee of Ministers finding Italy in breach of Article 6 for the same reason.
>
> (*Bottazzi v. Italy*, Judgment of 28 July 1999, paragraph 22)

The ECtHR also noted that Article 6(1) 'imposes on the Contracting States the duty to organise their judicial systems in such a way that their courts can meet the requirements of this provision',[186] and reaffirmed 'the importance of administering justice without delays which might jeopardize its effectiveness and credibility'.[187] Finally, it recalled that the Committee of Ministers of the Council of Europe, in its Resolution DH (97) 336 of 11 July 1997 (*Length of civil proceedings in Italy: supplementary measures of a general character*) had affirmed that 'excessive delays in the administration of justice constitute an important danger, in particular for the respect of the rule of law'.[188]

184. *Ibid.*, paragraph 53.
185. See, *ex multis*, *Johansen v. Norway*, Judgment of 7 August 1996, paragraph 88.
186. *Bottazzi v. Italy*, cited above, paragraph 22; see also *Salesi v. Italy*, Judgment of 26 February 1993, paragraph 24, cited by the Court.
187. *Bottazzi v. Italy*, cited above, paragraph 22; see also *Katte Klitsche de la Grange v. Italy*, Judgment of 27 October 1994, paragraph 61, cited by the Court.
188. *Bottazzi v. Italy*, cited above, paragraph 22.

On the above premises, the Court concluded for a violation of the right to a reasonable length of proceedings, emphasizing that the continuing violations constitutes a 'practise incompatible with the Convention':

> The frequency with which violations are found shows that there is an accumulation of identical breaches which are sufficiently numerous to amount not merely to isolated incidents. Such breaches reflect a continuing situation that has not yet been remedied and in respect of which litigants have no domestic remedy.
>
> This accumulation of breaches accordingly constitutes a practice that is incompatible with the Convention.
>
> The Court has examined the facts of the present case in the light of the information provided by the parties and the above-mentioned practice. Having regard to its case-law on the subject, the Court considers that in the instant case the length of the proceedings was excessive and failed to meet the 'reasonable time' requirement.
>
> (*Bottazzi v. Italy*, Judgment of 29 July 1999, paragraphs 22-23)

The high number of judgments against Italy, wherein the ECtHR remarked the repeated and non-accidental breach of the right of a decision within a reasonable time, led the Italian legislator to the adoption of a special law against delays in proceedings (so called '*Legge Pinto*'), which entitled victims of unjustified delayed proceedings to the right of compensation.

However, the new law did not solve the problem completely, as observed by the ECtHR – among others – in *Apicella v. Italy*,[189] either because the compensation awarded by the Italian government under the new law[190] was not fully satisfactory, due to the relatively insignificant sums awarded as compensation, or because further delays followed, in the stage of executing the decisions:

> Hundreds of cases are currently pending before the Court in respect of awards made by the courts of appeal in 'Pinto' proceedings prior to the Court of Cassation's departure from precedent and/or the delay in payment of the amounts in question. The Court, while acknowledging with satisfaction the favourable developments in Italian case-law, and particularly the recent judgment of the plenary Court of Cassation (see paragraph 27 above), regrets to observe that where a deficiency that has given rise to a violation has been put right, another one related to the first one appears: in the present case the delay in executing decisions. It cannot over-emphasise the fact that States must equip themselves with the means necessary and adequate to ensure that all the conditions for providing effective justice are guaranteed.
>
> (*Apicella v. Italy*, [Grand Chamber], Judgment of 29 March 2006, paragraph 124)

Similarly, in *Scordino v. Italy*,[191] the ECtHR noted that the compensation awarded by the Italian Court of Appeal following the Pinto Act was not sufficient, if compared to the standard of compensation awarded by the ECtHR in similar cases:

189. *Apicella v. Italy*, Judgment of 10 November 2004, and *Apicella v. Italy*, (Grand Chamber), Judgment of 29 March 2006.
190. Law no. 89 of 24 March 2001, known as the 'Pinto' Act.
191. *Scordino v. Italy*, (Grand Chamber), Judgment of 29 March 2006.

> Even if the method of calculation provided for in domestic law does not correspond exactly to the criteria established by the Court, an analysis of the case-law should enable the courts of appeal to award sums that are not unreasonable in comparison with the awards made by the Court in similar cases.
>
> In the instant case the Court notes that the Court of Appeal did not find that the conduct of the applicants had had a significant effect on the length of the proceedings. Nor did it find that the case was particularly complex. The Court of Appeal's decision appears to take account only of the excessive length, assessed at three years and six months, and the stakes involved in the dispute. The Court reiterates that the stakes involved in the dispute cannot be assessed with regard only to the final outcome, otherwise proceedings that are still pending would have no value. Regard has to be had to the overall stakes involved in the dispute for the applicants.
>
> With regard to the amount awarded, it would appear that EUR 2,450 for a delay of three and a half years amounts to applying a rate of EUR 700 per annum, that is, EUR 175 for each applicant. The Court observes that this amount is approximately 10% of what it generally awards in similar Italian cases. That factor in itself leads to a result that is manifestly unreasonable having regard to its case-law. It will return to this matter in the context of Article 41 (see paragraphs 272-73 below).
>
> In conclusion, and having regard to the fact that various requirements have not been satisfied, the Court considers that the redress was insufficient. As the second condition – appropriate and sufficient redress – has not been fulfilled, the Court considers that the applicants can in the instant case still claim to be 'victims' of a breach of the 'reasonable time' requirement.
>
> (*Scordino v. Italy* [Grand Chamber], Judgment of 29 March 2006, paragraphs 213-215)

[B] When the Length of Proceedings Is 'Reasonable'

The reasonableness of the timeframe required to fully adjudicate a case is conducted on a case by case basis according to the factual circumstances presented by each case. However, in order to assess when time is 'reasonable', the ECtHR has laid down the following criteria: the complexity of the case, the conduct of the parties and of the State authorities, and the importance of what was at stake for the applicant in the litigation.[192]

> The reasonableness of the length of the proceedings is to be assessed in the light of the particular circumstances of the case, regard being had to the criteria laid down in the Court's case-law, in particular the complexity of the case, the applicants' conduct and that of the competent authorities, and the importance of what was at stake for the applicants in the litigation.
>
> (*Gast and Popp v. Germany*, Judgment of 25 February 2000, paragraph 70)

192. See also, among other authorities, *Veliyev v. Russia*, Judgment of 24 June 2010, paragraph 173; *Uhl v. Germany*, Judgment of 10 February 2005, paragraph 27; *Pélissier and Sassi v. France*, (Grand Chamber), Judgment of 25 March 1999, paragraph 67; *Kemmache v. France*, Judgment of 27 November 1991, paragraph 60.

[1] Responsibility of the Parties for the Delay

Delay can also be attributable to litigants or the accused. When delay is attributable to a non-state party, this amount of delay is offset against the total time considered in a reasonableness inquiry, as such for the purposes of Article 6(1) only delays attributable to the State are relevant.[193]

For example, in *Vernillo v. France*,[194] the ECtHR noted that 'the parties showed little alacrity in filing their submissions' and that they 'did much to prolong the proceedings', and concluded that no breach of Article 6(1) with respect of the reasonableness of length of proceedings had occurred.

In *Proszak v. Poland*,[195] the applicant complained, *inter alia*, of the length of the civil proceedings brought in the Stalowa Wola District Court. The ECtHR remarked that the conduct of the applicant played a significant role in the total length of the proceedings:

> ... it notes that the applicant groundlessly challenged the reporting judge on three occasions, once even after judgment had been given at first instance (see paragraph 23 above). Her failures to attend the hearings, only some of which were justified by her state of health, and her refusal to attend for the third psychiatric examination contributed decisively to slowing down the proceedings. Had she undergone the third psychiatric examination, the case could have been concluded within a short space of time. Furthermore, the applicant and her counsel seem to have coordinated their actions poorly. Although the lawyer had accepted the court's appointment of a fresh psychiatrist as an expert (see paragraph 10 above), Mrs Proszak did not attend on the day appointed for the examination (see paragraph 11 above). That was scarcely consistent with the diligence which must be shown by the plaintiff in civil proceedings.
>
> (*Proszak v. Poland*, Judgment of 16 December 1997, paragraph 40)

Then, having regard to all the circumstances of the case and, in particular, to the part played by the applicant in the conduct of the proceedings, concluded that the length of time could not be regarded as unreasonable, and that Article 6(1) was not violated:

> The Court notes that almost the whole period falling within its jurisdiction ratione temporis was essentially taken up with the search for an expert with sufficient specialist qualifications, as the applicant herself had wished. It observes in this connection that experts work in the context of judicial proceedings supervised by a judge, who remains responsible for the preparation and speedy conduct of proceedings (see, mutatis mutandis, the Billi v. Italy judgment of 26 February 1993, Series A no. 257-G, p. 89, § 19). In the instant case it was reasonable to take the view that a third opinion on Mrs Proszak's mental health was necessary. The District Court did everything possible to obtain it. Admittedly, the length of time complained of may at first sight seem excessive, but the evidence does not disclose any significant period of inactivity. The District Court even went so far as to offer to take evidence from her at her home in view of her bad health (see paragraph 20 above). Furthermore, once the expert was appointed, the applicant refused to

193. See, *ex multis*, *Ringeisen v. Austria*, Judgment of 16 July 1971, paragraph 110.
194. *Vernillo v. France*, Judgment of 20 February 1991, paragraph 34.
195. *Proszak v. Poland*, Judgment of 16 December 1997.

> undergo examination on 23 January 1996 despite being requested to do so (see paragraph 19 above).
>
> (*Proszak v. Poland*, Judgment of 16 December 1997, paragraph 44)

On the contrary, in *Mikulić v. Croatia*,[196] where only one of the parties – the defendant – caused delaying of the proceedings by not appearing for six consecutive times for the scheduled DNA test, the Court held the State responsible for the excessive length of the proceedings:

> The Court reiterates that particular diligence is required in cases concerning civil status and capacity (see *Bock v. Germany*, judgment of 29 March 1989, Series A no. 150, p. 23, § 49). In view of what was at stake for the applicant in the present case, that is her right to have her paternity established or refuted and thus to have her uncertainty as to the identity of her natural father eliminated, the Court considers that the competent national authorities were required by Article 6 § 1 to act with particular diligence in ensuring the progress of the proceedings.
>
> The Court notes that in the period to be taken into account the proceedings were altogether pending before the first-instance court for about four years and have been pending before the appellate court for about four months. The first-instance court scheduled fifteen hearings, six of which were adjourned owing to the defendant's absence. Not a single hearing was adjourned on account of the applicant's conduct. The first-instance court scheduled six appointments for DNA tests and the defendant did not attend any of those appointments. As to the Government's contention that the first-instance court was impeded in progressing with the proceedings because the defendant did not comply with the court's orders to attend the hearings and the DNA tests, the Court reiterates that it is for Contracting States to organise their legal systems in such a way that their courts can guarantee the right of everyone to obtain a final decision on disputes relating to civil rights and obligations within a reasonable time (see, among other authorities, *G.H. v. Austria*, no. 31266/96, § 20, 3 October 2000).
>
> In the light of the criteria laid down in its case-law and having regard to all the circumstances of the case, the Court considers that the length of the proceedings complained of, which are still pending, failed to satisfy the reasonable time requirement. There has, accordingly, been a violation of Article 6 § 1 of the Convention.
>
> (*Mikulić v. Croatia*, Judgment of 7 February 2002, paragraphs 44-46)

[2] Conduct of State Authorities

If delay is caused by the State, for the purposes of Article 6(1), generally without exception the delay will become a part of the reasonableness of time calculation.[197]

Thus, the ECtHR has often stressed that, even in cases where the conduct of the parties has a relevant role in the delay of the proceedings, the domestic courts are not

196. *Mikulić v. Croatia*, Judgment of 7 February 2002. Similar conclusions were reached by the ECtHR in *Beaumartin v. France*, Judgment of 24 November 1994 (see, in particular, paragraphs 29-33).
197. See, among many others, *Ciricosta and Viola v. Italy*, Judgment of 4 December 1995, paragraph 28.

exempted from organizing their judicial system in a way that ensures compliance with the right to a decision in a reasonable time.[198]

This principle was remarked, among others, in *Scopelliti v. Italy*,[199] where the period taken into consideration by the ECtHR was from 10 December 1980 to 14 January 1988:

> The Court reiterates that in Italy civil proceedings are subject to the 'principio dispositivo', according to which it is for the parties to take the initiative with regard to the progress of the proceedings. However, that principle does not dispense the courts from ensuring compliance with the requirements of Article 6 (art. 6) as regards reasonable time (see the Guincho v. Portugal judgment of 10 July 1984, Series A no. 81, p. 14, para. 32, and the Capuano judgment, cited above, Series A no. 119, p. 11, para. 25). In any event, Article 175 of the Code of Civil Procedure provides that the judge responsible for preparing the case for trial 'shall take all possible steps to ensure that the proceedings are conducted with the utmost speed and fairness' (see the Capuano judgment, cited above, ibid.).
>
> (*Scopelliti v. Italy*, Judgment of 23 November 1993, paragraph 25)

In *Hentrich v. France*,[200] where the period taken into consideration by the ECtHR began on 31 March 1980, when proceedings were instituted in the Strasbourg *Tribunal de Grande Instance*, and ended on 16 June 1987, when the Court of Cassation delivered the final judgment, the Court stated that the backlog of domestic courts cannot excuse the excessive length of proceedings:[201]

> Like the Commission, the Court notes that while the proceedings at first instance progressed at an acceptable pace, there were delays especially on appeal (the proceedings took four years), and to a lesser extent in the Court of Cassation (where the proceedings lasted two years). For the most part, the length of the appeal proceedings was due to the backlog of business in the Colmar Court of Appeal, a factor which, as the Court has consistently held in the past, cannot excuse it. On the other hand, the length of the proceedings in the Court of Cassation was attributable primarily to that court's wish to hear together four cases that raised similar issues - an approach which is understandable but which, under Article 6 (art. 6) of the Convention, cannot justify substantial delay.
>
> That being so, and having regard to what was at stake for the applicant, the Court cannot regard the lapse of time in the instant case as having been 'reasonable'.
>
> There has therefore been a breach of Article 6 para. 1 (art. 6-1) in this respect.
>
> (*Hentrich v. France*, Judgment of 22 September 1994, paragraph 61)

198. See, *ex multis*, *Neves e Silva v. Portugal*, Judgment of 27 April 1989, paragraphs 44-46; *Manieri v. Italy*, Judgment of 27 February 1992, paragraphs 18-19.
199. *Scopelliti v. Italy*, Judgment of 23 November 1993.
200. *Hentrich v. France*, Judgment of 22 September 1994.
201. Similarly, in *Vocaturo v. Italy*, Judgment of 24 May 1991, paragraph 17, the Court did not consider the backlog of cases as a valid justification for the length of proceedings, recalling the principle according to which Article 6(1) imposes on the Contracting States the duty to organize their legal systems in such a way that their courts can meet each of its requirements.

[3] The Importance of the Dispute for the Parties

The importance of the matter to the applicant is another factor to be considered with regard to the reasonableness of time to adjudicate cases. Thus, a case important to the applicant will require closer scrutiny to the time expended adjudicating the case. Conversely, outcomes which are less vital to the applicant will be viewed under a less strict standard, whereby the court may allow for a longer time to adjudicate the case.[202]

The ECtHR has held that importance necessitates a strict reading of the reasonableness requirement. For example, pension disputes,[203] child custody litigation,[204] disputes arising from an alleged wrongful termination of employment,[205] pre-trial criminal detention cases,[206] and cases involving compensation for personal injury related to automobile accidents have been considered as of significant importance.[207]

In *Obermeier v. Austria*,[208] where employment related proceedings before the national court lasted for nine years, the ECtHR observed:

> The parties discussed various criteria which the Court has applied in such cases, such as the exact period to be taken into consideration, the degree of complexity of the case, the parties' conduct, and so on. The Court notes, however, that its case-law is based on the fundamental principle that the reasonableness of the length of proceedings is to be determined by reference to the particular circumstances of the case. In this instance those circumstances call for a global assessment so that the Court does not consider it necessary to consider these questions in detail.
>
> It stresses that an employee who considers that he has been wrongly suspended by his employer has an important personal interest in securing a judicial decision on the lawfulness of that measure promptly. The proceedings in question were clearly of some complexity, involving as they did the interaction between the administrative and judicial proceedings concerning dismissal of disabled persons and a large number of different sets of proceedings; the fact remains, however, that a period of nine years without reaching a final decision exceeds a reasonable time.
>
> (*Obermeier v. Austria*, Judgment of 28 June 1990, paragraph 72)

202. According to the consistent case law of the Court of Strasbourg, what was at stake for the applicant before the domestic court has always to be taken into account in assessing the reasonableness of the length of proceedings (see, among many others, *X v. France*, Judgment of 31 March 1992, paragraph 32; *H. v. the United Kingdom*, Judgment of 8 July 1987, paragraph 71).
203. *Docevski v. The former Yugoslav Republic of Macedonia*, Judgment of 1 March 2007, paragraph 35; *Pocuca v. Croatia*, Judgment of 29 June 2006, paragraph 46.
204. *Niederboster v. Germany*, Judgment of 27 February 2003.
205. *Dumanovski v. The former Yugoslav Republic of Macedonia*, Judgment of 8 December 2005, paragraph 49.
206. *Kreps v. Poland*, Judgment of 26 July 2001, paragraphs 52-54.
207. *Silva Pontes v. Portugal*, Judgment of 23 March 1994, paragraph 39.
208. *Obermeier v. Austria*, Judgment of 28 June 1990.

The same principle was applied by the Court in *Stamoulakatoes v. Greece*,[209] concerning a disability pension dispute:

> Bearing in mind the overall length of time taken by the proceedings, namely nine and a half years already, and the importance of what was at stake for the applicant, namely his entitlement to a disability pension and thus a significant portion of his livelihood, the Court is of the opinion that the length of proceedings went beyond what can be considered 'reasonable' under Article 6 § 1. There has accordingly been a violation of that provision.
>
> (*Stamoulakatoes v. Greece*, Judgment of 26 November 1997, paragraph 39)

With specific regard to criminal cases, the ECtHR has consistently remarked that when an accused person is in detention pending trial, the reasonableness of the length of the proceedings must be assessed with particular attention.[210]

> The Court concludes that where a person is kept in detention pending the determination of a criminal charge against him, the fact of his detention is a factor to be considered in assessing whether the requirement of a decision on the merits within a reasonable time has been met.
>
> The time required on both occasions for transmission of the documents to the Supreme Court totals more than twenty-one months of the fifty-two which it took to deal with the case. The Court finds such protracted periods of inactivity unacceptable, especially where, as in the present case, the accused is detained; in its opinion, they go well beyond what can still be considered 'reasonable' for the purposes of Article 6 paragraph 1 (Article 6-1).
>
> (*Abdoella v. The Netherlands*, Judgment of 25 November 1992, paragraph 24)

[4] The Complexity of the Case

The complexity of the case will often impact the rate at which litigation is adjudicated by domestic courts.

A case can be considered complex, according to the Court of Strasbourg's case law, when it involves a greater depth of issues or concerns numerous factual circumstances to be determined, such as a vast number of charges to be determined in a criminal case joining various alleged offences. At the same time, a case can be considered complex as a result of the legal complexity of the proceedings that may arise, for example, from the application of a fresh piece of legislation.

Where the proceedings have been established as complex, the ECtHR as a rule will consider that a longer period of time for the authorities to finalize the case does not violate Article 6.[211]

---

209. *Stamoulakatoes v. Greece*, Judgment of 26 November 1997.
210. See also, in the context of Article 5(3) ECHR, *Herczegfalvy v. Austria*, Judgment of 24 September 1992, paragraph 71.
211. See, however, *Lorenzi, Bernardini and Gritti v. Italy*, Judgment of 27 February 1992, paragraph 16, where the complexity of the case did not justify – according to the ECtHR – the excessive length of the proceedings.

For example, in *Vaivada v. Lithuania*,[212] the Court firstly highlighted the complexity of the criminal proceedings against the applicants, for the reason that they involved a joint examination of eight different criminal offences, allegedly committed by the applicants against various victims at different periods of time:

> The authorities were thus faced with a very difficult task in conducting the trial and summoning numerous victims and witnesses, the proceedings having been adjourned a number of times in view of the failure of some of these participants to appear at trial.
>
> (*Vaivada v. Lithuania*, Appl. No., Decision of 24 November 2005)

Therefore, the Court concluded, the principle of reasonable length of proceedings was not violated:

> To the extent that the applicants have alleged the excessive length of the impugned proceedings, the Court notes that the total length of the proceedings at three levels of jurisdiction was slightly more than 4 years and 9 months. The Court reiterates its finding above, in the context of the applicants' complaint about the length of their detention, that the proceedings could be regarded as complex, and that the authorities were faced with a very difficult task in conducting the trial and questioning various victims and witnesses, the case being adjourned a number of times because of the failure of certain victims or witnesses to appear at trial. It is also to be noted that the second applicant's treatment from tuberculosis constituted a factor which had prevented the investigation from proceeding quicker for more than a year. Furthermore, no significant delay could have been attributed to the authorities during the investigation or trial. The Court concludes therefore that the proceedings viewed as a whole may not be deemed unduly long.
>
> (*Vaivada v. Lithuania*, Appl. No., Decision of 24 November 2005)

§3.08 THE RIGHT TO A REASONED JUDGMENT

The right to a fair hearing pursuant to Article 6 places an affirmative duty on a court, tribunal or jury to provide reasoned judgments, specifically a judgment that adequately outlines the legal and factual basis of the decision. This principle is derived from the concept that a final reasoned judgment provides the parties protection from arbitrary decisions veiled behind ambiguous and incomplete reasoning, in that the parties should be provided with all the data needed to make a fully informed decision regarding whether to lodge an appeal or not.

Despite this protection, Article 6 does not require that a domestic court provide detailed answers to every argument raised by the parties.[213] However, the court's judgment should provide, at a minimum, sufficient reply to the foundational element(s) of the factual or legal claim.

> The Court then reiterates that, according to its established case-law reflecting a principle linked to the proper administration of justice, judgments of courts and

212. *Vaivada v. Lithuania*, Appl. No., Decision of 24 November 2005.
213. See, *ex multis*, *Van de Hurk v. the Netherlands*, Judgment of 19 April 1994, paragraph 61; and *Hiro Balani v. Spain*, Judgment of 9 December 1994, paragraph 27.

> tribunals should adequately state the reasons on which they are based. Article 6 § 1 obliges courts to give reasons for their judgments, but cannot be understood as requiring a detailed answer to every argument. The extent to which this duty to give reasons applies may vary according to the nature of the decision. It is moreover necessary to take into account, *inter alia*, the diversity of the submissions that a litigant may bring before the courts and the differences existing in the Contracting States with regard to statutory provisions, customary rules, legal opinion and the presentation and drafting of judgments. That is why the question whether a court has failed to fulfil the obligation to state reasons, deriving from Article 6 of the Convention, can only be determined in the light of the circumstances of the case (see Ruiz Torija v. Spain, judgment of 9 December 1994, Series A no. 303-A, § 29).
>
> (*Suominen v. Finland*, Judgment of 1 July 2003, paragraph 34)

Hence, if a court addresses the main arguments submitted by the parties, then the requirements of Article 6(1) will be deemed satisfied.

Specific applications of the right to reasoned judgment can be found in cases involving decisions exclusively issued by a court or a tribunal. For example, in *Baucher v. France*, the ECtHR found a violation of the right to a reasoned judgment because of domestic court's practice of reading the verdict during the last hearing and of providing the reasons of the judgment only after the deadline for lodging an appeal had expired.[214]

In *García Ruiz v. Spain*,[215] the ECtHR found no violation of the right to a reasoned judgment in a case where the Spanish higher court (*Audiencia Provincial*) endorsed the first instance court's decision without stating any additional reasons. The ECtHR observed that, even though it would have been desirable 'a more substantial statement of reasons', the proceedings before the domestic courts, taken as a whole, were fair for the purposes of Article 6(1):

> The factual and legal reasons for the first-instance decision dismissing his claim were set out at length. In the judgment at the appeal stage the Audiencia Provincial endorsed the statement of the facts and the legal reasoning set out in the judgment at first instance in so far as they did not conflict with its own findings. The applicant may not therefore validly argue that this judgment lacked reasons, even though in the present case a more substantial statement of reasons might have been desirable.
>
> (*García Ruiz v. Spain*, Judgment of 21 January 1999, paragraph 29)

The ECtHR's approach to jury trials is somewhat different. The Court's jurisprudence is in the sense States are free to determine the mechanisms by which their judicial

214. *Baucher v. France*, Judgment of 24 July 2007 ('*La Cour relève qu'en droit français, le tribunal correctionnel est soumis à l'obligation de motiver ses décisions (article 485 du code de procédure pénale). Une telle motivation doit apparaître dans la minute qui est déposée au plus tard dans les trois jours qui suivent le prononcé du jugement (article 486 du code précité). En l'espèce, le fait que le jugement comprenant la motivation n'a pas été communiqué au requérant faute d'avoir été retranscrit par écrit par le greffe dans le délai d'appel de dix jours constituait donc une anomalie que le Gouvernement reconnaît d'ailleurs puisqu'il l'explique par la surcharge de travail que connaissent les tribunaux*'; from the original in French).
215. *García Ruiz v. Spain*, Judgment of 21 January 1999.

systems achieve compliance with the Convention. Therefore, a domestic law allowing juries to deliver a verdict without legal reasoning is not, *per se*, a breach of Article 6.

However, the accused and the public must be able to understand the verdict that has been given. For example, in *Taxquet v. Belgium*,[216] the applicant complained that his right to a fair trial had been violated because his conviction by the Assize Court had been based on a verdict which did not contain any reasoning and, furthermore, could not be appealed.

The Court firstly observed that the decision of a State to adopt the jury system cannot be questioned, as 'a State's choice of a particular criminal justice system is in principle outside the scope of the supervision carried out by the Court at European level, provided that the system chosen does not contravene the principles set forth in the Convention:'[217]

> The Court notes that several Council of Europe Member States have a lay jury system, guided by the legitimate desire to involve citizens in the administration of justice, particularly in relation to the most serious offences. The jury exists in a variety of forms in different States, reflecting each State's history, tradition and legal culture; variations may concern the number of jurors, the qualifications they require, the way in which they are appointed and whether or not any forms of appeal lie against their decisions.
>
> (*Taxquet v. Belgium*, Judgment of 16 November 2010, paragraph 83)

The Court then, recalling its case law on the subject matter, reiterated that Article 6 does not preclude trials by jury, even where reasons are not given, but that a vital safeguard against arbitrariness is that the accused and the public must be able to understand the verdict:

> Such procedural safeguards may include, for example, directions or guidance provided by the presiding judge to the jurors on the legal issues arising or the evidence adduced (...), and precise, unequivocal questions put to the jury by the judge, forming a framework on which the verdict is based or sufficiently offsetting the fact that no reasons are given for the jury's answers (see *Papon*, cited above). Lastly, regard must be had to any avenues of appeal open to the accused.
>
> (*Taxquet v. Belgium*, Judgment of 16 November 2010, paragraph 92)

In the case under examination, however, the ECtHR found that the right to a reasoned judgment was violated, considering - *inter alia* - that 'neither the indictment nor the questions to the jury contained sufficient information as to the applicant's involvement in the commission of the offences of which he was accused', and that no ordinary appeal was granted by the Belgian system against judgments of the Assize Court.

216. *Taxquet v. Belgium*, [Grand Chamber], Judgment of 16 November 2010.
217. *Ibid.*, paragraph 83.

§3.09 ACCESS TO JUDICIAL REMEDIES AND THE EUROPEAN UNION COURT OF JUSTICE

European Union (EU) law often claims to be 'supra-national' law, balancing somewhere between national and international law. Indeed, as a law system created by a regional organization, it is very specific and not fitting into ordinary frames. Such principles as supremacy over national law, including national constitutional law, the principle of primacy, direct effect and direct application highlights the totally different approach to traditional system of law and inherent hierarchy in it.

EU institutions adopt a variety of different acts, which affect not only EU Member States, but also natural and legal persons within their jurisdiction. Thus, directly or with the interference of national laws, the EU law regulates rights and obligations of private persons, giving rise to the need of consistent interpretation of EU law as well as of the possibility of its judicial review.

As regards the control of legality of EU legal acts exercised by the Court of Justice of the European Union (ECJ)[218] and national courts, the ECJ, stressing the importance of effective judicial protection, has stated:

> 39. Individuals are ... entitled to effective judicial protection of the rights they derive from the Community legal order, and the right to such protection is one of the general principles of law stemming from the constitutional traditions common to the Member States. That right has also been enshrined in Articles 6 and 13 of the European Convention for the Protection of Human Rights and Fundamental Freedoms ...
>
> 40. ... the Treaty has established a complete system of legal remedies and procedures designed to ensure judicial review of the legality of acts of the institutions, and has entrusted such review to the Community Courts ... Under that system, where natural or legal persons cannot, by reason of the conditions for admissibility laid down in the fourth paragraph of Article 173 of the Treaty [present Article 263(4)], directly challenge Community measures of general application, they are able, depending on the case, either indirectly to plead the invalidity of such acts before the Community Courts ... or to do so before the national courts and ask them, since they have no jurisdiction themselves to declare those measures invalid ..., to make a reference to the Court of Justice for a preliminary ruling on validity.
>
> (Case C-50/00 P *Unión de Pequeños Agricultores* v. *Council* [2002] ECR I-6677)

Two issues linked to the ECJ and right of access to court will be discussed here: [A] standing before the ECJ (the right to initiate direct actions against EU measures before the ECJ); [B] the possibility to raise EU law interpretation or validity questions before the ECJ through the preliminary reference procedure.

It has to be noted that after the Lisbon Treaty came into force, Article 6(2) of the Treaty on European Union (TEU) provides that EU shall accede to the ECHR, while

218. The Court of Justice of the European Union consists of three courts: the Court of Justice, the General Court (created in 1988) and the Civil Service Tribunal (created in 2004). It is the judicial authority of the European Union and, in cooperation with the courts and tribunals of the EU Member States, ensures the uniform application and interpretation of EU law.

Protocol 8 to the Lisbon Treaty established the guidelines of such participation.[219] The accession process is still ongoing, however, in April 2013 the final version of the Draft Agreement on Accession of the EU to the ECHR was finally adopted. As a result of acceding to the ECHR, the EU will be formally bound by the ECHR and placed under the control of the European Court of Human Rights.

Even though the EU is not currently a party to the ECHR and its acts cannot be the subject of applications to the ECtHR, EU law related questions have been raised regularly with the Court of Strasbourg. To some extent the ECtHR has also touched the issue of effectiveness of judicial protection against potentially illegal EU legal acts.

[A] Standing before the ECJ

The ECJ in its case law has consistently stressed the importance of access to judicial remedies, effective judicial protection, and fundamental rights in general, often referring to the practice of the ECtHR. It widely interpreted fundamental rights in the cases brought to its attention; however, when judicial protection of individuals within the EU legal order came into question, the ECJ was much stricter.[220]

The ECJ is empowered by the Treaties[221] to consider whether legally binding measures adopted by EU institutions, bodies, offices or agencies violate procedural or substantive rules. For this purpose, there are several types of actions that may be brought directly before the ECJ: annulment actions (Article 263 of the Treaty on the Functioning of the European Union (TFEU); 'plea of illegality' (Article 277 TFEU); and actions for 'failure to act' (Article 265 TFEU).

219. For an analysis of the initial version and critics, see Xavier Groussot, Tobias Lock & Laurent Pech, *EU Accession to the European Convention on Human Rights: A Legal Assessment of the Draft Accession Agreement of 14th October 2011*. Robert Schuman Foundation, Policy papers, European issues No. 218, http://www.robert-schuman.eu/doc/questions_europe/qe-218-en.pdf, accessed 21 October 2013.

220. See, for example, Albertina Albors-Llorens, *Private Parties in European Community Law. Challenging Community Measures* (New York: Oxford University Press, 1996); Albertina Albors-Llorens, *The Standing of Private Parties to Challenge Community Measures: Has the European Court Missed the Boat?*, 62(1) Cambridge Law Journal, 72–92 (2003); Alan Dashwood & Angus Johnston, *The Future of the Judicial System of the European Union* (Oxford: Hart Publishing, 2001); Anthony Arnull, *Private Applicants and the Action for Annulment since Codorniu*, 38 Common Market Law Review 7–52 (2001); Stefan Enchelmaier, *No-One Slips Through the Net? Latest Developments, and Non-Developments, in the European Court of Justice's Jurisprudence on Art. 230(4) EC*, 24 Yearbook of European Law 173–221 (2005); Koen Lenaerts, Tim Corthaut, *Judicial Review as a Contribution to the Development of European Constitutionalism*, 22(1) Yearbook of European Law 1–43 (2003); Angela Ward, *Locus Standi under Article 230(4) of the EC Treaty: Crafting an Coherent Test for a 'Wobbly Polity'*, 22 Yearbook of European Law 45–77 (2003); Angela Ward, *Judicial Review and the Rights of Private Parties in EC Law*, 2nd edn (New York: Oxford University Press, 2007).

221. Treaty establishing the European Coal and Steel Community (signed on 18 April 1951) and Treaties of Rome (European Economic Community and EURATOM treaties, signed on 25 March 1957) are the EU founding Treaties. After the Treaty of Lisbon came into force on 1 December 2009, the EU is based on two Treaties: Treaty on the Functioning of the European Union (Official Journal C 326, 26 October 2012) and Treaty on European Union (Official Journal C 326, 26 October 2012).

The action for annulment is the main instrument by which the legality of binding EU legal acts can be judicially reviewed. Comparing to national law, annulment actions correspond to actions for judicial and constitutional review of laws, to actions for annulment of administrative acts, and to *Organstreit* actions (in disputes between constitutional organs).

The action for annulment is introduced by Article 263 TFEU (former Article 230 EC Treaty). Ensuring the right to judicial protection against potentially deficient EU legal acts, besides other possible applicants, it allows natural or legal person to 'institute proceedings against an [EU] act addressed to that person or which is of direct and individual concern to them, and against a regulatory act which is of direct concern to them and does not entail implementing measures'. Thus, any natural or legal person may institute annulment proceedings:

- against an EU act addressed to that person;[222] or
- against an EU act which is of direct and individual concern to them; or
- against an EU regulatory act which is of direct concern to them and does not entail implementing measures.

However, in practice standing of private applicants to challenge EU measures directly before the ECJ is considerably restrictive. The conditions set by the ECJ to satisfy the requirement of being 'individually and directly concerned' harshly limit the possibilities for natural or legal persons to fulfil the admissibility criteria, especially in cases where an individual concern is required.

The requirement of direct concern determines if rights and obligations of a private person are affected by a certain EU legal act. Thus, to establish direct concern the applicant must show a direct link or straight chain of causation between the act and the damage sustained. The direct concern is usually established by the Court if: (i) an EU institution, body, office or agency adopts a legal act; and (ii) it directly affects the interest of private party; and (iii) there is no actual/possible/future interference of a third party, which acted/might act using its discretion to implement that EU legal act. If the measure leaves its addressee (usually a Member State) discretion in implementation, it is presumed that the applicant is affected not by the act itself but by a national legal act implementing such EU legal act.[223]

222. With respect to such act, an addressee has a clear right of standing, direct and individual concern are presumed, and admissibility is unproblematic. Such measures in EU law may be challenged by their addressees without restrictions, provided they are brought within the two-month time limit (limitation period for annulment actions).

223. See Case 294/83 *Les Verts v. Parliament* [1986] ECR 1339; Cases 41–44/70 *International Fruit Company v. Commission* [1971] ECR 411; Case 62/70 *Bock v. Commission* [1971] ECR 897; Case 11/82 *Piraiki-Patraiki v. Commission* [1985] ECR 207; Joined Cases T-172/98 and T-175/98 to T-177/98 *Salamander AG and Others v. European Parliament and Council* [2000] ECR II-2487.

Proving individual concern is even more complicated. The ECJ defined the requirement of individual concern in the *Plaumann* case[224] in 1963, by what was later called the 'Plaumann formula':

> Persons other than those to whom a decision is addressed may only claim to be individually concerned if that decision affects them by reason of certain attributes which are peculiar to them or by reason of circumstances in which they are differentiated from all other persons and by virtue of these factors distinguishes them individually just as in the case of the person addressed. In the present case the applicant is affected by the disputed decision as an importer of clementines, that is to say, by reason of a commercial activity which may at any time be practised by any person and is not therefore such as to distinguish the applicant in relation to the contested decision as in the case of the addressee.
>
> (Case 25/62 *Plaumann v. Commission* [1963] ECR 95, paragraph 9)

In this respect, in *Plaumann* and in later cases, the Court linked granting of standing to closed categories and open categories of persons affected by a certain EU measure. According to its case law, an open category is one that is not determined at the time when the measure is adopted, while a closed category is one that is fixed at that time, i.e., it cannot be enlarged after the decision is taken.[225] The number of persons in the group or possibility to identify them at the time the measure is adopted is irrelevant, as the Court has denied standing considering that the group was open even in cases where only one person was actually affected.[226] Moreover, in accordance with the ECJ's case law, to establish individual concern it is required that the EU institution, body, office or agency which adopted the measure had a duty to take into account the effects of an act to the closed group.[227]

Despite constant criticism, the ECJ adhered to its case law on standing, confirming it in particular in *Unión de Pequeños Agricultores*[228] and *Jégo-Quéré*,[229] and claiming that to change the practice the change of Treaties was necessary. The call for change was finally heard and the Treaty of Lisbon introduced relaxed standing in case of regulatory acts not entailing implementing measures - private applicants seeking annulment of such acts are not required to prove individual concern. This should open the door to the ECJ at least to a larger amount of applicants.

Interestingly, the question of limited standing before the ECJ was also considered by the ECtHR. Of particular importance in this context is the *Bosphorus* Judgment. In this case, having analysed, *inter alia*, standing rules before the ECJ and having recognized that access of individuals to the ECJ is limited, the Court held that the EU

224. Case 25/62 *Plaumann v. Commission* [1963] ECR 95.
225. See D. Chalmers, *European Union Law. Volume I. Law and EU Government*, 552 (Aldershot: Ashgate Dartmouth, 1998); and Paul Craig, *Legality, Standing and Substantive Review in Community Law*, 14(4) Oxford Journal of Legal Studies 507–537 (1994).
226. See, for example, Case 231/82 *Spijker v. Commission* [1983] ECR 2559.
227. Case C-152/89 *Sofrimport v. Commission* [1990] ECR I-2477; Case T-489/93 *Unifruit Hellas v. Commission* [1994] ECR II-1201.
228. Case C-50/00 P *Unión de Pequeños Agricultores v. Council* [2002] ECR I-6677.
229. Case C-263/02 P *Commission v. Jégo-Quéré* [2004] ECR I-3425.

law provides protection of fundamental rights which can be considered as 'equivalent' to the ECHR system:

> In such circumstances, the Court finds that the protection of fundamental rights by Community law can be considered to be, and to have been at the relevant time, 'equivalent' ... to that of the Convention system.
>
> (*Bosphorus Airways v. Ireland*, Appl. No. 45036/98, Decision of 30 June 2005)

On the other hand, as noted Judge Ress in his concurring opinion, the Court has not addressed the question of whether limited access of individuals to the ECJ is really in accordance with Article 6(1) ECHR and whether the EU provisions on standing should not be interpreted more extensively in the light of Article 6(1).

[B] Access to Court and Preliminary References

Another issue important for this context is the preliminary reference procedure provided for in Article 267 TFEU. This procedure establishes a possibility (in certain cases – a duty) for a national court to question the ECJ on the interpretation or validity of acts adopted by institutions, bodies, offices or agencies. As non-referral for a preliminary ruling may infringe the right to a fair trial, a few aspects of it should be mentioned.

Firstly, neither EU law, nor the case law of the ECtHR confirms the absolute right of the parties to have the question of EU law discussed before the ECJ.

The preliminary ruling procedure is based on cooperation between the ECJ and the courts and tribunals of the Member States. Hence, according to the ECJ's practice, although parties involved in a dispute may request a national court to refer EU law questions to the ECJ, the decision to do so rests with the national court only. In its Recommendations to national courts and tribunals in relation to the initiation of preliminary ruling proceedings,[230] the ECJ has firmly stated:

> Whether or not the parties to the main proceedings have expressed the wish that it do so, it is for the national court or tribunal alone to decide whether to refer a question to the Court of Justice for a preliminary ruling.

The ECtHR also supports such approach. It has consistently reiterated in its case law that the ECHR does not guarantee, as such, an absolute right to have a case referred to the ECJ for a preliminary ruling.[231]

In *Peter Moosbrugger v. Austria* [232] the applicants complained, *inter alia*, that the domestic courts' refusal to seek a preliminary ruling by the ECJ had violated their right to a fair trial. The ECtHR recalled its earlier decision in *Societe Divagsa v. Spain*[233] and

230. EU Official Journal C 338 of 6 November 2012.
231. *Societe Divagsa v. Spain*, Appl. No. 20631/92, Decision of 12 May 1993; *Schweighofer and Others v. Austria*, Appl. No. 35673/97, 35674/97, 36082/97 and 37579/97, Decision of 24 August 1999; *Peter Moosbrugger v.* Austria, Appl. No. 44861/98, Decision of 25 January 2000; *Herma v. Germany*, Appl. No. 54193/07, Decision of 8 December 2009; etc.
232. *Peter Moosbrugger v. Austria*, Appl. No. 44861/98, Decision of 25 January 2000.
233. *Societe Divagsa v. Spain*, Appl. No. 20631/92, Decision of 12 May 1993.

other cases, and found that there had been no arbitrariness in the case at hand, declaring the application inadmissible:

> The Court recalls that an absolute right to have a case referred to the Court of Justice of the European Communities cannot be derived from the provisions of the Convention. Nevertheless, there may be certain circumstances in which such a refusal by a national court might infringe the principle of the fairness of judicial proceedings, as set forth in Article 6 § 1 of the Convention, particularly when it appears to be arbitrary
>
> (*Peter Moosbrugger v. Austria*, Appl. No. 44861/98, Decision of 25 January 2000, paragraph 2)

However, the refusal of such a request may infringe the fairness of proceedings 'if it appears to be arbitrary'.[234] In *Ullens de Schooten and Rezabek v. Belgium*,[235] the applicants maintained that, last-instance courts have the obligation to refer matters to the ECJ for a preliminary ruling on any question of interpretation of the Treaty, and that the denial of their request for a preliminary ruling had arbitrarily deprived them of the protection of Community law and of their access to a 'tribunal established by law'.[236] Disagreeing with them, the ECtHR found that no violation of Article 6 had taken place, on the ground that the domestic courts had given reasoned justification for having refused the applicants' request. In particular, the Court, after recalling the established principle according to which 'it is primarily for the national authorities, notably the courts, to interpret and apply domestic law, if necessary in conformity with Community law',[237] observed that the obligation of national courts to refer a question concerning the interpretation of the Treaty is not absolute,[238] and reminded that the ECHR does not guarantee any right to have a case referred by a domestic court to another (national or international) authority for a preliminary ruling.[239]

In *Ullens de Schooten and Rezabek v. Belgium*, the ECtHR also linked arbitrariness to the obligation to motivate the decisions:

> It should further be observed that the Court does not rule out the possibility that, where a preliminary reference mechanism exists, refusal by a domestic court to grant a request for such a referral may, in certain circumstances, infringe the fairness of proceedings – even if that court is not ruling in the last instance –,

234. See, *ex multis*, *Matheis v. Germany*, Appl. No. 73711/01, Decision of 1 February 2005; *Bakker v. Austria*, Appl. No. 43454/98, Decision of 13 June 2002; *John v. Germany*, Appl. No. 15073/03, Decision of 13 February 2007.
235. *Ullens de Schooten and Rezabek v. Belgium*, Appl. No. 3989/07 and 38353/07, Judgment of 20 September 2011.
236. *Ibid.*, paragraph 47.
237. *Ibid.*, paragraph 54.
238. The ECtHR recalled the ECJ jurisprudence (notably, the case *S.r.l. CILFIT and Lanificio di Gavardo S.p.a. v. Ministry of Health* [283/81, Rec. 1982, 3415]), according to which 'it is for the national courts against whose decisions there is no judicial remedy under national law, like other national courts, to decide "whether a decision on a question of Community law is necessary to enable them to give judgment"' (*Ullens de Schooten and Rezabek v. Belgium*, cited above, paragraph 56).
239. The ECtHR cited, among others, *Ernst and Others v. Belgium*, Judgment of 15 July 2003, paragraph 74.

> whether the preliminary ruling would be given by a domestic court or a Community court. The same is true where the refusal proves arbitrary, that is to say where there has been a refusal even though the applicable rules allow no exception to the principle of preliminary reference or no alternative thereto, where the refusal is based on reasons other than those provided for by the rules, and where the refusal has not been duly reasoned in accordance with those rules.
>
> Article 6 § 1 thus imposes, in this context, an obligation on domestic courts to give reasons, in the light of the applicable law, for any decisions in which they refuse to refer a preliminary question, especially where the applicable law allows for such a refusal only on an exceptional basis.
>
> (*Ullens de Schooten and Rezabek v. Belgium*, Judgment of 20 September 2011, paragraphs 59-60)

In this case, the Court, after examining all the specific circumstances of the case concluded that the obligation of the domestic courts to give reasons had been fulfilled:

> In conclusion, having regard to the reasons given by the Court of Cassation and the *Conseil d'Etat* in support of their refusal to grant the applicants' requests to refer to the Court of Justice preliminary questions on the interpretation of Community law that they had submitted in the course of the proceedings before those courts, and considering those proceedings as a whole, the Court finds that there has been no violation of the applicants' right to a fair hearing within the meaning of Article 6 § 1 of the Convention.
>
> (*Ullens de Schooten and Rezabek v. Belgium*, Judgment of 20 September 2011, paragraph 67)

CHAPTER 4

The Right to a Fair Trial in Criminal Proceedings

Piero Leanza

§4.01 THE PRESUMPTION OF INNOCENCE

> Article 6(2) – *Everyone charged with a criminal offence shall be presumed innocent until proved guilty according to law.*

One of the fundamental principles of criminal law, recognized not only in the ECHR, but also in other human rights treaties, as well as in State constitutional charters,[1] is the 'presumption of innocence': 'Everyone charged with a criminal offence shall be presumed innocent until proved guilty according to law.'

1. Article 14(2) of the International Covenant on Civil and Political Rights (ICCPR) provides that 'everyone charged with a criminal offence shall have the right to be presumed innocent until proved guilty according to law'. Article 7(1)(b) of the African Charter on Human and Peoples' Rights (ACHRP) grants every individual 'the right to be presumed innocent until proved guilty by a competent court or tribunal'. Article 8(2) of the American Convention on Human Rights (ACHR) provides that 'every person accused of a criminal offense has the right to be presumed innocent so long as his guilt has not been proven according to law'. Article 11(1) of the Universal Declaration of Human Rights (UDHR) reads: 'Everyone charged with a penal offence has the right to be presumed innocent until proved guilty according to law in a public trial at which he has had all the guarantees necessary for his defence.' Article 20(3) of the Statute of the International Criminal Tribunal for the former Yugoslavia (ICTY) and Article 21(3) of the International Criminal Tribunal for Rwanda (ICTR) contain the same provision, according to which 'the accused shall be presumed innocent until proved guilty according to the provisions of the present Statute'. The Statute of the International Criminal Court (ICC) provides for a more detailed article (Article 66 – *Presumption of innocence*), which reads: '1. Everyone shall be presumed innocent until proved guilty before the Court in accordance with the applicable law. 2. The onus is on the Prosecutor to prove the guilt of the accused. 3. In order to convict the accused, the Court must be convinced of the guilt of the accused beyond reasonable doubt.'

In accordance with this principle, no one can be considered guilty until the intervention of a final verdict, with the logic corollary that it is unacceptable an anticipation of such verdict before it is given by the competent judicial authorities according to the law.

This principle can be violated in various ways, such as, among others: when state officers, including judicial authorities, anticipate an assessment of guilt pending investigation; when a judicial body issues a procedural decision, during either criminal or civil proceedings; by statements made by state officials to the press; etc.

In *Lavents v. Latvia*, the Court, after recalling that the presumption of innocence enshrined in Article 6(2) ECHR requires that also members of the court, in carrying out their duties, must not act with the preconceived idea that the accused is guilty, remarked that the judges assigned to the case must refrain from declaring publicly that the accused is guilty of the offence charged until his guilt has been duly established by the court.[2]

The principle of the presumption of innocence is a 'typical' one, and it can be frequently found in the ECtHR's jurisprudence.

In *Butkevičius v. Lithuania*,[3] the applicant complained that the statements of the Prosecutor General, and the statements of the Chairman of the *Seimas* (the Lithuanian Parliament) published in the press violated the guarantee under Article 6(2).[4]

The Court, recalling the principles previously affirmed in *Daktaras v. Lithuania*,[5] remarked that the presumption of innocence 'may be infringed not only by a judge or court but also by other public authorities' and reaffirmed 'the importance of the choice of words by public officials in their statements before a person has been tried and found guilty of an offence'. Then, after noting that in order to ascertain whether a statement of a public official is in breach of the presumption of innocence it is necessary to examine the particular circumstances in which the statement was made,[6] the Court concluded that the statements of the Chairman of the *Seimas* had violated Article 6(2):

> Of more concern are the statements made by the Chairman of the Seimas to the effect that he entertained no doubt that the applicant had accepted a bribe, that he

2. *Lavents v. Latvia*, Judgment of 28 February 2002, paragraph 125. From the original, in French language: '*La Cour rappelle que la présomption d'innocence, consacrée par l'article 6 § 2 de la Convention, exige notamment qu'en remplissant leurs fonctions les membres du tribunal ne partent pas de l'idée préconçue que le prévenu a commis l'acte incriminé; la charge de la preuve pèse sur l'accusation et le doute profite à l'accusé (voir l'arrêt Barberà, Messegué et Jabardo c. Espagne du 6 décembre 1988, série A no 146, p. 31, § 77). Par conséquent, l'article 6 § 2 exige que les représentants de l'Etat – les juges chargés de l'affaire en premier lieu, mais également les représentants des autres autorités investies du pouvoir publique – s'abstiennent de déclarer en public que l'accusé est coupable d'avoir commis l'infraction incriminée, avant que sa culpabilité ait été régulièrement établie par le tribunal (voir l'arrêt Allenet de Ribemont c. France du 10 février 1995, série A no 308, p. 16, §§ 36-37, et Butkevičius c. Lituanie, no 48267/99, § 49, 26 mars 2002, non publié).*'
3. *Butkevičius c. Lithuania*, Judgment of 26 March 2002.
4. In particular, while the Prosecutor General had stated that the applicant had 'enough sound evidence of the guilt' of the applicant, the Chairman of the *Seimas* had declared that the applicant had taken money 'while promising criminal services', and that he was a 'bribe-taker'.
5. *Daktaras v. Lithuania*, Judgment of 10 October 2000.
6. See, *ex multis*, *Adolf v. Austria*, Judgment of 26 March 1982, paragraphs 36-41.

> had taken money 'while promising criminal services', and that he was a 'bribe-taker'. In this respect the Court has had particular regard to the fact that the Seimas had lifted the applicant's parliamentary immunity to enable criminal proceedings to be instituted against him.
>
> The Court does not agree with the Government that all the Chairman's references to 'bribery' were irrelevant to this application. It is undisputed that the facts of the offence committed by the applicant, whilst subsequently classified by the prosecutors and the courts as an attempt to cheat, had frequently been interpreted by the media and the general public, prior to the applicant's conviction, as 'bribery' (see, for instance, § 30 above). It has not been contended by the Government that, by stating that the applicant was a 'bribe-taker', the Chairman of the Seimas was not referring to the criminal proceedings in question. In the Court's view, this remark could therefore be interpreted as confirming the Chairman's view that the applicant had committed the offences of which he was accused.
>
> While the impugned remarks of the Chairman of the Seimas were in each case brief and made on separate occasions, in the Court's opinion they amounted to declarations by a public official of the applicant's guilt, which served to encourage the public to believe him guilty and prejudged the assessment of the facts by the competent judicial authority.
>
> There has therefore been a breach of Article 6 § 2 of the Convention.
>
> (*Butkevičius v. Lithuania*, Judgment of 26 March 2002, paragraphs 53-54)

In the above-mentioned *Daktaras v. Lithuania* the Court observed that infringements of the presumption of innocence may derive, not only by statements of judges, but also of the prosecutor, in particular when he performs a 'quasi-judicial' function (such as, when ruling on the applicant's request to dismiss the charges at the stage of the pre-trial investigation).

In the case at hand, the Court found no violation of Article 6(2). Indeed, the Prosecutor had stated in one of his decisions during the preliminary stages of the proceedings – thus, not in a press conference or in any occasion out of the proceedings – that the applicant's guilt had been 'proved' by the evidence in the case file, while the applicant had contended that his guilt had not been 'proved', using the same terminology. The Court concluded that:

> (...) While the use of the term 'proved' is unfortunate, the Court considers that, having regard to the context in which the word was used, both the applicant and the prosecutor were referring not to the question whether the applicant's guilt had been established by the evidence – which was clearly not one for the determination of the prosecutor – but to the question whether the case file disclosed sufficient evidence of the applicant's guilt to justify proceeding to trial.
>
> (*Daktaras v. Lithuania*, Judgment of 10 October 2000, paragraph 44)

In *Allenet de Ribemont v. France*,[7] some of the highest-ranking officers in the French police had referred to the applicant, without any reservation, as one of the instigators of a murder.

The ECtHR, after acknowledging that freedom of expression, guaranteed by Article 10 of the Convention, 'includes the freedom to receive and impart information'

7. *Allenet de Ribemont v. France*, Judgment of 10 February 1995.

and that Article 6(2) 'cannot therefore prevent the authorities from informing the public about criminal investigations in progress', remarked that this must be done 'with all the discretion and circumspection necessary if the presumption of innocence is to be respected'.[8]

The Court found that the statements in question had been made in a press conference when the applicant had not been formally charged. This represented not only a clear declaration of the applicant's guilt, in violation of Article 6(2), but had also prejudged the assessment of the facts by the competent judicial authority:

> The Court notes that in the instant case some of the highest-ranking officers in the French police referred to Mr Allenet de Ribemont, without any qualification or reservation, as one of the instigators of a murder and thus an accomplice in that murder (see paragraph 11 above). This was clearly a declaration of the applicant's guilt which, firstly, encouraged the public to believe him guilty and, secondly, prejudged the assessment of the facts by the competent judicial authority. There has therefore been a breach of Article 6 para. 2 (art. 6-2).
>
> (*Allenet de Ribemont v. France*, Judgment of 10 February 1995, paragraph 41)

In *Bohmer v. Germany*,[9] the applicant had been sentenced in 1991 to two years of imprisonment, the execution of which had been 'suspended'. He complained that the Court of Appeal's decision contained a finding of guilt with regard of a criminal charge which formed part of other criminal proceedings, pending before another court, which was a violation of Article 6(2).

The ECtHR reaffirmed the principle according to which a finding of guilt for an offence outside the criminal proceedings where such an offence is to be examined, is a violation of the presumption of innocence, and stressed that it is sufficient, to have such a violation, that the reasoning suggests that the court considered the accused as guilty:

> The presumption of innocence will be violated if a judicial decision or a statement by a public official concerning a person charged with a criminal offence reflects an opinion that he is guilty before he has been proved guilty according to law. It suffices, even in the absence of any formal finding, that there is some reasoning suggesting that the court or the official regards the accused as guilty (...)
>
> (*Bohmer v. Germany*, Judgment of 3 October 2001, paragraph 54)

In some occasions, the ECtHR ruled that the presumption of innocence was violated when criminal proceedings were stayed, because of a time bar or similar reasons.

For example, in *Minelli v. Switzerland*,[10] the Court examined the question whether the presumption of innocence is violated when an individual is obliged to pay procedural costs and expenses for proceedings in which he has been acquitted, or which have been discontinued, discharged, or terminated due to the fact that prosecution was time-barred.

8. *Ibid.*, paragraph 38.
9. *Bohmer v. Germany*, Judgment of 3 October 2001.
10. *Minelli v. Switzerland*, Judgment of 25 March 1983.

In the case at hand, the applicant alleged that the decision by which the Chamber of the Canton of Zürich Assize Court had terminated the prosecution against him on account of limitation, but had nevertheless ordered him to pay two-thirds of the costs of the investigation and trial and compensation in respect of the private prosecutors' expenses, violated the principle of presumption of innocence (he alleged, in particular, that this decision amounted to 'a punishment on suspicion').

The Court first recalled the general principle according to which:

> (...) the presumption of innocence will be violated if, without the accused's having previously been proved guilty according to law and, notably, without his having had the opportunity of exercising his rights of defence, a judicial decision concerning him reflects an opinion that he is guilty. This may be so even in the absence of any formal finding; it suffices that there is some reasoning suggesting that the court regards the accused as guilty.
>
> (*Minelli v. Switzerland*, Judgment of 25 March 1983, paragraph 37)

Then it examined the particular circumstances of the case. In particular, focusing on the fact that the domestic court had found that 'the incidence of the costs and expenses should depend on the judgment that would have been delivered' had the statutory period of limitation not expired,[11] it found that Article 6(2) was violated:

> Notwithstanding the absence of a formal finding and despite the use of certain cautious phraseology ('in all probability', 'very probably'), the Chamber proceeded to make appraisals that were incompatible with respect for the presumption of innocence.
>
> (*Minelli v. Switzerland*, Judgment of 25 March 1983, paragraph 38)

A similar analysis was made by the ECtHR in *Sekanina v. Austria*,[12] where the applicant alleged that, by refusing to award compensation in respect of his detention on remand, the Linz Regional Court and the Linz Court of Appeal had violated the principle of presumption of innocence.

The applicant had been acquitted for the murder of his wife by the Assize Court sitting at the Linz Regional Court, by a judgment which had become final. However, notwithstanding this decision, the domestic courts rejected his claim for compensation, on the basis of elements contained in the Assize Court file, from which they found that strong indications of the applicant's guilt remained.

The Court held that such decisions, when relying on an individual's suspicion of guilt, even after a final decision of acquittal, violated Article 6(2):

> Despite the fact that there had been a final decision acquitting Mr Sekanina, the courts which had to rule on the claim for compensation undertook an assessment of the applicant's guilt on the basis of the contents of the Assize Court file. The voicing of suspicions regarding an accused's innocence is conceivable as long as the conclusion of criminal proceedings has not resulted in a decision on the merits of the accusation. However, it is no longer admissible to rely on such suspicions once an acquittal has become final. Consequently, the reasoning of the Linz

11. *Ibid.*, paragraph 38.
12. *Sekanina v. Austria*, Judgment of 25 August 1993.

> Regional Court and the Linz Court of Appeal is incompatible with the presumption of innocence.
>
> (*Sekanina v. Austria*, Judgment of 25 August 1993, paragraph 30)

§4.02 MINIMUM DEFENCE RIGHTS IN CRIMINAL PROCEEDINGS AS PARTICULAR ASPECTS OF THE RIGHT TO A FAIR TRIAL

> Article 6(3) – *Everyone charged with a criminal offence has the following minimum rights:*
>
> *a to be informed promptly, in a language which he understands and in detail, of the nature and cause of the accusation against him;*
> *b to have adequate time and facilities for the preparation of his defence;*
> *c to defend himself in person or through legal assistance of his own choosing or, if he has not sufficient means to pay for legal assistance, to be given it free when the interests of justice so require;*
> *d to examine or have examined witnesses against him and to obtain the attendance and examination of witnesses on his behalf under the same conditions as witnesses against him;*
> *e to have the free assistance of an interpreter if he cannot understand or speak the language used in court.*

The guarantees provided by Article 6(3) represent the minimum threshold of rights available to a defendant in criminal proceedings, and – according to the Court of Strasbourg's case law and the predominant literature – they represent specific aspects of the more general 'right to a fair trial' under Article 6(1).[13]

The ECtHR has always examined a complaint alleging a violation of one of the defence rights set forth in Article 6(3), in light of the general principle of fairness of proceedings set forth in Article 6(1), thus considering the violation of the right to a fair trial in the criminal proceedings considered as a whole.

In *T. v. Austria*,[14] for example, the applicant complained that the District Court, before imposing a fine for abuse of process, had not informed him of its suspicion that he had made false or incomplete statements in his legal aid request and maintained, for this reason, that he could not defend himself. He therefore claimed that his defence rights under Article 6(3), (a) and (b), had been violated.

The Court, recalling that 'the guarantees in paragraph 3 of Article 6 are specific aspects of the right to a fair trial set forth in paragraph 1', held that there had been a violation 'of Article 6 § 1 taken in conjunction with Article 6 § 3 (a) and (b) of the Convention', for the following reasons:

> Like the Commission, the Court notes that the District Court, on 11 April 1994, ordered the applicant to supplement his legal aid request, but did not indicate that

13. Also the specific minimal defence rights listed in Article 6(3) can be found in a number of human rights treaties, such as the International Covenant on Civil and Political Rights, the American Convention on Human Rights, etc. (see above, footnote 1).
14. *T. v. Austria*, Judgment of 14 November 2000. In the same sense, *ex multis*, see also *Kremzow v. Austria*, Judgment of 21 September 1993, paragraph 44.

> it suspected him of having committed the offence punishable under section 69 of the Code of Civil Procedure. Without having held a hearing, it found him guilty of this offence on 5 May 1994 and imposed a fine for abuse of process. Thus, the applicant only learned about the accusations levelled against him when the District Court's decision was served on him. Contrary to the Government's assertion, the applicant did appeal from this decision (see paragraph 40 above). However, the appeal was not capable of remedying the shortcomings of the first instance proceedings, because the Regional Court confirmed the District Court's decision on 28 February 1995 without a hearing and rejected the submissions made by the applicant in his defence as constituting new facts which were inadmissible on appeal.
>
> (*T. v. Austria*, Judgment of 14 November 2000, paragraph 71)

In the following sections will be examined the specific rights under Article 6(3) (a), (b), (c), (d) and (e).

[A] The Right to a Proper Notification of Charges

> Article 6(3)(a) – *[The right] to be informed promptly, in a language which he understands and in detail, of the nature and cause of the accusation against him.*

According to the vast case law of the ECtHR in the subject matter, a proper notification of the criminal charge to the accused person must make detailed reference to both the factual and legal basis of such charge, since it is from the moment of the service of the charge that the accused is put in the position to prepare his defence:

> The Court observes that the provisions of paragraph 3 (a) of Article 6 point to the need for special attention to be paid to the notification of the 'accusation' to the defendant. Particulars of the offence play a crucial role in the criminal process, in that it is from the moment of their service that the suspect is formally put on notice of the factual and legal basis of the charges against him (see the *Kamasinski v. Austria* judgment of 19 December 1989, Series A no. 168, pp. 36-37, § 79). Article 6 § 3 (a) of the Convention affords the defendant the right to be informed not only of the cause of the accusation, that is to say the acts he is alleged to have committed and on which the accusation is based, but also the legal characterization given to those acts. That information should, as the Commission rightly stated, be detailed.
>
> (*Pélissier and Sassi v. France*, Grand Chamber, Judgment of 25 March 1999, paragraph 51)

The ECtHR also considers that 'sub-paragraphs (a) and (b) of Article 6 § 3 are connected and that the right to be informed of the nature and the cause of the accusation must be considered in the light of the accused's right to prepare his defence'.[15]

15. *Pélissier and Sassi v. France*, Grand Chamber, Judgment of 25 March 1999, paragraph 54.

It is worth quoting some passages of the Court's Judgment in *Mattoccia v. Italy*,[16] wherein the Judges of Strasbourg examined in detail the main aspects of the rights under Article 6(3) (a) and (b), in connection with Article 6(1).

In the case at hand, the applicant complained on the fact that he had not been afforded an opportunity to properly defend himself in the criminal proceedings initiated against him. In particular, he alleged that the judicial notification of the charges of which he was accused was vague and imprecise (time and place of the offence were not specified), which 'had adversely affected his right to defend himself, since he had been unable to reach a considered decision as to what line of defence to adopt'.[17]

The Court, recalling the principle established in its case law, observed that 'the requirements of paragraph 3 of Article 6 represent particular aspects of the right to a fair trial guaranteed in paragraph 1' and that these two provisions must be examined together:

> Paragraph 3 (a) of Article 6 points to the need for special attention to be paid to the notification of the 'accusation' to the defendant; particulars of the offence play a crucial role in the criminal process, in that it is from the moment of their service that the suspect is formally put on notice of the factual and legal basis of the charges against him (see, mutatis mutandis, the Kamasinski v. Austria judgment of 19 December 1989, Series A no. 168, pp. 36-37, § 79). The accused must be made aware 'promptly' and 'in detail' of the cause of the accusation, that is, the material facts alleged against him which are at the basis of the accusation, and of the nature of the accusation, namely, the legal qualification of these material facts. The Court considers that in criminal matters the provision of full, detailed information concerning the charges against a defendant is an essential prerequisite for ensuring that the proceedings are fair (see, mutatis mutandis, Pélissier and Sassi v. France [GC], no. 25444/94, §§ 51-52, ECHR 1999-II).
>
> While the extent of the 'detailed' information referred to in this provision varies depending on the particular circumstances of each case, the accused must at any rate be provided with sufficient information as is necessary to understand fully the extent of the charges against him with a view to preparing an adequate defence.
>
> In this respect, the adequacy of the information must be assessed in relation to sub-paragraph (b) of paragraph 3 of Article 6, which confers on everyone the right to have adequate time and facilities for the preparation of their defence, and in the light of the more general right to a fair hearing embodied in paragraph 1 of Article 6 (see Pélissier and Sassi cited above, § 54).
>
> As concerns the changes in the accusation, including the changes in its 'cause', the accused must be duly and fully informed thereof and must be provided with adequate time and facilities to react to them and organize his defence on the basis of any new information or allegation.
>
> (*Mattoccia v. Italy*, Judgment of 25 July 2000, paragraphs 59-61)

16. *Mattoccia v. Italy*, Judgment of 25 July 2000.
17. *Ibid.*, paragraph 51.

The Court, however, does not require that the notification of the criminal charge must be in writing:

> Article 6 § 3 (a) does not impose any special formal requirement as to the manner in which the accused is to be informed of the nature and cause of the accusation against him.
>
> (*Pélissier and Sassi v. France*, Grand Chamber, Judgment of 25 March 1999, paragraph 53)

A proper notification must be made in a language which the accused understands.

In *Brozicek v. Italy*,[18] the applicant, a resident of Germany, complained - *inter alia* - that he had not been informed of the criminal proceedings against him, in a language which he understood. The institution of criminal proceedings had in fact been provided twice in Italian, notwithstanding that, after receiving the first notice, the applicant had expressly requested to receive notifications in a language he could understand or in an official language of the United Nations.[19]

The Court found that the right to be properly informed of criminal charges had been violated, on the basis of the following facts:

> The applicant was not of Italian origin and did not reside in Italy. He informed the relevant Italian judicial authorities in an unequivocal manner that because of his lack of knowledge of Italian he had difficulty in understanding the contents of their communication. He asked them to send it to him either in his mother tongue or in one of the official languages of the United Nations.
>
> On receipt of this request, the Italian judicial authorities should have taken steps to comply with it so as to ensure observance of the requirements of Article 6 § 3 (a) (art. 6-3-a), unless they were in a position to establish that the applicant in fact had sufficient knowledge of Italian to understand from the notification the purport of the letter notifying him of the charges brought against him.
>
> No such evidence appears from the documents in the file or the statements of the witnesses heard on 23 April 1989 (...).
>
> (*Brozicek v. Italy*, Judgment of 19 December 1989, paragraph 41)

In *T. v. Italy*,[20] where the 'judicial notification' of an indictment for the offence of rape was not received by the applicant who at the time of the notification had changed official residence (from Saudi Arabia to Sudan, for work reasons), the Court found a lack of a proper notification, since it was not made according to the relevant procedural rules. As a consequence of that, the applicant was sentenced in absentia.

18. *Brozicek v. Italy*, Judgment of 19 December 1989.
19. The applicant, after receiving the first 'judicial notification', sent the Italian Public Prosecutor a note stating the following (translation from Germany):

> I return the enclosed document to the sender as I find it difficult to understand. In lodging my detailed complaint of 14 August - on which no action has yet been taken even though the facts complained of could have far-reaching consequences - and in all correspondence to date with the Italian authorities, I have always expressly requested that either the mother tongue of the persons concerned or one of the international official languages of the United Nations be used, in order to avoid from the outset any risk of misunderstanding (see *Brozicek v. Italy*, cited above, paragraph 16).

20. *T. v. Italy*, Judgment of 12 October 1992.

In the case at hand, even though the applicant had indirectly known about the criminal proceedings instituted against him, the Court found that Article 6(1) was violated, because informing someone of a prosecution brought against him is 'a legal act of such importance that it must be carried out in accordance with procedural and substantive requirements capable of guaranteeing the effective exercise of the accused's rights, as is moreover clear from Article 6 para. 3 (a)', with the consequence that 'vague and informal knowledge cannot suffice'.[21]

However, if the accused's conduct is the main reason why he has not received the notification of a criminal charge, he cannot complain that his right of access to court has been violated.

In *Hennnigs v. Germany*,[22] the applicant complained that he had been denied access to a court in breach of Article 6(1) and (3) (a), (b) and (c), alleging that the prosecuting authorities had 'failed to ensure that he was in actual receipt of the penal order through personal service and that due to the shortness of the time-limit for lodging an objection to it he was deprived of the possibility of getting legal assistance in time'.[23]

The Court, recalling that the guarantees under Article 6(3) are constituent elements of the 'general notion of a fair trial', concluded that there had been no violation of Article 6(1), for the following reasons:

> The Court, like the Commission and the Government, considers that the applicant could reasonably have been expected to obtain a key to his letter-box in order to have ready access to any mail addressed to him, particularly since he must have foreseen that proceedings would be brought against him as a result of his failure to reply to the letter of 9 August 1984 from the public prosecutor's office (see paragraph 10 above). The authorities cannot be held responsible for barring his access to a court because he failed to take the necessary steps to ensure receipt of his mail and was thereby unable to comply with the requisite time-limits laid down under German law.
>
> (*Hennings v. Germany*, Judgment of 16 December 1992, paragraph 26)

[B] The Right to Have Adequate Time and Facilities for the Preparation of a Defence

> Article 6(3)(b) – *[Right] to have adequate time and facilities for the preparation of his defence.*

The right to have adequate 'time' and 'facilities' for the preparation of one's defence is strictly linked, as it happens for the other rights under Article 6(3), with the general right to have a 'fair' trial under Article 6(1). Moreover, it is also linked to the specific defence rights under lit. (a) ['to be informed promptly, in a language which he understands and in detail, of the nature and cause of the accusation against him'] and

21. *Ibid.*, paragraph 28.
22. *Hennings v. Germany*, Judgment of 16 December 1992.
23. *Ibid.*, paragraph 24.

lit. (c) ['to defend himself in person or through legal assistance of his own choosing or, if he has not sufficient means to pay for legal assistance, to be given it free when the interests of justice so require].

The ECtHR has therefore always examined such specific rights in connection with the general principle of fairness of proceedings taken as a whole.

For example, in *Krempovskij v. Lithuania*,[24] the applicant complained – *inter alia* – that Article 6(3)(a)-(d) of the Convention had been violated, alleging that 'at the stage of pre-trial investigation he had not been informed of the cause of the accusation against him, that he had had no time or facilities for the preparation of his defence, that he had not been able to defend himself through legal assistance of his own choosing, and that the courts had not examined all the witnesses that he wanted'.[25]

Firstly, the Court noted that the applicant's complaints concerned his arrest and the following detention on remand which ended on 23 December 1992, and the pre-trial investigation which continued until 7 September 1993, and therefore it lacked competence *ratione temporis* on such complaints, having the Convention entered into force with respect to Lithuania only on 20 June 1995. However - it noted - since the guarantees under Article 6(3) must be interpreted in connection with the general principle under Article 6(1), the respect of the principles laid down in Article 6(3) must be assessed examining the proceedings as a whole, and not with regard to just one or more stages.

The Court therefore considered the applicant's complaints taking in consideration the proceedings as a whole after 20 June 1995, and concluded that 'the isolated aspects alleged by the applicant neither constitute breaches of the requirements of Article 6 §§ 3 (a) to (d) of the Convention, nor have an impact on the fairness of the proceedings as a whole', thus rejecting this part of the application for the following reasons:

> [...] The Court notes that, following the conclusion of the pre-trial investigation, the applicant and his lawyer were able to submit various applications and pleadings contesting the arguments presented by the prosecution in support of his alleged guilt. The Court observes that thus the applicant was in fact aware of the nature and cause of the accusation against him as required by Article 6 § 3 (a) of the Convention.
>
> As regards the alleged interference with the applicant's defence rights in breach of Article 6 §§ 3 (b) and (c) of the Convention, the Court notes that the applicant only complains in this connection that he could not have the assistance of official counsel of his own choosing at the stage of the pre-trial investigation. However, the applicant has not substantiated in any way that the officially appointed representative at the pre-trial investigation failed to perform his functions satisfactorily. Moreover, at the appellate trial, when the case was reheard in full, the applicant was represented by counsel of his choice. The applicant has not shown that any possible defects at the first stage were not thereby subsequently rectified by the applicant's second lawyer. In these circumstances, the Court does not find any indication that the applicant's defence rights laid down in Article 6 §§ 3 (b) and (c) were breached in the instant case.

24. *Krempovskij v. Lithuania*, (Appl. No. 37193/97), Decision of 20 April 1999.
25. *Ibid.*, paragraph 6.

> As regards the applicant's allegation that the courts did not examine all the witnesses of his choice in violation of Article 6 § 3 (d) of the Convention, the Court recalls that the above provision does not give the defence an absolute right to question any witnesses it wishes to call (see e.g., Eur. Court HR, Vidal v. Belgium judgment of 22 April 1992, Series A no. 235-B, p. 32, § 33). Furthermore, the admissibility of evidence is primarily a matter for regulation by national law and, as a general rule, it is for the domestic courts to assess the evidence before them. The Court's task is to determine whether the proceedings considered as a whole – including the way in which evidence was taken – were fair (see e.g., Eur. Court HR, Kostovski v. the Netherlands judgment of 20 November 1989, Series A no. 166, p. 19, § 39).
>
> On the facts of the case, the Court notes that 29 witnesses were questioned in the course of the trial. It must be noted that, in his subsequent appeals against the conviction, the applicant contested the courts' assessment of evidence, including the statements made by certain witnesses. He did not suggest however that he was unable to examine the witnesses in question, or that the failure to call any particular witness would have had a decisive impact on the courts' conclusions as to his guilt. The Court observes that many of the participants in the events of 1990-1991, including the former Head of the LSPO Mr P., were beyond the reach of Lithuanian authorities as they lived in other countries and could not reasonably be expected to testify at the applicant's trial in Lithuania when faced with similar charges themselves. Thus the Court does not consider that the possible failure by the courts to invite a particular witness was of such a nature or degree as render the trial unfair as a whole. Nor is it established that the manner in which the witnesses' evidence was taken was contrary to the requirements of Article 6 § 3 (d) of the Convention.
>
> (*Krempovskij v. Lithuania*, Appl. No. 37193/97, Decision of 20 April 1999, paragraph 7)

In *Hadjianastassiou v. Greece*,[26] instead, the Court found that the applicant's right to be provided with sufficient time and facilities to prepare his defence was violated.

In the case at hand, the applicant, who was subject to court-martial proceedings, complained that, despite the fact that the judgment read out on 22 November 1985 by the President of the Courts-Martial Appeal Court did not include the reasons for his conviction, he had only five days to file an appeal against the decision. He further alleged that he received a reasoned judgment only on 10 January 1986, when the time limit for filing the appeal had already expired. His subsequent request to expand the grounds of his appeal, once he had received a copy of a properly reasoned judgment, was however rejected.

The Court, recalling that the Contracting States 'enjoy considerable freedom in the choice of the appropriate means to ensure that their judicial systems comply with the requirements of Article 6', remarked however that the national courts have the duty to 'indicate with sufficient clarity the grounds on which they based their decision', in order to make it possible for the accused to exercise his right of appeal.[27]

In light of the above, and considering that the request to expand the grounds of the appeal before the Court of Cassation had been rejected, the Court held that the

26. *Hadjianastassiou v. Greece*, Judgment of 16 December 1992.
27. *Ibid.*, paragraphs 33-37.

applicant had not been given sufficient time, or facilities to prepare his defence, and that therefore Article 6(3) (b) had been violated.

A well-known case where the ECtHR found a violation - *inter alia* - of the right of defence under Article 6(3)(b) in *Öcalan v. Turkey*.[28]

After numerous transfers through from Syria to Greece, Russia, Italy and Kenya, and repeated attempts to obtain political asylum, all to no avail, Mr Abdullah Öcalan, leader of the PKK (Workers' Party of Kurdistan), was finally arrested in Kenya on 15 February 1999, and taken on a aircraft whereby Turkish officers arrested him and transported him to Turkey, where he was taken into custody at İmralı Prison on 16 February 1999.[29]

The applicant alleged that Article 6 ECHR had been violated by Turkish judicial authorities, for various reasons.[30] However, we will focus, for the purpose of this section, on the complaints directly related to the violation of the right under Article 6(3)(b).

The applicant maintained that he had not been given the possibility to have a copy of the trial papers or any other documents he needed to prepare his defence. He had been obliged to write out his defence by hand, having access only to the bill of indictment. Moreover, he had been given access to the court file regarding him (composed of 17.000 pages) only on 4 June 1999, and his trial was finalized on 29 June 1999. On the other hand, his lawyers were not provided with a copy of the case file, and obtained access to it only on 7 May 1999, with the consequence that it took them, only to make copies of the case file, until 15 May 1999. He also complained on the fact that restriction on proper communications between him and his lawyers had been placed throughout the investigation, which made even more difficult for his lawyers to prepare his defence. Therefore, the applicant concluded that he had not enjoyed equality of arms with the prosecution in preparing his defence.

Although the multiple complaints raised by the applicants involve the more general principle of equality of arms (on which see Chapter 3, §3.04), the issues examined by the Court in the *Öcalan* case are relevant, in particular, to the right to have sufficient time and facilities to prepare one's defence (as well as to the right to legal representation provided for by Article 6(3)(c), on which see, *infra*, section §4.02[D]).

With regard to the violation of this specific provision, the Court first recalled the principles stated in *Kremzow v. Austria*,[31] emphasizing that 'respect for the rights of the defence requires that limitations on access by an accused or his lawyer to the court file

28. *Öcalan v. Turkey*, (Grand Chamber), Judgment of 12 May 2005.
29. Mr Öcalan was wanted by Turkish authorities, since a number of warrants ordering his arrest had been issued by Turkish courts (and a wanted notice also by Interpol), with the charge of founding an armed gang in order to destroy the territorial integrity of the Turkish State and of instigating various terrorist acts.
30. The applicant, with regard to the alleged violation of Article 6 complained on the following facts: that he had not been tried by an independent and impartial tribunal, since a military judge had sat on the bench during part of the proceedings in the National Security Court; that he and his lawyers encountered difficulties and restrictions in having access to the case file, in calling defence witnesses, and in accessing all the information held by the prosecution; that the media had influenced the judges to his detriment.
31. *Kremzow v. Austria*, cited above.

must not prevent the evidence being made available to the accused before the trial and the accused being given an opportunity to comment on it through his lawyer in oral submissions'.[32] The ECtHR then, made a distinction between the case at hand and the *Kremzow* and *Kamasinsky* cases, for the following reasons:

> The Grand Chamber therefore considers that the present case is distinguishable from Kremzow, in which the applicant had twenty-one days in which to examine forty-nine pages, in contrast to Mr Öcalan, who had twenty days in which to examine a case file containing some 17,000 pages. The present case is also distinguishable from Kamasinski, in which the applicant's lawyer was able to pass on to his client copies of all the documents he considered relevant. Mr Öcalan's lawyers were not able to provide him with any documents before submitting their comments on the prosecution evidence.
>
> (*Öcalan v. Turkey*, [Grand Chamber], Judgment of 12 may 2005, paragraph 142)

The Court concluded that, had the applicant been permitted to study the prosecution evidence directly for a sufficient period, he would have been able to better prepare his defence:

> (...) It is thus reasonable to assume that, had he been permitted to study the prosecution evidence directly for a sufficient period, the applicant would have been able to identify arguments relevant to his defence other than those his lawyers advanced without the benefit of his instructions.
>
> The Court therefore holds that the fact that the applicant was not given proper access to any documents in the case file other than the bill of indictment also served to compound the difficulties encountered in the preparation of his defence.
>
> (*Öcalan v. Turkey*, [Grand Chamber], Judgment of 12 may 2005, paragraphs 143-144)

The Grand Chamber also agreed with the Chamber's findings that difficulties met by the applicant's lawyers in obtaining access to the court file had impaired the applicant's right of defence,[33] and concluded that, taking in consideration all the violations

32. *Öcalan v. Turkey*, cited above, paragraph 140.
33. By Judgment of 12 March 2003, a Chamber of the First Section of the ECtHR unanimously decided that there had been a violation of Article 6(1), taken in conjunction with Article 6(3)(b) and (c), in that the applicant had not had a fair trial. The Chamber's findings on the difficulties encountered by the applicant's lawyers – quoted in the Grand Chamber's Judgment of 12 May 2005, paragraph 147 – read as follow:

> the applicant's lawyers received a 17,000-page file approximately two weeks before the beginning of the trial in the National Security Court. Since the restrictions imposed on the number and length of their visits made it impossible for the applicant's lawyers to communicate the documents in the file to their client before 2 June 1999 or to involve him in its examination and analysis, they found themselves in a situation that made the preparation of the defence case particularly difficult. Subsequent developments in the proceedings did not permit them to overcome those difficulties: the trial proceeded apace; the hearings continued without interruption until 8 June 1999; and on 23 June 1999 the applicant's lawyers were invited to present their submissions on all the evidence in the file, including that taken at the hearings.

of the right of defence as a whole, the right to a fair trial of the applicant had been violated:

> Accordingly, the applicant's trial was unfair for the following reasons: he had no assistance from his lawyers during questioning in police custody; he was unable to communicate with his lawyers out of the hearing of third parties; he was unable to gain direct access to the case file until a very late stage in the proceedings; restrictions were imposed on the number and length of his lawyers' visits; and, lastly, his lawyers were given proper access to the case file belatedly. The Court finds that the overall effect of these difficulties taken as a whole so restricted the rights of the defence that the principle of a fair trial, as set out in Article 6, was contravened. There has therefore been a violation of Article 6 § 1 of the Convention, taken in conjunction with Article 6 § 3 (b) and (c).
>
> (*Öcalan v. Turkey*, [Grand Chamber], Judgment of 12 may 2005, paragraph 148)

[C] The Right Not to Incriminate Oneself

In *Saunders v. The United Kingdom*,[34] the applicant alleged that his statements previously made, under compulsion, to the inspectors appointed by the Department of Trade and Industry during their investigation were afterward admitted as evidence against him in the following criminal trial. The applicant recalled the principles affirmed by the Court of Strasbourg in *Funke v. France*[35] and *John Murray v. the United Kingdom*,[36] and maintained that using his statements constituted a violation of the right not to incriminate oneself - which is strictly linked to the presumption of innocence - since they were used as evidence by the prosecutor during the trial.

The Court reaffirmed the established principle according to which, although not specifically mentioned in Article 6, 'the right to silence and the right not to incriminate oneself are generally recognized international standards which lie at the heart of the notion of a fair procedure under Article 6',[37] but stressed that such right concerns, principally, the respect of the will of the accused to remain silent, and does not extend to 'the use in criminal proceedings of material which may be obtained from the accused through the use of compulsory powers but which has an existence independent of the will of the suspect such as, *inter alia*, documents acquired pursuant to a warrant, breath, blood and urine samples and bodily tissue for the purpose of DNA testing'.[38]

In the case at hand, considering the context of the specific circumstances, the Court concluded that there had been an infringement of the right not to incriminate oneself, and thus a violation of Article 6(2), because the applicant's statements before the inspectors - which the accused had the obligation to make, since a refusal to answer could have led to a finding of contempt of court - had been used in the course of the proceedings to incriminate the applicant.

34. *Saunders v. The United Kingdom*, (Grand Chamber), Judgment of 17 December 1996.
35. *Funke v. France*, Judgment of 25 February 1993, paragraph 44.
36. *John Murray v. the United* Kingdom, Judgment of 8 February 1996, paragraph 45.
37. *Saunders v. The United Kingdom*, cited above, paragraph 68.
38. *Ibid.*, paragraph 69.

[D] The Right to Legal Representation and Legal Aid

> Article 6(3)(c) – *[The right] to defend himself in person or through legal assistance of his own choosing or, if he has not sufficient means to pay for legal assistance, to be given it free when the interests of justice so require.*

In the previous section we have seen that the ECtHR has often examined the right to adequate time and facilities to prepare one's defence together with the right to legal representation.[39]

Article 6(3)(c), however, contains three specific manifestations of such right: the right to defend oneself in person, the right to choose a lawyer, and – if the accused has 'not sufficient means to pay for legal assistance' and 'when the interest of justice so require' – the right to free legal assistance.[40]

The principle according to which an accused person can defend himself has been expressed by the ECtHR in a number of cases,[41] wherein the Court has stressed that the Convention requires that a 'person charged with a criminal offence who does not wish to defend himself in person must be able to have recourse to legal assistance of his own choosing'.

This interpretation is illustrated in *Pakelli v. Germany*,[42] where the Court makes an interesting analysis on the wording of Article 6(3)(c) both in the English and in the French translation. It is worth quoting the relevant paragraphs of the Court's reasoning in their entirety:

> Article 6 para. 3 (c) (art. 6-3-c) guarantees three rights to a person charged with a criminal offence: to defend himself in person, to defend himself through legal assistance of his own choosing and, on certain conditions, to be given legal assistance free. To link the corresponding phrases together, the English text employs on each occasion the disjunctive 'or'; the French text, on the other hand, utilises the equivalent – 'ou' – only between the phrases enouncing the first and the second right; thereafter, it uses the conjunctive 'et'. The 'travaux préparatoires' contain hardly any explanation of this linguistic difference. They reveal solely that in the course of a final examination of the draft Convention, on the eve of its signature, a Committee of Experts made 'a certain number of formal corrections and corrections of translation', including the replacement of 'and' by 'or' in the English version of Article 6 para. 3 (c) (art. 6-3-c) (Collected Edition of the 'Travaux préparatoires', vol. IV, p. 1010). Having regard to the object and purpose of this paragraph, which is designed to ensure effective protection of the rights of the defence (see the above-mentioned Artico judgment, Series A no. 37, p. 16, para. 33; see also, mutatis mutandis, the Adolf judgment of 26 March 1982, Series A no. 49, p. 15, para. 30, and the Sunday Times judgment of 26 April 1979,

39. See, in particular, *Ocalan v. Turkey*, cited above.
40. This right, as it happens for the presumption of innocence and other basic defence rights, is granted also by other human rights treaties. Among those, it is interesting to mention Article 8(2)(d) of the American Convention on Human Rights, which provides also that during criminal proceedings every accused person has the right 'to communicate freely and privately with his counsel', a specific right that is not listed in Article 6 ECHR.
41. See, *ex multis*, *Pakelli v. Germany*, Judgment of 25 April 1983, paragraph 31; *Campbell and Fell v. The United Kingdom*, Judgment of 28 June 1984, paragraph 99.
42. *Pakelli v. Germany*, cited above.

> Series A no. 30, p. 30, para. 48), the French text here provides more reliable guidance; the Court concurs with the Commission on this point. Accordingly, a 'person charged with a criminal offence' who does not wish to defend himself in person must be able to have recourse to legal assistance of his own choosing; if he does not have sufficient means to pay for such assistance, he is entitled under the Convention to be given it free when the interests of justice so require.
>
> (*Pakelli v. Germany*, Judgment of 25 April 1983, paragraph 31)

However, the Court recognized that the national law of each State can regulate differently the right to legal representation. According to this principle, the domestic legislation can provide that the accused cannot defend himself without the assistance of a professional lawyer, on the grounds that representation by a lawyer is necessary in the interest of justice.

Among others, the Italian criminal law obliges a person accused in criminal proceedings to be represented by a professional lawyer. This rule has been considered legitimate not only by the Italian Constitutional Court (its first judgment on this issue dates back to 1980), but also by the ECtHR in numerous decisions and judgments.[43]

For example, in *Sannino v. Italy*,[44] the Court reiterated the principle according to which, although Article 6(3)(c) grants the accused the right to 'defend himself in person or through legal assistance', it 'does not specify the manner of exercising this right', leaving to the Contracting States 'the choice of the means of ensuring that it is secured in their judicial systems'.[45] It is up to the ECtHR to verify whether the method chosen by the States is in line with the requirements of a fair trial.[46]

In *Artico v. Italy*,[47] the applicant – who had been previously represented by a lawyer of his own choice – filed an application to the Court of Cassation, before which applications to quash previous sentences against him were pending, requesting free legal aid in connection with the applications to quash. The request was granted by the President of the Second Criminal Section, who appointed a lawyer from Rome. This lawyer, however, informed the applicant, a first time, that he had learned of the appointment only on his return from holidays and that he could not accept it due to other commitments, and, a second time, that health reasons prevented him to accept such a demanding and onerous task. Mr Artico filed several requests to the Court of Cassation, asking to appoint a substitute legal aid lawyer, and stressing that he lacked of legal assistance, but to no avail, having the Court repeatedly informed him that the first legal aid lawyer was still acting (since a lawyer appointed for legal aid was not entitled by law to refuse the appointment).

The ECtHR remarked that, save certain exceptions not pertinent to the case at hand, 'anyone who is in a state of poverty is entitled under Italian law to free legal aid in criminal matters', and that 'in any event, here the interests of justice did require the

43. See, in the Italian case law, *ex multis*, Constitutional Court No. 180/1980; Constitutional Court No. 8/2007; Court of Cassation No. 7786/2008; Court of Cassation No. 17400/2008; Court of Cassation No. 1890/2013.
44. *Sannino v. Italy*, Judgment of 27 April 2006.
45. *Ibid.*, paragraph 48.
46. See, *ex multis*, *Quaranta v. Switzerland*, Judgment of 24 May 1991, paragraph 30.
47. *Artico v. Italy*, Judgment of 13 May 1980.

provision of effective assistance',[48] and concluded that a violation of Article 6(3)(c) had occurred in this case:

> (...) Admittedly, a State cannot be held responsible for every shortcoming on the part of a lawyer appointed for legal aid purposes but, in the particular circumstances, it was for the competent Italian authorities to take steps to ensure that the applicant enjoyed effectively the right to which they had recognised he was entitled.
>
> (*Artico v. Italy*, Judgment of 13 May 1980, paragraph 36)

In *Quaranta v. Switzerland*,[49] the applicant complained on the fact that he had been refused free legal assistance, not only during the trial, but also during the proceedings before the investigating judge, and that, in doing so, the Swiss authorities had violated his right to defence under Article 6(3)(c).

In the case at hand, the Swiss authorities had denied to grant the applicant free legal assistance with the reason that the case was not complex and that the interest of justice did not require to grant legal aid.

The ECtHR, however, examining the criteria set forth in Article 6(3)(c) - complexity of the case and interest of justice -took into consideration several factors: firstly, it considered not the punishment that was concretely applied to the applicant (six months of imprisonment), but the maximum penalty that could have been imposed (three years of imprisonment). In addition, the Court took into account - among others - the age of the applicant, whether he was a foreigner, the circumstance that the alleged offence had occurred during a probationary period, his long criminal record, and the lack of means to support himself.

Considering the factors outlined above, the Court concluded that the applicant's right of defence was violated by denying him free legal assistance before the investigating judge, as well as before the trial judge. The Court reasoned:

> (...) In order to determine whether the 'interests of justice' required that the applicant receive free legal assistance, the Court will have regard to various criteria. To a large extent they correspond to those put forward by the Government. However, the way in which the Swiss authorities appear to apply them may differ - and in the present case did differ - from the Court's approach.
>
> In the first place, consideration should be given to the seriousness of the offence of which Mr Quaranta was accused and the severity of the sentence which he risked. He was accused of use of and traffic in narcotics and was liable to 'imprisonment or a fine' (section 19 para. 1 of the 1951 Act - see paragraph 19 above).
>
> According to the Government, there was nothing in the file to indicate that the Criminal Court was likely to impose a sentence exceeding eighteen months, the maximum for a suspended sentence. By sentencing the applicant to six months' imprisonment, the court did not reach this limit, even if the sentence imposed in 1982 is taken into account (see paragraph 8 above).

48. *Ibid.*, paragraph 34.
49. *Quaranta v. Switzerland*, Judgment of 24 May 1991.

The Court notes however that this was no more than an estimation; the imposition of a more severe sentence was not a legal impossibility. Under section 19 para. 1 of the Federal Misuse of Drugs Act, in conjunction with Article 36 of the Swiss Criminal Code, the maximum sentence was three years' imprisonment (see paragraph 20 above). In the present case, free legal assistance should have been afforded by reason of the mere fact that so much was at stake.

An additional factor is the complexity of the case. The Court agrees with the Government that the case did not raise special difficulties as regards the establishment of the facts, which the applicant had moreover admitted immediately at his only examination by the investigating judge. However, the outcome of the trial was of considerable importance for the applicant since the alleged offence had occurred during the probationary period to which he was made subject in 1982 (see paragraph 8 above). The Criminal Court therefore had both to rule on the possibility of activating the suspended sentence and to decide on a new sentence. The participation of a lawyer at the trial would have created the best conditions for the accused's defence, in particular in view of the fact that a wide range of measures was available to the Court.

Such questions, which are complicated in themselves, were even more so for Mr Quaranta on account of his personal situation: a young adult of foreign origin from an underprivileged background, he had no real occupational training and had a long criminal record. He had taken drugs since 1975, almost daily since 1983, and, at the material time, was living with his family on social security benefit.

In the circumstances of the case, his appearance in person before the investigating judge, and then before the Criminal Court, without the assistance of a lawyer, did not therefore enable him to present his case in an adequate manner.

This defect was not cured either in the Criminal Court of Cassation of the Canton of Vaud, despite the presence of a lawyer paid by the applicant, or in the Federal Court, although he was accorded free legal assistance before that court, because of the limits on the scope of the review, which may be carried out by those two courts (see, as the most recent authority, mutatis mutandis, the Weber judgment of 22 May 1990, Series A no. 177, p. 20, para. 39).

In conclusion, there has been a violation of Article 6 para. 3 (c) (art. 6-3-c).

(*Quaranta v. Switzerland*, Judgment of 24 May 1991, paragraphs 32-38)

In *John Murray v. The United Kingdom*,[50] the applicant complained that he had been denied access to a lawyer during the first stage of the criminal proceedings against him (the first 48 hours of police questioning). He stressed that in Northern Ireland the initial phase of detention is of crucial importance, due to the possibility of inferences that the trial judge can subsequently draw under Articles 3, 4 and 6 of the Criminal Evidence (Northern Ireland) Order 1988.

The Court ruled that there was a violation of Article 6(1) taken together with Article 6(3)(c).

The Court, in order to assess whether Article 6(3)(c) is to be applied during the preliminary investigation, examined the features of the specific proceedings involved, observing that in the specific case the initial stage of police interrogation was of paramount importance:

The Court is of the opinion that the scheme contained in the Order is such that it is of paramount importance for the rights of the defence that an accused has access

50. *John Murray v. The United Kingdom*, Judgment of 8 February 1996.

> to a lawyer at the initial stages of police interrogation. It observes in this context that, under the Order, at the beginning of police interrogation, an accused is confronted with a fundamental dilemma relating to his defence. If he chooses to remain silent, adverse inferences may be drawn against him in accordance with the provisions of the Order. On the other hand, if the accused opts to break his silence during the course of interrogation, he runs the risk of prejudicing his defence without necessarily removing the possibility of inferences being drawn against him.
>
> (*John Murray v. The United Kingdom*, Judgment of 8 February 1996, paragraph 66)

Therefore, it noted that the principle of fairness as guaranteed by Article 6 requires that the accused have the right to the assistance of a lawyer already at the initial stages of police interrogation, and concluded that to deprive the accused of such assistance in the above mentioned circumstance is incompatible with the rights of the accused under Article 6(1) in conjunction with 6(3)(c), 'whatever the justification for such denial'.[51]

Similar reasoning was adopted by the Court in *Berlinski v. Poland*,[52] where the applicants complained on the fact that – despite their application – they were not granted free legal assistance for one year, and were eventually convicted:

> The Court observes that it is undisputed that the applicants lacked means to employ a private representative in the context of criminal proceedings against them. It is also uncontested that the applicants' request for an official lawyer to be appointed was ignored by the authorities, with the result that they had no defence counsel for more than a year. Given that a number of procedural acts, including questioning of the applicants and their medical examinations, were carried out during that period (see §§ 40-45 above), the Court finds no justification for this restriction which deprived the applicants of the right to adequately defend themselves during the investigation and trial.
>
> (*Berlinski v. Poland*, Judgment of 20 June 2002, paragraph 77)

Another interesting aspect of the right to legal representation is related to the right of the accused to communicate with his lawyer in private. Such right, as mentioned above, is not explicitly listed in Article 6 ECHR – differently from what happens in other Conventions, such as in Article 8(2)(d) of the American Convention on Human Rights, which provides that during criminal proceedings every accused person has also the right 'to communicate freely and privately with his counsel'. The ECtHR, however, has recognized that one of the basic aspects of the right of an accused to legal representation is to the confidentiality of the consultations with his lawyer, although it may be restricted where specific circumstances so require.

51. *Ibid.*, paragraphs 66 and 70. Similar reasoning and conclusions were expressed, among others, in *Averill v. The United Kingdom*, Judgment of 6 June 2006; *Magee v. The United Kingdom*, Judgment of 6 June 2000. *Contra*, see *Latimer v. The United Kingdom*, (Appl. No. 12141/04), Decision of 31 May 2005.
52. *Berlinski v. Poland*, Judgment of 20 June 2002.

For example, in *Brennan v. The United Kingdom*,[53] the Court found that Article 6(3)(c) was violated, for the following reasons:

> The Court has noted above (see paragraph 45) that Article 6 § 3 normally requires that an accused be allowed to benefit from the assistance of a lawyer at the initial stages of an interrogation. Furthermore, an accused's right to communicate with his advocate out of hearing of a third person is part of the basic requirements of a fair trial and follows from Article 6 § 3 (c). If a lawyer were unable to confer with his client and receive confidential instructions from him without surveillance, his assistance would lose much of its usefulness, whereas the Convention is intended to guarantee rights that are practical and effective (see S. v. Switzerland, judgment of 28 November 1991, Series A no. 220, p. 16, § 48). The importance to be attached to the confidentiality of such consultations, in particular that they should be conducted out of hearing of third persons, is illustrated by the international provisions cited above (see paragraphs 38-40). However, the Court's case-law indicates that the right of access to a solicitor may be subject to restrictions for good cause and the question in each case is whether the restriction, in the light of the entirety of the proceedings, has deprived the accused of a fair hearing. While it is not necessary for the applicant to prove, assuming such were possible, that the restriction had a prejudicial effect on the course of the trial, the applicant must be able to be claim to have been directly affected by the restriction in the exercise of the rights of the defence.
>
> (*Brennan v. The United Kingdom*, Judgment of 16 October 2001, paragraph 58)

Similarly, the Court decided in the previously mentioned *Öcalan v. Turkey*,[54] where it found that the accused's right to communicate in private with his lawyer had been violated because the applicant and his lawyers were unable to consult out of hearing of the authorities at any stage:

> Consequently, the Court holds that the fact that it was impossible for the applicant to confer with his lawyers out of the hearing of members of the security forces infringed the rights of the defence.
>
> (*Öcalan v. Turkey*, [Grand Chamber], Judgment of 12 May 2005, paragraph 133)

[E] The Right to Attendance and Examination of Witnesses

> Article 6(3)(d) – *[The right] to examine or have examined witnesses against him and to obtain the attendance and examination of witnesses on his behalf under the same conditions as witnesses against him.*

Article 6(3)(d) represents a specific aspect of the general principle of equality of arms, with regard to the right to witnesses' examination. It does not imply, that the accused has the right to examine all witnesses he intends to call in the proceedings, but that he should have the opportunity to challenge witnesses against him, either when he is

53. *Brennan v. The United Kingdom*, Judgment of 16 October 2001.
54. *Öcalan v. Turkey*, cited above.

making his statement or at a later stage of the proceedings.[55] Moreover, all evidence should be produced at a public hearing, in the presence of the accused, 'with a view to adversarial argument'.[56]

> Article 6 § 3 (d) enshrines the principle that, before an accused can be convicted, all evidence against him must normally be produced in his presence at a public hearing with a view to adversarial argument. The underlying principle is that the defendant in a criminal trial should have an effective opportunity to challenge the evidence against him. Exceptions to this principle are possible but must not infringe the rights of the defence, which, as a rule, require not merely that a defendant should know the identity of his accusers so that he is in a position to challenge their probity and credibility but that he should be able to test the truthfulness and reliability of their evidence, by having them orally examined in his presence, either at the time the witness was making the statement or at some later stage of the proceedings.
>
> (*Sievert v. Germany*, Judgment of 19 July 2012, paragraph 58)

It is important to note that the ECtHR is generally quite cautious when dealing with evidence issues. This is due to the fact that rules of evidence vary from State to State, and that a general European 'law of evidence' is still far from being established. In particular, such rules are very different depending on the criminal procedural system adopted by a State: the traditional distinction between adversarial and inquisitorial proceedings is probably the main obstacle to the realization of a uniform model of criminal trial in Europe.[57]

As previously noted, domestic courts assess the relevance of evidence brought before them and, therefore, can refuse to allow one or more witnesses deemed as not relevant.[58]

In this sense, the ECtHR has often remarked that its task is not to decide whether statements of witnesses have properly been admitted by national courts as evidence, but 'rather to ascertain whether the proceedings as a whole, including the way in which evidence was taken, were fair'.[59] It is therefore up to the national courts to decide whether or not to allow a party to call and examine witnesses.[60] The logical consequence of this principle is that it is not sufficient for the accused to complain that he has not been allowed to call one or more witnesses, being also needed that he demonstrates that such evidence is necessary to the establishment of the truth.[61]

---

55. See, among others, *Isgrò v. Italy*, Judgment of 19 February 1991, paragraph 34; *Van Mechelen and Others v. The Netherlands*, Judgment of 23 April 1997, paragraph 51.
56. See, among others, *PK v. Finland*, Appl. No. 37442/97, Decision of 9 July 2002.
57. For an interesting analysis on this subject, see, among others, Sarah J. Summers, *Fair Trials: The European Criminal Tradition and the European Court of Human Rights* (Oxford and Portland, Oregon: Hart Publishing, 2003), 132-136.
58. *Barberà, Messegué and Jabardo v. Spain*, Judgment of 6 December 1988, paragraph 68; *Asch v. Austria*, Judgment of 26 April 1991, paragraph 25; *Engel and Others v. the Netherlands*, Judgment of 8 June 1976, paragraph 91; *Vidal v. Belgium*, Judgment of 22 April 1992, paragraph 33.
59. See, among others, *Perna v. Italy* (Grand Chamber), Judgment of 6 May 2006, paragraph 29; *Van Mechelen and Others v. the Netherlands*, Judgment of 23 April 1997, paragraph 50.
60. *Vidal v. Belgium*, Judgment of 22 April 1992, paragraph 33.
61. See *Perna v. Italy*, cited above, paragraph 29; *Engel and Others v. the Netherlands*, Judgment of 8 June 1976, paragraph 91; *Bricmont v. Belgium*, Judgment of 7 July 1989, paragraph 89.

A fundamental principle in adversarial proceedings is – as it has been said – that evidence must be produced in the presence of the accused. However, the ECtHR has ruled that this does not mean that the witnesses' statements must be made during the trial. They can, on the contrary, also be collected in the pre-trial stage, provided that the accused right was protected in this stage, giving him the possibility to examine the witnesses.

In *Unterpertinger v. Austria*,[62] the applicant complained on that he had been convicted on the basis of statements made by his former wife and step-daughter to the police. He alleged that the witnesses had refused to give evidence during the trial (being close relatives), the consequence of which was that he had not had any possibility to examine them.

The ECtHR found that the domestic provisions (Article 152(1)(1) of the Austrian Code of Criminal Procedure) entitling the applicant's relatives to refuse evidence was not in contrast with the ECHR, because it was aimed at protecting the witness to face the 'moral dilemma':

> This accordingly prevented the trial judge from hearing them as witnesses and prevented the defence – and the prosecution – from examining them during the oral proceedings. As such, the provision manifestly is not incompatible with Article 6 §§ 1 and 3 (d) (art. 6-1, art. 6-3-d) of the Convention: it makes allowance for the special problems that may be entailed by a confrontation between someone 'charged with a criminal offence' and a witness from his own family and is calculated to protect such a witness by avoiding his being put in a moral dilemma; furthermore, there are comparable provisions in the domestic law of several member States of the Council of Europe.
>
> (*Unterpertinger v. Austria*, Judgment of 24 November 1986, paragraph 30)

In the case at hand, both the trial court and the Court of Appeal were unable to hear evidence from the applicant's relatives, but their statements – as previously given to the police – were read out during the trial upon request of the prosecution.

The ECtHR found that the reading out of the statements in itself is not inconsistent with Article 6(1) and (3)(d), provided that the use of such statements as evidence comply with the rights of the defence:[63]

> This is especially so where the person 'charged with a criminal offence', who has the right under Article 6 § 3 (d) (art. 6-3-d) to 'examine or have examined' witnesses against him, has not had an opportunity at any stage in the earlier proceedings to question the persons whose statements are read out at the hearing.
>
> (*Unterpertinger v. Austria*, Judgment of 24 November 1986, paragraph 31)

The Court then noted that it was clear from the judgment that the Court of Appeal had based the applicant's conviction mainly on the statements made by the applicant's relatives to the police, and concluded that the applicant's defence rights had been violated:

62. *Unterpertinger v. Austria*, Judgment of 24 November 1986.
63. On this principle, see also *Kostovski v. The Netherlands*, Judgment of 20 November 1989, paragraph 41.

> It did not treat these simply as items of information but as proof of the truth of the accusations made by the women at the time. Admittedly, it was for the Court of Appeal to assess the material before it as well as the relevance of the evidence which the accused sought to adduce; but Mr. Unterpertinger was nevertheless convicted on the basis of 'testimony' in respect of which his defence rights were appreciably restricted.
>
> That being so, the applicant did not have a fair trial and there was a breach of paragraph 1 of Article 6 (art. 6-1) of the Convention, taken together with the principles inherent in paragraph 3 (d) (art. 6-3-d).
>
> (*Unterpertinger v. Austria*, Judgment of 24 November 1986, paragraph 33)

Although the Court affirmed that examination of witnesses in a pre-trial stage is not, in itself, inconsistent with the principles enshrined in Article 6 ECHR, it cannot be underestimated that such practice seems to be incompatible with the principle of 'immediacy', e.g., the guarantee that in criminal proceedings the accused has the right to be confronted with the witnesses before an impartial judge, who will decide the case.

The importance of the principle of immediacy has been recalled by the ECtHR in some of its decisions. For example, in *PK v. Finland*[64] the Court, in declaring the application inadmissible, observed:

> The Court considers that an important element of fair criminal proceedings is also the possibility of the accused to be confronted with the witness in the presence of the judge who ultimately decides the case. Such a principle of immediacy is an important guarantee in criminal proceedings in which the observations made by the court about the demeanour and credibility of a witness may have important consequences for the accused. Therefore, normally a change in the composition of the trial court after the hearing of an important witness should lead to the rehearing of that witness.
>
> (*PK v. Finland*, Appl. No. 37442/97, Decision of 9 July 2002)

Another principle affirmed by the Judges of Strasbourg is that a conviction based on the testimony of anonymous witnesses constitutes a breach of Article 6(3)(d). In *Krasniki v. The Czech Republic*,[65] the applicant complained that his conviction had been based exclusively on the declarations of an anonymous witness, and that his lawyer had been denied the possibility either to see the anonymous witnesses during their testimony or to know their identity.

The ECtHR recalled the principles already affirmed in its previous case law,[66] according to which that 'the use of statements made by anonymous witnesses to found

64. *PK v. Finland*, Appl. No. 37442/97, cited above.
65. *Krasniki v. The Czech Republic*, Judgment of 28 February 2006.
66. *Van Mechelen and Others v. The Netherlands*, Judgment of 23 April 1997, paragraph 52; *Doorson v. the Netherlands*, Judgment of 26 March 1996, paragraphs 69-76. See, in particular, the following passage of the *Doorson* Judgment:

> It is true that Article 6 (art. 6) does not explicitly require the interests of witnesses in general, and those of victims called upon to testify in particular, to be taken into consideration. However, their life, liberty or security of person may be at stake, as may interests coming generally within the ambit of Article 8 (art. 8) of the Convention. Such interests of witnesses and victims are in principle protected by other, substantive

a conviction is not in all circumstances incompatible with the Convention', provided that 'the handicaps under which the defence operates ... be sufficiently counterbalanced by the procedures followed by the judicial authorities'.[67] The Court then remarked that 'no conviction should be based either *solely or to a decisive extent* on anonymous statements'[68] (author's italics), and – considering all the circumstances of the specific case – concluded that the proceedings as a whole were unfair:

> In addition, the Court observes that the District Court based the applicant's conviction solely or at least to a decisive extent on the anonymous testimonies. Yet the Court notes that the decision of the Regional Court upholding the first-instance judgment was not based on any new evidence from identified sources.
>
> In the light of the above conclusion, the Court does not find it necessary to examine further whether the procedures introduced by the judicial authorities could have sufficiently counterbalanced the difficulties faced by the defence as a result of the anonymity of the witnesses (see, mutatis mutandis, Visser v. the Netherlands, cited above, § 51, with further references to Kok v. the Netherlands, cited above).
>
> The Court thus concludes that the proceedings as a whole were unfair.
>
> (*Krasniki v. The Czech Republic*, Judgment of 28 February 2006, paragraphs 84-86)

[F] The Right to the Free Assistance of an Interpreter

> Article 6(3)(e) – *[The right] to have the free assistance of an interpreter if he cannot understand or speak the language used in court.*

As previously discussed, according to Article 6(3)(a), any person charged with a criminal offence has the right 'to be informed promptly, in a language which he understands and in detail, of the nature and cause of the accusation against him'.

The ECtHR noted that the above provision does not specify whether the information should be given in writing, but remarked that the notification of the indictment to the defendant plays a crucial role in criminal proceedings, with the consequence that 'a defendant not familiar with the language used by the court may be at a practical disadvantage if the indictment is not translated into a language which he understands'.[69]

Paragraph 3(e) of Article 6 goes further, and provides that the defendant has the right to the free assistance of an interpreter, if he cannot 'understand' or 'speak' the language used in the court. This guarantee applies, according to the jurisprudence of the ECtHR, not only to oral statements made during the trial hearing, but also to

> provisions of the Convention, which imply that Contracting States should organise their criminal proceedings in such a way that those interests are not unjustifiably imperilled. Against this background, principles of fair trial also require that in appropriate cases the interests of the defence are balanced against those of witnesses or victims called upon to testify. (paragraph 70).

67. *Krasniki v. The Czech Republic*, cited above, paragraph 76.
68. *Ibid.*, paragraph 76; *Van Mechelen and Others*, cited above, paragraphs 54-55.
69. See, *ex multis*, *Hermi v. Italy* (Grand Chamber), Judgment of 18 October 2006, paragraph 68.

documentary evidence and to the pre-trial stage in general. It does not imply, however, that the defendant has the right to have 'translated' all the written documents in the procedure, but only that he must be put in the position 'to have knowledge of the case against him and to defend himself':

> This means that an accused who cannot understand or speak the language used in court has the right to the free assistance of an interpreter for the translation or interpretation of all those documents or statements in the proceedings instituted against him which it is necessary for him to understand or to have rendered into the court's language in order to have the benefit of a fair trial (see *Luedicke, Belkacem and Koç v. Germany*, 28 November 1978, § 48, Series A no. 29).
>
> However, paragraph 3 (e) does not go so far as to require a written translation of all items of written evidence or official documents in the procedure. In that connection, it should be noted that the text of the relevant provisions refers to an 'interpreter', not a 'translator'. This suggests that oral linguistic assistance may satisfy the requirements of the Convention (see *Husain v. Italy* (dec.), no. 18913/03, 24 February 2005). The fact remains, however, that the interpretation assistance provided should be such as to enable the defendant to have knowledge of the case against him and to defend himself, notably by being able to put before the court his version of the events.
>
> (*Hermi v. Italy* [Grand Chamber], Judgment of 18 October 2006, paragraphs 69-70)

In *Cuscani v. the United Kingdom*,[70] the applicant complained that he had not been granted an interpreter during the proceedings against him, and that, therefore, he had not been able to understand and follow the trial proceedings. In particular, he alleged that the trial judge had been clearly informed by his lawyer that he had a 'very poor' command of English,[71] after which the judge decided to grant him an interpreter. However, the interpreter failed to appear at the scheduled hearing, and the judge directed to proceed anyway (also relying on the possibility for the defendant to avail of the linguistic assistance of the brother).

The ECtHR found that Article 6(1) and (3)(e) were violated, on the grounds that it was task of the trial judge – who is the actual 'guardian of the fairness of the proceedings' – to ensure that the absence of an interpreter at a crucial hearing would not prejudice the applicant's right to a fair trial:

> The Court observes that the applicant's alleged lack of proficiency in English and his inability to understand the proceedings became a live issue for the first time on 4 January 1996 when the trial court was informed by his legal team that the applicant wished to enter a guilty plea to the charges brought against him. At the request of the applicant's counsel, the trial judge directed that an interpreter be present at the hearing on sentence to be held on 26 January 1996 (see paragraphs 15 and 16 above). The judge was thus put on clear notice that the applicant had problems of comprehension. However, notwithstanding his earlier concern to ensure that the applicant could follow the subsequent proceedings it would appear

70. *Cuscani v. The United Kingdom*, Judgment of 24 September 2002.
71. *Ibid.*, paragraphs 14 and 37.

that the judge allowed himself to be persuaded by the applicant's counsel's confidence in his ability to 'make do and mend' (see paragraph 17 above). Admittedly, the trial judge left open the possibility of the applicant having recourse to the linguistic assistance of his brother if the need arose. However, in the Court's opinion the verification of the applicant's need for interpretation facilities was a matter for the judge to determine in consultation with the applicant, especially since he had been alerted to counsel's own difficulties in communicating with the applicant. It is to be noted that the applicant had pleaded guilty to serious charges and faced a heavy prison sentence. The onus was thus on the judge to reassure himself that the absence of an interpreter at the hearing on 26 January 1996 would not prejudice the applicant's full involvement in a matter of crucial importance for him. In the circumstances of the instant case, that requirement cannot be said to have been satisfied by leaving it to the applicant, and without the judge having consulted the latter, to invoke the untested language skills of his brother.

It is true that the conduct of the defence is essentially a matter between the defendant and his counsel, whether counsel be appointed under a legal aid scheme as in the applicant's case or be privately financed (see the Kamasinski v. Austria judgment of 19 December 1989, Series A no. 168, pp. 32-33, § 65; the Stanford v. the United Kingdom judgment of 23 February 1994, Series A 282-A, p. 11, § 28). However, the ultimate guardian of the fairness of the proceedings was the trial judge who had been clearly apprised of the real difficulties which the absence of interpretation might create for the applicant. It further observes that the domestic courts have already taken the view that in circumstances such as those in the instant case, judges are required to treat an accused's interest with 'scrupulous care' (see paragraphs 32 and 33 above).

Having regard to the above considerations, the Court concludes that there has been a violation of Article 6 § 1 of the Convention taken in conjunction with Article 6 § 3(e).

(*Cuscani v. The United Kingdom*, Judgment of 24 September 2002, paragraphs 38-40)

The wording of Article 6(3)(e) is clear in stating that the accused has right to the 'free' assistance of an interpreter. Therefore, granting the assistance of an interpreter but charging at the same time its costs on the accused has been considered a violation of the provision under examination.

In *Luedicke, Belkacem and Koc v. Germany*,[72] the Commission unanimously reached the conclusion that Article 6(3)(e) had been violated by the German courts, which had granted the three accused the assistance of interpreters, and ordered the applicants - after their conviction - to pay the related costs.

The Court agreed with the findings of the Commission, on the grounds that 'free' assistance ('*gratuitement*' in the French text) means nothing but free of any charge, once and for all, and not only temporarily (consequently, the accused person cannot be obliged to pay the costs of interpretation once he has been convicted):

The Court finds, as did the Commission, that the terms 'gratuitement'/'free' in Article 6 para. 3 (e) (art. 6-3-e) have in themselves a clear and determinate meaning. In French, 'gratuitement' signifies 'd'une manière gratuite, qu'on donne pour rien, sans rétribution' (Littré, Dictionnaire de la langue française), 'dont on jouit sans payer' (Hatzfeld et Darmesteter, Dictionnaire général de la langue

72. *Luedicke, Belkacem and Koc v. Germany*, Judgment of 28 November 1978.

> française), 'à titre gratuit, sans avoir rien à payer', the opposite of 'à titre onéreux' (Larousse, Dictionnaire de la langue française), 'd'une manière gratuite; sans rétribution, sans contrepartie' (Robert, Dictionnaire alphabétique et analogique de la langue française). Similarly, in English, 'free' means 'without payment, gratuitous' (Shorter Oxford Dictionary), 'not costing or charging anything, given or furnished without cost or payment' (Webster's Third New International Dictionary).
>
> Consequently, the Court cannot but attribute to the terms 'gratuitement' and 'free' the unqualified meaning they ordinarily have in both of the Court's official languages: these terms denote neither a conditional remission, nor a temporary exemption, nor a suspension, but a once and for all exemption or exoneration. It nevertheless remains to be determined whether, as the Government contend the context as well as the object and purpose of the provision in issue negative the literal interpretation.
>
> (*Luedicke, Belkacem and Koc v. Germany*, Judgment of 28 November 1978, paragraph 40)

The Court went further, affirming that the right to the assistance of an interpreter is not limited to the hearing, but applies also to other stages of the proceedings, and therefore to other interpretation costs:

> Before the Court a difference of opinion emerged between the Government and the Commission as to which costs come within the scope of Article 6 para. 3 (e) (art. 6-3-e). In the Government's submission, Article 6 para. 3 (e) (art. 6-3-e) 'unambiguously and expressly settles the assistance of an interpreter at the oral hearing (audience)' but does not apply to other interpretation costs.
>
> The Government's contention, the correctness of which is contested by the Delegates, cannot be accepted by the Court. Article 6 para. 3 (e) (art. 6-3-e) does not state that every accused person has the right to receive the free assistance of an interpreter at the oral hearing (à l'audience); it states that this right is accorded to him 'if he cannot understand or speak the language used in court' ('s'il ne comprend pas ou ne parle pas la langue employée à l'audience'). As was pointed out by the Delegates, the latter words do no more than indicate the conditions for the granting of the free assistance of an interpreter. Furthermore, the English text 'used in court', being wider than the French expression 'employée à l'audience' (literally translated as 'used at the hearing'), furnishes an additional argument in this respect.
>
> Construed in the context of the right to a fair trial guaranteed by Article 6, paragraph 3 (e) (art. 6-3-e) signifies that an accused who cannot understand or speak the language used in court has the right to the free assistance of an interpreter for the translation or interpretation of all those documents or statements in the proceedings instituted against him which it is necessary for him to understand in order to have the benefit of a fair trial.
>
> (*Luedicke, Belkacem and Koc v. Germany*, Judgment of 28 November 1978, paragraph 48)

[G] The Prohibition of a Double Jeopardy

The principle prohibiting 'double jeopardy', e.g., the repetition of criminal proceedings that have been concluded by a final decision, is not included in Article 6 ECHR, but in Article 4 of Protocol No. 7 to the Convention, which reads as follows:

(1) No one shall be liable to be tried or punished again in criminal proceedings under the jurisdiction of the same State for an offence for which he has already been finally acquitted or convicted in accordance with the law and penal procedure of that State.
(2) The provisions of the preceding paragraph shall not prevent the reopening of the case in accordance with the law and penal procedure of the State concerned, if there is evidence of new or newly discovered facts, or if there has been a fundamental defect in the previous proceedings, which could affect the outcome of the case.
(3) No derogation from this Article shall be made under Article 15 of the Convention.

The principle in question is, however, undoubtedly connected with the right to a fair trial and, in fact, in several occasions the ECtHR has examined it conjointly with Article 6(3) (in particular with the presumption of innocence). For example, among others, in *Sievert v. Germany* the Court remarked that 'the presumption of innocence is consubstantial with and thus inseparable from the banning of double jeopardy (*ne bis in idem*)'.[73]

The ECtHR established jurisprudence is in the sense that 'the aim of Article 4 of Protocol No. 7 is to prohibit the repetition of criminal proceedings that have been concluded by a final decision'.[74]

In defining when a decision is 'final', the Court recalls the explanatory report to Protocol No. 7, stating that a decision is 'final' when it has acquired the force of *res judicata* and is therefore 'irrevocable' (when no further ordinary remedies are available to the parties):

> According to the explanatory report to Protocol No. 7, which itself refers back to the European Convention on the International Validity of Criminal Judgments, a 'decision is final "if, according to the traditional expression, it has acquired the force of *res judicata*. This is the case when it is irrevocable, that is to say when no further ordinary remedies are available or when the parties have exhausted such remedies or have permitted the time-limit to expire without availing themselves of them"'.
>
> (*Nikitin v. Russia*, Judgment of 29 July 2004, paragraph 37)

In *Menelaou v. Cyprus*,[75] the ECtHR considered the applicant's complaint manifestly ill-founded and thus declared the application as inadmissible. This decision is however interesting for the analysis made by the Court on the scope and purpose of Article 4 of Protocol No. 7 to the Convention.

The applicant complained on the fact that, notwithstanding the discharge of the case by the Assize Court on 24 October 2003, the Supreme Court had subsequently ordered the Assize Court to re-hear his case.

73. *Sievert v. Germany*, Judgment of 19 July 2012, paragraph 11.
74. See, *ex multis*, *Oliveira v. Switzerland*, Judgment of 30 July 1998; *Sundqvist v. Finland*, Appl. No. 75602/01, Decision of 22 November 2005; *Muller v. Germany* (2), Judgment of 18 September 2008.
75. *Menelaou v. Cyprus*, Appl. 34071/04, Decision of 12 June 2008.

The ECtHR, recalling its established case law on the subject matter,[76] determined that in the case in question no 'final' decision (*res judicata*) had been issued by the domestic courts, with the consequence that the principle of double jeopardy had not been violated:

> The Court observes that the judgment of the Assize Court, by which the discharge of the applicant was ordered, was not final but remained subject to the right of the prosecution to contest it by lodging an appeal before the Supreme Court. The prosecution did lodge such an appeal, which was in fact successful, leading to the setting aside of the decision of the Assize Court. Hence, Article 4 of Protocol No. 7 has no application to the facts of the present case.
>
> Accordingly, the Court considers that this complaint is manifestly ill-founded and must be rejected in accordance with Article 35 §§ 3 and 4 of the Convention.
>
> (*Menelaou v. Cyprus*, Appl. No. 34071/04, Decision of 12 June 2008, paragraph B[1])

[H] The Right of Appeal to an Higher Court

Article 2 of Protocol No. 7 to the Convention reads as follows:

1. Everyone convicted of a criminal offence by a tribunal shall have the right to have his conviction or sentence reviewed by a higher tribunal. The exercise of this right, including the grounds on which it may be exercised, shall be governed by law.
2. This right may be subject to exceptions in regard to offences of a minor character, as prescribed by law, or in cases in which the person concerned was tried in the first instance by the highest tribunal or was convicted following an appeal against acquittal.

The right provided by Article 2 of Protocol No. 7 to the Convention is, like the principle of *ne bis in idem* under Article 4 of the same Protocol, often connected with the right to a fair trial in general, and as such it has been often examined by the ECtHR.[77]

Moreover, the explanatory report of Protocol No. 7 states, *inter alia*, that Article 2, as compared with the wording of the corresponding provisions of the United Nations Covenant (Article 14, paragraph 5), contains in addition the word 'tribunal', 'to show clearly that this provision does not concern offences which have been tried by bodies which are not tribunals within the meaning of Article 6 of the Convention'.

As far as the relation between the provision in question and Article 13 ECHR is concerned, the Court has often noted that Article 13 of the Convention does not, as such, guarantee a right of appeal or a right to a second level of jurisdiction,[78] but, when the impugned proceedings are to be considered as criminal in the meaning of the Convention, Article 2 of Protocol No. 7 shall apply.[79]

---

76. See, other than the already mentioned *Sundqvist v. Finland*, *Gradinger v. Austria*, Judgment of 23 October 1995, paragraph 53.
77. See, *ex multis*, *Gurepka v. Ukraine*, Judgment of 6 September 2005, paragraphs 41-46.
78. See, among others, *Kopczynski v. Poland*, Appl. No. 28863/95, Decision of 1 July 1998; *Csepyová v. Slovakia*, Appl. No. 67199/01, Decision of 14 May 2002.
79. *Gurepka v. Ukraine*, cited above, paragraphs 50-56.

In *Krombach v. France*,[80] the applicant was convicted *in absentia* by the Paris Assize Court, for the offence of involuntary homicide. The applicant complained - *inter alia* - that according to Article 636 of the Code of Criminal Procedure, it was impossible to appeal to the Court of Cassation against a conviction by an assize court after a trial *in absentia*, which violated the provision under Article 2 of Protocol No. 7 to the Convention.

The ECtHR recalled the principle according to which it is left to the Contracting States a wide margin of discretion in determining how the right under Article 2 of Protocol No. 7 shall be exercised. However - the Court noted - similarly to what happens with the right of access to a court under Article 6(1), possible restrictions by national law must pursue a legitimate aim and not infringe the very essence of the right in question.

The Court then observed that, although French law allowed appeals against a verdict of the Court of Assize only on points of law (and therefore, it complied *in abstracto* with Article 2 of Protocol No. 7), in the specific case the applicant had no right of appeal to the Court of Cassation against defects in the trial *in absentia* itself, and therefore concluded that there had been a violation of Article 2 of Protocol No. 7:

> By virtue of Articles 630 and 639 of the Code of Criminal Procedure taken together (see paragraph 59 above) the applicant, on the one hand, could not be and was not represented in the Assize Court by a lawyer (see paragraph 46 above), and, on the other, was unable to appeal to the Court of Cassation as he was a defendant *in absentia*. He therefore had no real possibility of being defended at first instance or of having his conviction reviewed by a higher court.
>
> (*Krombach v. France*, Judgment of 13 February 2001, paragraph 100)

In a number of cases against Bulgaria, where the applicant complained of not having been allowed to file an appeal against a verdict of guilty for an offence considered by Bulgarian law as an administrative offence, the ECtHR found that certain administrative violations under Bulgarian law were to be considered as criminal offences within the meaning of Article 2 of Protocol No. 7 (in particular, the offence in question was almost identical to the criminal offence of 'hooliganism' and led to a penalty of imprisonment). The Court then noted that under the Bulgarian law at that time, there was no possibility to appeal against a conviction under that law, and concluded that there had been a breach of Article 2 of Protocol No. 7.[81]

80. *Krombach v. France*, Judgment of 13 February 2001.
81. See *Zhelyazkov v. Bulgaria*, Judgment of 9 October 2012, paragraphs 39-45; *Kambourov v. Bulgaria (no. 2)*, Judgment of 23 April 2009, paragraphs 22-27; *Stanchev v. Bulgaria*, Judgment of 1 October 2009, paragraphs 44-49.

CHAPTER 5

Conflict between Particular Aspects of the Right to a Fair Trial

Ondrej Pridal

In Chapter 3, we described the distinctive features of the right to a fair trial. In an ideal situation, the individual elements of the right to a fair trial are mutually supportive. Sometimes, however, a situation occurs when they are in conflict, and this conflict has to be resolved. Since particular aspects of the right to a fair trial are of equivalent or even identical nature, we can in theory use the same methods for the resolution of a conflict of principles.[1]

A conflict of principles occurs if the actions of the court fulfil one or more principles but at the same time violate[2] one or more other principles. This means that one or more principles support particular acts of the court, while - at the same time - other principle(s) support different acts. The judge must then decide which of the principles will prevail. It must be emphasized that no principle, and no fundamental right, has an absolute character. In this sense also, their applicability is limited, as it is their enforceability, since other legally protected - general or individual interests - must be respected as well.

The possibility of conflict between individual aspects of the right to a fair trial was foreseen by the drafters.[3] An example can be seen in Article 6, paragraph 1, last sentence of the Convention, where the right to a publicly pronounced judgment is deemed to potentially conflict with other principles:

1. Other Authors also deal with procedural principles of a fair trial. We are aware of some simplifications, which this leads to. See, on the subject matter: P. Holländer, *Základy všeobecné státovědy* [*Introduction to the General Theory of State*] (Plzeň: Aleš Ceněk, 2009), 127.
2. The word 'violates' should be treated with caution, because quite often even experienced lawyers do not agree on what the content of this or that principle is. It might therefore suffice to say that one principle withdrew to another, without being derogated.
3. Conflict of principles, of course, has its own importance in law-making.

> Judgment shall be pronounced publicly but the press and public may be excluded from all or part of the trial in the interests of morals, public order or national security in a democratic society, where the interests of juveniles or the protection of the private life of the parties so require, or to the extent strictly necessary in the opinion of the court in special circumstances where publicity would prejudice the interests of justice.

Conflicting principles may be decided through compromise. However, this conflict is usually solved by giving preference to one of the conflicting principles over the other(s), which can be called the 'subordination' of a principle. Court decisions could then be challenged by focusing on the alleged improper suppression of a principle, as this would constitute a violation of fundamental human rights and freedoms.

In the following sections we will describe possible conflicts between particular aspects of the right to a fair trial, as they might occur especially in civil proceedings. We will not examine a specific model of a particular State, since each national judicial system has its own peculiarities, but we will try to highlight how the main principles apply, as a general rule, and how they may go into conflict.

§5.01 INDIVIDUAL CONFLICTS

Compliance with any principle is always linked to compliance with certain rules, procedures, and legal institutions in order to give all parties the opportunity to make use of the principle. But this often occurs at the cost of time, and affects the swiftness of proceedings. Thus, it can be said that any principle detrimentally affects the swiftness of proceedings and is therefore in conflict with the right to receive a decision within a reasonable time. The question immediately arises, whether it is acceptable or not acceptable to violate some of the principles in certain situations, just in order to expedite the proceedings (which anyway would have the same result). This question is intended to provoke a theoretical scientific discussion with an ethical dimension, while it is certainly not our intention to give instructions on how and when to violate one of these principles. We believe that results from this discussion could have a possible outcome *de lege ferenda*.

Similarly, the duty of the court to instruct the parties is inherent in all the principles and is their important adjunct, because without it the participants in some situations would have been unable to exercise the given principle at all. Granting precedence of one principle over the other would constitute a violation of the principle of 'perception of conduct of proceedings as fair by parties,' in case a violation of the principle were to be perceived by the participants.

[A] Rules of Evidence versus Equality of Arms

According to the rules of evidence present in the national legislation of all states, the one who is alleging something is the one who has to prove the allegation – the burden of proof rests with him (*affirmanti incumbit probation*). Anti-discrimination laws have usually reversed this burden of proof in favour of a party alleging that he was directly or indirectly discriminated due to his sex, racial or ethnic origin, religion, belief, worldview, disability, age or sexual orientation. Article 1 § 4 of Council Directive 97/80/EC of 15 December 1997 reads:

> Member States shall take such measures as are necessary, in accordance with their national judicial systems, to ensure that, when persons who consider themselves wronged because the principle of equal treatment has not been applied to them establish, before a court or other competent authority, facts from which it may be presumed that there has been direct or indirect discrimination, it shall be for the respondent to prove that there has been no breach of the principle of equal treatment.

It is, therefore, sufficient that the claimant allege discrimination and be able to provide facts from which the form of discrimination could be presumed. Then the respondent has to prove the opposite: i.e., that there had been no discrimination since he had fulfilled all requirements to prevent it. The respondent can thus find himself in the difficult situation of having to prove so-called negative facts.

Accordingly, discrimination cases are an example of a conflict between two aspects of the right to a fair trial: the rules of evidence (as part of the right to a fair hearing) and the principle of equality of arms. When balancing these two aspects, the criterion of suitability has to be applied, based on which we can conclude that restricting rules of evidence will facilitate achievement of the goal: i.e., protecting people facing discrimination by improving their position in evidentiary proceedings. There is no other possibility for accomplishing that goal, because there are often no witnesses in cases of discrimination.

We can assess this conflict by applying the principle of proportionality.[4] When examining the gravity of both aspects, we find that they are *prima facie* of the same value. Nevertheless, discrimination is nowadays a serious problem, which causes not only tremendous grief, but also has a serious economic impact (empirical argument). If the burden of proof is not shifted, there is the risk that courts will not be able to decide otherwise than to reject discrimination claims: discrimination often occurs without witnesses and places the victim in a difficult life situation. The claimant may be suffering severely and shy away from speaking about it. Thus, procedural 'help' is necessary to equalize his position with the respondent. This is often called the principle of protecting the weaker (systemic and contextual argument).

Conclusion: There are more arguments than not for shifting the burden of proof to the respondent. This result was repeatedly confirmed by the ECtHR; for example, the ruling in the case of *D.H. and Others v. The Czech Republic*[5] stated:

> Where an applicant alleging indirect discrimination thus establishes a rebuttable presumption that the effect of a measure or practice is discriminatory, the burden then shifts to the respondent State, which must show that the difference in treatment is not discriminatory (see, mutatis mutandis, Nachova and Others, cited above, § 157).Regard being had in particular to the specificity of the facts and the nature of the allegations made in this type of case (ibid., § 147), it would be

4. See in detail below, subchapter §5.02 Conflict resolutions.
5. *D.H. and Others v. The Czech Republic*, Judgment of 13 November 2007.

extremely difficult in practice for applicants to prove indirect discrimination without such a shift in the burden of proof.

(*D.H. and Others v. The Czech Republic*, Judgment of 13 November 2007, paragraph 189)

[B] Hearing versus Economy of Proceedings

Article 6(1) ECHR provides: 'In the determination of his civil rights and obligations... everyone is entitled to a fair ... hearing ...'.

In some types of civil proceedings, however, conducting a proper hearing involves serious difficulties. For example, in a class action, properly conducting a hearing with numerous claimants, and always giving each of them the floor, might be impossible or, at least, extremely time-consuming and contrary to the principle of the economy of proceedings.

Or, in the event that a participant is imprisoned, a conflict may arise between the right to a hearing and the economy of proceedings.[6] A resolution of this conflict was reached by the ECtHR in *Pashayev v. Azerbaijan*,[7] where the ECtHR reiterated that the right to attend proceedings in a civil court in person is not guaranteed *per se* by Article 6:

> Article 6 of the Convention does not guarantee the right to attend a civil court in person, but rather a more general right to present one's case effectively before a court and to enjoy equality of arms with the opposing side. Article 6 § 1 leaves to the State a choice of the means to be used in guaranteeing litigants these rights (see Steel and Morris v. the United Kingdom, no. 68416/01, §§ 59-60, ECHR 2005-II).
>
> (*Pashayev v. Azerbaijan*, Judgment of 28 February 2012, paragraph 64)

This means that a hearing is not always necessary if the rights of the litigants are guaranteed by other means. Thus, a State can organize its class action even without a hearing, or make other arrangements, such as compulsory representation, joint representation, limited speech of each participant, mandatory joinder of parties when the actions of one are valid also for the others, etc.

When comparing the right to a hearing with the economy of proceedings (taking into account the relative gravity and hierarchy of the principles), different types of arguments can be brought. From an empirical point of view, courts are facing an ever increasing caseload. A systemic argument shows that the right to a fair trial constitutes a general instrument for the protection of fundamental rights. A contextual argument indicates that not having a hearing might lead to a serious infringement of the right to a fair trial.

Therefore, usually the hearing is a desideratum for with at least some claimants in the case of class actions. This is especially true when the claim is based on the

6. In *Schuler-Zgraggen v. Switzerland*, Judgment of 24 June 1993, paragraph 58, the ECtHR considered as legitimate that the national authorities should have regard to the demands of efficiency and economy in the sense of not having a hearing.
7. *Pashayev v. Azerbaijan*, Judgment of 28 February 2012.

personal experience of the claimant, and his testimony can be decisive for the resolution of his claim and cannot be replaced by documentary evidence.

In *Kovalev v. Russia,*[8] the claimant intended to defend himself by stating that he had been ill-treated while in police custody. The ECtHR found that that there had been a violation of the applicant's right to a fair hearing, as guaranteed by Article 6(1) ECHR, because the nature of the claim required the claimant's presence at the hearing:

> A distinction must be made, in this respect, between claims that are not genuine and serious (see Skorobogatykh v. Russia, cited above, and the Court's finding in paragraphs 28 and 29 above) and claims that are unlikely to succeed for lack of evidence. Given that the applicant's claim was, by its nature, largely based on his personal experience, his statement would have been an important part of the plaintiff's presentation of the case, and virtually the only way to ensure adversarial proceedings. In refusing to order his attendance, the domestic courts therefore failed to ensure a fair hearing of the applicant's claim.
>
> (*Kovalev v. Russia*, Judgment of 10 May 2007, paragraph 37)

In some types of cases, it is justifiable not to have a hearing: for example, in cases concerning benefits under social-security schemes, because the nature of these cases is rather technical, involving numerous figures and often depending upon expert written opinions. This was reiterated in *Miller v. Sweden:*[9]

> The exceptional character of the circumstances that may justify dispensing with an oral hearing essentially comes down to the nature of the issues to be decided by the competent national court, not to the frequency of such situations. It does not mean that refusing to hold an oral hearing may be justified only in rare cases. For example, the Court has recognised that disputes concerning benefits under social security schemes are generally rather technical, often involving numerous figures, and their outcome usually depends on the written opinions given by medical doctors. Many such disputes may accordingly be better dealt with in writing than in oral argument. Moreover, it is understandable that in this sphere the national authorities should have regard to the demands of efficiency and economy. Systematically holding hearings could be an obstacle to the particular diligence required in social-security cases (see the following judgments cited above: Schuler Zgraggen pp. 19 20, § 58; Salomonsson, § 38; Lundevall, § 38; and Döry, § 41).
>
> (*Miller v. Sweden*, Judgment of 8 February 200, paragraph 29)

For the above reasons, courts dealing with class actions always have to consider carefully whether to conduct proceedings without a hearing. In such cases, it is first necessary to evaluate the nature of the claim and determine whether proceedings without the presence of the participants, respectively their representatives, would infringe their right to a fair trial, and whether the advantages, such as saved time and means, would justify this decision. In other words, it is important to carefully weigh up both principles. Still, the party must have the possibility to apply for a hearing. Finally,

8. *Kovalev v. Russia*, Judgment of 10 May 2007.
9. *Miller v. Sweden*, Judgment of 8 February 2005.

it should be noted that even for class actions, having a hearing is the preferred way to conduct proceedings.

[C] Swiftness versus Lawful Judge

The principle of 'no one shall be denied his lawful judge' provides a fundamental guarantee of a fair trial. It entails that selection of courts and judges 'ad hoc' – for different reasons and different purposes – may not be implemented. Multiple factors must be applied to ensure that this principle is fully realized: numerous procedural provisions of the subject matter, functional and territorial jurisdiction, and composition of panels. Naturally, this sometimes causes unnecessary delays, publicly known as 'Judicial Ping-Pong,' when the courts toss cases from one to another. Procedural Codes and related regulations usually provide for mechanisms establishing which court and judge is in charge of deciding a case. The question, however, is whether delays in the proceedings[10] are worthwhile, and whether it would be preferable for the case to be decided by the first court, which would mean that priority is given to the right to a decision within a reasonable time.

The conflict is further highlighted by the following example: A petty monetary claim is filed, involving the non-payment of utilities bills or fares in public transport where the respondent's place of residence is located within the judicial circuit of a different court. First, a certain period of time elapses before the first court will deal with the matter. Then the court finds it has no territorial jurisdiction and rules accordingly. Afterwards, the decision is served, and when the decision is effective, the case is forwarded to another court. More time elapses. The second court will now consider the possibility of disagreeing with the transfer of the case and several additional months are lost. At first glance, it seems that no negative consequence would arise if the dispute were resolved by the initial court; moreover, the time and work of the second court's staff would have been saved. However, further scrutiny shows that such an outcome would mean that the dispute has been decided by an unlawful judge, with which goes the possibility of manipulation in the choice of the judge and the possible loss of the specialization of a particular judge. While it could be argued that these facts would not constitute a major problem in petty cases, there is nevertheless the breach of a principle, making it difficult to draw a line: when it is possible to violate the principle of being tried by a lawful judge in one case, it may be possible also in other cases.

We can establish that weakening the principle of lawful judge is capable of accelerating the proceedings following a criterion of suitability. Using a second criterion (of necessity) should provide an answer as to whether there are other possibilities for a lawmaker to solve this issue. This answer is unclear, as there could be a provision which prevents the court from referring cases *ex officio* to another court. In comparing the gravity of both particular aspects of the right to a fair trial, we can conclude that the principle of a lawful judge cannot be sacrificed in favour of swiftness,

10. It is well-known that referrals between courts cause delays in the proceedings. *Ex plurimis*, see the case of *Korbel v. Poland*, Judgment of 21 September 2004, paragraph 45.

because more convincing arguments are in favour of the principle of a lawful judge; namely, the systemic argument, where the principle of a lawful judge prevents being tried by a judge ad hoc; and the contextual argument, which warns not to misuse a law through 'forum shopping' and thus choosing the judge. On the other hand, only one argument, the empirical argument - an increase in the caseload - supports a solution based on the possibility of trying a case more swiftly.

Another example of this *Ping-Pong* is the referral to a more suitable forum. It is based on the consideration that the referring court, despite being the competent court, refers the case to another court because the former is of the opinion that the latter will be able to deal with the case faster or in a more efficient manner. This approach is practical in cases where one or more witnesses living in the jurisdiction of another court have to be heard, as the complete referral of the case to that other court makes it superfluous to file successive requests for hearings and results in a quicker consolidation of the case. As this approach violates territorial jurisdiction, it has to be seen as an exception that must be applied restrictively,[11] and the court has to give reasons for the referral. If a referral was undertaken without adequate reason, this would constitute a breach of the principle that no one shall be denied his lawful judge.

It can thus be concluded that it is possible to weaken the principle of lawful judge in favour of accelerating proceedings. Yet, this possibility has to rest with the lawmaker, who *de lege ferenda* shall preclude the courts to refer cases *ex officio* to other courts. As a consequence, the respondent shall be enabled, by his own initiative, to ask for a change of the territorial jurisdiction. Generally, the principle of lawful judge shall prevail.

[D] Deprivation of the Right to Act before the Court versus Swiftness

The so-called 'deprivation of the right to act before the court' means to deny a party the right to present their arguments orally in a court session, or to deny the submission of evidence or the ability to comment on it. In civil proceedings, one of the most common examples is the appointment of an 'incorrect' guardian for participants of unknown residence; i.e., a guardian from among the employees of the court (legal secretaries, judge-to-be etc.), who then does not act sufficiently and causes the party to lose the dispute. Other cases of deprivation include an insufficient court searching for the party's place of residence when the place is unknown, or incorrectly holding a hearing *in absentia* although a party is duly excused. Nevertheless, it has to be admitted that all of these errors have a 'positive' effect, too - saved time.

Appointing a guardian from among the employees of the court is economical, not only because of the difficulties and considerable time delays when trying to appoint such persons - relatives regularly refuse to be called upon - but also due to time savings for the proceedings. A legal base is usually lacking for the appointment of any other persons or entities, such as municipalities; therefore, an attorney-at-law paid by

11. Cf. Judgment of the Constitutional Court of the Czech Republic of 15 November 2001, sp. No. I. CC 144/2000.

the state would have to be appointed.[12] It may be of theoretical interest to appoint employees of the court, especially for petty claims, where even an attorney-at-law does not have an effective opportunity to raise relevant objections. In this context, we also have to ask ourselves whether the appointment of the attorney-at-law as a guardian for a person of unknown residence is not a violation of the principle of equality. This is based on the argument that the respondent is a person of unknown residence, he does not want to pay its obligations, court proceedings are not of interest to him, and yet he is helped by receiving the assistance of an attorney-at-law at the expense of the state.

It could also be controversial to disrespect a party's reasonable excuse by having a hearing in his absence in cases where the final decision is in his favour. This saves time in the proceedings, as the hearing will not be adjourned. On the other hand, the damaged party may wish to attend the hearing for the purpose of obtaining moral satisfaction, and then even a decision in his favour, in his absence, might be regarded as unsatisfactory.

It must be emphasized again that the importance of a fair trial is utmost; swiftness of the proceedings ranks only second. Such an important principle cannot be violated just for the sake of a fast procedure.

[E] The Right to Use One's Mother Tongue versus Swiftness and Principle of the Economy of Proceedings

The right to use one's mother tongue is an important tool for ensuring equality between the parties. A party incapable of self-expression in one language shall be permitted to use another language, and important documents must be translated into that mother tongue by a court interpreter. To appoint an interpreter, however, has its downsides. Above all, the proceedings are delayed by the need to issue a decision on the appointment of an interpreter and about his remuneration. Further delays are caused by having lengthy interpretations during the hearing. Appointing an interpreter means increased costs for the proceedings, given the interpreter's fee and the higher costs for lengthier proceedings. Sometimes also, the spontaneity of a witness's statement may be distorted, especially if the witness understands the foreign language and can thus prepare an answer before the interpretation of the question. Consequently, we face a conflict between the right to use one's mother tongue and the economy and swiftness of proceedings.

When dealing with this conflict we know that weakening the right to use one's mother tongue will speed up proceedings and help save some money; therefore, this would allow the goal to be achieved (the suitability criterion). However this could also be achieved by different means: e.g., employing more support staff and judges. When comparing these two principles in conflict, we can assess that both rights are *prima facie* of the same value, and at the same time we cannot sacrifice the right to the use of one's mother tongue, because otherwise the proceedings could be considered unfair as a whole.

12. There were unsuccessful attempts to appoint as guardian the Ombudsman in judicial practice.

Then again, we can posit whether, in some cases, it would be appropriate to weaken the right to use the mother tongue in order to expedite and streamline court proceedings. This might be possible only in petty cases, where a judge determines that weakening a party's possibility to use his mother tongue is not in any way able to influence the litigation against him. It might be sufficient to translate the judgment only, and so forth.[13]

A specific problem related to the right to use the one's mother tongue arises in so-called 'hybrid courts'. Hybrid courts are courts where mixed panels composed of international and local judges decide cases, usually in post-conflict countries.[14] In this case, a specific language issue immediately arises, because everything must be translated into one or several local languages in order to enable both international and local judges to work on cases. This high volume of translations is not only time-consuming, but also costly and demanding on the personal resources of the court. Law-makers usually solve the problem by imposing a translation fee on the parties.[15] The result is that it is not sufficient to submit the claim in the party's mother tongue. Rather, the claim must be accompanied by a translation into the working language of the international judges; otherwise, it will be dismissed as inadmissible.

There is again an apparent conflict between the right to use one's the mother tongue and the swiftness as well as economy of the proceedings at the hybrid courts. For the purpose of preserving the right to a fair trial, this conflict should be resolved in favour of the right to use the mother tongue. There are strong arguments in favour of this solution. The issue is especially problematic if the constitution of a country or territory in which a hybrid court is established provides for the local language as being the official language. Then, filing a claim in an official language must be seen as sufficient, and it is the responsibility of the State to arrange its judicial system in such a way as to be capable of handling translation issues. Moreover, to consider insufficient that a party, who is a citizen of that State, file submissions in an official language of the state - his mother tongue - sounds absurd and must, therefore, be rejected as absurd (*argumentum ad absurdum*).

[F] The Duty of the Court to Instruct versus Perception of Conduct of Proceedings as Fair by the Parties and Swiftness

The court's task is to provide parties with equal opportunities to exercise their rights. For this purpose, the court's duty to instruct precludes someone suffering harm in the proceedings out of disregard for procedural law. When the court is consistent in implementing its duty to instruct, one party may have the feeling that the other one is 'favoured' by the court's 'advice.' In particular, this may be the case when the court is

13. Of course, in the absence of request of the party for translation of other documents.
14. This is what happened, for example, in Sierra Leone, Lebanon, East Timor, Cambodia, and Kosovo.
15. See, for example, Article 25.2., *Annex to Law No. 04/L-033 on the Special Chamber of the Supreme Court of Kosovo on Privatization Agency Related Matters.*

instructing about the lack of argument or evidence or other possible legal opinions on the matter.

Each exercise of the duty to instruct slows down the procedure, sometimes even twice - firstly by the instruction itself and its recording, and secondly due to the response of the instructed party, who, for example, may propose additional pieces of evidence or ask for the appointment of a representative, thus potentially delaying a final decision.

When evaluating both aspects, we find that there is no alternative but to fulfil the court's duty to instruct about procedural law. Otherwise, the principle of impartiality would be breached, and a party would be impaired in the exercise of his right (criterion of necessity), even if this takes time. The fact that the other party might perceive this as unjustly helping the opponent could be mitigated by limiting advice strictly to procedural law, in an appropriate situation in the proceeding when the need to advice occurs, and then giving advice also to the other party in another procedural situation.

The only solution would be that lawmakers narrow the duty to instruct in such a way that parties would have to be more responsible for knowing the procedural law. As a consequence, civil proceedings would become even more professionalized, with more parties being represented by an attorney-at-law and with more demands on judges.[16]

[G] The Principle of Directness versus Swiftness

The principle of directness means that evidentiary proceedings are carried out before the court and that the court may consider only the evidence adduced directly before it. The appellate court does not then have to repeat the collection of evidence and can rely on protocols recorded by the first court. In civil proceedings, moreover, there is no need to repeatedly produce evidence even if a panel's composition is changed. Not having to reproduce the evidence saves time. A notable exception, developed by jurisprudence, exists, however: if a Court of Appeal intends to deviate from the fact-findings made by the Court of First Instance on the basis of interpreting evidence produced by the Court of First Instance, it has to require the repetition of the testimony of witnesses, and so provide itself a basis for the possibly different assessment of the witnesses' testimony.[17] Similarly, any court generally favours direct evidence over indirect evidence, which means that an examination of a witness takes precedence over reading his affidavit.

When one court asks another court to hear a witness, which is crucial for the outcome of the case, it also causes a problem in terms of directness. The court from which the hearing has been requested may hear the witness through a junior judge. While this might accelerate the case, such a procedure could burden the proceedings with procedural errors, as such an inappropriate request might restrict the court

16. It has however to be noted that in some countries representation of parties by a lawyer is compulsory.
17. See, for example, Judgment of the Constitutional Court of the Czech Republic of 29 May 2000, sp. No. IV. ÚS 275/98.

charged with the proceedings by having to rely solely on the recorded protocol. This is because for the evaluation of evidence, and in addition to the substance of testimony, other information exists, which - although important for the assessment of the credibility of testimony - cannot be expressed in the minutes.[18]

This again shows another example of a conflict between the swiftness of the proceedings and a fair production of evidence.[19] There is always an alternative to this conflict: to interrogate witnesses directly before the court charged with the proceedings or to repeat the interrogation of the witness. On the other hand, it could be very time-consuming, uneconomical, and harsh on a citizen to be forced to give testimony again.[20] Accordingly it is not clear whether the criterion of necessity is fulfilled. Both aspects - directness and swiftness - are *prima facie* of the same value. However, it is clear that we cannot sacrifice the principle of directness without real safeguards for the right to a fair trial.

[H] Perception of Conduct of Proceedings as Fair by the Parties versus the Principle of Equality

In civil proceedings, a party may not perceive as fair the fact that the opponent is exempt from the payment of court fees,[21] which is one of the instruments to ensure equality of the parties. A party to complex proceedings in which representation is not compulsory and who is able to afford a lawyer will also perceive it as unfair if the opposing party is represented by a court-appointed attorney at the State's expense.

When assessing this conflict, we see at a first glance that exemption from court fees and the appointment of a representative paid by the State are effective means to achieve the goal; namely, to ensure that a participant without financial means is in a position to defend his rights (criterion of suitability). Also the criterion of necessity is fulfilled, as generally both exemption and legal aid are necessary to achieve the goal, the defence of a party's right. However, it has to be borne in mind that there are exceptions, as it might be sufficient, in some States and for simple cases not requiring representation by an attorney, to appoint as a representative a person who is not necessarily a lawyer, such as a family member. Both aspects are *prima facie* of the same value (criterion of gravity).

Nevertheless, based on an empirical argument, we can reach the conclusion that not granting exemption from court fees or not appointing a lawyer at the State's

18. See Decision of the Supreme Court of the Czech Republic of 27 June 1968, Rc 92/68.
19. With reference to the balancing between swiftness and the principle of directness, thus ruled the Supreme Court of the Czech Republic in its Judgment of 10 February 2004, sp. No. 22 Cdo 2475/2003: Neither of the principles, directness or oral proceedings, can be applied without exceptions in civil proceedings, but in conjunction with other principles, in particular with the requirement that the protection of rights is swift and efficient.
20. It has to be noted, however, that rules on the subject matter are different in each signatory State to the Convention, and also vary depending on whether they apply to civil or criminal proceedings.
21. Not only a natural person but also a legal person can be exempted: cf. Judgment of the Constitutional Court of the Czech Republic of 3 September 1998, No. IV. ÚS 13/98.

expenses can – depending on the circumstances of the specific case – impair the very essence of the parties' right to equality under the law.[22]

> In that context, the Court underlines that a restriction placed on access to a court or tribunal will not be compatible with Article 6 § 1 unless it pursues a legitimate aim and there is a reasonable relationship of proportionality between the means employed and the legitimate aim sought to be achieved.
>
> (*Kreuz v. Poland*, Judgment of 19 June 2001, paragraph 55)

This right, however, is not absolute. Thus, the lawmaker has to strike a balance between the principle of equality, based on which one party would be at a substantial disadvantage in comparison to its opponent, and the principle of perception of conduct of proceedings as fair by the parties.

The rules governing exemption from court fees should therefore take into consideration that the denial of exemption from court fees would make it impossible for a party to claim or defend his rights, due to his financial situation: the burden of proof is with the applicant. Parties' rights could find further limitations, such as an exemption not being granted for cases of arbitrary claims or for cases when defending a right is obviously going to be unsuccessful. These cases include a situation in which already from the allegations of the facts of a case it is obvious that no relief can be granted, or a situation when the party's aim is obviously to delay a condemnation to pay, in monetary cases.

An exemption from court fees may be partly granted, and can even be removed, retroactively, which can also result in proceeding with the case, and collecting the fees in a further stage, when the applicant's financial situation has improved.[23]

> The Court also observes that under Polish law an exemption from payment of court fees can at any time be revoked by the courts if the basis therefor has ceased to exist. Allowing the applicants to proceed with their claim at the initial phase of the proceedings would not therefore have prevented the Polish courts from collecting court fees if at some further stage their financial situation had improved.
>
> (*Jedamski and Jedamska v. Poland*, Judgment of 26 July 2005, paragraph 65)

In regard to the appointment of a representative, limitations could result in the fact that an attorney paid by the State should be appointed to a party only in a situation when it is necessary to protect his legal interests. Also, the court may withdraw the appointment of a representative paid by the State with retroactive effect if it finds that the personal situation of the party has developed sufficiently to enable him to bear the costs of legal representation.

22. *Ex plurimis*, see *Kreuz v. Poland*, Judgment of 19 June 2001, paragraphs 55-67; *Tinnelly & Sons Ltd and Others and McElduff and Others v. the United Kingdom*, Judgment of 10 July 1998, paragraph 72.
23. See, for example, *Jedamski and Jedamska v. Poland*, Judgment of 26 July 2005, paragraph 65.

[I] The Perception of Conduct of Proceedings as Fair by Parties versus Swiftness

If the parties are to perceive conduct of proceedings as fair, the court has to provide them the full opportunity to exercise their rights and, in addition, to make an extra effort so that the parties are able to perceive the proceedings as being fair. It is understood that these efforts are time-consuming.

For example, if the court adjourns a hearing based on one party's request, the counterparty may reasonably expect that a hearing will also be adjourned upon its request, and thus perceive the proceedings as fair. If the court rejects that party's request for adjournment in order not to further delay the proceedings, the rejected party may see the courts' decision as unfair.

When weighing both aspects, the necessity criterion should be strictly applied: is the adjournment really necessary, or is there an alternative? For example, appointing a substitute lawyer who is able to represent the party? The proceedings have to move forward as much as possible (systemic argument).

In most cases, the ECtHR has assessed decisions of national courts granting adjournments to the detriment of the states, arguing that the Contracting States have the duty to organize their judicial systems in such a way that their courts can meet each of its requirements, including the obligation to hear cases within a reasonable time:[24]

> (...) the Court recalls that Article 6 § 1 imposes on the Contracting States the duty to organise their judicial systems in such a way that their courts can meet each of its requirements, including the obligation to hear cases within a reasonable time
>
> (*Deak v. Romania and the United Kingdom*, Judgment of 3 June 2008, paragraph 80)

From the above, we might deduce that the ECtHR would support the argument that swiftness is favoured over the party's perception of conduct of proceedings as fair.

Another example is that of one of the parties requesting the referral of the case, pending before the domestic court, to the Court of Justice of the European Union (ECJ) for a preliminary ruling. While on the one hand this will delay the proceedings significantly, on the other hand rejecting this request would be in contradiction with the principle of perception of conduct of proceedings as fair. Here again, it is necessary to balance swiftness of the proceedings with the perception of conduct of proceedings as fair.

A solution can be found by applying the criterion of necessity: if the national court is not the court of last instance in the Member State, it is not necessary to grant the request. If the national court is the court of last instance, arbitrarily refusing the request for a preliminary ruling may infringe the right to a fair trial. For example, the ECtHR held in *Herma v. Germany*:[25]

24. See, among many others, *Deak v. Romania and the United Kingdom*, Judgment of 3 June 2008, paragraph 80; *Kyrtatos v. Greece*, Judgment of 22 May 2003, paragraph 42).
25. *Herma v. Germany*, Appl. No. 54193/07, Decision of 8 December 2009, fifth last paragraph.

> The Court reiterates that the Convention does not guarantee, as such, any right to have a case referred to the ECJ for a preliminary ruling under Article 234 (former Article 177) of the EC Treaty (which has become Article 267 of the Treaty on the Functioning of the EU since 1 December 2009). Nevertheless, refusal of a request for such a referral may infringe the fairness of proceedings if it appears to be arbitrary (Schweighofer and Others v. Austria (dec.), nos. 35673/97, 35674/97, 36082/97 and 37579/97, 24 August 1999; Canela v. Spain (dec.), no. 60350/00, 4 October 2001; Bakker v. Austria (dec.), no. 43454/98, 13 June 2002; John v. Germany (dec.), no. 15073/03, 13 February 2007).
>
> (*Herma v. Germany*, Appl. No. 54193/07, Decision of 8 December 2009, fifth last paragraph)

In this situation, a national court should consider all the circumstances of the case, including the length of the proceedings, whether one of the parties requested an adjournment repeatedly and purposefully or not, and whether the court is the last instance for the case or not.

Above all, however, the desired outcome is to avoid a) granting an inappropriate request for adjournment, or b) the court referring the party's ill-founded request for preliminary ruling to the ECJ.

[J] Reasoned Judgment versus Economy of Proceedings

As we have seen in Chapter 3, the right to a reasoned judgment is one important aspect of the right to a fair trial. Only by allowing the parties to know why the court came to a certain conclusion can the process be regarded as fair.

In petty civil cases, lawmakers often exempt judges from a lengthy legal reasoning, and allow them to limit judgments to their very essence, as otherwise it would not be economical. When dealing with class actions, a detailed reasoning for each participant involved may not be feasible and it might be more reasonable a common legal reasoning for multiple participants. This illustrates the conflict between the right to a reasoned judgment and the economy of proceedings.

When comparing the right to a reasoned judgment with the principle of economy of proceedings, we can establish that from an empirical point of view the legal system is facing an ever increasing case load. The systemic argument shows that the right to a fair trial serves as a general instrument for the protection of fundamental rights. The contextual argument indicates that not receiving a reasoned judgment might constitute an infringement of the right to a fair trial and might lead to misusing the concept of abridged judgments. It is preferable for the parties to receive a reasoned judgment.

In light of these arguments, the solution of this conflict is exemplified in *Klemeco Nord AB v. Sweden*,[26] where the ECtHR held that:

> According to its established case-law reflecting the need for the effective administration of justice, courts and tribunals should adequately state the reasons on which they base their decisions. The extent to which this obligation applies may vary according to the nature of the decision and must be determined in the light of

26. *Klemeco Nord AB v. Sweden*, Judgment of 19 December 2006.

> the circumstances of the case. However, it cannot be understood as requiring a detailed answer to every argument.
>
> (*Klemeco Nord AB v. Sweden*, Judgment of 19 December 2006, paragraph 39)

One thing is clear – there must be a legal reasoning. The extent of the reasoning, however, depends on the nature and circumstances of the particular case. Accordingly, the reasoning might be shorter in petty cases, even limited to the very substance of the case, tailored according to the participants and their submission, thus balancing between fully reasoned judgment and the principle of the economy of proceedings.

[K] Publicly Pronounced Judgment versus Reasoned Judgment

Article 6(1), second sentence, reads: 'Judgment shall be pronounced publicly ...'. At the same time, the judgment must be reasoned.[27] A well-reasoned, public pronouncement is especially difficult in very complex cases. Lawmakers sometimes allow oral reasoning to be postponed until written reasoning is issued, and judges tend to simplify reasoning by saying that more details will be provided in written form. These practices create conflict between the right to a publicly pronounced judgment and the right to a reasoned judgment.

One could argue that restricting public oral reasoning may lead to better reasoning in writing. The necessity criterion shows that it is not necessary to restrict the public access to full reasoning; for example, allowing the public to see the reasoning in written form in the registry of the court. Both rights are *prima facie* of the same importance. It is especially not desirable for justice to be viewed as secret and removed from public scrutiny.

This position was held by the ECtHR, for example, *Pretto and others v. Italy*:[28]

> The public character of proceedings before the judicial bodies referred to in Article 6 § 1 (art. 6-1) protects litigants against the administration of justice in secret with no public scrutiny; it is also one of the means whereby confidence in the courts, superior and inferior, can be maintained. By rendering the administration of justice visible, publicity contributes to the achievement of the aim of Article 6 § 1 (art. 6-1), namely a fair trial, the guarantee of which is one of the fundamental principles of any democratic society, within the meaning of the Convention (see the Golder judgment of 21 February 1975, Series A no. 18, p. 18, § 36, and also the Lawless judgment of 14 November 1960, Series A no. 1, p. 13).
>
> (*Pretto and others v. Italy*, Judgment of 8 December 1983, paragraph 21)

A solution could be based on the case of *Ryakib Biryukov v. Russia*.[29] In this case, the Court of First Instance examined the case on the merits at a public hearing. At the end of the hearing, the court read the enacting clause of the judgment under which the applicant's claim was dismissed. The reasoned judgment was served on the parties later. Neither oral nor written reasons were accessible to the public because the public had no

27. See, among others, the case of *Klemeco Nord AB v. Sweden*, Judgment of 19 December 2006.
28. *Pretto and others v. Italy*, Judgment of 8 December 1983.
29. *Ryakib Biryukov*, Judgment of 17 January 2008.

access to the files. The ECtHR found that there had been a violation of Article 6(1), in that the State failed to comply with the requirement of making judgments public:

> The Court has had on several occasions to assess situations in which the decisions of superior courts, dismissing appeals on points of law, were not pronounced in open court. In finding no violation of Article 6 § 1, the Court paid particular attention to the stage of the proceedings and the role of the courts in question, which was confined to the issues of law, and to their decisions, which made lower courts' judgments final and changed nothing in respect of the consequences for the applicants. Having such considerations in mind, it found that the requirement of the public pronouncement of judgments was satisfied where the full text of the decision deposited in the court registry was available to everyone (see *Pretto and Others*, cited above, §§ 27-28), or where the lower court held public hearings and the lower court's judgment was pronounced in open court (see *Axen*, cited above, § 32), or where anyone who established an interest could obtain the full text of judgments of the court, the most important judgments of which were subsequently published in an official collection (see *Sutter*, cited above, § 34).
>
> (*Ryakib Biryukov v. Russia*, Judgment of 17 January 2008, paragraph 34)

> The Court considers that the object pursued by Article 6 § 1 in this context – namely, to ensure scrutiny of the judiciary by the public with a view to safeguarding the right to a fair trial – was not achieved in the present case, in which the reasons which would make it possible to understand why the applicant's claims had been rejected were inaccessible to the public.
>
> (*Ryakib Biryukov v. Russia*, Judgment of 17 January 2008, paragraph 45)

When applying the necessity criterion, we found that it is not necessary to restrict the public from reading or hearing the reasoning. Therefore, two possibilities exist: either to provide the reasoning during the public session or to give it in written form, in legal systems where the public has access to written decisions. In other words, it is necessary for the court to provide its reasoning immediately, unless the public can read the judgment later on.

§5.02 CONFLICT RESOLUTIONS

When solving a conflict of principles, the judge must decide which principle or group of principles is to be given priority over any other principle or group of principles. The solution must lie in careful consideration of which principle is more appropriate, and which is less, under certain circumstances. But this does not mean that the less appropriate principle is not valid. On the contrary, such a principle might, under different circumstances, outweigh the other principle. That is exactly why it is said that principles have different weight in different cases.[30] In the following section, we will try to outline the options and processes in the resolutions of conflict between principles.

First, it is worth exploring the possibility of avoiding conflict of principles. Can a solution be found to keep principles intact? If so, that solution should be taken. An

30. R. Alexy, *A Theory of Constitutional Rights* (Julian Rivers, Oxford: Oxford University Press, 2002), 50.

exception would be in situations leading to gross violation of another protected interest.[31] When we cannot leave both principles untouched, and a real conflict between principles exists, then it is important to avoid sacrificing one principle for the sake of the other. By definition, both principles are considered important, and they normally have priority in relation to other protected interests. That is why it is undesirable for one of the principles to be completely negated by another.

When weighing up the two principles, the role of the court – and the preferred solution – is to find a balance between them before favouring one of them. Therefore, the priority solution is the one that does not make one principle subordinate to another, but rather finds a compromise on both sides in order to guarantee maximum protection of both principles.

In many cases, however, finding such a compromise is not possible. The conflict of principles is then resolved by giving preference to one of the principles in conflict. Attempts have been made in the literature to create a hierarchy of principles based on human rights protection. The problem with this method is that there is no consensus at all on the status of each principle in this hierarchy.

When giving preference to one of the principles, the judge dealing with the conflict is on thin ice. The judgment is then easily challenged merely by pointing to the suppression of a principle and the related violations of fundamental human rights and freedoms.

Some of the methods and procedures for solving this difficult issue will be examined below.

[A] Conflict between an Unwritten Principle and the Principle Enshrined in a Legal Norm

If an unwritten legal principle is in conflict with the principles enshrined in a legal norm, then the norm takes precedence because legal principles have the character of *praeter legem* –'outside of the written law'. An exception to this rule is an extreme case of non-compliance of the legal norm with fundamental principles of justice, when the legal norm must be considered as 'non-law' and rejected. This situation is known as 'Radbruch's formula,'[32] from a German jurist reacting against the Nazi era of legalized

31. E. Brems, *Conflicting Human Rights: An Exploration in the Context of the Right to a Fair Trial in the European Convention for the Protection of Human Rights and Fundamental Freedoms*, Vol. 27, Human Rights Quarterly (2005), 303.
32. The formula reads as follow: '*Der Konflikt zwischen der Gerechtigkeit und der Rechtssicherheit dürfte dahin zu lösen sein, daß das positive, durch Satzung und Macht gesicherte Recht auch dann den Vorrang hat, wenn es inhaltlich ungerecht und unzweckmäßig ist, es sei denn, daß der Widerspruch des positiven Gesetzes zur Gerechtigkeit ein so unerträgliches Maß erreicht, daß das Gesetz als, unrichtiges Recht' der Gerechtigkeit zu weichen hat*' (Radbruch, G., *Gesetzliches Unrecht und übergesetzliches Recht* [Legal Injustice and Supralegal Law], Süddeutsche Juristen-zeitung, I, 1946, 105). P. Holländer, *Nástin filosofie práva* [*Outline of the Philosophy of Law*] (Praha: Všehrd, 2000), 63, defined the Radbruch's formula as follows: The conflict between justice and legal certainty could probably be solved except that the positive law, guaranteed by laws and power, has precedence even if the content is unfair and ineffective, only, if the discrepancy between positive law and justice reaches so intolerable an extent that the law must as 'non-law' [*unrichtiges Recht*] justice withdraw.

criminality. The contradiction must be evident, it must be a contradiction with key principles of justice, and it must reach an unbearable level.

[B] Conflicting Unwritten Principles

[1] Lex specialis derogat legi generali

The principle in question states that where there are two laws governing the same factual situation, the law that regulates a specific aspect (*lex specialis*) always prevails over a law that regulates only general aspects (*lex generalis*). Thus the special principle for the case at hand takes precedence over the general one; for example, the principle of obligation of the State to provide functional criminal-law protection (the need to perform a forensic autopsy) is special to the principle of protection of personality,[33] and therefore forensic autopsy may be performed even against the will of relatives of deceased.

[2] *The Principle of Proportionality*

The principle of proportionality is designed to be used in practice to resolve the collision of two or more fundamental rights and freedoms, and it establishes the conditions under which it is possible to limit one fundamental right for the benefit of another.

The principle of proportionality is widely used by Constitutional courts. In a similar manner, the principle of proportionality is also applicable for conflict resolution principles, because legal principles are largely grounded at constitutional level.

A first criterion consists in mutually examining the principles for the suitability: i.e., whether a principle allows one individual to achieve his goal (protection of other fundamental rights) and contribute to a fair trial. A second criterion consists in examining necessity: i.e., whether for achieving the goal this or that principle is needed or whether the goal can be achieved by other means. Third, it must be assessed by the gravity (the importance and significance) of this or that principle within the empirical, systemic, contextual and value arguments.

An empirical argument can be understood as the factual importance of the social phenomenon being protected by the principle (e.g., whether some negative effect would be increased). The systemic argument means considering the meaning and the position of each principle in the legal system. The contextual argument can be explained as another negative effect from the limitation of one principle due to the preference of another. The value argument implies considering the positive aspects of the conflicting principles according to the generally accepted hierarchy of values. For a

33. This example is taken from P. Holländer, *Základy všeobecné státovědy* [*Introduction to the General Theory of State*] (Plzeň: Aleš Čeněk, 2009), 63.

more detailed explanation, reference could be made to the jurisprudence of constitutional courts.[34]

[3] Arbiters[35]

Conflict principles may also be solved by using other principles or methods, such as an imaginary adjudicator, which is called an '*arbiter*.'

A reliable arbiter is the *argumentum ad absurdum*.

The *Argumentum ad absurdum* will exclude one of the principles because its application is senseless or does not give us a reasonable sense. Its application would indeed lead to a factually or legally impossible outcome that we would describe as 'absurd'. Another *arbiter* we can use is a constitutionally conforming interpretation, which is a directive ordering an interpretation that is best suited to the constitutional order.[36] Priority will be given to the principle that is most compliant with the constitutional order, taking into account that inhibiting another principle means the least interference with the constitutional order. Other arguments and methods, such as logical interpretation, are not as reliable in the role of arbiter.

[4] Other Methods

These methods are essentially about various ways of balancing and testing conflicting principles. Alexy describes one option with help of the *Lebach* Judgment of the Constitutional Court of the Federal Republic of Germany.[37] The facts were as follows: German ZDF Television planned to broadcast the documentary 'Soldiers – Murder in Lebach.' The case involved a criminal offence, where four soldiers sleeping in an ammunition depot were murdered, and weapons were stolen for the purpose of committing another crime. At the scheduled broadcast date, only a short time remained until the release of an offender who was convicted of aiding in this crime. He was of the opinion that the documentary's disclosure of his name damaged his constitutional rights by destroying the possibility of his integration into society.

The Constitutional Court's decision can be divided into three parts. The first part recognized the conflict of the constitutional principles to protect an individual's personal rights and of freedom of expression, and the right to information (media reporting). That led to an adverse court decision because they could not be resolved by declaring the invalidity of any one of the principles. In the second part, the court held that freedom of expression and the right to information (media reporting) generally have priority over protection of individual personal rights when the information about

34. See, for example, in the Czech legal system, the Judgment of the Plenum of the Constitutional Court of the Czech Republic of 12 October 1994, sp. No. Pl. ÚS 4/94.
35. This notion is created by the Author.
36. Cf. Judgment of the Constitutional Court of the Czech Republic of 22 October 1996, sp. No. III. ÚS 277/96: *In a situation where a law provision allows different interpretations it is the task of all state authorities to interpret it in a constitutionally conforming way.*
37. See the Judgment of the Constitutional Court of the Federal Republic of Germany of 5 June 1973, BVerfGE 35, 202.

a crime is up-to-date. In the third part, the judgment was pronounced, and can be expressed as follows: F1 and F2 and F3 and F4 implies Q, which means repeated media coverage (F1) in situations where there is not a specific interest in actual information (F2) concerning a particularly serious crime (F3), in the situation when the media story threatens a prisoner's social rehabilitation, (F4) is constitutionally prohibited (Q).[38]

Another method could be based on the jurisprudence of the ECtHR and the article of Brems:[39] When a conflict of principles affecting fundamental rights occurs, it is necessary to examine a) how important the rights are, and b) the importance of the case at hand for the protection of fundamental human rights, as such. It is necessary to identify the essential (core) and peripheral aspects of the pertinent principle. If an essential aspect of principle (human rights) is in conflict with a more peripheral aspect, it is justifiable to give priority to the former. The notion 'the essence (core) of the fundamental right' regularly appears in the jurisprudence of the ECtHR. For example, an individual's name, gender, religion, sexual orientation, and ethnic identity constitute an essential aspect of the right to respect for private and family life according to Article 8.[40] Similarly, the ECtHR considered that high court fees impair the very essence of the right of access to a court.[41]

Another relevant factor is the severity of interference caused by the application of one principle (fundamental right) at the expense of another, and vice-versa. If the principle is completely ruled out, then it has more weight than if its application would be just difficult.

It is also necessary to determine whether additional fundamental rights are indirectly affected. This criterion is particularly important in the context of the right to a fair trial, which is a tool for the protection and enforcement of other fundamental rights.

In addition, procedural steps often affect more than two parties.

Finally, the restrictions imposed on one fundamental right in order to protect another one should not be evaluated separately. This criterion takes into account the general interest in fundamental rights, which are in the background of the case in hand. For example, the degree of restriction on freedom of expression does not only impact upon the individual fundamental right at stake, but also the background democracy.

[C] Conflict in Written Principles

When a conflict of written principles occurs, all the above solutions and procedures will apply. Additionally, one could also use the procedures usually adopted when dealing with conflicts of methods of interpretation (linguistic, logical, teleological, historical interpretation, ...), but this goes beyond the scope of this book.

38. Example taken from Alexy, R., *A Theory of Constitutional Rights*, cited above, 54-56.
39. E. Brems, *Conflicting Human Rights: An Exploration in the Context of the Right to a Fair Trial in the European Convention for the Protection of Human Rights and Fundamental Freedoms*, cited above, 303-304.
40. See, among others, *Ciubotaru v. Moldova*, Judgment of 27 April 2010, paragraph 53.
41. See, *ex multis*, *Georgel and Georgeta Stoicescu v. Romania*, Judgment of 26 July 2011, paragraph 70.

[D] Conclusions about Conflicts between Particular Aspects of the Right to a Fair Trial

The more legally sophisticated a society is, the more frequent conflicts of principles concerning particular aspects of the right to a fair trial will be.

While this legal sophistication will lead to a decrease in the number of lawsuits, it will lead to an increase in the number of lawsuits in which principles are in conflict. Also, constitutions, charters, protocols, and other international treaties foster the proliferation of fundamental rights and freedoms affecting more and more individual cases, which again increases the importance of the principles. Finally, the composition of judicial bodies by international judges from different legal background also increases the importance of principles as a tool for unification.

For the issue of conflict of principles, the ECtHR often leaves the legislator of each signatory State a broad range for general considerations. There are strong arguments for this: Given the fact that both contested principles are equally important, this flexibility enables legislators to take into account local, cultural, or religious views on the matter, forming the basis for finding the best or at least most acceptable solutions in a particular context.

The challenge is to look for the degree of conflicting principles: i.e., which principle shall have priority and why. Conflicts of principles were and always will be a big challenge for legislators, judges, and the judiciary in general. A major task of the legal theory is to create a reasonable set of tools for conflict resolution.

Court procedures are disputable when they deliberately cause a conflict of legal principles and prefer one over another. Typically, the preferred one is swiftness or economy of the proceedings for 'practical reasons.' This occurs surprisingly often in the practice of lower courts, which are overwhelmed by cases. For example, in a situation in which it is practically certain that the claimant is going to win the dispute, the court may override a principle actually benefiting the claimant, which leads to an acceleration of the proceedings and the rendering of a factually correct decision. This decision to override a principle is taken with the expectation that the winning party would not be concerned by the infringement of a principle, and that it benefits the proceedings as whole, because faster proceedings are more valuable than an 'unfair' trial.

However, the affected party may not be pleased by the outcome of the case and may actually favour a hearing, to gain moral satisfaction. In this situation, and although the final decision will be rendered in his favour, the claimant could perceive the proceedings as insufficient and erroneous. In addition, it is of paramount importance not to overlook the important ethical dimension of this issue.

It has therefore to be noted that the judge involved in such decisions is on thin ice and has to weigh, exercising extraordinary care, all circumstances in the case. In the vast majority of cases, the truth is that a fair judgment not only has to be correct in merits, but it must be preceded by fair proceedings. Both aspects of justice condition themselves to the extent that in the absence of one of its components, we cannot talk about justice.[42]

Wrongly giving preference to one of the conflicting principles may constitute a violation of the right to a fair trial and thus there is the risk that the decision will be annulled. This will make it necessary to conduct a retrial and will result in an additional delay for adjudicating the case, thus also increasing the costs of the procedure. Another consequence would be the liability of the State for damages and non-proprietary damages. The intention to accelerate and economize judicial proceedings by giving preference to one principle may thus be foiled and result in the opposite. It is therefore necessary that courts be ready and prepared to deal with conflicts of principles in a professional and careful manner.

42. P. Lavický, *Funkční vazby občanského práva hmotného a procesního* [*Functional Bindings in Substantive and Procedural Civil Law*] (Ph.D. Thesis, Faculty of Law, Brno: Masaryk University, 2006/7), 192.

CHAPTER 6

The Right to a Fair Trial in Practice

Ondrej Pridal

§6.01 INTRODUCTION

It is one thing to theoretically define what a fair trial should be, and it is anothers to apply this knowledge in practice. It should be noted that judges are only humans, and that decision-making often takes place in a stressful atmosphere and within a limited time frame. Courts are furthermore overwhelmed by the sheer number of cases, which not only puts increased demands on the swiftness of the trial (having to deal with so many cases, the risk of undue delays rises proportionally), but also leaves the judges little time to study jurisprudence and to their professional development. Judges are also entrusted with the managing of several different agendas, which increases the volume of material that must be examined. One may well ask how all of the principles of a fair trial can reasonably be applied.

Another element which must be taken into consideration is the fact that a party is often unwilling to cooperate with the court, as in the case of the defendant (in criminal proceedings) or the respondent (in civil proceedings), who usually prefer to have a lengthier trial, so as to put off the enforcement of the judgment as long as possible. This is reflected in the coarser form of ignoring proceedings and refusing to receive summons and other acts and in the more subtle form of filing various submissions and proposals, and appealing with the sole purpose of delaying the final judgment. This 'non-cooperation' necessarily impacts on a fair trial and requires a specific reaction to be taken by the court.

The guarantees of the right to a fair trial will normally be applied from the commencement of the proceedings. There are some exceptions to this principle, such as the right to consult a solicitor before launching the suit. The 'reasonable time' may also start running before the commencement of the proceedings when there is a preceding administrative procedure[1] or other important issues. For example, in the already-mentioned *Golder v. the United Kingdom*[2] the Court reaffirmed that:

> While the right to a fair, public and expeditious judicial procedure can assuredly apply only to proceedings in being, it does not, however, necessarily follow that a right to the very institution of such proceedings is thereby excluded; the Delegates of the Commission rightly underlined this at paragraph 21 of their memorial. Besides, in criminal matters, the 'reasonable time' may start to run from a date prior to the seizing of the trial court, of the 'tribunal' competent for the 'determination ... of (the) criminal charge' (Wemhoff judgment of 27 June 1968, Series A no. 7, pp. 26-27, para. 19; Neumeister judgment of 27 June 1968, Series A no. 8, p. 41, para. 18; Ringeisen judgment of 16 July 1971, Series A no. 13, p. 45, para. 110). It is conceivable also that in civil matters the reasonable time may begin to run, in certain circumstances, even before the issue of the writ commencing proceedings before the court to which the plaintiff submits the dispute.
>
> (*Golder v. the United Kingdom*, Judgment of 21 February 1975, paragraph 32)

§6.02 HOW TO CONDUCT A FAIR TRIAL IN CIVIL PROCEEDINGS

A civil fair trial should of course be a combination of all of the particular aspects of the right to a fair trial mentioned in Chapter 3. It is interesting and challenging to find a 'proper' degree of application of each particular aspect of the right to a fair trial and all aspects together. At first glance, the right to a decision within a reasonable time must be highlighted – slow justice can be equal to no justice. In *Salesi v. Italy*,[3] for example, the Court stated:

> It must not be forgotten that Article 6 para. 1 (art. 6-1) imposes on the Contracting States the duty to organise their judicial systems in such a way that their courts can meet each of its requirements (...).
>
> (*Salesi v. Italy*, Judgment of 26 February 1993, paragraph 24)

However, it is important to realize that the swiftness of proceedings can be at the expense of justice (less accurate fact-finding, and breach of certain guarantees).[4] In this way of thinking, each aspect of the right to a fair trial has its place in the proceedings, for which an approach that placed an exaggerated stress on swiftness would be wrong as well. The aim is therefore to have a process provided with all the safeguards but which will end in a reasonable time.

For the entire duration of the trial, one deals with facts and observations. It all starts when the claimant encrypts the factual background of the case in a wording of his choice and puts it in writing. The judge then reads it and decrypts it into his own language. This 'mini-process' could itself cause some misunderstanding, further

1. *Konig v. Germany*, Judgment of 28 June 1978, paragraph 94.
2. *Golder v. the United Kingdom*, Judgment of 21 February 1975.
3. *Salesi v. Italy*, Judgment of 26 February 1993; see also, among many others, *Tusa v. Italy*, Judgment of 27 February 1992, paragraph 17.
4. It is therefore necessary for a judge to be prepared to deal with conflict between particular aspects of the right to a fair trial – on which see in detail Chapter 5.

compounded by the fact that different interpretations of the concepts might arise (Wittgenstein refers to 'language games'[5]). It is consequently important that the concepts be formulated in a generally accepted way, with complete awareness of 'who one is dealing with'. The court should also refrain, according to some Authors, from an excessive use of Latin expressions.

This subchapter will study in particular the procedure prior to and during the hearing in the civil procedure, the order of the cases, and the use of modern technology in proceedings. Flowchart diagrams and their description are the core of this subchapter. The diagrams represent 'ideal' schemes of civil proceedings, e.g., how civil proceedings should be conducted in order to ensure the respect of all the aspects of the right to a fair trial, as guaranteed by Article 6 ECHR. It is not tailored on a specific domestic civil procedure, but it is based on common principles present in most of European jurisdictions.[6]

[A] The Procedure before the Hearing Takes Place[7]

One thing, therefore, is the due process defined in theory, as it should be, and quite another is its confrontation with the practice.

In practice, one would find that the adjudication of the case (and the application of the principles of a fair trial) is fundamentally limited by time, which is to be divided between the cases in hand and other cases. Considering that a month has about twenty-one working days and that the judge must deal with the conditions of proceedings, issue (in some Countries) orders for the payment of court fees, request the parties to amend possible errors in the pleadings, order – in some kinds of proceedings – to serve the claim on the respondent and, vice-versa, the respondent's defence on the claimant, conduct the trial and write the judgment, there remains very little time for a

5. See, on the point: A. Biletzki & A. Matar, 'Ludwig Wittgenstein', in *The Stanford Encyclopedia of Philosophy*, ed. Edward N. Zalta (Summer 2011 Edition), http://plato.stanford.edu/archives/sum2011/entries/wittgenstein/ > : '(...) the term "language-*game*" is meant to bring into prominence the fact that the *speaking* of language is part of an activity, or of a form of life' (*PI* 23). What enables language to function and therefore must be accepted as 'given' is precisely forms of life. In Wittgenstein's terms, agreement is required 'not only in definitions but also (queer as this may sound) in judgments' (*PI* 242), and this is 'not agreement in opinions but in form of life' (*PI* 241). Used by Wittgenstein sparingly – five times in the *Investigations* – this intriguing concept has given rise to interpretative quandaries and subsequent contradictory readings. Forms of life can be understood as changing and contingent, dependent on culture, context, history, etc.; this appeal to forms of life grounds a relativistic reading of Wittgenstein'.
6. It is not easy to give an exact answer on what are the common grounds of European civil procedures. Important are, in this respect, experiences of Authors, as among others, G.C. Hazard et al., *Draft Rules of Transnational Civil Procedure (with Comments)*, UNIDROIT Study LXXVI – Doc. 12, International Institute for the Unification of Private Law, 2004.
7. This subchapter was published with specifics of the Czech procedure: O. Pridal, *Postup soudu před nařízením jednání* [*The Particular Steps of the Court before Hearing Takes Place*], Bulletin advokacie [Attorney's Bulletin], 2009, No. 5, 25 et seq.

particular case itself.[8] That same time frame should also accommodate further study of changing legislation, case law, and participation in legal training. As a result, every judge sooner or later 'creates or experiences' a sequence of steps disciplining the manner in which to proceed in the vast majority of his cases. Such a procedure is shown in the flowchart diagrams.

The flowcharts shown in this chapter depict the effective sequence of steps that are specifically arranged so that the written proceedings may be completed, and the hearing be summoned as soon as possible, while respecting the procedural rights of all the participants. It should be noted that every aspect of the right to a fair trial has been examined. A selection of multiple variants has been provided for the proceedings, to cover the most frequently occurring situations.

The following types of flowcharts have been employed: the rectangle signifies the progress in the case; the diamond (rhomboid) represents decision-making, assessment of certain conditions, or the choice between different variants; and the oval marks the closing of the case. The arrows departing from each flowchart indicate substantial opportunities that have been chosen to be illustrative and transparent.

Scheme 6.1

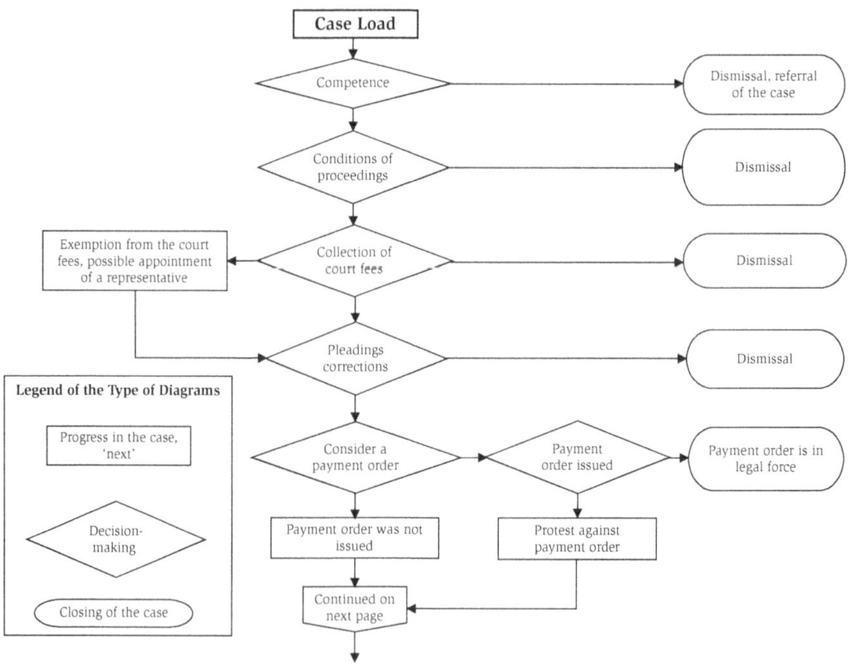

8. The above listing has been simplified, as some cases will end by withdrawal, while others are repeatedly postponed and require several days' hearing.

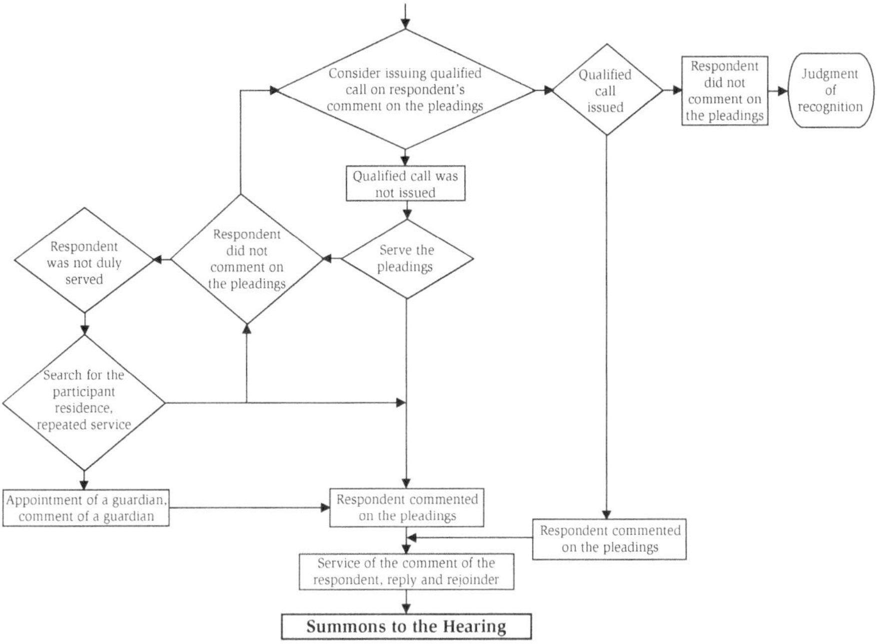

[1] The Case Load, Competence and Other Conditions of the Proceedings

After the case load, the court examines its competence and jurisdiction, which sometimes leads to a suspension of the proceedings (or dismissal of the case on grounds of inadmissibility) or to referral to another competent court or authority. This may occur for various reasons, e.g., organization of the court system, right to a lawful judge, or competence of a different authority. In many judicial systems, there is a special procedure for certain case referrals, such as between different court instances, compulsory referral, or referral to a more convenient forum.[9] Finally, a judge may consider himself biased in a particular case, for which the case must be brought before the president of the court (or to the higher court instance), who might assign the case to another judge (seldom to another court, unless all the judges are biased) to adjudicate the case. It is the duty of every court to examine whether, as constituted, it is 'an impartial tribunal'. This was decided, for example, by ECtHR in *Remli v. France*:[10]

> Article 6 para. 1 (art. 6-1) of the Convention imposes an obligation on every national court to check whether, as constituted, it is 'an impartial tribunal' within the meaning of that provision (art. 6-1) where, as in the instant case, this is disputed on a ground that does not immediately appear to be manifestly devoid of merit'.
>
> (*Remli v. France*, Judgment of 23 April 1996, paragraph 48)

9. It should be mentioned that every referral slows the procedure and therefore it is the duty of each state to organize its judicial system to work effectively in this regard.
10. *Remli v. France*, Judgment of 23 April 1996.

The next step for the court will be to check the conditions of the proceedings. There may be a lack of legal capacity before the commencement of the proceedings (for example, the participant died before they began), in which case the deficiency cannot be amended and the proceedings must be dismissed as inadmissible. A plea of *res judicata* or *lis pendens* in the event of an adjudicated case or previously commenced proceedings will also lead to the dismissal of the proceedings. The fact that a matter should be tried before arbitrators will similarly result in the dismissal of the proceedings. On the contrary, other pleas after the commencement of the proceedings, such as a successive loss of legal capacity of one party or succession in rights or obligations (or cession), will usually cause suspension of the proceedings and appropriate decision has to be issued.

[2] Collection of Legal Fees: Pleadings Corrections

At this point, the court may ask the plaintiff to pay the court fees (which can preferably be processed by an order, or by an informal notice), but which, once again, may lead to a dismissal of the proceedings if the plaintiff fails to do so. A secondary option is exemption from the court fees upon request of the participant, after examining his financial means. This is an important aspect of the right to a fair trial, because no one shall be prevented from bringing his matter to the court due to lack of money (right of access to the court). In *Kreuz v. Poland*,[11] for example, the Court affirmed:

> (...) the amount of the fees assessed in the light of the particular circumstances of a given case, including the applicant's ability to pay them, and the phase of the proceedings at which that restriction has been imposed are factors which are material in determining whether or not a person enjoyed his right of access and had 'a ... hearing by [a] tribunal' (see Tolstoy-Miloslavsky, cited above, and Aït-Mouhoub, cited above, pp. 80-81, § 63 et seq., and p. 3228, § 57, respectively)'.
>
> (*Kreuz v. Poland*, Judgment of 19 June 2001, paragraph 60)

Moreover, the participant may apply to the court for the granting of legal aid. An attorney will then be appointed for this purpose, and this will preserve another aspect of the right to a fair trial, the principle of equality. This is what was decided, for instance, in *Airey v. Ireland*:[12]

> Article 6 para. 1 (art. 6-1) may sometimes compel the State to provide for the assistance of a lawyer when such assistance proves indispensable for an effective access to court either because legal representation is rendered compulsory, as is done by the domestic law of certain Contracting States for various types of litigation, or by reason of the complexity of the procedure or of the case'.
>
> (*Airey v. Ireland*, Judgment of 9 October 1979, paragraph 26)

11. *Kreuz v. Poland*, Judgment of 19 June 2001.
12. *Airey v. Ireland*, Judgment of 9 October 1979.

As soon as the court fees have been paid, or the claimant has been exempted from paying them, the court proceeds - where needed - with the pleadings corrections and, if necessary, issues an order to amend the pleadings. Non-compliance with this order could again lead to the dismissal of the proceedings. There is an apparent question, as to whether to collect the court fees first, or to proceed with the pleadings corrections. The preferable option is to collect the court fees and after that to deal with the pleadings corrections, as amending the claim can sometimes be a very time-consuming task, which could be proven ineffective in the event of failure of the payment of the court fees. In addition, if, after exempting a participant from paying the court fees, the court has successively appointed an attorney, the corrections of the pleadings will obviously be faster.

There may infrequently present a situation in which, due to errors in the pleadings, it is not possible to conclude what the subject of the proceedings is and thus identify the decisive criterion for determining the amount of the court fees. In this case, the errors will first have to be removed by the court and the participant (this applies equally to the court with regard to errors in the determination of its competence). Finally, the errors could be irreparable (e.g., the participant died before the commencement of the proceedings, *lis pendens*, etc.), for which the court will have to dismiss the proceedings as inadmissible. Therefore, in a minority of cases (depending on an estimate of the judge) it will be preferable to reverse the process, i.e., first eliminate the procedural errors and then collect the legal fees.

[3] Consideration of Issuing a Payment Order

If the pleadings are free from errors, the court may then consider the issuing of a payment order. It will take into account, in particular, the nature of the action, the likelihood of successful service of the payment order, and the likelihood of submitting a complaint against the payment order to ensure that the payment order is an appropriate and effective mean to end the proceedings. With the payment order, the court can already 'incorporate' a so-called 'qualified call' on the respondent's comment on the pleadings (see below). This may again accelerate the proceedings because the respondent will not only submit the complaint against the payment order, but also its defence.

[4] Consideration of Issuing a 'Qualified Call' on the Respondent's Comment on the Pleadings: Respondent Was Not Duly Served – Appointment of a Guardian

Unless a payment order is issued, or is abolished following a complaint of the respondent, the court considers the issuing of an order requesting from the respondent his response on the pleadings ('qualified call'). The aim of the court in this case is to obtain the opinion of the respondent, under penalty of a 'judgment of recognition'.

Issuing this call is not always appropriate. In particular, it is necessary to evaluate-whether this step is required by the nature or the circumstances of the case. If the court issues a qualified call, the case may end up with a judgment of recognition, should the respondent fail to comment on the pleadings. It must be noted that not every defence (comment) of the respondent can preserve him from a judgment of recognition; the defence must be proper and relevant, a simple disagreement with the claim is not sufficient. If the qualified call is not issued, the claim shall be served on the respondent, who, in simple cases, may be summoned to the hearing with the other parties.

Upon serving of the claim, the respondent will file his defence. If he fails to do so, the court may find it appropriate to re-issue a qualified call on the respondent, with a possible judgment of recognition.

If, instead, the serving of the claim on the respondent is not successful, the court will try to locate the respondent's residence in order to deliver the claim, and if the respondent is a person of unknown residence, the court may appoint a guardian.[13] This guardian could be one of his relatives or an attorney paid by the State, but not a person working within the same court (such as a judicial trainee, a legal officer, etc.), because they could be seen as not impartial.[14] The guardian institution is another fair trial guarantee. The court should then appoint a guardian who will be paid by the State, which will allow the trial to proceed with a duly represented participant.

[5] Service of the Defence, Reply and Rejoinder: Summons to the Hearing

If the participant (or his guardian) files a defence, the court will serve it on the claimant. The reply and rejoinder should be treated accordingly. Afterwards, the parties should be summoned to the hearing.[15]

It should be noted that the procedural steps of the court outlined above apply to the vast majority of cases. There are exceptions confirming this rule, of course; for example, in cases of agreed divorce proposed by both spouses with a contract for the distribution of their property, the hearing could be ordered immediately. Likewise, some of these steps and procedural situations may occur at any moment of the proceedings, and will be followed contextually by specific acts of the court and the participants, such as recusal, changes of the claim, withdrawal of the claim, legal succession, etc.

13. This procedure, as others mentioned in this chapter, may vary from one country to another.
14. See, for example, Judgment of the Constitutional Court of the Czech Republic of 31 March 2005, sp. No. II. ÚS 629/04.
15. As noted in the literature, the parties can also waive implicitly their right to be present at the hearing, for example not attending it after having received notice (see R. Clayton & H. Tomlinson, *Fair Trial Rights* (New York: Oxford University Press, 2010), 158).

[6] Conclusion: The Importance of Scheme 1

The above scheme illustrates the steps the court should take before the hearing takes place. The steps of the court outlined in the flowcharts are applicable to the vast majority of cases and aim at finalizing the case appropriately and effectively in due time, with full respect for the procedural rights of the participants.

As the flowcharts show, a considerable number of routine tasks should be undertaken by the court (especially in cases of typically recurrent claims). The whole procedure may be made even more efficient by setting up mini-teams, where the vast majority of these routine operations can be handled by an assistant of the judge/legal officer. However, after the summons to the hearing, the role of the judge is already indispensable.

[B] Particular Steps of the Court during the Hearing[16]

The court hearing is the peak of the judicial activity. Full exercise of the right to a fair trial is accomplished only during the hearing, in which the judge must particularly pay attention that his impartiality is not questioned, and should restrain any kind of sympathy, antipathy or different kind of treatment towards participants. At almost every step, the judge is closely scrutinized by the participant, who creates himself an image of how the dispute is developing for him.

The court hearing is oral[17] and public. The ECtHR reiterated in *Diennet v. France*[18] that:

> (...) the holding of court hearings in public constitutes a fundamental principle enshrined in paragraph 1 of Article 6 (art. 6-1) (see, as the most recent authority, the Schuler-Zgraggen v. Switzerland judgment of 24 June 1993, Series A no. 263, p. 19, para. 58). This public character protects litigants against the administration of justice in secret with no public scrutiny; it is also one of the means whereby confidence in the courts can be maintained. By rendering the administration of justice transparent, publicity contributes to the achievement of the aim of Article 6 para. 1 (art. 6-1), namely a fair trial, the guarantee of which is one of the fundamental principles of any democratic society, within the meaning of the Convention (see, for example, the Sutter v. Switzerland judgment of 22 February 1984, Series A no. 74, p. 12, para. 26).
>
> (*Diennet v. France*, Judgment of 31 August 1995, paragraph 33)

However, Article 6(1) provides a number of express restrictions from the principle of right to a public hearing – 'the press and public may be excluded from all or part of the

16. This subchapter was published with specifics of the Czech procedure: O. Pridal, *Postup soudu po nařízení jednání* [*The Particular Steps of the Court during the Hearing*], Bulletin advokacie [Attorney's Bulletin], 2009, No. 6, 39 et seq.
17. See, *ex multis*, *Fisher v. Austria*, Judgment of 26 April 1995, paragraph 44.
18. *Diennet v. France*, Judgment of 31 August 1995.

trial in the interests of morals, public order or national security[19] in a democratic society, where the interests of juveniles or the protection of the private life of the parties so require, or to the extent strictly necessary in the opinion of the court in special circumstances where publicity would prejudice the interests of justice.' There are other restrictions in the Court's jurisprudence. In *Osinger v. Austria*,[20] for example, the Court already considered that:

> In the course of proceedings where exclusively legal or highly technical questions are at stake, the requirements of Article 6 may be fulfilled even in the absence of a hearing. Moreover, neither the letter nor the spirit of this provision prevents a person from waiving of his own free will, either expressly or tacitly, the entitlement to have his case heard in public (see *Schuler-Zgraggen v. Switzerland*, Judgment of 24 June 1993, Series A no. 263, p. 19, § 58; and *Varela Assalino v. Portugal* (dec.), no. 64336/01, 25 April 2002).
>
> (*Osinger v. Austria*, Judgment of 25 March 2005, paragraph 45)

Scheme 6.2

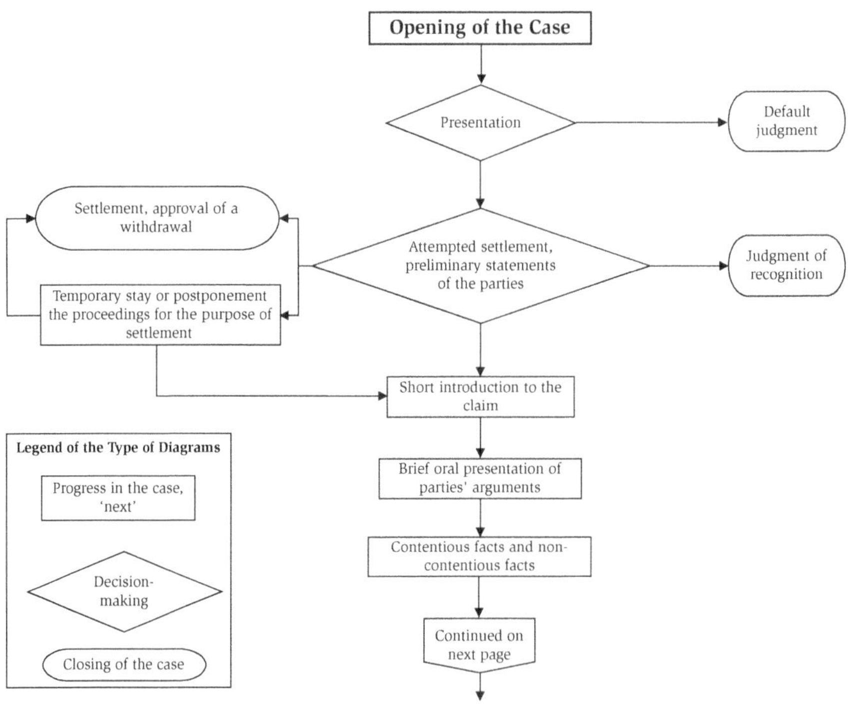

19. The Court accepted that there were sufficient reasons of public order and security justifying the exclusion of the press and public from the disciplinary proceedings held in prison in *Campbell and Fell v. the United Kingdom*, Judgment of 28 June 1984, paragraph 88.
20. *Osinger v. Austria*, Judgment of 25 March 2005.

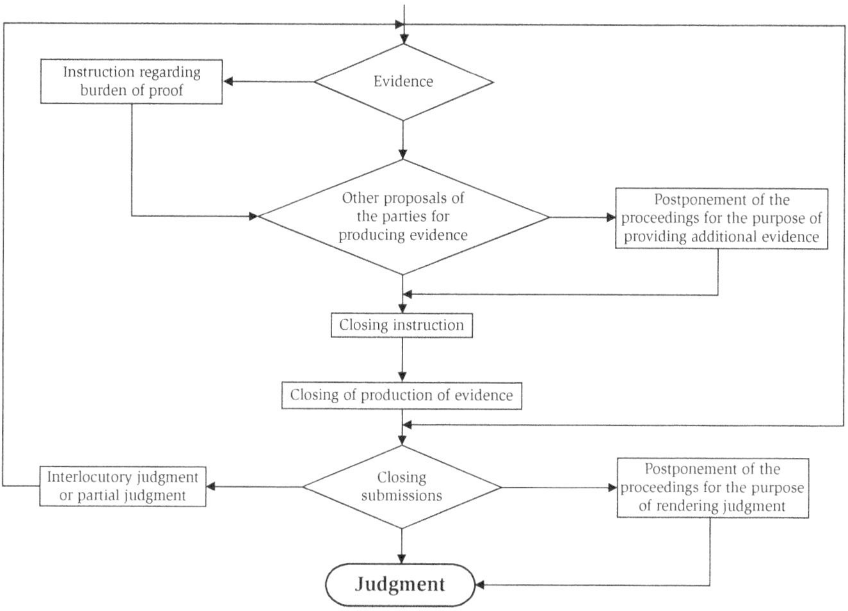

[1] Opening the Case, Presentation

The hearing starts with the stating of the case, which should be done in a loud and clear manner. This is followed by a presentation of the participants, with verification of their identity and, where applicable, their legal representation details. Participants have the right to be present at an oral hearing, and therefore they must be duly-summoned. It means that they have to be notified of the hearing according to the domestic[21] procedural law. If a duly-summoned participant fails to appear at the court hearing, the court may hear the case in his absence or otherwise issue a default judgment, which ends the proceedings.

If a duly-summoned participant (or his attorney) intends to achieve the adjournment of the hearing without the case being heard in his absence, he must either excuse himself or ask for an adjournment, and his excuse must also be justified and timely. Any request for adjournment of the hearing shall be made according to explicit conventional judicial practice. 'Timely excuse' means that a party excuses himself immediately upon learning the reason causing his absence, except when such reason itself prevents him from excusing himself (e.g., acute health problems); in such a case, timeliness shall be interpreted to mean as soon as an excuse can reasonably be

21. The way how to summon a participant differs from country to country. It could be done by various means during a proceeding hearing, by written notice, by mail, by e-mail, fax or phone, by police etc. Important is that national procedural law is respected and therefore the participant cannot object that he was truly surprised that a hearing was held.

submitted. The most frequently cited reason for an excuse is a health problem - which must be accompanied by a sick note - but it is possible to distinguish between a medical problem preventing the participation in the trial and one which does not (e.g., a fractured finger).

Another very common reason for an excuse is when two hearings of the participant's attorney coincide. For example, the case law of several jurisdictions is in the sense that the party must notify the court and submit specific information about why he cannot attend the hearing, specifying which other hearing would prevent his participation and when he has learned about it (in other words, that his summons to the other hearing arrived prior to the one from which he excuses himself) and that the collision cannot be solved otherwise, including by means of substitution.[22]

In the event that an adjournment of the hearing is not granted, the court is not obliged to notify the party of non-compliance; in this matter, each participant must ascertain for himself that his proposal for adjournment has been approved.[23] If the court hears the case in the absence of a participant without complying with the rules mentioned above, it violates the participant's right to a fair trial by deprivation of the opportunity to act before the court and the affected participant may appeal the decision.

[2] Attempted Settlement: Preliminary Statements of the Parties

After the commencement of the proceedings, the court attempts to settle the dispute. The institute of settlement is, in practice, quite underestimated. For example, the court limits itself to one or two sentences, which has to be considered as not sufficient, because settlement is considered one of the best civil procedure practices.[24] It is appropriate to know the preliminary views of the participants for the purpose of the settlement, and to make the participants familiar with the court's jurisprudence. A less well-known option is the conclusion of a conditional settlement (when the settlement is bound to a specific condition), such as when the claimant may, within one month after the conclusion, withdraw the settlement in case the respondent has not paid the required sum of money, at which time the court would continue with the proceedings.

An interesting alternative for the participants may also be to agree that the claimant will withdraw the claim and receive full or partial payment of the required sum of money from the respondent. After the withdrawal of the claim, the proceedings shall end and the court fees shall also be returned to the claimant. The court can have quite an active role in the settlement; it can lead the participants to settle the case, give

22. See, for example, Judgment of the Supreme Court of the Czech Republic of 25 May 1999, R 38/2000.
23. See, among others, Judgment of the Supreme Court of the Czech Republic of 14 October 2003, 22 Cdo 1962/2003.
24. A settlement can be considered a better solution than a judgment by the court, because a compromise is reached and accepted by both parties. On the contrary, the judgment might be for one party (and sometimes for both) an unfavourable solution. Furthermore, the settlement of a dispute can sometimes lead to the restoration of a business cooperation between the parties.

them a preliminary non-binding opinion on the merits or postpone[25] the hearing for the purpose of negotiating the settlement. Finally, the third and not entirely exceptional option is the recognition of the claim, which leads to a judgment of recognition.

[3] Short Introduction to the Claim, Oral Presentation of the Parties' Arguments

If the settlement fails, a short introduction to the claim shall follow, detailing what has been done so far by the court. This is important because it lets the participants know that the court is aware of all their submissions and opinions. The program of the hearing should then be announced, which helps the parties to understand what will follow. After that, the parties are allowed to make brief oral presentations of their arguments. The parties may also refer to written documents and the court may ask a participant to elaborate more closely on certain facts or to clarify some facts if his previous presentation was not sufficient.

[4] Contentious Facts and Non-contentious Facts

The court will discuss contentious and non-contentious facts with the participants. This activity is sometimes underestimated in practice; with proper implementation, it can reasonably simplify the fact-finding process, because the allegations regarding the substantial sum of facts will coincide. This will help saving time and energy for all the actors. Moreover, the court can then focus the fact-finding process on contentious facts.

An important issue and often unsolved by civil procedures concerns the 'unopposed' facts, i.e., the claimant alleges certain facts which the respondent does not oppose. Judicial practice quite often comes out of unopposed facts, which may sometimes be seen as problematic, due to the fact that the parties cannot anticipate what will happen. Occasionally, there is no need of a fact-finding process at all, in the case where no relief could be granted even if all the claimant's allegations were proven.[26]

[5] Evidence, Closing of the Production of Evidence

The next stage is the production of evidence. Here, the participants propose and introduce evidence, and the court decides which evidence can be produced. Both parties have the right to have knowledge of, and to comment on, the evidence and observations, both on the evidence proposed (why it cannot be produced) and also on

25. For the purpose of assessing whether the case was decided in a 'reasonable time', the period of negotiation required to reach a settlement is not taken into account (*Lithgow and Others v. the United Kingdom*, Judgment of 8 July 1986, paragraph 199).
26. See, for example, the Judgment of the Supreme Court of the Czech Republic of 30 January 2008, 25 Cdo 214/2006.

the evidence already produced, thereby contributing with their evaluation to the discretionary weighing of evidence by the court and to the formation of its conclusion on fact[27] (right to adversarial proceedings).

Another important aspect of the right to a fair trial is that of 'equality of arms' (no substantial disadvantage vis-à-vis his or her opponent), already examined in Chapter 3. Among many others, in *Anket v. Switzerland*,[28] for example, the ECtHR reiterated that:

> (...) 'equality of arms', in the sense of a 'fair balance' between the parties, applies also to litigation in which private interests are opposed; in such instances 'equality of arms' implies that each party must be afforded a reasonable opportunity to present his case – including his evidence -under conditions that do not place him at a substantial disadvantage vis-à-vis his opponent (see the Dombo Beheer B.V. Judgment previously cited, p. 19, paras. 32-33).
>
> (*Anket v. Switzerland*, Judgment of 23 October 1996, paragraph 38)

For every proposed piece of evidence, the participant is obliged to state clearly and unequivocally which allegation this evidence is aimed to prove. Only thus can the principles of predictability of court procedure and of economy of the proceedings be satisfied. If a participant does not state unambiguously and clearly what should be proven by the proposed evidence, he will risk that the proposed evidence will not be authorized, for which he will not be able to prove the particular facts and will risk to be unsuccessful in the lawsuit.

The court does not allow the proposed evidence if this clearly cannot prove material facts.[29] A problem, viewed from the perspective of the right to a fair trial, can be that of evidence which has been obtained by illegal means ('fruit of the poisonous tree doctrine'), on which see, *amplius*, Chapter 3. What counts is whether the proceedings as a whole, including the unlawfully obtained evidence, may be considered as fair. This was, *inter alia*, pronounced by the ECtHR in *Khan v. the United Kingdom*:[30]

> It is not the role of the Court to determine, as a matter of principle, whether particular types of evidence – for example, unlawfully obtained evidence – may be admissible or, indeed, whether the applicant was guilty or not. The question which must be answered is whether the proceedings as a whole, including the way in which the evidence was obtained, were fair. This involves an examination of the 'unlawfulness' in question and, where violation of another Convention right is concerned, the nature of the violation found.'
>
> (*Khan v. the United Kingdom*, Judgment of 12 May 2000, paragraph 34)

27. Compare with *Lobo Machado v. Portugal*, Judgment of 20 February 1996, paragraph 31.
28. *Anket v. Switzerland*, Judgment of 23 October 1996.
29. On the other hand, when the proposed evidence relates to relevant facts, then court cannot deny this evidence on the grounds that it would still not confirm the truth of the particular fact (see, for example, Decision of the Constitutional Court of the Czech Republic of 13 September 1999, sp. No. I. ÚS 236/98) or deny proposed evidence with reference to its unreliability (see Judgment of the Supreme Court of the Czech Republic of 9 October 2002 R 40/2003).
30. *Khan v. the United Kingdom*, Judgment of 12 May 2000.

Torture evidence is completely inadmissible. For instance, in *Othman v. the United Kingdom*[31] the ECtHR considered that:

> The admission of torture evidence is manifestly contrary, not just to the provisions of Article 6, but to the most basic international standards of a fair trial. It would make the whole trial not only immoral and illegal, but also entirely unreliable in its outcome.
>
> (*Othman [Abu Qatada] v. the United Kingdom*, Judgment of 17 January 2012, paragraph 267)

Likewise, the court would not allow evidence where the participant failed to demonstrate which allegation should be proven, and when the evidence has apparently been proposed to purposefully prolong the proceedings. If the court does not produce proposed evidence, it is obliged to properly justify this in its decision on the merits.[32]

The court instructs the participants as to how to meet their burden of proof and on their duty to allege material facts. Other participants' proposals (in consequence of the court's instruction) may require an adjournment of the hearing, for instance when there is the need to summon witnesses or obtain documents. However, the court should try to avoid adjournments by careful preparation.

Upon conclusion of the process of producing evidence, instruction regarding the necessity to apply the relevant facts and evidence before the announcement of the decision on the merits takes place. The way in which the participants respond to this instruction must be annotated in the proceedings record. It is then appropriate to close the phase of evidence production, for example by resolution to reject any unnecessary and redundant evidence.

[6] Closing Submissions

Finally, the court grants the floor, for the purpose of closing submissions, at which point the participants should comment on the facts and on the legal aspects as well.[33] Some participants express themselves in a somewhat lengthy manner in this closing speech, the essential content of which is noted down by the court recorder. It should be mentioned that the court may postpone the hearing for the purpose of rendering the judgment, and thus gaining some time for the deliberation. An additional possibility could be to return to the stage of producing evidence, should this be deemed necessary.

The court may also issue an interlocutory judgment or partial judgment and decide, for example, that the claimant's right for damages is to be granted and that the amount of damages will be decided after this interlocutory judgment shall be in full legal force. An interlocutory or partial judgment complies with the terms of the principle of the economy of proceedings.

31. *Othman [Abu Qatada] v. the United Kingdom*, Judgment of 17 January 2012.
32. See, for example, Judgment of the Constitutional Court of the Czech Republic of 13 June 2006, sp. No. I. ÚS 50/03.
33. It has to benoted that in some States the closing submissions are written and not oral.

[7] Judgment

The closing submissions are followed by a suspension of the proceedings for the purpose of deliberating the judgment. Judgment is to be public to ensure scrutiny of the judiciary by the public, with a view to safeguarding the right to a fair trial. Nevertheless, it is possible in some countries to make the judgment available in the court registry, rendering its full text available to everyone. For example, as it has already been said in Chapter 3, in *Pretto and Others v. Italy*[34] the ECtHR did not interpret the words 'pronounced publicly' literally:

> However, many member States of the Council of Europe have a long-standing tradition of recourse to other means, besides reading out aloud, for making public the decisions of all or some of their courts, and especially of their courts of cassation, for example deposit in a registry accessible to the public. (...)The Court therefore does not feel bound to adopt a literal interpretation. It considers that in each case the form of publicity to be given to the 'judgment' under the domestic law of the respondent State must be assessed in the light of the special features of the proceedings in question and by reference to the object and purpose of Article 6 § 1 (art. 6-1). (...) In the opinion of the Court, the object pursued by Article 6 § 1 (art. 6-1) in this context - namely, to ensure scrutiny of the judiciary by the public with a view to safeguarding the right to a fair trial - is, at any rate as regards cassation proceedings, no less achieved by a deposit in the court registry, making the full text of the judgment available to everyone, than by a reading in open court of a decision dismissing an appeal or quashing a previous judgment, such reading sometimes being limited to the operative provisions.
>
> (*Pretto and Others v. Italy*, Judgment of 8 December 1983, paragraphs 26 and 27)

According to the right to a reasoned judgment, the judgment itself must be properly justified. A written reasoning of a scant two sentences would therefore constitute malpractice. A reasoned judgment requires that every decisive factor be elucidated, but on the other hand does not mean that detailed answers must be given to every argument. This was reiterated, among others, by the ECtHR in *Hiro Balani v. Spain*:[35]

> (...) Article 6 para. 1 (art. 6-1) obliges the courts to give reasons for their judgments, but cannot be understood as requiring a detailed answer to every argument (see the Van de Hurk v. the Netherlands judgment of 19 April 1994, Series A no. 288, p. 20, para. 61). The extent to which this duty to give reasons applies may vary according to the nature of the decision. It is moreover necessary to take into account, inter alia, the diversity of the submissions that a litigant may bring before the courts and the differences existing in the Contracting States with regard to statutory provisions, customary rules, legal opinion and the presentation and drafting of judgments. That is why the question whether a court has failed to fulfil the obligation to state reasons, deriving from Article 6 (art. 6) of the Convention, can only be determined in the light of the circumstances of the case.
>
> (*Hiro Balani v. Spain*, Judgment of 9 December 1994, paragraph 27)

34. *Pretto and Others v. Italy*, Judgment of 8 December 1983.
35. *Hiro Balani v. Spain*, Judgment of 9 December 1994.

However, the court must indicate with sufficient clarity the grounds on which it based its decision[36] with the aim of making its reasoning persuasive. After the announcement of the judgment, the court usually asks the participants whether they wish to waive an appeal against it.

[8] Conclusion: The Importance of Scheme 2

The above scheme illustrates the course of a hearing, i.e., the individual steps taken by the court and the participants until the judgment is rendered. The steps of the court in the flowcharts are applicable to the vast majority of cases;[37] their objective is to end the case appropriately and effectively within a reasonable time, with full respect of the right to a fair trial.

The scheme illustrates how a considerable number of steps must be carried out in order to render a judgment, and highlights the importance of the order of these steps. One may consider whether this or that procedure is well-suited for each type of claim. English civil procedure, for example, could provide interesting solutions in this context, as claims are distinguished as appertaining to a small claims track, a fast track or a multi-track (see below). One important principle common to all claims is to be mentioned at the end: *justice must not only be done, it must also be seen to be done.*

§6.03 THE ORDER OF THE CASES

The order of the cases is generally not subject to regulation in civil procedure; however, precedence should be given to cases of special importance and to old cases. Cases of special importance are those with social significance (judicial care of minors, personal status, cases with an elevated number of participants) and those which are especially important for specific categories of individuals (labour disputes, claims concerning damage to health, pension insurance schemes, etc.).

For example, in *Nuutinen v. Finland*[38] the ECtHR stated:

> On the latter point, the importance of what is at stake for the applicant in the litigation has to be taken into account. It is thus essential that custody cases be dealt with speedily (see, for example, the *Hokkanen v. Finland* Judgment of 23 September 1994, Series A no. 299-A, p. 25, § 69)'.
>
> (*Nuutinen v. Finland*, Judgment of 27 June 2000, paragraph 110)

The special importance of a case is generally found where a delayed adjudication of the same would determine significant and irreparable damage. After claims of special importance, older cases should be adjudicated. In this regard, it should be

36. *Hadjianastassiou v. Greece*, Judgment of 16 December 1992, paragraph 32.
37. The hearing may obviously be adjourned at any stage, and the next steps undertaken successively. Likewise, in certain proceedings other situations not covered by the scheme may occur (e.g., legal succession, the withdrawal of the claim, the unknown residence of a participant - see also the preceding subsection 'The Procedure before the Hearing Takes Place').
38. *Nuutinen v. Finland*, Judgment of 27 June 2000.

mentioned that older cases are often supervised by the State court administration, and are thus systemically accelerated. Cases are often accelerated also judicially: constitutional courts are frequently authorized to render a decision that a case shall have priority over other cases, because it has not been adjudicated in a reasonable time and there have been particular undue delays. Next come the cases ordered according to their date. By respecting the above-mentioned rationale, a hearing of cases of the same type and involving the same parties may be efficiently summoned on the same day.

A fair trial would certainly benefit from a case resolution of small cases (small claims track), medium cases (fast track) and complex cases (multi-track), as it has been done, for example, in the English civil procedure. As noted by an eminent Author, 'small claims tracks' (most claims up to £. 5.000.00) have simplified the procedure, which develops faster because the preparation of the case is limited and fact-findings are accelerated. A similarly simplified procedure also characterizes the 'fast track' cases (from £. 5.000.00 to £. 25,000.00; however, some claims within this amount can fall within the 'multi-track' cases when they are particularly complex), where hearings have to be held in 30 weeks. The most time is taken by the so-called 'multi-track' cases (over £. 25,000), where the full procedure is applied with all the guarantees, since they involve the most important cases in terms of the value of the claim or the public interest.[39]

§6.04 THE USE OF MODERN TECHNOLOGY

It is beneficial to use modern technology to provide a fair and swift trial. The use of computers can now be taken for granted (although a few years back, they were not available to all courts and judges). It is thus possible to communicate with participants via electronic means. These are widely used nowadays by lawyers, whose submissions are filed in electronic form.[40] A submission transmitted by fax or e-mail and guaranteed by an electronic signature[41] is self-standing; without the latter, the electronic communication must be followed by a written submission for it to be validated. The courts are also sending more and more correspondence by email, for example to send out the minutes of a hearing.

39. See, among others, S. Sime, *A Practical Approach to Civil Procedure* (New York: Oxford University Press, 2006), 279, 283 and 290. For a systematic and detailed account of the English civil procedure, see N. Andrews, *English Civil Procedure: Fundamentals of the New Civil Justice System* (New York: Oxford University Press, 2003).
40. In *Lawyer Partners, a.s. v. Slovakia,* Judgment of 16 June 2009, paragraphs 49-56, the ECtHR found it inappropriate and a violation of Article 6 ECHR to refuse the claimant's actions filed on DVD, even though about 70,000 actions had been filed electronically, necessitating their being printed at the expense of the Slovak state. The Court reiterated that the Convention is intended to guarantee rights that are not theoretical or illusory, but practical and effective. This is particularly relevant with regard to Article 6(1), in view of the prominent place held in a democratic society by the right to a fair trial.
41. The guaranteed electronic signature is the digital data that the signatory created using his private key and which ensures the integrity and origin of the signed data. See S. Stedron, *Contested Civil Procedure and Use of Information Technology and Legal Information Systems (E-Justice)* (Linde Praha, a.s., 2008), 46.

A lawyer may also be obliged – if it is necessary for the conduct of the proceedings – to produce certain documents in electronic form. Authoritative literature – with regard to the English civil procedure – observed that in the judge may even order the submission of evidentiary documentation in electronic form, noting – however – that the Court of Appeal (of England and Wales) had the occasion to remark that technology should be used in order to save time and money, and only if it does not put any party in position of disadvantage.[42]

Some tasks can be accomplished by telephone as well, such as a summons to the hearing, adjournment of the hearing or other minor procedural acts. With regard to the merits, however, the judge should act only in the presence of both parties. *De lege ferenda*, video conferencing may, for example, be used to hear a witness at another court (without compelling him to travel a great distance to the site of the proceedings or even in a foreign country) or to interrogate a witness in prison.

Judges already have at their disposal a variety of computer programs, including electronic jurisprudence databases (with advanced search features), databases of written law, various calculators for calculating interest on late payment, travel expenses, etc. It is of course possible to use the internet as a source of information or sometimes to provide a piece of evidence.

The idea of an electronic file has been outlined for the future. Participants w be able to inspect the file remotely, accessing their file with a password, in order to prevent the leaking of sensitive information. The use of such a file will be convenient and reduce the risk of losing documents as well. Other courts and authorities would be able to see it without the necessity of its being sent, and every access will be monitored, to maximize the security of the remote approach. Another advantage of the electronic file would lie in the economy of its use and it would also be 'ecological', as it will not be necessary to print and copy every document. A search engine will enable particular information to be obtained rapidly. In several countries, some information from files, for example the terms of hearings, are already available on internet.

Modern technology has already affected judges, the evaluation of evidence, and the issuing of judgments. Participants sometimes submit as evidence a video record, an internet page, an email or even an SMS. This evidence cannot be overestimated, on the other hand emails or any other electronic document is full-fledged evidence, which, if proposed, can be produced by the court and has no less probative value than a written document a priori.[43] Unjustified failure to produce such evidence could therefore lead to a violation of the right to a fair trial.

Accompanying the development of modern technologies is an increasing risk of automation of the judiciary. Views are emerging[44] in society that the work of a judge can be replaced by a computer or by a combination of a computer and an expert computer system (intelligent system created by lawyers and programmers). The most frequently expressed advantage is the swiftness of the proceedings. This opinion is ill-founded. One can immediately point to its deviation from the basic purpose of the

42. See, in this sense, S. Sime, cited above, 23-24.
43. See *Lawyer Partners a.s. v. Slovakia*, cited above.
44. In particular from people working in IT.

court trial: a fair protection of fundamental rights and interests. No computer is capable of this protection; the program can only compare pre-specified criteria. And no program is minimally capable of making judicial deliberations and a sensitive assessment of the situation in a particular individual case (the right to a fair trial is the judge-made-law). Society and human behaviour are so highly differentiated (and the same is true of the structure of the language with which the parties communicate) that it is impossible to assume all of the possible situations, and thus impossible to adequately equip a computer with the necessary knowledge for solving claims.

Another risk in the use of modern technology is an exaggerated monitoring of the performance of judges, connected with the prioritization of the number of finalized cases over the quality of adjudication. The information systems established in the courts, in fact, allow very accurate monitoring of the work of a judge with regard to his performance, but delays in the proceedings. As explained above, the quality of judgment is necessarily an essential value for a fair trial.

Modern civil procedure should be able to assimilate technological innovations in order to better fulfil the criteria of the right to a fair trial and, consequently, the common interest of society. The traditional problem in this context – together with that of lack of funding – is the considerable conservative nature of judicial practice, which is often reluctant to give up its 'beaten paths'. The process of digitalization is further impeded by the fact that the law is always one step behind social-technological development. But, in the end, judicial practice will inevitably have to adopt modern technologies, due to the simple fact that it must necessarily follow real life changes and needs.

APPENDIX

Convention for the Protection of Human Rights and Fundamental Freedoms*

Rome, 4.XI.1950

The governments signatory hereto, being members of the Council of Europe,

Considering the Universal Declaration of Human Rights proclaimed by the General Assembly of the United Nations on 10th December 1948;

Considering that this Declaration aims at securing the universal and effective recognition and observance of the Rights therein declared;

Considering that the aim of the Council of Europe is the achievement of greater unity between its members and that one of the methods by which that aim is to be pursued is the maintenance and further realisation of human rights and fundamental freedoms;

Reaffirming their profound belief in those fundamental freedoms which are the foundation of justice and peace in the world and are best maintained on the one hand by an effective political democracy and on the other by a common understanding and observance of the human rights upon which they depend;

Being resolved, as the governments of European countries which are like-minded and have a common heritage of political traditions, ideals, freedom and the rule of law, to take the first steps for the collective enforcement of certain of the rights stated in the Universal Declaration,

Have agreed as follows:

Article 1 - Obligation to respect human rights

The High Contracting Parties shall secure to everyone within their jurisdiction the rights and freedoms defined in Section I of this Convention.

---

* Text as amended by Protocol No. 11 and Protocol No. 14.

Section I – Rights and freedoms

Article 2 – Right to life

1 Everyone's right to life shall be protected by law. No one shall be deprived of his life intentionally save in the execution of a sentence of a court following his conviction of a crime for which this penalty is provided by law.
2 Deprivation of life shall not be regarded as inflicted in contravention of this article when it results from the use of force which is no more than absolutely necessary:
  a in defence of any person from unlawful violence;
  b in order to effect a lawful arrest or to prevent the escape of a person lawfully detained;
  c in action lawfully taken for the purpose of quelling a riot or insurrection.

Article 3 – Prohibition of torture

No one shall be subjected to torture or to inhuman or degrading treatment or punishment.

Article 4 – Prohibition of slavery and forced labour

1 No one shall be held in slavery or servitude.
2 No one shall be required to perform forced or compulsory labour.
3 For the purpose of this article the term 'forced or compulsory labour' shall not include:
  a any work required to be done in the ordinary course of detention imposed according to the provisions of Article 5 of this Convention or during conditional release from such detention;
  b any service of a military character or, in case of conscientious objectors in countries where they are recognised, service exacted instead of compulsory military service;
  c any service exacted in case of an emergency or calamity threatening the life or well-being of the community;
  d any work or service which forms part of normal civic obligations.

Article 5 – Right to liberty and security

1 Everyone has the right to liberty and security of person. No one shall be deprived of his liberty save in the following cases and in accordance with a procedure prescribed by law:
  a the lawful detention of a person after conviction by a competent court;

b the lawful arrest or detention of a person for non-compliance with the lawful order of a court or in order to secure the fulfilment of any obligation prescribed by law;
c the lawful arrest or detention of a person effected for the purpose of bringing him before the competent legal authority on reasonable suspicion of having committed an offence or when it is reasonably considered necessary to prevent his committing an offence or fleeing after having done so;
d the detention of a minor by lawful order for the purpose of educational supervision or his lawful detention for the purpose of bringing him before the competent legal authority;
e the lawful detention of persons for the prevention of the spreading of infectious diseases, of persons of unsound mind, alcoholics or drug addicts or vagrants;
f the lawful arrest or detention of a person to prevent his effecting an unauthorised entry into the country or of a person against whom action is being taken with a view to deportation or extradition.

2 Everyone who is arrested shall be informed promptly, in a language which he understands, of the reasons for his arrest and of any charge against him.
3 Everyone arrested or detained in accordance with the provisions of paragraph 1.c of this article shall be brought promptly before a judge or other officer authorised by law to exercise judicial power and shall be entitled to trial within a reasonable time or to release pending trial. Release may be conditioned by guarantees to appear for trial.
4 Everyone who is deprived of his liberty by arrest or detention shall be entitled to take proceedings by which the lawfulness of his detention shall be decided speedily by a court and his release ordered if the detention is not lawful.
5 Everyone who has been the victim of arrest or detention in contravention of the provisions of this article shall have an enforceable right to compensation.

Article 6 – Right to a fair trial

1 In the determination of his civil rights and obligations or of any criminal charge against him, everyone is entitled to a fair and public hearing within a reasonable time by an independent and impartial tribunal established by law. Judgment shall be pronounced publicly but the press and public may be excluded from all or part of the trial in the interests of morals, public order or national security in a democratic society, where the interests of juveniles or the protection of the private life of the parties so require, or to the extent strictly necessary in the opinion of the court in special circumstances where publicity would prejudice the interests of justice.
2 Everyone charged with a criminal offence shall be presumed innocent until proved guilty according to law.

3 Everyone charged with a criminal offence has the following minimum rights:
   a to be informed promptly, in a language which he understands and in detail, of the nature and cause of the accusation against him;
   b to have adequate time and facilities for the preparation of his defence;
   c to defend himself in person or through legal assistance of his own choosing or, if he has not sufficient means to pay for legal assistance, to be given it free when the interests of justice so require;
   d to examine or have examined witnesses against him and to obtain the attendance and examination of witnesses on his behalf under the same conditions as witnesses against him;
   e to have the free assistance of an interpreter if he cannot understand or speak the language used in court.

Article 7 – No punishment without law

1 No one shall be held guilty of any criminal offence on account of any act or omission which did not constitute a criminal offence under national or international law at the time when it was committed. Nor shall a heavier penalty be imposed than the one that was applicable at the time the criminal offence was committed.

2 This article shall not prejudice the trial and punishment of any person for any act or omission which, at the time when it was committed, was criminal according to the general principles of law recognised by civilised nations.

Article 8 – Right to respect for private and family life

1 Everyone has the right to respect for his private and family life, his home and his correspondence.

2 There shall be no interference by a public authority with the exercise of this right except such as is in accordance with the law and is necessary in a democratic society in the interests of national security, public safety or the economic well-being of the country, for the prevention of disorder or crime, for the protection of health or morals, or for the protection of the rights and freedoms of others.

Article 9 – Freedom of thought, conscience and religion

1 Everyone has the right to freedom of thought, conscience and religion; this right includes freedom to change his religion or belief and freedom, either alone or in community with others and in public or private, to manifest his religion or belief, in worship, teaching, practice and observance.

2 Freedom to manifest one's religion or beliefs shall be subject only to such limitations as are prescribed by law and are necessary in a democratic society

in the interests of public safety, for the protection of public order, health or morals, or for the protection of the rights and freedoms of others.

Article 10 – Freedom of expression

1 Everyone has the right to freedom of expression. This right shall include freedom to hold opinions and to receive and impart information and ideas without interference by public authority and regardless of frontiers. This article shall not prevent States from requiring the licensing of broadcasting, television or cinema enterprises.
2 The exercise of these freedoms, since it carries with it duties and responsibilities, may be subject to such formalities, conditions, restrictions or penalties as are prescribed by law and are necessary in a democratic society, in the interests of national security, territorial integrity or public safety, for the prevention of disorder or crime, for the protection of health or morals, for the protection of the reputation or rights of others, for preventing the disclosure of information received in confidence, or for maintaining the authority and impartiality of the judiciary.

Article 11 – Freedom of assembly and association

1 Everyone has the right to freedom of peaceful assembly and to freedom of association with others, including the right to form and to join trade unions for the protection of his interests.
2 No restrictions shall be placed on the exercise of these rights other than such as are prescribed by law and are necessary in a democratic society in the interests of national security or public safety, for the prevention of disorder or crime, for the protection of health or morals or for the protection of the rights and freedoms of others. This article shall not prevent the imposition of lawful restrictions on the exercise of these rights by members of the armed forces, of the police or of the administration of the State.

Article 12 – Right to marry

Men and women of marriageable age have the right to marry and to found a family, according to the national laws governing the exercise of this right.

Article 13 – Right to an effective remedy

Everyone whose rights and freedoms as set forth in this Convention are violated shall have an effective remedy before a national authority notwithstanding that the violation has been committed by persons acting in an official capacity.

Article 14 – Prohibition of discrimination

The enjoyment of the rights and freedoms set forth in this Convention shall be secured without discrimination on any ground such as sex, race, colour, language, religion, political or other opinion, national or social origin, association with a national minority, property, birth or other status.

Article 15 – Derogation in time of emergency

1 In time of war or other public emergency threatening the life of the nation any High Contracting Party may take measures derogating from its obligations under this Convention to the extent strictly required by the exigencies of the situation, provided that such measures are not inconsistent with its other obligations under international law.
2 No derogation from Article 2, except in respect of deaths resulting from lawful acts of war, or from Articles 3, 4 (paragraph 1) and 7 shall be made under this provision.
3 Any High Contracting Party availing itself of this right of derogation shall keep the Secretary General of the Council of Europe fully informed of the measures which it has taken and the reasons therefor. It shall also inform the Secretary General of the Council of Europe when such measures have ceased to operate and the provisions of the Convention are again being fully executed.

Article 16 – Restrictions on political activity of aliens

Nothing in Articles 10, 11 and 14 shall be regarded as preventing the High Contracting Parties from imposing restrictions on the political activity of aliens.

Article 17 – Prohibition of abuse of rights

Nothing in this Convention may be interpreted as implying for any State, group or person any right to engage in any activity or perform any act aimed at the destruction of any of the rights and freedoms set forth herein or at their limitation to a greater extent than is provided for in the Convention.

Article 18 – Limitation on use of restrictions on rights

The restrictions permitted under this Convention to the said rights and freedoms shall not be applied for any purpose other than those for which they have been prescribed.

Section II – European Court of Human Rights

Article 19 – Establishment of the Court

To ensure the observance of the engagements undertaken by the High Contracting Parties in the Convention and the Protocols thereto, there shall be set up a European Court of Human Rights, hereinafter referred to as 'the Court'. It shall function on a permanent basis.

Article 20 – Number of judges

The Court shall consist of a number of judges equal to that of the High Contracting Parties.

Article 21 – Criteria for office

1 The judges shall be of high moral character and must either possess the qualifications required for appointment to high judicial office or be jurisconsults of recognised competence.
2 The judges shall sit on the Court in their individual capacity.
3 During their term of office the judges shall not engage in any activity which is incompatible with their independence, impartiality or with the demands of a full-time office; all questions arising from the application of this paragraph shall be decided by the Court.

Article 22 – Election of judges

The judges shall be elected by the Parliamentary Assembly with respect to each High Contracting Party by a majority of votes cast from a list of three candidates nominated by the High Contracting Party.

Article 23 – Terms of office and dismissal

1 The judges shall be elected for a period of nine years. They may not be re-elected.
2 The terms of office of judges shall expire when they reach the age of 70.
3 The judges shall hold office until replaced. They shall, however, continue to deal with such cases as they already have under consideration.
4 No judge may be dismissed from office unless the other judges decide by a majority of two-thirds that that judge has ceased to fulfil the required conditions.

Article 24 – Registry and rapporteurs

1 The Court shall have a registry, the functions and organisation of which shall be laid down in the rules of the Court.
2 When sitting in a single-judge formation, the Court shall be assisted by rapporteurs who shall function under the authority of the President of the Court. They shall form part of the Court's registry.

Article 25 – Plenary Court

The plenary Court shall

a elect its President and one or two Vice-Presidents for a period of three years; they may be re-elected;
b set up Chambers, constituted for a fixed period of time;
c elect the Presidents of the Chambers of the Court; they may be re-elected;
d adopt the rules of the Court;
e elect the Registrar and one or more Deputy Registrars;
f make any request under Article 26, paragraph 2.

Article 26 – Single-judge formation, committees, Chambers and Grand Chamber

1 To consider cases brought before it, the Court shall sit in a single-judge formation, in committees of three judges, in Chambers of seven judges and in a Grand Chamber of seventeen judges. The Court's Chambers shall set up committees for a fixed period of time.
2 At the request of the plenary Court, the Committee of Ministers may, by a unanimous decision and for a fixed period, reduce to five the number of judges of the Chambers.
3 When sitting as a single judge, a judge shall not examine any application against the High Contracting Party in respect of which that judge has been elected.
4 There shall sit as an *ex officio* member of the Chamber and the Grand Chamber the judge elected in respect of the High Contracting Party concerned. If there is none or if that judge is unable to sit, a person chosen by the President of the Court from a list submitted in advance by that Party shall sit in the capacity of judge.
5 The Grand Chamber shall also include the President of the Court, the Vice-Presidents, the Presidents of the Chambers and other judges chosen in accordance with the rules of the Court. When a case is referred to the Grand Chamber under Article 43, no judge from the Chamber which rendered the judgment shall sit in the Grand Chamber, with the exception of the President of the Chamber and the judge who sat in respect of the High Contracting Party concerned.

Article 27 – Competence of single judges

1 A single judge may declare inadmissible or strike out of the Court's list of cases an application submitted under Article 34, where such a decision can be taken without further examination.
2 The decision shall be final.
3 If the single judge does not declare an application inadmissible or strike it out, that judge shall forward it to a committee or to a Chamber for further examination.

Article 28 – Competence of committees

1 In respect of an application submitted under Article 34, a committee may, by a unanimous vote,
  a declare it inadmissible or strike it out of its list of cases, where such decision can be taken without further examination; or
  b declare it admissible and render at the same time a judgment on the merits, if the underlying question in the case, concerning the interpretation or the application of the Convention or the Protocols thereto, is already the subject of well-established case-law of the Court.
2 Decisions and judgments under paragraph 1 shall be final.
3 If the judge elected in respect of the High Contracting Party concerned is not a member of the committee, the committee may at any stage of the proceedings invite that judge to take the place of one of the members of the committee, having regard to all relevant factors, including whether that Party has contested the application of the procedure under paragraph 1.b.

Article 29 – Decisions by Chambers on admissibility and merits

1 If no decision is taken under Article 27 or 28, or no judgment rendered under Article 28, a Chamber shall decide on the admissibility and merits of individual applications submitted under Article 34. The decision on admissibility may be taken separately.
2 A Chamber shall decide on the admissibility and merits of inter-State applications submitted under Article 33. The decision on admissibility shall be taken separately unless the Court, in exceptional cases, decides otherwise.

Article 30 – Relinquishment of jurisdiction to the Grand Chamber

Where a case pending before a Chamber raises a serious question affecting the interpretation of the Convention or the protocols thereto, or where the resolution of a question before the Chamber might have a result inconsistent with a judgment previously delivered by the Court, the Chamber may, at any time before it has rendered its judgment, relinquish jurisdiction in favour of the Grand Chamber, unless one of the parties to the case objects.

Article 31 – Powers of the Grand Chamber

The Grand Chamber shall

a determine applications submitted either under Article 33 or Article 34 when a Chamber has relinquished jurisdiction under Article 30 or when the case has been referred to it under Article 43;
b decide on issues referred to the Court by the Committee of Ministers in accordance with Article 46, paragraph 4; and
c consider requests for advisory opinions submitted under Article 47.

Article 32 – Jurisdiction of the Court

1 The jurisdiction of the Court shall extend to all matters concerning the interpretation and application of the Convention and the protocols thereto which are referred to it as provided in Articles 33, 34, 46 and 47.
2 In the event of dispute as to whether the Court has jurisdiction, the Court shall decide.

Article 33 – Inter-State cases

Any High Contracting Party may refer to the Court any alleged breach of the provisions of the Convention and the protocols thereto by another High Contracting Party.

Article 34 – Individual applications

The Court may receive applications from any person, non-governmental organisation or group of individuals claiming to be the victim of a violation by one of the High Contracting Parties of the rights set forth in the Convention or the protocols thereto. The High Contracting Parties undertake not to hinder in any way the effective exercise of this right.

Article 35 – Admissibility criteria

1 The Court may only deal with the matter after all domestic remedies have been exhausted, according to the generally recognised rules of international law, and within a period of six months from the date on which the final decision was taken.
2 The Court shall not deal with any application submitted under Article 34 that

a is anonymous; or
b is substantially the same as a matter that has already been examined by the Court or has already been submitted to another procedure of international investigation or settlement and contains no relevant new information.

3 The Court shall declare inadmissible any individual application submitted under Article 34 if it considers that:
a the application is incompatible with the provisions of the Convention or the Protocols thereto, manifestly ill-founded, or an abuse of the right of individual application; or
b the applicant has not suffered a significant disadvantage, unless respect for human rights as defined in the Convention and the Protocols thereto requires an examination of the application on the merits and provided that no case may be rejected on this ground which has not been duly considered by a domestic tribunal.

4 The Court shall reject any application which it considers inadmissible under this Article. It may do so at any stage of the proceedings.

Article 36 – Third party intervention

1 In all cases before a Chamber or the Grand Chamber, a High Contracting Party one of whose nationals is an applicant shall have the right to submit written comments and to take part in hearings.

2 The President of the Court may, in the interest of the proper administration of justice, invite any High Contracting Party which is not a party to the proceedings or any person concerned who is not the applicant to submit written comments or take part in hearings.

3 In all cases before a Chamber or the Grand Chamber, the Council of Europe Commissioner for Human Rights may submit written comments and take part in hearings.

Article 37 – Striking out applications

1 The Court may at any stage of the proceedings decide to strike an application out of its list of cases where the circumstances lead to the conclusion that
a the applicant does not intend to pursue his application; or
b the matter has been resolved; or
c for any other reason established by the Court, it is no longer justified to continue the examination of the application.

However, the Court shall continue the examination of the application if respect for human rights as defined in the Convention and the protocols thereto so requires.

2 The Court may decide to restore an application to its list of cases if it considers that the circumstances justify such a course.

Article 38 – Examination of the case

The Court shall examine the case together with the representatives of the parties and, if need be, undertake an investigation, for the effective conduct of which the High Contracting Parties concerned shall furnish all necessary facilities.

Article 39 – Friendly settlements

1 At any stage of the proceedings, the Court may place itself at the disposal of the parties concerned with a view to securing a friendly settlement of the matter on the basis of respect for human rights as defined in the Convention and the Protocols thereto.
2 Proceedings conducted under paragraph 1 shall be confidential.
3 If a friendly settlement is effected, the Court shall strike the case out of its list by means of a decision which shall be confined to a brief statement of the facts and of the solution reached.
4 This decision shall be transmitted to the Committee of Ministers, which shall supervise the execution of the terms of the friendly settlement as set out in the decision.

Article 40 – Public hearings and access to documents

1 Hearings shall be in public unless the Court in exceptional circumstances decides otherwise.
2 Documents deposited with the Registrar shall be accessible to the public unless the President of the Court decides otherwise.

Article 41 – Just satisfaction

If the Court finds that there has been a violation of the Convention or the protocols thereto, and if the internal law of the High Contracting Party concerned allows only partial reparation to be made, the Court shall, if necessary, afford just satisfaction to the injured party.

Article 42 – Judgments of Chambers

Judgments of Chambers shall become final in accordance with the provisions of Article 44, paragraph 2.

Article 43 – Referral to the Grand Chamber

1 Within a period of three months from the date of the judgment of the Chamber, any party to the case may, in exceptional cases, request that the case be referred to the Grand Chamber.
2 A panel of five judges of the Grand Chamber shall accept the request if the case raises a serious question affecting the interpretation or application of the Convention or the protocols thereto, or a serious issue of general importance.
3 If the panel accepts the request, the Grand Chamber shall decide the case by means of a judgment.

Article 44 – Final judgments

1 The judgment of the Grand Chamber shall be final.
2 The judgment of a Chamber shall become final
 a when the parties declare that they will not request that the case be referred to the Grand Chamber; or
 b three months after the date of the judgment, if reference of the case to the Grand Chamber has not been requested; or
 c when the panel of the Grand Chamber rejects the request to refer under Article 43.
3 The final judgment shall be published.

Article 45 – Reasons for judgments and decisions

1 Reasons shall be given for judgments as well as for decisions declaring applications admissible or inadmissible.
2 If a judgment does not represent, in whole or in part, the unanimous opinion of the judges, any judge shall be entitled to deliver a separate opinion.

Article 46 – Binding force and execution of judgments

1 The High Contracting Parties undertake to abide by the final judgment of the Court in any case to which they are parties.
2 The final judgment of the Court shall be transmitted to the Committee of Ministers, which shall supervise its execution.
3 If the Committee of Ministers considers that the supervision of the execution of a final judgment is hindered by a problem of interpretation of the judgment, it may refer the matter to the Court for a ruling on the question of interpretation. A referral decision shall require a majority vote of two thirds of the representatives entitled to sit on the Committee.
4 If the Committee of Ministers considers that a High Contracting Party refuses to abide by a final judgment in a case to which it is a party, it may, after serving formal notice on that Party and by decision adopted by a majority vote of two

thirds of the representatives entitled to sit on the Committee, refer to the Court the question whether that Party has failed to fulfil its obligation under paragraph 1.

5 If the Court finds a violation of paragraph 1, it shall refer the case to the Committee of Ministers for consideration of the measures to be taken. If the Court finds no violation of paragraph 1, it shall refer the case to the Committee of Ministers, which shall close its examination of the case.

Article 47 – Advisory opinions

1 The Court may, at the request of the Committee of Ministers, give advisory opinions on legal questions concerning the interpretation of the Convention and the protocols thereto.

2 Such opinions shall not deal with any question relating to the content or scope of the rights or freedoms defined in Section I of the Convention and the protocols thereto, or with any other question which the Court or the Committee of Ministers might have to consider in consequence of any such proceedings as could be instituted in accordance with the Convention.

3 Decisions of the Committee of Ministers to request an advisory opinion of the Court shall require a majority vote of the representatives entitled to sit on the Committee.

Article 48 – Advisory jurisdiction of the Court

The Court shall decide whether a request for an advisory opinion submitted by the Committee of Ministers is within its competence as defined in Article 47.

Article 49 – Reasons for advisory opinions

1 Reasons shall be given for advisory opinions of the Court.

2 If the advisory opinion does not represent, in whole or in part, the unanimous opinion of the judges, any judge shall be entitled to deliver a separate opinion.

3 Advisory opinions of the Court shall be communicated to the Committee of Ministers.

Article 50 – Expenditure on the Court

The expenditure on the Court shall be borne by the Council of Europe.

Article 51 – Privileges and immunities of judges

The judges shall be entitled, during the exercise of their functions, to the privileges and immunities provided for in Article 40 of the Statute of the Council of Europe and in the agreements made thereunder.

Section III – Miscellaneous provisions

Article 52 – Inquiries by the Secretary General

On receipt of a request from the Secretary General of the Council of Europe any High Contracting Party shall furnish an explanation of the manner in which its internal law ensures the effective implementation of any of the provisions of the Convention.

Article 53 – Safeguard for existing human rights

Nothing in this Convention shall be construed as limiting or derogating from any of the human rights and fundamental freedoms which may be ensured under the laws of any High Contracting Party or under any other agreement to which it is a Party.

Article 54 – Powers of the Committee of Ministers

Nothing in this Convention shall prejudice the powers conferred on the Committee of Ministers by the Statute of the Council of Europe.

Article 55 – Exclusion of other means of dispute settlement

The High Contracting Parties agree that, except by special agreement, they will not avail themselves of treaties, conventions or declarations in force between them for the purpose of submitting, by way of petition, a dispute arising out of the interpretation or application of this Convention to a means of settlement other than those provided for in this Convention.

Article 56 – Territorial application

1 Any State may at the time of its ratification or at any time thereafter declare by notification addressed to the Secretary General of the Council of Europe that the present Convention shall, subject to paragraph 4 of this Article, extend to all or any of the territories for whose international relations it is responsible.
2 The Convention shall extend to the territory or territories named in the notification as from the thirtieth day after the receipt of this notification by the Secretary General of the Council of Europe.

3 The provisions of this Convention shall be applied in such territories with due regard, however, to local requirements.
4 Any State which has made a declaration in accordance with paragraph 1 of this article may at any time thereafter declare on behalf of one or more of the territories to which the declaration relates that it accepts the competence of the Court to receive applications from individuals, non-governmental organisations or groups of individuals as provided by Article 34 of the Convention.

Article 57 – Reservations

1 Any State may, when signing this Convention or when depositing its instrument of ratification, make a reservation in respect of any particular provision of the Convention to the extent that any law then in force in its territory is not in conformity with the provision. Reservations of a general character shall not be permitted under this article.
2 Any reservation made under this article shall contain a brief statement of the law concerned.

Article 58 – Denunciation

1 A High Contracting Party may denounce the present Convention only after the expiry of five years from the date on which it became a party to it and after six months' notice contained in a notification addressed to the Secretary General of the Council of Europe, who shall inform the other High Contracting Parties.
2 Such a denunciation shall not have the effect of releasing the High Contracting Party concerned from its obligations under this Convention in respect of any act which, being capable of constituting a violation of such obligations, may have been performed by it before the date at which the denunciation became effective.
3 Any High Contracting Party which shall cease to be a member of the Council of Europe shall cease to be a Party to this Convention under the same conditions.
4 The Convention may be denounced in accordance with the provisions of the preceding paragraphs in respect of any territory to which it has been declared to extend under the terms of Article 56.

Article 59 – Signature and ratification

1 This Convention shall be open to the signature of the members of the Council of Europe. It shall be ratified. Ratifications shall be deposited with the Secretary General of the Council of Europe.
2 The European Union may accede to this Convention.
3 The present Convention shall come into force after the deposit of ten instruments of ratification.

4 As regards any signatory ratifying subsequently, the Convention shall come into force at the date of the deposit of its instrument of ratification.

5 The Secretary General of the Council of Europe shall notify all the members of the Council of Europe of the entry into force of the Convention, the names of the High Contracting Parties who have ratified it, and the deposit of all instruments of ratification which may be effected subsequently.

Done at Rome this 4th day of November 1950, in English and French, both texts being equally authentic, in a single copy which shall remain deposited in the archives of the Council of Europe. The Secretary General shall transmit certified copies to each of the signatories.

Bibliography

Albors-Llorens, A., *Changes in the Jurisdiction of the European Court of Justice in the Treaty of Amsterdam*, Common Market Law Review, 1998, vol. 35.

Albors-Llorens, A., *Private Parties in European Community Law. Challenging Community Measures* (Oxford: Oxford University Press, 1996).

Albors-Llorens, A., *The Standing of Private Parties to Challenge Community Measures: Has the European Court Missed the Boat?*, Cambridge Law Journal, 2003, vol. 62, no. 1.

Alexy, R., *A Theory of Constitutional Rights* (Julian Rivers, Oxford: Oxford University Press, 2002).

Andrews, N., *English Civil Procedure: Fundamentals of the New Civil Justice System* (New York: Oxford University Press, 2003).

Arnull, A., Barnard, C., Dougan, M. & Spaventa, E. (eds), *Constitutional Order of States: Essays in EU Law in Honour of Alan Dashwood* (Oxford: Hart Publishing, 2011).

Arnull, A., *Private Applicants and the Action for Annulment since Codorniu*, Common Market Law Review, 2001, vol. 38.

Arnull, A., *Private Applicants and the Action for Annulment under Article 173 of the EC Treaty*, Common Market Law Review, 1995, vol. 32.

Bailey, D., *Scope of Judicial Review under Article 81 EC*, Common Market Law Review, 2004, vol. 41.

Barents, R., *The Court of Justice after the Treaty of Lisbon*, Common Market Law Review, 2010, vol. 47.

Berger, V., *Judikatura Evropského soudu pro lidská práva* [*Case Law of the European Court of Human Rights*], vol. I, 7th French edn, 1th Czech Release (Prague: Éditions Dalloz, 2000).

Biletzki, A. & Matar, A. 'Ludwig Wittgenstein', *The Stanford Encyclopedia of Philosophy*, Edward N. Zalta (ed.), http://plato.stanford.edu/archives/sum2011/entries/wittgenstein/, Summer 2011 Edition.

Bodenhamer, D.J. & Ely, J.W., Jr. (eds), *The Bill of Rights in Modern America* (Bloomington: Indiana University Press, 2008).

Boguszak, J., *Právní principy*, kolokvium, Vydavatelství 999, Pelhřimov 999.

Brems, E., *Conflicting Human Rights: An Exploration in the Context of the Right to a Fair Trial in the European Convention for the Protection of Human Rights and Fundamental Freedoms*, Human Rights Quarterly (2005), vol. 27.

Bubík, T., *Filosoficky o spravedlnosti* (Pardubice: Univerzita Pardubice, 2007).

Chalmers, D., Davies, G. & Monti, G., *European Union Law. Text and Materials*. 2nd edition (New York: Cambridge University Press, 2010).

Chalmers, D., *European Union Law. Volume I. Law and EU Government* (Aldershot: Ashgate-Dartmouth, 1998).

Charrier, J., *Code de la Convention Europenne des Droit de l'Homme*, 2nd edition (Paris: Litec, 2002).

Chiavario, M. (in Bartole, Conforti, Raimondi), *Commentario alla convenzione europea per al tutela dei diritti dell'uomo e delle libertà fondamentali* (Padova: Cedam, 2001).

Clayton, R. & Tomlinson, H., *Fair Trial Rights* (New York: Oxford University Press, 2010).

Corthaut, T., *An Effective Remedy for All? Paradoxes and Controversies in Respect of Judicial Protection in the Field of the CFSP under the European Constitution*, Tilburg Foreign Law Review, 2005, vol. 12.

Craig, P., *Legality, Standing and Substantive Review in Community Law*, Oxford Journal of Legal Studies, 1994, vol. 14, no. 4.

Curtis, F. & Doebbler, J., *Introduction to International Human Rights Law* (Washington: CD Publishing, 2006).

Dashwood, A. & Johnston, A., *The Future of the Judicial System of the European Union* (Oxford: Hart Publishing, 2001).

Dougan, M., *The Treaty of Lisbon 2007: Winning Minds, Not Hearts*, Common Market Law Review, 2008, vol. 45.

Dworkin, R., *Když se práva berou vážně. Přeložil Zdeněk Masopust* (Pragua: Oikoymenh, 2001).

Enchelmaier, S., *No-One Slips Through the Net? Latest Developments, and Non-Developments, in the European Court of Justice's Jurisprudence on Art. 230(4) EC*, Yearbook of European Law, 2005, vol. 24.

Fawcett, J.E.S., *The Application of the European Convention on Human Rights* (Oxford: Clarendon Press, 1987).

Fekete, L., *Public versus Private Domain: Knowledge and Information in the Global Communications Network*, in Zsolnai L., Boda Z. & Fekete L. (eds), *Ethical Prospects. Economy, Society and Environment* (Berlin: Springer, 2009).

Frédéric, E., *The Length of Civil and Criminal Proceedings in the Case-Law of the European Court of Human Rights* (Human Rights Files No. 16), Council of Europe publishing (1996-2007).

Galligan, D.J., *Due Process and Fair Procedures: A Study of Administrative Procedures* (New York: Oxford University Press, 1996).

Giunio, M., *Arbitration and the Right to a Fair Trial: Right to Fair Trial and Efficiency of Arbitration Proceedings*, Croatian Arbitration Yearbook, Croatian Chamber of Commerce, 2000.

Groussot, X., *The EC System of Legal Remedies and Effective Judicial Protection: Does the System Really Need Reform?*, Legal Issues of Economic Integration, 2003, vol. 30, no. 3.

Harris, D.J., O'Boyle, M., Bates E. & Buckley, C., *Harris, O'Boyle & Warbrick: Law of the European Convention on Human Rights*, 2nd edn (New York: Oxford University Press, 2009).

Hart, H.L.A., *The Concept of Law*, 2nd edn (New York: Oxford University Press, 1994).

Hartley, T.C., *The Foundations of European Community Law. An Introduction to the Constitutional and Administrative Law of the European Community*, 5th edn (New York: Oxford University Press, 2003).

Hazard, G.C., Stürner, R., Taruffo, M. & Gidi, A., *Draft Rules of Transnational Civil Procedure (with Comments)*, UNIDROIT Study LXXVI - Doc. 12, International Institute for the Unification of Private Law (2004).

Hofmann, H.C.H., *Legislation, Delegation and Implementation under the Treaty of Lisbon: Typology Meets Reality*, European Law Journal, 2004, vol. 15, no. 4.

Holländer, P., *Nástin filosofie práva* [*An Outline of the Philosophy of Law*] (Prague: Všehrd, 2000).

Hubálková, E., *Evropská úmluva o lidských právech a Česká republika* (Prague: Linde, 2003).

Jaksic, A., *Arbitration and Human Rights* (Frankfurt am Main: Peter Lang, 2002).

Janis, M.W., Kay, R.S. & Bradley, A.W., *European Rights Law (Text and Materials)*, 3rd edn (New York: Oxford University Press, 2008).

Jhering, R., *Boj o právo. Přeložila Lenka Bezoušková, nakladatelství Aleš Čeněk* (s.r.o. 2009).

Knapp, V., *Teorie práva, 1. Vydání* (Prague: C.H. Beck, 1995).

Koch, Ch., *Locus Standi of Private Applicants under the EU Constitution: Preserving Gaps in the Protection of Individuals' Right to an Effective Remedy*, European Law Review, 2005, vol. 30.

Labunski, R.E., *James Madison and the Struggle for the Bill of Rights* (New York: Oxford University Press, 2006).

Lambert P., *L'arbitrage et l'article 6, 1° de la Convention européenne des droits de l'homme*, in Cambi Favre-Bulle, A., Dal, G.-A., Flécheux, G. & Lambert, P. (eds), *L'arbitrage et la Convention européenne des droits de l'homme*, Droit et Justice, No. 31 (Bruxelles: Nemesis, Bruylant, 2001).

Lavický, P., *Funkční vazby občanskeho práva hmotného a procesního* [*Functional Bindings in Substantive and Procedural Civil Law*] (Ph.D. Thesis, Faculty of Law, Brno: Masaryk University, 2006/7).

Leanza, P. (ed.), *Le prove civili* (Turin: Giappichelli, 2012).

Leanza; P., *L'istruzione probatoria nel processo civile* (Turin: Giappichelli, 2009).

Lemmens, P., *Geschillen over burgerlijke rechten en verplichtingen* (Antwerpen: Kluwer, 1989).

Lenaerts, K. & Corthaut, T., *Judicial Review as a Contribution to the Development of European Constitutionalism*, Yearbook of European Law, 2003, vol. 22, no. 1.

Letsas, G., *A Theory of Interpretation of the European Convention on Human Rights* (New York: Oxford University Press, 2007).

Letsas, G., *The Truth in Autonomous Concepts: How to Interpret the ECHR*, European Journal of International Law, 2004, vol. 15, no. 2.

Levy, L.W., *Origin of the Bill of Rights* (Yale University Press, 2001).

Lorenzmeier, S., *The Right to a Fair Trial in Europe? – Procedural Guarantees under the European Convention on Human Rights*, Journal of the Institute of Justice and International Studies 7/2007.

Mason, D.S., *A Concise History of Modern Europe: Liberty, Equality, Solidarity*, 2nd edn (Plymouth: Rowman & Littlefield Publishers, 2011).

Matscher, F., *'L'arbitrage et la Convention,'* in Petititi – Decaux – Imbert, *La Convention européenne des droits de l'homme – Commentaire article par article*, 2nd edn (Paris: Economica, 1999).

Merrills, J.G. & Robertson, A.H., *Human Rights in Europe: A Study of the European Convention on Human Rights*, 4th edn (Manchester: Manchester University Press, 2001).

Öberg, U., *The Concept of 'Harmonious Interpretation'. Reflections from a Practitioner on the Case Law of the ECJ.* Conference Access to justice (Praha: 15-16.4.2008).

Olivier, C., *Revisiting General Comment No. 29 of the United Nations Human Rights Committee: About Fair Trial Rights and Derogations in Times of Public Emergency*, Journal of International Law, 17/2004.

Ovey, C. & White, R.C.A., *The European Convention on Human Rights*, 4th edn (New York: Oxford University Press, 2006).

Pallister, A., *Magna Carta: The Heritage of Liberty* (Oxford: Oxford University Press, 1971).

Partsch, K.J., *Die Rechte und Freiheiten der europäischen Menschenrechtskonvention* (Berlin: Duncker & Humblot, 1966).

Pieper, J., *The Four Cardinal Virtues* (Notre Dame, IN: University of Notre Dame Press, 1966).

Pirrone, P., *Il Caso Pellegrini dinanzi alla Corte europea dei diritti dell'uomo: efficacia in Italia delle sentenze ecclesiastiche ed equo processo*, in *Diritto pubblico comparato ed europeo*, IV (2001).

Pittman, R.C., *The Creation of the Sixth Amendment Right to a Fair Trial*, in *The Right to a Fair Trial* (series *'The Bill of Rights'*), Enid W. Langbert, Esq. (eds) (Famington Hills: Greenhaven Press [Thomson Gale corp.], 2005).

Plato, *Republic* [translated by John Llewelyn Davies and David James Vaughan, in *Wordsworth Classics of World Literature*] (Ware: Wordsworth Editions Ltd., 1997).

Pridal, O., *Postup soudu po nařízení jednání* [*The Particular Steps of the Court during the Hearing*], Bulletin advokacie [Attorney's Bulletin], no. 6, 2006.

Pridal, O., *Postup soudu před nařízením jednání* [*The Particular Steps of the Court before Hearing Takes Place*], Bulletin advokacie [Attorney's Bulletin], no. 5, 2009.

Pridal, O., *Pravo na spravedlivy proces v civilnim rizeni (The Right to a Fair Trial in Civil Procedure)*, Ph.D. Thesis, Masaryk University in Brno, 2011.

Radbruch, G., *Gesetzliches Unrecht und übergesetzliches Recht [Legal Injustice and Supralegal Law]*, Süddeutsche Juristenzeitung, I, 1946.

Rawls, J.A., *Theory of Justice* (The Belknap Press of Harvard University Press, 1971).

Rawls, J., *Justice as Fairness: A Restatement* (Harvard University Press, 2001).

Rawls, J., *Political Liberalism* (New York: Columbia University Press, 1996).

Reed Amar, A., *The Bill of Rights: Creation and Reconstruction* (Yale University Press, 1998).

Repík, B., *Implicitní procesní ochrana základních materiálních práv v judikatuře Evropského soudu pro lidská práva*, Právník 9/2008.

Repík, B., *Ľudské práva v súdnom konání* (Bratislava: Manz Bratislava, 1999).

Schwartz, B., *The Great Rights of Mankind: A History of the American Bill of Rights* (Lanham: Rowman & Littlefield, 2002).

Šimáčková, K. & Koláčková, J., *Právo na spravedlivý proces v prostoru Evropských společenství*, Právní Fórum 11/2005.

Sime, S., *A Practical Approach to Civil Procedure* (New York: Oxford University Press, 2006).

Šišková, N., *Dimenze ochrany lidských práv v Evropské unii* (Praha: Linde, 2008).

Slapper, G. & Kelly, D., *Sourcebook on the English Legal System* (London: Cavendish Publishing Limited, 2001).

Spooner, L., *An Essay on the Trial by Jury* (BostonL Cleveland, 1852).

Stedron, S., *Contested Civil Procedure and Use of Information Technology and Legal Information Systems (E-Justice)* (Praha: Linde, 2008).

Sudre, J., *L'interprétation de la Convention européenne des droits de l'homme* (Bruxelles: Brylant, 1998).

Trechsel, S. & Summers, S.J., *Human Rights in Criminal Proceedings (Collected Courses in the Academy of European Law)* (New York: Oxford University Press, 2006).

Van Dijk, P. & Hoof, G.J.H., *Theory and Practice of the European Convention on Human Rights* (The Hague: Kluwer Law International, 1998).

Van Dijk, P., *The Right of the Accused to a Fair Trial under International Law* (Utrecht: S.I.M., 1983).

Večeřa, M., *Spravedlnost v právu* (Brno: Masarykova Univerzita, 1997).

Velu, J. & Ergec, R., *La Convention europeenne des droits de l'homme* (Bruxelles: Brylant, 1990).

Villiger, M., *Fair Trial and Excessive Length of Proceedings as Focal Points of the ECtHR's Increasing Caseload in The European Court of Human Rights Overwhelmed by Applications: Problems and Possible Solutions* (Heildeberg: Springer, 2007).

Ward, A., *Locus Standi under Article 230(4) of the EC Treaty: Crafting an Coherent Test for a 'Wobbly Polity'*, Yearbook of European Law, 2003, vol. 22.

Table of Cases

ECtHR, Commission

Court of Justice of the European Union

National Constitutional and Supreme Courts

Index

EUROPEAN MONOGRAPH SERIES

1. Lammy Betten (ed.), *The Future of European Social Policy,* 1991 (ISBN 90-654-4585-4).
2. Annemarie Loman, Kamiel Mortelmans, Harry H.G. Post & Stewart Watson, *Culture and Common Law: Before and After Maastricht,* 1992 (ISBN 90-654-4638-9).
3. John A.E. Vervaele, *Fraud against the Community: The Need for European Fraud Legislation,* 1994 (ISBN 90-654-4634-6).
4. Philip Raworth, *The Legislative Process in the European Community,* 1993 (ISBN 90-654-4690-7).
5. Jules Stuyck, *Financial and Monetary Integration in the European Economic Community,* 1993 (ISBN 90-654-4718-0).
6. Jules Stuyck & A.J. Vossestein (eds), *State Entrepreneurship, National Monopolies and European Community Law,* 1993 (ISBN 90-654-4773-3).
7. Jules Stuyck & A. Looijestijn-Clearie (eds), *The European Economic Area EC-EFTA,* 1994 (ISBN 90-654-4815-2).
8. Rosita B. Bouterse, *Competition and Integration: What Goals Count?,* 1995 (ISBN 90-654-4816-0).
9. René Barents, *The Agricultural Law of the EC: An Inquiry into the Administrative Law,* 1994 (ISBN 90-654-4867-5).
10. Nicholas Emiliou, *Principles of Proportionality in European Law: A Comparative Study,* 1996 (ISBN 90-411-0866-1).
11. Eivind Smith, *National Parliaments as Cornerstones of European Integration,* 1996 (ISBN 90-411-0898-X).
12. Jan H. Jans, *European Environmental Law,* 1996 (ISBN 90-411-0877-7).
13. Síofra O'Leary, *The Evolving Concept of Community Citizenship: From the Free Movement of Persons to Union Citizenship,* 1997 (ISBN 90-411-0878-5).
14. Laurence W. Gormley (ed.), *Current and Future Perspectives on EC Competition Law,* 1983 (ISBN 90-411-0691-X).
15. Simone White, *Protection of the Financial Interests of the European Communities: The Fight against Fraud and Corruption,* 1998 (ISBN 90-411-9647-1).
16. Morten P. Broberg, *Broberg on the European Commission's Jurisdiction to Scrutinise Mergers*, 4th Edition, 2013 (ISBN 978-90-411-3339-7).
17. Doris Hildebrand, *The Role of Economic Analysis in the EC Competition Rules: The European School,* 2nd Edition, 2002 (ISBN 90-411-1706-7).
18. Christof R.A. Swaak, *European Community Law and the Automobile Industry,* 1999 (ISBN 90-411-1140-9).

19. Dorthe Dahlgaard Dingel, *Public Procurement: A Harmonization of the National Judicial Review of the Application of European Community Law,* 1999 (ISBN 90-411-1161-1).
20. John A.E. Vervaele (ed.), *Compliance and Enforcement of European Community Law,* 1999 (ISBN 90-411-1151-4).
21. Martin Trybus, *European Defence Procurement Law: International and National Procurement Systems as Models for a Liberalized Defence Procurement Market in Europe,* 1999 (ISBN 90-411-1167-0).
22. Helen Staples, *The Legal Status of Third Country Nationals Resident in the European Union,* 1999 (ISBN 90-411-1277-4).
23. Damien Geradin (ed.), *The Liberalization of State Monopolies in the European Union and Beyond,* 1999 (ISBN 90-411-1264-2).
24. Katja Heede, *European Ombudsman: Redress and Control at Union Level,* 2000 (ISBN 90-411-1413-0).
25. Ulf Bernitz & Joakim Nergelius (eds), *General Principles of European Community Law,* 2000 (ISBN 90-411-1402-5).
26. Michaela Drahos, *Convergence of Competition Laws and Policies in the European Community,* 2002 (ISBN 90-411-1562-5).
27. Damien Geradin (ed.), *The Liberalization of Electricity and Natural Gas in the European Union,* 2001 (ISBN 90-411-1560-9).
28. Gisella Gori, *Towards an EU Right to Education,* 2001 (ISBN 90-411-1670-2).
29. Brendan P.G. Smith, *Constitution Building in the European Union,* 2001 (ISBN 90-411-1695-8).
30. Friedl Weiss & Frank Wooldridge, *Free Movement of Persons within the European Community,* 2nd Edition, 2007 (ISBN 978-90-411-2545-3).
31. Ingrid Boccardi, *Europe and Refugees: Towards an EU Asylum Policy,* 2002 (ISBN 90-411-1709-1).
32. John A.E. Vervaele & André Klip (eds), *European Cooperation Between Tax, Customs and Judicial Authorities,* 2001 (ISBN 90-411-1747-4).
33. Wouter P.J. Wils, *The Optimal Enforcement of EC Antitrust Law: Essays in Law and Economics,* 2002 (ISBN 90-411-1757-1).
34. Damien Geradin (ed.), *The Liberalization of Postal Services in the European Union,* 2002 (ISBN 90-411-1780-6).
35. Nick Bernard, *Multilevel Governance in the European Union,* 2002 (ISBN 90-411-1812-8).
36. Jill Wakefield, *Judicial Protection through the Use of Article 288(2) EC,* 2002 (ISBN 90-411-1823-3).
37. Sebastiaan Princen, *EU Regulation and Transatlantic Trade,* 2002 (ISBN 90-411-1871-3).

38. Amaryllis Verhoeven, *The European Union in Search of a Democratic and Constitutional Theory*, 2002 (ISBN 90-411-1872-1).
39. Paul L.C. Torremans, *Cross Border Insolvencies in EU, English and Belgian Law*, 2002 (ISBN 90-411-1888-8).
40. Malcolm Anderson & Joanna Apap (eds), *Police and Justice Cooperation and the New European Borders*, 2002 (ISBN 90-411-1893-4).
41. Christin M. Forstinger, *Takeover Law in EU and USA: A Comparative Analysis*, 2002 (ISBN 90-411-1919-1).
42. Antonio Bavasso, *Communications in EU Antitrust Law: Market Power and Public Interest*, 2003 (ISBN 90-411-1974-4).
43. Fiona G. Wishlade, *Regional State Aid and Competition Policy in the European Union*, 2003 (ISBN 90-411-1975-2).
44. Gareth Davies, *Nationality Discrimination in the European Internal Market*, 2003 (ISBN 90-411-1998-1).
45. René Barents, *The Autonomy of Community Law*, 2003 (ISBN 90-411-2251-6).
46. Gerhard Dannecker & Oswald Jansen (eds), *Competition Law Sanctioning in the European Union*, 2004 (ISBN 90-411-2100-5).
47. Nauta Dutilh (ed.), *Dealing with Dominance: The Experience of National Competition Authorities*, 2004 (ISBN 90-411-2211-7).
48. Stefaan van den Bogaert, *Practical Regulation of the Mobility of Sportsmen in the EU Post Bosman*, 2005 (ISBN 90-411-2327-X).
49. Katalin Judit Cseres, *Competition Law and Consumer Protection*, 2005 (ISBN 90-411-2380-6).
50. Philipp Kiiver, *The National Parliaments in the European Union: A Critical View on EU Constitution Building*, 2006 (ISBN 978-90-411-2452-4).
51. Alexander Turk, *The Concept of Legislation in European Community Law*, 2006 (ISBN 978-90-411-2472-2).
52. Dimitrios Sinaniotis, *The Interim Protection of Individuals before the European and National Courts*, 2006 (ISBN 978-90-411-2498-2).
53. M. Holoubek & D. Damjanovic, M. Traimer (eds), *Regulating Content: The European Regulatory Framework for the Media and Related Creative Sectors*, 2006 (ISBN 978-90-411-2597-2).
54. Anneli Albi & Jacques Ziller (eds), *The European Constitution and National Constitutions: Ratification and Beyond*, 2006 (ISBN 978-90-411-2524-8).
55. Gustavo E. Luengo, *Regulation of Subsidies and State Aids in WTO and EC Law: Conflicts in International Trade Law*, 2007 (ISBN 978-90-411-2547-7).
56. Eniko Horvath, *Mandating Identity: Citizenship, Kinship Laws and Plural Nationality in the European Union*, 2007 (ISBN 978-90-411-2662-7).

57. Rass Holdgaard, *External Relations Law of the European Community: Legal Reasoning and Legal Discourses*, 2007 (ISBN 978-90-411-2604-7).
58. Jill Wakefield, *The Right to Good Administration*, 2007 (ISBN 978-90-411-2697-9).
59. Dimitry Kochenov, *EU Enlargement and the Failure of Conditionality: Pre- accession Conditionality in the Fields of Democracy and the Rule of Law*, 2008 (ISBN 978-90-411-2696-2).
60. Despina Mavromati, *The Law of Payment Services in the EU: The EC Directive on Payment Services in the Internal Market*, 2008 (ISBN 978-90-411-2700-6).
61. Anne Meuwese, *Impact Assessment in EU Lawmaking*, 2008 (ISBN 978-90-411-2720-4).
62. Ulf Bernitz, Joakim Nergelius & Cecilia Cardner (eds), *General Principles of EC Law in a Process of Development*, 2008 (ISBN 978-90-411-2705-1).
63. Johan van de Gronden (ed.), *The EU and WTO Law on Services: Limits to the Realisation of General Interest Policies within the Services Markets?*, 2008 (ISBN 978-90-411-2809-6).
64. Alina Tryfonidou, *Reverse Discrimination in EC Law*, 2009 (ISBN 978-90-411-2751-8).
65. Mikael Berglund, *Cross-Border Enforcement of Claims in the EU: History Present Time and Future*, 2009 (ISBN 978-90-411-2861-4).
66. Theodore Konstadinides, *Division of Powers in European Union Law: The Delimitation of Internal Competence between the EU and the Member States*, 2009 (ISBN 978-90-411-2615-3).
67. Mattias Derlén, *Multilingual Interpretation of European Union Law*, 2009 (ISBN 978-90-411-2853-9).
68. René Barents, *Directory of EU Case Law on the Preliminary Ruling Procedure*, 2009 (ISBN 978-90-411-3150-8).
69. Yan Luo, *Anti-dumping in the WTO, the EU and China: The Rise of Legalization in the Trade Regime and its Consequences*, 2010 (ISBN 978-90-411-3207-9).
70. Patrick Birkinshaw & Mike Varney (eds), *The European Union Legal Order after Lisbon*, 2010 (ISBN 978-90-411-3152-2).
71. Thomas Gr. Papadopoulos, *EU Law and Harmonization of Takeovers in the Internal Market*, 2010 (978-90-411-3340-3).
72. Bas van Bockel, *The* Ne Bis In Idem *Principle in EU Law*, 2010 (978-90-411-3156-0).
73. Veljko Milutinović, *The 'Right to Damages' under EU Competition Law: From* Courage v. Crehan *to the White Paper and Beyond*, 2010 (978-90-411-3235-2).

74. Amandine Garde, *EU Law and Obesity Prevention*, 2010 (978-90-411-2706-8).
75. Leonard Besselink, Frans Pennings & Sacha Prechal (eds), *The Eclipse of the Legality Principle in the European Union*, 2011 (978-90-411-3262-8).
76. Sacha Garben, *EU Higher Education Law: The Bologna Process and Harmonization by Stealth*, 2011 (978-90-411-3365-6).
77. Dimitry Kochenov (ed.), *EU Law of the Overseas: Outermost Regions, Associated Overseas Countries and Territories, Territories Sui Generis*, 2011 (978-90-411-3445-5).
78. Pablo Ibáñez Colomo, *European Communications Law and Technological Convergence: Deregulation, Re-regulation and Regulatory Convergence in Television and Telecommunications*, 2012 (978-90-411-3829-3).
79. Elise Muir, *EU Regulation of Access to Labour Markets: A Case Study of EU Constraints on Member State Competences*, 2012 (978-90-411-3823-1).
80. Tim Corthaut, *EU Ordre Public*, 2012 (978-90-411-3232-1).
81. Oana Ştefan, *Soft Law in Court: Competition Law, State Aid and the Court of Justice of the European Union*, 2013 (978-90-411-3997-9).
82. Francesco Rossi dal Pozzo, *Citizenship Rights and Freedom of Movement in the European Union*, 2013 (978-90-411-4660-1).
83. Jens Hartig Danielsen, *EU Agricultural Law*, 2013 (978-90-411-3280-2).
84. Ulf Bernitz, Xavier Groussot & Felix Schulyok (eds), *General Principles of EU Law and European Private Law*, 2013 (978-90-411-4683-0).
85. Michelle Everson, Cosimo Monda & Ellen Vos (eds), *European Agencies in between Institutions and Member States*, 2014 (978-90-411-2843-0).
86. Stefan Leible & Matthias Lehmann (eds), *European Contract Law and German Law*, 2014 (978-90-411-2588-0).
87. Piero Leanza & Ondrej Pridal, *The Right to a Fair Trial: Article 6 of the European Convention on Human Rights*, 2014 (978-90-411-4855-1)